TEARS

of

MERMAIDS

ALSO BY STEPHEN G. BLOOM

Postville: A Clash of Cultures in Heartland America

The Oxford Project (with Peter Feldstein)

Inside the Writer's Mind

The
Secret Story
of Pearls

TEARS
of
MERMAIDS

Stephen G. Bloom

ST. MARTIN'S PRESS
New York

www.stmartins.com

Design by Kathryn Praise

LIBRARY OF CONGRESS CATALOGING-IN-PUBLICATION DATA

Bloom, Stephen G.
    Tears of mermaids : the secret story of pearls / Stephen G. Bloom.—1st ed.
         p. cm.
    Includes bibliographical references and index.
    ISBN 978-0-312-36326-0
 1. Pearl industry and trade.   2. Cultured pearls.   I. Title.
    HD9678.P4B66 2009
    338.3'71412—dc22

                                  2009019933

First Edition: December 2009

10 9 8 7 6 5 4 3 2 1

For Iris and Mikey,
the adventure continues

CONTENTS

Introduction: From Diver's Hand to Woman's Bosom   1

1   In the Beginning   7
2   A Pearl Primer: Some of What You Need to Know   17
3   Entranced   28
4   Into the Mix   35
5   The Rana of Fresno   42
6   Pearl City   56
7   Hong Kong—Dealers' Paradise   75
8   The Traders   85
9   Across the Chinese Border to the Transformatron   105
10 Faye's World   117
11 Tammy and a (Sort of) Barbara Bush Sighting
    at the Hongqiao Pearl Market   126
12 Miss Pearl   136
13 The Way of the Internet: A Trek from the Neighborhood
    Jewelry Store to the Rural Chinese Villages of Haian and Xuwen   140
14 To the Source   153
15 Karaoke-Krazy   161

Contents • x

16 A Dog in My Crotch   165
17 On JB's Farm   173
18 Sold!   187
19 French Polynesia: The Pearl that Got Away   206
20 Snakes & Crocs   230
21 Australia's First Family of Pearls   237
22 Fight for Pearl Supremacy: The Strange Case of the
    Otto Gerdau Co.   249
23 Life as a Deckhand   266
24 On Board   276
25 At Sea   285
26 The Show   292
27 The Comer   301
28 The Payoff   311
29 Where It All Began   319
30 The Dogs of Cubagua   329
31 El Señor Sixto of Cubagua   336
32 Nicholas El Gato's Legacy   342

Acknowledgments   349
Endnotes   357
Index   367

Kino deftly slipped his knife into the edge of the shell. Through the knife he could feel the muscle tighten hard. He worked the blade lever-wise and the closing muscle parted and the shell fell apart. The lip-like flesh writhed up and then subsided. Kino lifted the flesh, and there it lay, the great pearl, perfect as the moon. It captured the light and refined it and gave it back in silver incandescence. It was as large as a sea-gull's egg. It was the greatest pearl in the world.
—*The Pearl*, by John Steinbeck, November 1947

What symmetry! What art! They are the tears of mermaids!
—Jeweler Aristide Duvalle describing a strand of pearls
in the 1936 film *Desire*, starring Marlene Dietrich
and Gary Cooper

All art is autobiographical; the pearl is the oyster's autobiography.
—Federico Fellini, 1965

TEARS

of

MERMAIDS

INTRODUCTION

From Diver's Hand to
Woman's Bosom

Twenty-five years ago, I wrote a quirky newspaper story about a year in the life of a down-at-the-heels rental tuxedo. The jacket, model 18214, had gone on four Caribbean cruises, to not just a few weddings, and a slew of proms. The tuxedo story was a gimmicky yarn that began in a rental shop and from there moved forward. But years later, I wondered if my direction had been wrong. What would have happened had I moved backward in time—to where the jacket's fibers had been grown, who gathered the crop and how, where the threads had been spun into cloth, who had sewn on the buttons?

Tracking the hopscotch world route from creation to consumption was a concept that stayed with me, and not just for tuxedo jackets. Who were the nurturers at whose hands any object took shape? What kinds of lives did each along the global assembly line lead? What were their stories? Did the goods these laborers produced have any meaning to them? After the products were manufactured, how many middlemen traded them along the way, and by what amount did each hike the price?

As the Western world becomes less and less a consortium of producer nations, we forget (or ignore) that the objects we wear, consume, and surround ourselves with come to us from a spiderweb network of laborers, processors, managers, brokers, agents, jobbers, and distributors, usually in faraway places. The closer to the raw material, the less the pay usually is (straight out of Economics 101, I know, but nonetheless something I still find nutty). Some workers earn practically nothing, like Kino in *The Pearl*. Others further up the line are rewarded quite handsomely. All share hopes and dreams, occasional desperation and heartbreak. Yet we know nothing about these anonymous laborers, toiling to bring necessities, convenience, and luxury to our insular, cozy lives. Who are they all? Those at the beginning of the global chain seldom know anything about those in the middle or those at the end; those in the middle and at the end know little, if anything, about those at the beginning. The genius of the global economy, of course, is to insure that we'll never know anything about any of them. Indeed, part of that genius is to dissociate any human intervention whatsoever in the creation and transit of the commodities to which we're so fiercely attached.

The idea behind *Tears of Mermaids* is to provide a genuine sense of provenance to an organic object—in this case, pearls. Provenance means place of origin. I can't begin to guess how many times I'd be at a pearl convention, show, or auction when a drop-dead gorgeous woman would stun everyone by strutting in, wearing a spectacular strand of pearls. Given the audience at these events, every head would swivel toward the necklace (not the woman). Within a nanosecond, the dealers would have assessed the pearls' orient, lustre, surface quality, size, shape, and match—and, if they were as grand as they looked at first blush, the dealers' eyes would dilate. Without a moment's hesitation, the first thing they'd sputter to the woman would be, "May I ask the provenance of your pearls?" It was all a game, of course, since the dealers already knew, but a popular diversion nonetheless, since the wearer almost never had a clue.

For me provenance, though, was never merely about where pearls come from. It was more about the zigzag path the pearls took, merrily plinking their way in time along a global route of tens of thousands of miles—from the moment an elegant woman in New York (Hong Kong, Geneva, Paris, or Buenos Aires, etc.) wrapped a dazzling strand of glistening pearls around her neck, all the way back to the instant a diver off the coast of Australia (China, Mexico, Tahiti, Indonesia, or the Philippines) scooped up from the ocean floor an oyster, to be implanted with a bead to form the core of one of those pearls. (Natural pearls are extraordinarily rare these days, by the way; and the idea that a pearl is created by a grain of sand has as much veracity as the story of the tooth fairy, but more on that later.) My interest was to follow each step of the route, from diver's hand to woman's bosom—and everywhere and everyone in between. My plan was to get at the source of these pricey little orbs, then to track them to the end-consumer. I wanted to learn where pearls came from, to meet the owners of the multitude of hands that had touched the pearls all along the way, and, in doing so, to enter the lives of workers whose livelihoods were governed by the fickle world of fashion.

Take, for instance, the itinerary of a AAA opera-length necklace of cultured pearls, born in the translucent warm waters surrounding Palawan Island, 250 miles north of an active al Qaeda cell carved from the overgrown Philippine jungle. After a Japanese technician inserts a Mississippi River clam bead and local mantle tissue into the *Pinctada maxima* oyster's gonad, the oyster is returned to the sea, where a single pearl as large as 18 millimeters (the size of a very large gumball) develops inside the submerged shell over the course of three to five years. Armed guards in offshore sentry towers patrol the fecund oyster beds around the clock. Once harvested, hundreds of loose kan[1] of pearls are helicoptered to Manila for sorting and grading. The best are then couriered via Learjet to Hong Kong for a private showing. After further culling, the pearls might travel to Kobe, Japan, where dealers drum up international interest, then to Paris for stringing and wholesale display. Of the original crop, only 100 or so pearls are of extraordinary quality and size, and these are made into three exquisite strands. The necklaces are displayed at an exclusive dealer show in Basel, Switzerland, then in New York, then in London for auction at Christie's or Sotheby's, then back to Hong Kong, where a dealer breaks up one of the strands. He might hire a German designer to fashion the pearls into three brooches and a choker strand with a diamond *pavé*[2] clasp—all of which go on display at another invitation-only show, perhaps in Geneva, Abu Dhabi, or Paris. Within a year, a São Paulo coffee trader gives one of the brooches to his Bahian mistress; a San Francisco venture capitalist gives the second brooch to his wife over dinner at Chez Panisse; a Tel Aviv banker buys the third brooch as a wedding present for his new daughter-in-law. The choker necklace goes to a Russian oligarch who presents it to his granddaughter for her twenty-first birthday. One of the remaining two strands ends up in a Dutch industrialist's vault, the other is auctioned off in Dubai, where a trader buys it for a twice-Oscar-winning Hollywood filmmaker.

Alas, I soon realized that my dreamy odyssey to trace a single pearl or pearl necklace back to its source would be nearly impossible. There's no sure way to mark specific pearls. And even if I could, such pearls might take years to reach their final destination, and with no guarantee they'd come back with a story.

I pondered my next move. I'd flip the pearl equation. If I couldn't track a single pearl or strand, I'd track the thousands of people who coaxed the pearls along their way.

It was a trip that took four years and thirty thousand miles. Through some manic perseverance (and flexible airline tickets), I turned into a modern Marco Polo, searching for the world's most spectacular pearls and the laborers who made them possible. Almost all of the world's pearl farms were way off the beaten path, inaccessible by any transportation except company plane or boat. As with the thirteenth-century Venetian explorer, no one had ever traveled to so many distant pearl outposts or been allowed to see what I saw.

For me, what started as a novel way to tell a story, as well as a naïve fascination with the world's oldest gem, turned into a pilgrimage and ended as an obsession. I hired myself out as a pearl deckhand, rising with the ship's crew at 5:00 a.m. and going to bed exhausted at 8:00 p.m. I sorted pearls on a rigger as humpback whales breached off our trawler's starboard side. I found the spot off the coast of Venezuela where Columbus took sight of twelve Indians wearing priceless pearls the size of walnuts. I sailed in outlets so remote they are unidentified on any topographical map. I flew in too many precarious Tinkertoy planes that took off and landed on bumpy dirt roads that doubled as runways. Whenever I sleepwalked into yet another hostel or hovel on my four-continent odyssey, these items were on my list of hopeful requirements: a lock on the door, no cockroaches or rats, no smell of urine or feces. I was successful only part of the time. I shared rooms with animals (medium-sized if I was lucky, small if I was not). I drove hard bargains with cagey pearl dealers and got ripped off (at least in the beginning) before I learned to haggle with the best in the world. I became pearl-crazed, spending hours studying individual pearls till I got dizzy. Pearls were all I thought about. Wherever I went, I had vivid dreams about them. I still do.

Unexpected things happen on such open-ended, months-long global peregrinations. Maybe it was over the vast blue expanse of the South Pacific near Tahiti, or in the calm of the Timor Sea off Australia while sorting pearls moments after they had emerged from their watery wombs. As I got more and more entranced by these perfect little spheres, my fascination paradoxically became less about pearls and more about what they ultimately represented. Pearls embody how humans can trick Mother Nature into producing some of the world's most expensive objects. That was a nifty trick, but it wasn't what ultimately drew me so fully and inexorably to pearls. Pearls had grown into metaphors, prisms through which I could view global economics, the environment, fashion, wealth, greed, exploitation, adventure, and indomitable human spirit.

But why pearls? Why not some other object (diamonds, coffee beans, chocolate, really almost any good would have worked) to observe the world's interconnections? What exactly was it about pearls that led me on this four-year orbit?

My affection for pearls is curious. I'm not a jewelry person. I've never worn a watch. I hate diamonds and gold. Too showy, too glittery. Too much of a neon sign. Pearls are altogether different. Plucked from a live oyster, pearls are at once shiny, lustrous, ready to wear. They need no polishing, no treatment whatsoever. Pearls are the coal-mine canaries of the world's seas and oceans. The environment pearls come from (at least for saltwater pearls) has to be absolutely pristine for them to grow.

I've carried a torch for pearls ever since I was a little boy. My favorite book as a youngster was a dog-eared copy of *The Pearl*, which I must have read twenty times. I had (and still have) a wild crush on Holly Golightly, the Audrey Hepburn character in the 1961 film *Breakfast at Tiffany's*, bedecked in those exquisite pearl strands while peering into Tiffany's window. Princess Grace, Jackie Kennedy, and Princess Diana all were beautiful women, yes, but what sealed their sophistication and charm for me wasn't their looks, it was the pearls girding their necks.

Not everyone "gets" pearls. Few men do because pearls are so fundamentally distinctive when it comes to quantifying, grading, and pricing. Men seem to prefer a fail-safe system that matches specific characteristics with corresponding prices. Pearls don't have the four Cs (carat, clarity, cut, and color) as diamonds do to determine quality. Pricing a pearl is wholly subjective. Maybe that's one of the reasons I like them so much. Their beauty lies wholly with the beholder. While a dealer can boast of a pearl's color, lustre, skin purity, orient, shape, there's absolutely no universal grading system. The same strand can go for three thousand dollars or thirty thousand dollars. Some circumspect buyers might seek an official appraisal of a pearl necklace, but even the best appraisals are sketchy and subjective.

Some people have visions of Jesus, Rolexes, Rolls-Royces, the eighteenth hole at St. Andrews. My visions have always been of pearls. Big, beautiful, shiny, luminescent ones. The best have orient, a depth that allows a connoisseur to look into the pearl and see the different layers of conchiolin, or calcium carbonate. It's like looking into a pearl's soul. Let me play with pearls any day. It's my grown-up version of marbles. There's something so tactilely satisfying about rolling them around on your palms, pushing them atop a white cloth to see if they wobble, or spinning them between your index finger and thumb to distinguish the perfect round pearl from the near-round.

There's also a deeply personal reason for my love of pearls, and it has to do with my mother. When I was a child, my mother used to wear, only on special occasions, her one and only pearl necklace. The strand was modest and frugal, as was my family, a reflection of a post-Depression, post–World War II mindset. The necklace had been given to my mother by *her* mother as a wedding present. Preparing to go out for a reserved night on the town, perhaps to celebrate their anniversary, my father would dress in a suit and somber tie, my mother would wear a cheerful but demure dress. Following the age-old pearl dictum, "last on, first off," my mother would fix her hair and slip into her dress. Then she'd take the glass stopper of a bottle of Shalimar perfume and dab behind each earlobe. It was only when she was finally ready that my mother would ask my father to fasten the clasp to her one extravagance: the pearl necklace. This was always an ordeal, my father struggling with the clasp, my mother waiting anxiously till he got it right. "Stand still," he'd instruct my mother, sternly and genially.

I was mesmerized by what I thought were mysterious white marbles on a string. I'd marvel at their sheen, but what I remember most was the clean, clicking sound the pearls made when they collided with each other. They had a certain weight and density, they had symmetry, but most of all, they seemed to still be alive. To a little boy, they had magical powers.

Once a year, there they'd be, my parents—two ordinary Americans in the 1950s, arm in arm, strolling out the front door of an ordinary suburban home, headed to celebrate another year together, a single strand of pearls leading their way to the future.

1

In the Beginning

The story everyone knows goes like this:

On a clear night on October 11, 1492, Christopher Columbus gazed westward into the horizon from the *Santa María* and saw a faint light, "like a small wax candle that rose and lifted up," as he would write in his ship's log. The next morning the Genoese navigator and his men would be greeted by legions of adoring Caribbean Indians, and thus Columbus discovered the New World. The extraordinary first-ever meeting of Indians and Europeans would stir the greatest clash of cultures the world has ever known.[1]

But that's the official, sanitized version that details how Columbus brought prosperity and religion to tens of thousands of New World Indians and, in the process, set the course for the settlement of North and South America. It's also the version of Columbus's *first* voyage to the New World. Columbus's next three voyages to the New World—and the reasons for them—have largely been lost to modern readers of history.

Our story begins with *why* Columbus made these three subsequent trips across the Great Abyss, as the Atlantic was then called. Originally, his mandate from King Ferdinand and Queen Isabella was to find a route to the Orient so that the Spanish crown could access the reputed riches of Asia. But what specifically were Columbus and the Spanish monarchy looking for?

Columbus's charge was very specific, according to his ship's log: "to discover and acquire new lands," to set forth "the expansion of the Catholic Faith," and to secure "Pearls, Precious Stones, Gold, Silver, Spiceries, and other Things and Merchandise of whatever kind, name or description that may be."

That pearls led the list of commodities was not an accident. At the time, pearls fetched more per ounce than gold, and their scarcity led to a booming seller's market throughout Europe. While the king and queen were hopeful that Columbus's expedition would result in shiploads of gold and therefore finance greater expansion of the Spanish flag, it was pearls that particularly captivated the royalty of Spain, as well as the rest of Europe. Queen Isabella was almost a contemporary of England's Elizabeth, known as the Pearl Queen (for her coronation, Elizabeth draped herself with pearls; when she died, her corpse was swathed in them). Isabella, a strawberry-blonde fashion plate who often wore ornately spun satin and velvet gowns, was fascinated by pearls. With eyes described as a combination of jade and amethyst, Isabella collected hundreds of pearls, rubies, sapphires, and diamonds. When crowned queen of Castile in Segovia at age twenty-three, the fair-skinned princess wore a magnificent pearl necklace with a ruby pendant hanging from it. After Isabella and Ferdinand's first son, Juan, was baptized in Seville in 1478, riding high atop a white palfrey in a great procession, Isabella was dressed in a brocade shimmering with pearls. The queen took to wearing pearls woven into her flaxen hair. For the wedding of her oldest daughter, Isabel, in 1490, Isabella ordered a trousseau of tapestries, gowns, chemises, coats, and robes lined with pearls. When her religious confessor, the Hieronymite monk Fernando de Talavera, counseled Isabella against such excesses, Isabella replied that such show was necessary to demonstrate to other monarchies Spain's ascendant wealth and power. What Isabella neglected to say was simply that she adored pearls.

On his first voyage, Columbus returned to Spain with little to show for his New World expedition, except for fantastic stories that tantalized the royal court, as they did much of the nation.[2] The admiral presented to the king and queen seven naked Indians he had seized on Hispaniola, who were ceremoniously baptized and pronounced royal vassals. The troupe, accompanied by squawking parrots, was paraded on Palm Sunday in a thousand-kilometer procession from Seville to Barcelona to awestruck crowds lining the streets, craning to get a look. The Indians bounced a strange and marvelous ball that rebounded higher than anyone in Europe had ever seen. One of the Indians was chosen to remain as a personal valet to fifteen-year-old Prince Juan; the others were to receive religious training and then to return to the New World to serve as missionaries. Columbus was accorded a hero's welcome, and asked to sit in the presence of the king and queen, an extraordinary accommodation.

Despite the fantastic cavalcade, the king and queen were disappointed with Columbus's New World treasure chest. They urged Columbus to return to the mysterious land he had assured them was Asia, confident that a second voyage would surpass the riches of another explorer, Marco Polo, from the city-state of Venice. For his next expedition, the king and queen pulled out all stops, authorizing Columbus to be master of a fleet of seventeen ships that would carry as many as 1,500 men. A frenzy spread through Spain, and so many men wanted to accompany Columbus that only 200 crew members were paid salaries; the rest were volunteers hoping to cash in on the certain riches to be found on the other side of the world. This time Columbus's flotilla carried horses, cattle, sheep, pigs, and goats, all designed to sustain a settlement in the New World. With the crammed-packed ships went accountants and treasurers: Columbus was to keep for himself one tenth of all treasures, with almost all of the rest going to the Spanish crown.[3]

While pearls and gold may have been what the sovereigns were after, it was spices that Columbus brought back with him in the spring of 1496 when he returned from the second voyage. Spices by then had become thoroughly essential to Europeans. Salt, as well as pepper and other dried plants, was used to preserve meat and to conceal odors of spoiled foods. Spices such as cinnamon, nutmeg, cloves, vanilla, cassia, and saffron were indicators of wealth and status, and since most had to be imported through Venice and Egypt, Columbus's discovery was welcomed by the Spanish monarchs. Along with the spices, Columbus this time returned with 1,500 Taíno Indians, who were given Catholic training; almost all died of infectious diseases within six months back in Spain.

Spreading God's will to the natives may have been a noble undertaking, but what the king and queen particularly wanted—pearls and gold—Columbus was unable to provide his patrons. The most he could show for all the money the royals had fronted for both expeditions were several ornamental masks and belts accented with gold, along with crudely woven pieces of cotton. This time Isabella and Ferdinand did not ask Columbus to sit in their court.

The admiral returned to the New World two years later. On August 4, 1498, he sailed into the Gulf of Paria, at the mouth of the Orinoco, near the landmass now known as Venezuela. Columbus wrote in his diary that he was mesmerized by the lush lands he sailed by, believing that he had found the portals of the Garden of Eden on the forested islands he called Trinidad and Gracia, on either side of his ships. At about 9:00 a.m. on August 8, he anchored. Immediately, he was greeted by natives wearing strands of glistening pearls. Columbus promptly sent a boat ashore, where his crew was led to a chieftain's house for a gala feast. Columbus traded small brass bells, glass beads, and sugar for three pounds of pearls. When he inquired as to the pearls' source, the Indians told him that sumptuous, giant pearl oyster beds lay close by, to the immediate west and north, within a day's trip. At long last, Columbus was close to the Holy Grail.

Inexplicably, though, Columbus never sailed to the pearl-rich destination. In his diaries, he writes that he left immediately to sail to Hispaniola because food stock and supplies on his ship were spoiling. He also concedes that his health was deteriorating, "as a result of lack of sleep, I was suffering in my eyes." At the time, sunglasses had not been invented, nor had the relatively simple innovation of wide-brimmed hats; Columbus wrote that he was almost blind from nonstop squinting into the sun. He also suffered from aggravated arthritis and gout, and complained that he hadn't slept for more than a month. The physical ailments, as well as the worsening condition of his ships and the spoiled food in the holds, prompted him on August 8 to sail to the Spanish stronghold of Hispaniola without ever exploring the fertile gardens of luminescent pearls the queen so coveted. At least, that's what the admiral's diaries indicate.

Within a decade, the waters surrounding the islands of Cubagua, Margarita, and Coche would be discovered to contain the richest oyster beds in the world. No one knows how many pearls Columbus ever traded for or seized in the southeastern Caribbean near the coast of Venezuela, but in October he sent back to the king and queen a map of the Paria Gulf along with a sealed small cache of pearls, in an attempt to curry favor with his benefactors. Finally, the sovereigns had something tangible for all the money they had given Columbus.

News of Columbus's treasure chest, and his map pinpointing where to find more of what was inside, circulated to entrepreneurial European navigators and businessmen. Soon, the pearl rush was on. If there was little gold on the New World islands, pearls would do just fine. To Europeans, pearls meant the promise of staggering sums of money and opulence.

In 1499, Alonso de Ojeda, a gentleman (known as an *escudero*) volunteer on Columbus's second voyage, hired Juan de la Cosa, who had been on Columbus's first two expeditions and who had owned the *Santa María*, to lead a four-ship fleet to the area near Cubagua island to plunder the gulf's oyster beds. Along with Ojeda and Cosa, the Florentine merchant Amerigo Vespucci joined to assay the findings for the monarchs. The flotilla left in May 1499 and took just twenty-four days to cross the Atlantic. Vespucci wrote to a friend in Florence, Pedro Soderini, that on the expedition he found "a huge quantity of very good oriental pearls" weighing 119 marks, which he traded *"cascabeles, espejos y cuentas, diez balas y hojas de latón* (tiny bells, mirrors, and beads, ten shots of lead, and sheets of brass)" for.[4] In 1500, another pearl-seeking armada set sail, this one organized by a consortium of businessmen led by Cristóbal Guerra and Pedro Alonso Niño, who had been a crew member on Columbus's first two expeditions. Niño's ships were the more successful of the two flotillas, and returned to Spain with ninety-six pounds of magnificent pearls, "some as large as hazelnuts, very clear and beautiful, though poorly strung," according to historian Carl O. Sauer.[5] (One reason for the poor stringing was that the Indians did not possess Western instruments such as steel needles or drills necessary to pierce the delicate pearls without damaging them.)

In December 1499, the Spanish monarchy had authorized yet another voyage led by Vicente Yáñez Pinzón, the brother of Columbus antagonist Martín Alonzo Pinzón. All told, between May 1499 and June 1505, at least eleven flotillas left Spain in search of pearls and other riches in the New World. As word spread of vast pearl beds near Cubagua, more and more ships sailed from Spain for the New World. Ultimately, the waters surrounding Venezuela, and later, Colombia, were to produce more pearls in such a short period of time than any other region in the history of the world.

But the man who supposedly sailed into the pearl-producing water first was to realize none of the bounty of his successors. Columbus made a fundamental blunder when he first spotted the pearls in the Gulf of Paria. His contract with the king and queen as Admiral of the Ocean Sea mandated that he would personally receive 10 percent of the value of all goods seized on his voyages, and that he would be granted authority over all lands he discovered. What Columbus failed to do on his third voyage was not personally set foot on land. Instead, he sent his men to barter with the Indians, and thus he never performed the singular legal act of possession of the new territory. It was a technicality that was to undermine the rest of his career, providing a trump card for the king and queen to legally extricate themselves from Columbus, allowing the monarchs to license other navigators to explore what arguably should have been the exclusive domain of Columbus.

While this second crop of Spanish navigators, all following in Columbus's wake, was busy trading trinkets for increasingly large quantities of priceless pearls, enriching both themselves and the crown's coffers, Columbus had fallen into disfavor with the crown. The king and queen had commissioned a prosecutor by the name of Francisco de Bobadilla to get to the bottom of the squalid conditions and Columbus's mismanagement of affairs at Hispaniola. Bobadilla visited the island in the spring of 1500, by all accounts was horrified, and promptly had Columbus arrested and shipped back to Spain in chains. Thus, as scores of explorers, almost all of them antagonists of Columbus, were realizing huge profits from the procurement of New World pearls, the decommissioned admiral suffered the ignominy of hearing about their great fortunes while held under house arrest.

The Indians had initially regarded the Spanish as powerful, supernatural beings, who had arrived in mammoth ships never seen before, armed with such marvels as cannons, muskets, gunpowder, and axes. The Indians must have been awestruck, marveling at the enormous masts and huge sails. And metal. The Indians had never seen a substance as hard and durable, which, they were told, could be fashioned into everything, from knives, plates, cups, and utensils to needles and hooks. There was more: soft beds, finely crafted shoes, brightly colored flags. But of all the amazing items the Europeans brought with them, the most impressive to the Indians was glass.

In one of the world's most lopsided exchanges, the Spaniards heaped on the Indians inexpensive glass objects—beads, mirrors, glass shards, clear and colored bottles—for dazzling pearls that would fetch fortunes in Europe. It was the sparkle of glass, as well as its utility, that mesmerized the Indians.

Pearls were essential life elements to the Indians, but they were also plentiful in the southeast Caribbean waters. Their lack of scarcity reduced any sense of economic value to the Indians. The natives viewed pearls as material representations of a great ephemeral spirit. Pearls not only reflected light but transported light from within, and, as such, were viewed as giving strength and power to the wearer. "Light was life, light was mind, and light was great being," write historians Christopher L. Miller and George R. Hammell. Associated with water and life, pearls were a natural symbol of eternity to the Indians. Pearls were viewed as "sensuous, variably coloured embodiments of bright cosmic energy that energized the universe," writes anthropologist Nicholas J. Saunders. Shiny objects embodied brilliant luminescence and dazzling colors—values the Indians held as life-giving. Brilliant light brought structure, order, and reverence. Shimmering clear lakes, for instance, were viewed as portals through which the dead ascended to a spiritual realm.[6]

When the Spaniards opened up their chests full of glass beads, the Indians viewed the glass as even better than pearls. The man-made "jewels" provided an even greater concentration of light than pearls. To lure the Indians to part with pearls, the Spaniards employed, as Stephen Greenblatt writes in *Marvelous Possessions: The Wonder of the New World*, "the grossly unequal gift exchange." It went like this, writes Greenblatt: "I give you a glass bead and you give me pearls worth half your tribe."[7]

However skewed such a trade seems today, to the invaders there was little sense of inequality. In exchange for giving the Indians the glory of Catholicism and the privilege of being subjects of the royal court, the Spanish had the divine right to take as many pearls and other objects of economic worth as they wanted.[8] Once they realized the pearls' worth to the Spaniards, the Indians gladly traded more and more pearls for a chance to own such novel European goods as wine made from grapes, firearms, linen, and wheat bread (by 1516, wine and guns were prohibited from trade because they had led to violence and hostility). The Spanish let nothing get in the way of their mission to bring tens of thousands of pearls back to Spain. By the end of the first decade of the 1500s, pearls had become the New World's largest export, exceeding the value of all other goods combined. Navigators returned to present to Ferdinand and Isabella so many pearls that the king and queen took to plunging their hands into treasure chests, letting the gleaming white orbs pour through their splayed fingers.

The sovereigns' demand for pearls, as well as the sharply escalating market for them, soon became so great that within a decade whole Indian tribes were condemned to slavery and forced to dive for pearls. Especially prized for their diving were the Lucayans, capable of submerging more than 100 feet while holding their breath. To ensnare the Lucayans, the Spanish would announce with fanfare that they had just come from the spirit world and were willing to return there so the Lucayans would be able to visit their dead family members. Wholly unaccustomed to such wholesale deceit, the Lucayans swarmed the Spanish caravels, after which the ships' hatches would be locked, and the Indians would then be transported to outlying islands that had been transformed into labor camps, where they would be forced to dive for pearls.

Thousands of enterprising Spaniards sailed to the Gulf of Paria, by now known as the Golfo de Perlas (Gulf of Pearls). As an incentive to stay, the Spanish crown rewarded settlers with homesteads that included Indian slaves, provided the settlers converted the Indians to Catholicism. If the Indians resisted, they would be declared slaves by Spanish rule; to expedite matters, settlers reported that the Indians were cannibals and sodomites, and when so informed, the Spanish throne mandated that such infidels be legally taken as slaves anyway.

The descriptions of exploitation and subjugation of the native Indians to secure pearls is numbing. The most complete account comes from the Bishop Bartolomé de las Casas, a Spanish colonist whose father had accompanied Columbus on his second voyage. Las Casas turned into a well-known chronicler of Indian abuses in the New World, although scholars for years have contended that his account was exaggerated; perhaps because of that, it served as much-needed agitation for social reform.[9] In many ways, Casas is the forerunner of today's liberation theologists in Latin America. Here's just one paragraph of his numbing account, published in 1552, of pearl divers off the island of Trinidad—today the nation of Trinidad and Tobago:

One of the cruelest and most damnable things in the whole of Creation is the way in which the Spanish use natives to fish for pearls. The life of a pearl-fisher in these conditions is worse than any other on the face of the earth; it is even more dreadful and more terrible than that of the native gold-miner, ghastly though that undoubtedly is. They are in the water from dawn to dusk, often operating at depths of four or five fathoms. Seldom are they permitted to surface for air but must spend their time swimming under water and tearing at the oysters in which pearls grow. Once they have filled their nets they surface, gasping, and hand the oysters to the Spanish taskmaster who sits in a smak or canoe. If they spend more than a few seconds at the surface to get their breath back, he will punch or grab them by the hair and push them back under, making them dive once more. Their only food is fish—and then only oysters—plus, perhaps, some cassava bread (they bake with cassava flour of the region), the oysters providing little in the way of sustenance and the cassava being extremely hard to make. They are kept perpetually hungry. At night they are shackled to prevent them from escaping and they have to sleep on the hard ground. Often, when out fishing or searching for pearls, a man will dive never to resurface, for the poor wretches are easy prey to all manner of sharks, the most ferocious of sea creatures, capable of swallowing a man whole. One can see how closely the greed of those Spaniards involved in this profitable enterprise of pearl-fishing induces obedience to God's commandment to love Him and to love one's neighbors, for they place their fellow-creatures in peril of both body and soul (the wretches dying without learning of Christ and without the benefit of the Sacraments). On top of this, their victims are forced to spend their last days in agony, and the nature of the work is such that they perish in any case within a few days, for not many can spend long under water without coming up for air, and the water is so cold that it chills them to the marrow. Most choke on their own blood as the length of time they must stay under water without breathing and the attendant pressure upon their lungs makes them haemorrhage from the mouth; others are carried off by dysentery caused by the extreme cold to which they are subjected. Their hair, which is naturally jet black, takes on a singed appearance more typical of sea-wolves, and their backs come out in great salt sores, so that they look more like deformed monsters than men, or like members of another species altogether.[10]

All those pearls meant a continuing stream of fortune flowing back to the Spanish monarchy. When Charles V became king in 1519, the demand for pearls soared more as the Spanish court required more and more pearls be used as jewels and in clothing, to decorate churches, and as exchange for manufactured goods from more industrialized European nations. Spain's coffers so swelled that pearls helped underwrite a series of expansionist battles to seize lands belonging to France and Brittany.

From 1513 to 1530, an astonishing 113 million pearls were harvested near the island of Cubagua.[11] To regulate the commerce of pearls, the Spanish sovereignty officially founded Nueva Cádiz in 1528 on Cubagua, although the settlement dates back to 1509. Most of the pearls were shipped to Seville, which became Spain's center of pearl trade. One observer, Garcilaso de la Vega, noted that there was such an abundance of New World pearls in the Seville marketplace that, "they were sold in a heap . . . just as if there were some kind of seed."[12]

Columbus ultimately became a disgrace to the king and queen, his island outposts overrun with disease, filth, hunger, mutiny, and violence. But his discovery of New World pearls signaled a new chapter in Europe. The mariner who had opened Europe's eyes to the wealth and plenty of the New World died in 1506 at age fifty-five, broken in spirit (but financially well-off), after being released from house arrest for allegations of failure to declare all the treasures—most notably pearls—he had seized.

In less than thirty years, pearls had become a prime symbol of Spanish colonial dominance in the New World, a manifest Christian destiny that resulted in gaudy displays of pearls in thousands of European churches and scores of royal courts. Pearls had turned into a necessity for the well-dressed aristocratic woman and man from Lisbon to Copenhagen. Highly polished Venetian glass and imitation gems eventually put a dent in pearl consumption, but while skillfully made, the glass lacked the lustre and cachet of pearls. Glass beads (then and now) were no match for the real thing.

Pearls had become integral to fashionable European nobility, near-nobility, and the upper middle classes. Portraits and engravings of the era show members of the Hapsburgs, Medicis, Borgias, Tudors, and Stuarts all prominently wearing pearls to the exclusion of other gems. No longer accessories, pearls were essential elements that proclaimed success. The allure of pearls was a marketer's dream: their presence conferred instant status on the wearer. Europe couldn't get enough of them.

2

A Pearl Primer:
Some of What You Need to Know

Queen Isabella wasn't the first. For more than three thousand years, pearls have been an essential fashion element for the world's most powerful women. Cleopatra is said to have dissolved a magnificent pearl in wine; then, she drank the solution to demonstrate to her lover Antony the wealth of her kingdom.[1] Queen Isabella, Queen Elizabeth I, Catherine the Great, and Josephine Bonaparte revered pearls. All wore as many and as often as they could. Flash forward to the twentieth century. Any list of pearl lovers includes such icons as Jackie Kennedy Onassis, Princess Grace, Maria Callas, Coco Chanel, Marilyn Monroe, Diana Vreeland, Doris Duke, Katharine Graham, and Princess Diana.

These days, though, the type of woman who wears pearls is undergoing a makeover. To some, pearls used to be dowdy and Republican. Fueled in part by inexpensive Chinese pearls that started to flood the world market in the late 1990s, pearl wearers today no longer have to own a closet full of cashmere pashminas, graduate from a Seven Sisters college, marry old money, and live in Greenwich (winters in Palm Beach) to afford a strand. Barbara Bush still wears them, but so do secretaries, junior account executives, and middle-class mothers. Remade June Cleavers are just as likely to wear pearls today whether they're dressed in Vera Wang cocktail dresses and Jimmy Choo stilts or wearing Old Navy sweatpants and flip-flops.

An abbreviated registry of style makers for whom pearls are at the core of their fashion aesthetic includes Michelle Obama who showed up wearing a choker of big Australian beauties the night her husband clinched the Democratic nomination for president, Hillary Rodham Clinton, Nancy Pelosi—but also Madonna, Nicole Kidman, Oprah Winfrey, Jodie Foster, Angelina Jolie, Meryl Streep, Jennifer Lopez, Julia Roberts, even Paris Hilton and Nicole Richie. Pearls are hot. Your grandmother might still wear them, but probably not in a low-cut Versace gown with a thigh-high slit. As shoe-design king Manolo Blahnik put it: "Pearls give a gloss, a certain refinement, even if you're just a trashy girl."

Pearls project a series of paradoxes: innocence and power; simplicity and sophistication; youth and wisdom; integrity and drama; humility and conceit; tradition and haute couture; chastity and sexuality; modesty and wealth. What other single fashion item can do all that?

Pearls also make an undeniable political statement. When former New York Governor Eliot Spitzer resigned amid a sex scandal in March 2008, standing by his side was his wife, Silda Wall Spitzer, a Harvard-educated attorney, wearing a double strand of pearls. A week later, when Eliot Spitzer's replacement, David A. Paterson, explained to the press that he and his wife had engaged in infidelities, Michelle Paige Paterson, standing at her husband's side, also wore pearls. When New Jersey Governor James McGreevey stepped down from his post and announced that he had been carrying on a gay dalliance, wife Dina Matos McGreevey, also standing by her man, wore a single strand of pearls. And in 1998, when Hillary Clinton stood next to husband President Bill Clinton as he declared about Monica Lewinsky, "I did not have sexual relations with that woman," Mrs. Clinton wore a necklace known as a torsade, a braid of pearl strands. Pearls on these powerful women telegraphed to the world that while their husbands had lied, cheated, and sinned, the wives were still loyal and virtuous.

The value of pearls outstrips diamonds and gold because pearls can be worn more often and in more diverse settings. Gold or diamonds of the same price as the highest quality pearls probably would weigh too much to be worn. Something else distinguishes pearls from gold or diamonds: Gold shines, diamonds sparkle, but pearls actually glow. Their soft, warm luminescence quite literally lights up the wearer's face. Pearls also are elegantly neutral. They symbolize a bond between giver and wearer that transcends the ages of both, as well as the relationship each shares with the other. Try giving your daughter—or worse, your daughter-in-law—an ornate new diamond bracelet or necklace. If it's a man doing the giving, there's something creepy about it. Pearls are the classic present for bat mitzvahs, confirmations, milestone birthdays, graduations, weddings, and anniversaries (pearls are the traditional gift for the thirtieth anniversary), or any occasion worth celebrating.

Maybe that's because the pearl's aqueous origin makes for a natural connection to cleansings and new beginnings. Baby girls are traditionally given tiny pearl bracelets and pearl-stud earrings. Family customs call for presenting a daughter with one or two pearls on each birthday, so that by twenty-one, she'll have amassed enough pearls to string a complete strand. The concept was called Add-A-Pearl, started by the jewelry firm Juergens & Andersen. Today, some women announce their pre-engagements by wearing pearl rings; the word *pearl*, in fact, has become a verb—as in, *to pearl*, i.e., to present one's girlfriend with a pearl ring as a symbol of devotion. "She'll be the next to get engaged. She got pearled last summer."

It was fashion designer Coco Chanel who in the 1930s promoted the casual use of pearls. Chanel was hugely influential in spreading their gospel when she mixed ropes of faux pearls with real ones, whether she was kicking around in sneakers and Capri pants or wearing the little black dress she invented. Following World War II, tens of thousands of American GIs brought home strands of Japanese akoya pearls for their wives, girlfriends, and mothers, making pearls a fashion statement of the early 1950s. Meanwhile, Grace Kelly was telegraphing the sophistication of pearls when she wore a pearl choker during her 1956 wedding to Prince Rainier. Pearls became as much a trademark for the new princess as the handbag Hermès was to name after her. The princess made pearls de rigueur for millions of women around the world, a relationship furthered in 1961 with First Lady Jackie Kennedy's pearl chokers, consolidating her role as arbiter of style and elegance. The attraction between modern, elegant women and pearls was thus confirmed. All over again.

Long before Isabella of Spain started wrapping ropes of pearls around her neck, pearls had been part of our cultural DNA. Graves dating back seven thousand years in Umm al-Qaiwain (now in the United Arab Emirates) have yielded pearls, and pearl shells have been found at al-Dur (also in the UAE), stacked outside the entrances to tombs. They appeared in Egypt as early as 1550 BC, as evidenced by a pearl necklace unearthed from the tomb of Queen

Ahhotep. It makes no difference what country, era, or people: for centuries, pearls have been objects of cult adoration around the world. The genesis of the pearl, accepted the world over, used to be that the tiny reflective spheres were formed by dewdrops from heaven. Oysters rose to the water's surface, opened their shells, and imbibed droplets of dew that magically transformed into pearls. The world's scholars accepted this theory as indisputable fact for more than a thousand years.

Pearls reached a dizzying height of conspicuous consumption in ancient Rome when upper-class Roman women took to draping themselves in them. "By no gods or goddesses does she swear, but by her pearls," wrote the Roman poet Martial. "These she embraces and kisses. These she calls her brothers and sisters. She loves them more dearly than her sons. Should she by some chance lose them, the miserable woman would not survive an hour." That was during the day. At night, Roman women slept with their pearls as a precaution against theft, but also because pearls were thought to protect against evil spirits.

Gaudy displays of pearls declined after the birth of Christ and the spread of Christianity. Pearls were seen by the disciples as symbols of luxury and materialism, and therefore objects that detracted from spiritual life. The image of the profligate pearl, though, soon changed from defaming Christ to embodying him. By the seventh century, pearls had transformed into representations of Christ, personifying purity, virtue, and light. Church altars were festooned with them, as were prized bibles. Pearls served as a kind of uplifting white counterpoint to somber, black rosary beads. Priests advocated pious (and wealthy) supplicants to adorn themselves with pearls so they'd be able to hear the word of God.

With that admonition, pearls again reigned as the world's most popular embellishment. Diamonds had been mined since the eighth century, but it wasn't until 1450 that the process of faceting was invented. Even with the advent of cut diamonds and polished gold, though, pearls continued to rule as the choice personal object of adoration. Marco Polo fanned their popularity when he described going to India and meeting the king of Malabar, who wore a rosary of 104 oversized pearls, as well as pearl ankle bracelets and pearl toe rings. "The king desires to reserve all such [pearls] to himself, and so the quantity he had is almost incredible," Polo wrote in his travelogues.

Pearls reached such a frenzied height in Venice that from the fourteenth to the sixteenth century, the Venetian government resorted to enacting sumptuary laws to restrict the flaunting of them. Venice was at the vortex of trade between Europe and Asia, and because of its location and pearls' desirability, the shiny orbs from the East flooded the city. Venetian officials viewed pearls as reckless, extravagant scourges that had to be eradicated to return Venice to fiscal responsibility. When Venetian women refused to comply, lawmakers resorted to making their husbands accountable for their wives' pearl obsession. Men whose wives persisted were fined and faced banishment for three years. Other edicts were promulgated throughout western and northern Europe, given additional weight by the church's reversal, which inveighed (once again) against conspicuous material consumption. In Germany, a bishop in 1627 began excommunicating women who persisted in adorning themselves in pearls. Still, as in the past, despite the measures, women (and men) continued to drape themselves with as many pearls are they could afford (and then some), thus giving rise to the European era known as the Pearl Age (1524–1658). Pearls were in such demand that when available they were instantly bought or traded by Europe's nobility, near-nobility, aristocracy, and upper classes. Kings insisted on decorating their robes, vestments, and scepters with them. Pearl teardrops nestled in the cleavage of queens for all to marvel. Emperors and maharajas covered themselves from head to toe with as many pearls as they could hoard. Pearls were set in crowns, scrolls, tapestries, gowns, pendants, pins, rings, hair clips, bracelets, earrings, necklaces, buckles, even corsets. In portraits of royal family members, pearls were prominently displayed on both men and women. (European royalty today continues the custom. When Camilla Parker Bowles married Prince Charles at Windsor Castle in 2005, she wore a rare black pearl brooch set in fleur-de-lys.)

Artists' renditions of the times reflect the pearl's lofty status. Sandro Botticelli's 1486 painting *The Birth of Venus* shows a sultry redhead rising from an opened oyster shell, transformed from a pearl to a woman. In Flemish painter Peter Paul Rubens's 1615 portrait *Venus Before a Mirror*, Venus is shown with two different pearl earrings, one gray, the other white, perhaps expressing the dark and light sides of love. In Johannes Vermeer's 1667 canvas *Girl with a Pearl Earring*, one of eleven paintings in which Vermeer depicted pearls, the Dutch painter used the milky-white reflection of a pearl to accentuate his model's skin hue (and triggered endless speculation as to exactly why a commoner, albeit comely, would be wearing such expensive jewelry).

By the mid-nineteenth century, Paris had become the unrivaled fashion capital of the world, where a seemingly limitless supply of pearls and pearl-encrusted jewelry was worn with regularity by the aristocracy, as well as by anyone pretending to be wealthy, artistic, or both. Paris reigned as the world's pearl-trading epicenter, its marketplace at the intersection of rue Lafayette and rue Cadet. One reason for Paris's ascension as the matrix of pearl trade was its proximity to what were then three of the world's richest natural pearl beds: the Persian Gulf (the region today surrounded by Iran, Kuwait, Saudi Arabia, and Qatar); the Red Sea; and the Gulf of Mannar (between the southeastern coast of India and Ceylon). Once strung in Bombay, pearls would be shipped to Paris, where they'd fetch top prices, to be transported worldwide.

Following the Russian Revolution of 1917, thousands of White Russians flocked to Paris, many bringing family jewels (their only portable wealth), which they sold to French dealers to buy homes and apartments, or to continue their trek, often to America. From 1927 to 1936, the Soviet government auctioned off half of the jewels seized from the Czarist family of Nicholas and Alexandra, much of it consisting of pearl jewelry that ended up in Paris. With the advent of the cold war, many Soviet officials consolidated their personal wealth by off-market selling of antique natural pearls to Parisian dealers.

Natural pearls, exceedingly rare today, are exquisite accidents of nature, discovered by the laborious task of opening hundreds of thousands of oysters. A perfect natural pearl of extraordinary quality may be the product of one out of ten million oysters. Contrary to popular belief, seldom will a grain of sand produce a pearl, since mollusks constantly filter sand out of their organisms. Rather, almost all natural pearls are formed after a minuscule piece of coral, shell, bone, or (most likely) a tiny parasite finds its way inside an oyster. With the foreign matter unable to escape, the ensuing process is similar to a splinter on a finger: If the body can't extrude the sliver, the skin gradually covers it. In the case of a mollusk, the oyster's own natural defenses protect its soft, vulnerable flesh from the irritant by forming a smooth coating called nacre (pronounced NAY-ker). In a sense, the tiny unsuspecting trespasser becomes entombed in a spectacular sarcophagus we call a pearl.

For thousands of years, the only way to find pearls was through the prowess of divers. Greed, exploitation, and danger underscored the reality of procuring the rare adornments that ultimately would end up on a wealthy woman's neck, ears, fingers, wrists, or flowing tresses. Depending on the region, divers had to cope with sharks, crocodiles, giant clams, grouper, octopus, diamond fish, sawfish, jellyfish, rays, barracuda, dragon fish, and moray eels. If that wasn't enough, divers had to contend with a lethal disease known as the bends, or caisson disease, which happens when nitrogen bubbles form in the diver's bloodstream, not unlike fizz from a shaken bottle of pop.

Prior to the late 1800s, depending on where and when they lived and were employed, native divers dove nude (so as not to conceal any pearls), outfitted with a rope basket, a nose clip made from bone, beeswax earplugs, and finger-tip mittens. Many carried amulets—a strand of mother's hair, a child's nail clipping. Diving crews were often made up of men maimed by shark bites or ray-fish stings; some divers were blind, missing limbs, or deaf (an occupational hazard caused by burst eardrums from diving so deep, but a malady not unwelcomed since it allowed divers to dive even deeper). Many divers found themselves so much in debt to boat captains for food and necessities that when the divers died, their sons were forced to dive to erase their fathers' debts, which, of course, never could be paid off.

Divers were weighted with stones that allowed them to submerge fast. They hyperventilated, as well as trained themselves to hold their breath while being lowered by ropes. On the ocean floor, they'd scramble for as many oysters as they could grab, placing the mollusks in baskets before saltwater would burn their eyes or the air in their lungs would give out. The average length below was fifty to eighty seconds, at which time divers would tug on a rope and be pulled to the surface. When pressurized suits were introduced in the late 1800s, divers could stay down longer due to an air line, but the subsistence pay remained. Divers were paid a percentage of pearls found, which meant that, after their expenses were deducted, they usually ended up working for free. It was exceedingly rare if more than a single pearl was found per every thousand oysters hauled to the surface.

Natural pearls from the Arab world were (and still are) known in the trade as Oriental pearls. Wealthy Arabs and Indians are especially fond of such pearls, and today many flaunt lavish displays of pearls on their fingers, ears, noses, and toes. Pearl historian Jean Taburiaux writes that some Arab sheiks still collect pearls for the sheer pleasure of looking at them.

A sheik would take each jar and place it on a rich carpet covered by a white cloth so that nothing could change the colour of the pearls. The first few jars would contain pearls of rare quality but of small diameter. As more jars were taken from the chest, the diameter of the pearls increased. In a short while the guest, sitting cross-legged before about ten pearl jars, some more beautiful than others, would probably be seized by a strange emotion before the fairyland of gems.

Now for the greatest attraction: the sheik draws forth the final jar, containing a single pearl. What a joy! Alone, it is worth more than all the others. Watch the face of the sheik. He has let nothing show, but his eyes betray him; it is his pearl and he loves it more than anything in the world. But, as the visitor leaves the palace, he will be given, as a sign of friendship, a pearl which will remind him of an unforgettable spectacle.[2]

Such natural pearls today, though, have become nearly impossible to find. As early as 1890, many of the world's most plentiful centers of pearling began to feel the effects of pollution and overfishing. More remote habitats for pearl oysters had to be discovered to feed the world's voracious appetite. Thus pearlers moved to Japan, where inlets, seas, and oceans were pollutant-free. Among the most promising world regions were the shark-infested waters along the northwest coast of Australia, between Kimberley and Port Medland, with Broome (still known as the Port of Pearls) serving as the center of commerce. Pearls were also fished in New Guinea, Indonesia, the Cook Islands, Malaysia, and the Philippines, as well as in New Caledonia, Fiji, Samoa, and French Polynesia. Closer to the United States, the Sea of Cortez, off Baja California (where Steinbeck's *The Pearl* takes place), became a popular venue for pearl fishing. This region became known for lustrous black pearls, while the shores off Venezuela and Panama were known for small white and pink pearls.

Today, practically all pearls sold are cultured pearls, developed through a process pioneered in Japan in the early twentieth century by Kokichi Mikimoto. The son of a poor noodle-maker, Mikimoto is credited with creating the billion-dollar cultured-pearl industry. Mikimoto established his first pearl farm in 1888 on the Shinmei inlet, in Shima, and by 1906 he had developed the world's first round cultured pearl; two years later, the Japanese government granted Mikimoto a patent for the innovation of inserting into akoya oysters tiny mussel-shell beads that would form the nucleus of a pearl. To convince the world that cultured pearls were just as real as natural pearls, Mikimoto took to showcasing his goods through extravagant displays at world fairs, starting in St. Louis in 1904. Western visitors to Japan would return home with perfectly round pearls at a fraction of the cost of natural pearls. As fewer and fewer natural pearls were found around the world, the popularity of Mikimoto's economically priced cultured pearls soared.

Today's global process for culturing pearls is similar to how Mikimoto did it more than a century ago. A bead is inserted by a technician into the oyster's gonad, along with mantle tissue from the same species of oyster. The live oyster is then returned to its natural habitat, left to grow nacre around the bead to form a pearl. Almost all of the beads used as nuclei today, no matter where pearls are cultured, are made from ground-up and processed clamshells found in the Mississippi River Delta. The place where pearls were first cultured—in the Japanese prefecture of Shima—is so polluted today that few pearls grow there any longer.

While commerce of cultured pearls roared, the world's natural pearl industry began an inexorable death. The cost of finding natural pearls comparable to cultured pearls was astronomical, and natural pearls became increasingly scarce. The only real trading of natural pearls today is mainly through international auction houses. The centuries-old practice of diving for pearls, as depicted in *The Pearl*, no longer exists on any scale other than as family businesses on isolated islands and coastal regions.

Although the Japanese are the number-one consumer of pearls, Japanese production each year declines. Still, the Japanese port city of Kobe remains the global center of the pearl industry, where today tens of millions of pearls are cleaned, sorted, graded, drilled, processed, and exported each year. Kobe is still known as Pearl City, even though the vast majority of the pearls processed there come from elsewhere, mostly China.

The time-tested way to tell a real (natural or cultured) pearl from a fake is by rubbing it across the bottom of your teeth. Real pearls feel gritty, whereas fakes feel smooth. Another way, preferred by dealers, is to rub the pearls against each other. If they feel clean without drag, they are beads, not pearls. Whether natural or cultured, pearls are made up almost entirely of aragonite, or calcium carbonate, which coats the pearl's center in irregular concentric bands, not unlike the rings of a tree. Conchiolin (pronounced KONK-eye-oh-lin), an organic bond between the layers, and water account for the other material in pearls. Experts can distinguish only slight differences between natural and cultured pearls. One way is to observe the way each bounces: natural pearls bounce more rhythmically than cultured pearls, and cultured pearls tend to have a more rapidly diminishing rate of bounce, which often ends in a flat thud. Legend holds that following high-society dances in Paris during the Belle Époch, loose pearls from broken necklaces were often found on ballroom floors. Scavengers could tell real from imitation pearls by stamping on the jewelry: The paste would crush while the real pearls gave resistance.

Pearl-strand lengths vary and come in six standard styles: dog collar, multiple strands that fit tightly around the neck (they help to conceal wrinkles); choker, 14–16 inches; princess, 16–20 inches; matinée, 20–26 inches; opera, 30–36 inches; and rope, more than 36 inches. Other styles include: bib, three or more concentric stands of different lengths, and *torsade*, twisted strands. There are two pearl-stringing protocols: uniform (all pearls are the same size) and graduated, or chute (each succeeding pearl is larger, culminating with the largest pearl at the center of the strand; in this manner, the wearer can hide smaller, less expensive, often inferior pearls near the clasp behind the neck). No matter how long the strand, the string between each pearl is knotted for two reasons: to prevent abrasions from the pearls rubbing against each other and to prevent losing the pearls should the strand break.

Stored in a dry, airless vault, pearls will actually wither; constant dry heat will turn them brown. Pearls should be kept in a soft-cloth pouch, and ought to be slightly moisturized once a month. Vinegar is the one liquid that pearls must be kept away from; if dipped in vinegar, pearls will begin peeling and *eventually* dissolve (but not instantly, as Cleopatra's legend held). Pearls benefit from body oil, and the wearing of them against the skin enhances their longevity. "Last on, first off," the pearl wearer's maxim, is to remind wearers to protect pearls from perfumes and cosmetics, which can embed in a pearl strand. An enduring myth, which may or may not work, calls for pearls to be fed to closely watched hens for a thorough cleaning to restore their natural sheen.

Connoisseurs insist that the nature of pearls—that they are organic and plucked from the flesh of a live mollusk—is sensual. This may also be because the soft-tissue anatomy of oysters and mussels is suggestive of female genitalia. It might also have something to do with the persistent myth that when slurped and digested, oyster meat and ground-up pearls are thought to be aphrodisiacs.

For thousands of years, literature has showcased pearls, their meanings, and their significance. Several allusions: the Bible (the coats God gave Adam and Eve were as "beautiful as pearls"); the New Testament ("casting pearls before swine"); the Koran (mortals worthy of entering Paradise are greeted by virgins "resembling hidden pearls"); Shakespeare's *The Tempest* ("Why, then the world's mine oyster, which I with sword will open"); T. S. Eliot's *The Waste Land* (Madame Sosostris's tarot cards reveal a drowned Phoenician sailor with "pearls that were his eyes"). *The Pearl of Great Price*, which contains the writings of Joseph Smith, is one of the most revered tomes of the Mormon religion. So literally illuminating are pearls, they've come to represent shafts of light—thus the expression "pearls of wisdom." Pearls are often portrayed as omens, perhaps best represented by Steinbeck's Kino, who learns a gut-wrenching lesson about greed and avarice after he finds a huge pearl.

My own favorite pearl tale comes from the W. Somerset Maugham short story "A String of Beads." A pearl connoisseur notices at a London dinner party that a young, pretty governess is wearing an extraordinary natural pearl necklace he estimates to be worth 50,000 pounds. Midway through dinner, two men arrive and demand to see the governess. It seems a clerk at a jewelry store had mixed up the governess's necklace of beads for one of natural pearls. On the spot, the men exchange the pearls for the governess's fakes. The action sets forth a chain of events that includes the governess quitting her job, meeting a rich Argentine in Deauville, buying a house in Paris's Bois de Boulogne, driving around town in a Rolls Royce, dumping the Argentine for a Greek lover, and eventually becoming, in Maugham's words, "the smartest cocotte in Paris."

Pearls have that effect on some women.

3

Entranced

Bo knows. At least, that's what everyone who knows anything about pearls told me. The publisher of a journal called *Pearl World*, considered the Bible of the industry, Bo Torrey for more than a decade and a half has been an international authority on pearls. *Pearl World* is a high-priced, subscription-only, trade publication, and when I couldn't find it in any library or online, I called Bo at his home in Phoenix one morning in June to see if he'd sell me back issues.

"Hell, you don't need to buy them," he told me. "Come on down and I'll let you read 'em all. I'll lock you in a room and won't let you out till you've read every last issue." Bo cautioned me to wait till the winter, though. "It's an oven in Phoenix in the summer. I wouldn't wish this inferno on my worst enemy." I couldn't care less about the heat. Within twenty-four hours I was on a plane.

Bo, no surprise, is a bear of a man, six feet and pushing 250 pounds. He greeted me barefoot, with hairy chest, grayish beard, and nothing else on except a pair of very short shorts. Bo introduced me to his wife, Kumiko, a competitive volleyball player and runner whom Bo meet thirty years ago when he was an advertising executive in Japan, and to their two dogs, Mr. Pickles and

Bella, who sniffed at my ankles. Mr. Pickles was half wirehaired dachshund, half beagle; Bella was a full-blooded Japanese Shiba Inu. Both were nosey and intelligent in a Mr. Peabody sort of way. I imagined they too must have been perplexed what I was doing on their front step, inquiring about pearls.

Bo's physique (and attire) reminded me of a slimmed-down sumo wrestler. He graduated from Princeton in 1960, believes that both John McCain and CNN are *way* too liberal, and that Rush Limbaugh is "pretty damn right on almost everything." Bo thinks that women shouldn't be anchors on network news. "I love women," he explained over a five-course Japanese dinner Kumiko cooked. "I just don't want them to be giving me my news. Call me a male chauvinist pig. See if I care." Bo, who refuses to read books written by women, is the kind of guy who loathes Hillary Clinton, hates the Equal Rights Amendment ("Arizona was way out front on that one!"), and plasters his car with bumper stickers like "Prevent Forest Fires. Register Matches." All this from one of the world's great authorities on what drives so many women wild. Although his concealed weapon's permit expired years ago, Bo still makes pilgrimages to the Arizona desert with fellow militiamen to shoot Browning, Glock, and Sig Sauer automatics. Occasionally, someone brings a flamethrower or bazooka and everyone gets to go home happy.

A man of his word, Bo supplied me with seventeen years of *Pearl World*. As in any industry, Bo advised, there are hundreds of pearl insiders who are liars, cheats, grandstanders, sycophants, bullshitters, con artists, payola freaks— and that doesn't include thousands more who, as he put it, "will blow smoke up your ass. And not just a little smoke."

Bo and I spent the better part of three days looking at his pearl collection. He gave me a lesson in appraising pearls, showing me pearls that had been treated, dyed, tinted, polished, buffed, heated, bleached, irradiated, all to make inferior pearls look like collector's items. Throughout the tutorial, Bo praised Japanese and Filipino women. "You owe it to yourself to see them modeling pearls," he said with the arch of a bushy eyebrow. "You're going to have the time of your life on this little trip of yours. Your wife's not the jealous type, is she?"

I liked Bo. He was a combination college beer-drinking buddy, Bill O'Reilly (but sweet and likable), pearl expert, and pearl-industry watchdog, all rolled into one barrel-chested package. He had an ingratiating habit of calling me Babe, and I took that as a sign of trust.

Bo had been right about the Phoenix heat. The city was a pop-your-eyeballs sauna, 106 degrees and climbing. The constant whir of air conditioners was the city's mantra, and the only people I saw outdoors seemed to be poor, perspiring Hispanics waiting for buses that never arrived. Most streets in Phoenix's flat grid system didn't have sidewalks, and everyone in Bo's middle-class neighborhood had front yards of PX-green-painted concrete, Astroturf, volcanic moon rocks reminiscent of a Salvador Dali painting, or dump truck loads of rat-gray gravel. I became transfixed with Phoenix's Wild West saguaros and the local habit of drunk cowboys riddling them with bullets. The big thing was to shoot them so they'd eventually shrivel up and die. Go figure.

Bo said if I really was serious about my pearl odyssey, I'd absolutely have to get myself to Tucson at the end of February for the jewelry, gem, colored stone, and mineral show. The American Gem Trade Association exhibition probably has more loose pearls on display and for sale than any other convention anywhere. The event takes over Tucson for two weeks, and brings out tens of thousands of jewelry maniacs, many of them pearl freaks. "You gotta see it to believe it," Bo told me, sounding like a cross between P. T. Barnum and Paul Harvey. Every year, he said, there's something called the Pearl Walk at the AGTA, during which, as Bo explained, the pearl cognoscenti poke their noses into the booths of dozens of the world's most important pearl wholesalers and retailers. "You'll meet the whole pearl mafia under one roof," Bo promised.

Bo dropped me off at the Phoenix airport, and as I ran through the open-air terminal to make my flight back home, I heard him shout, "See you in Tucson in February, Babe!"

When I arrived at the convention seven months later, even in spite of Bo's hype, I hadn't prepared myself for how mega the show actually was. The convention is actually a conglomeration of thirty-eight *separate* mega shows, from the main event at the cavernous convention center downtown to a series of sleazy motels amid tumbleweeds on the wrong side of the freeway. Everything that anyone could conceivably call jewelry was there and then some, including meteorites guaranteed to have fallen from outer space. There were millions (maybe billions) of raw and finished stones and gems, including diamonds, peridots, amethysts, tourmalines, sapphires, garnets, topazes, emeralds, rubies, opals, amber, fluorite, malachite, chrysocolla, rhodochrosite, turquoise, ivory, fossils, petrified wood, quartz crystals and geodes (lots of them), coral, jade, chakra-tuned bowls, hand-tooled snuff bottles, even hand-carved ivory penises of all sizes. And of course, there were pearls. Lots of them.

As I made it to the convention center floor, a pasty guy with a pencil moustache and a string tie scanned my admittance badge before I passed through a phalanx of armed cops. Inside, I felt like James crawling into the Giant Peach.

Even with Bo's advisory, I couldn't quite fathom all that was before me—hundreds of booths, row after row, with all kinds of finished and unfinished jewelry, much of which was pearls. And this was less than 1 percent of the multi-ring offering. A jewelry thief could do well here, retiring forever on the Côte d'Azur, I thought, as I followed a queue of dealers pulling bulging black zippered wheelies filled with cut stones and pearls. As I meandered down the aisles, I noticed clusters of closed-circuit cameras strategically placed on walls and the ceiling, and that didn't include cameras concealed from view and the SWAT sentries armed with AK-47s on rooftops outside.

I was to find out from Skip Woodward, a Tucson police detective and head of security for AGTA, the way jewel thieves usually work is by "palming" a gem. "Whether they put glue on their fingers or they just have left-over maple syrup from their pancake breakfasts isn't my concern," said Woodward, a smiley Opie kind of guy with a mop of red hair, who looked like he used to lick spoons of molasses as a kid. During the first day of the show, Woodward had already gotten two complaints of men caught with stones stuck to their fingers. "Sometimes, it's really not as nefarious as it might seem. Pearls do stick to fingers. It *can* happen. Most times, though, these guys know exactly what they're doing. If you can make a quarter disappear behind your ear, then you can make a pearl disappear pretty easily," Woodward said, as he peered to my right to scan a large TV monitor split into six alternating screens.

The touted Pearl Walk Bo had promised turned out to be a motley assortment of collectors and pearl groupies. Among the group were Lois Berger, a pearl appraiser from McLean, Virginia; Eve Alfillé, the president of the Chicago-based Pearl Society of America; Elisabeth Strack, the affable author of the German-published encyclopedic *Pearls*, who had just flown in from Stuttgart; and two journalists who write about pearls, Gary Roskin from the jewelry-trade magazine *JCK* and Fred Ward, an entrepreneurial writer who seemed too important to have anything to do with me. Bo was there, too, striding around the maze of booths like a four-star general, nodding to everyone, cocked chin and pointed index finger at the ready.

The dealers had come with lockboxes filled with pearls in all shapes, colors, and sizes. We stopped in booth after booth to examine the largest pearls I'd ever seen, and I fell in love all over again. I felt guilty. My mother's modest pearl necklace would never be the same in my mind.

What I saw at one New York dealer's booth made me dizzy—a lustrous opera-length necklace of cream-white pearls from Broome, Australia; a sexy choker of peacock-colored (a green-blue-gray mélange) Tahitian pearls; an outrageous double strand of luscious, perfectly round gold pearls from the island of Palawan in the Philippines. These pearls strands were a trio to covet. Each was flawless. There were no prices posted, but these necklaces had to go for at least $50,000 apiece.

My eyes immediately went to the Australians, and almost instantly, a heavy-set dealer (replete with stubby fingers the size of sausages and pinky ring on one of those sausages) appeared. He nodded at me and without a single word unlocked a glass display case and handed me a necklace. I hadn't even asked. The dealer hadn't made me. My association with the Pearl Walkers had given me proximal legitimacy. Still, I felt like an imposter physician entering an examination room in which a patient nonchalantly unbuttons her blouse so he can examine her breasts.

I wasn't complaining. If I hadn't already been in a full swoon just by looking, I was when I held them. With thumb and forefinger, I lifted the necklace to eye level. I opened the clasp, so the strand reached down to the countertop, about twenty inches. I examined the necklace, looking at each pearl, paying close attention, as I had read, to lustre, orient, size, shape, and skin quality. All those criteria were through the roof on any scale, but in a single strand the skill is assembling pearls that match each other in *all* these qualities. Matching such over-the-top pearls could take five, ten, fifteen years. Fewer than fifty pearls per harvest probably were used in the necklace. They had to be the exact right size and color (white was the hardest to match). They also had to have identical lustre (the reflected sheen) and orient (the ability to look within the depth of the pearl). The necklace was not a graduated strand, which would have made it inferior. Each pearl in this particular strand was the same size, and my guess was close to an enormous 17 millimeters, about the size of an ample-sized maraschino cherry. I brought the strand to within two inches of my eyes. I could tell these pearls hadn't been dyed. There were no spots anywhere on them; in dyed or color-treated pearls (and even in untreated pearls), you often can make out barely visible marks like fingerprints or irregular-shaped shadows or faint blotches on the pearl's surface. The pearl's skin sometimes can be fractured slightly, too. I peered in these pearls' drill holes, where the silk thread goes through the widest part of the pearl, to check for evidence of layering or peeling, and there was none.

That all took just a minute or so. Then I positioned the palm of my left hand under the necklace, and slowly lowered the pearls so that they collapsed into a haphazard circular bunch. They carried a surprisingly dense weight. I loosely cupped my hand and tried to figure how much, ever so slightly moving my hand up and down.

"Who am I trying to fool?" ran through my mind. I have a hard time figuring out how many tomatoes make up a pound when I'm in the produce section at the grocery store, so how was I going to assay the weight of pearls (converted to momme)? Still I went through the motions. I was a virgin member of the pearl cognoscenti; I had a reputation to build. As I was to realize, theater often is at the heart of the pearl business, whether it's in bargaining for or merely admiring pearls. There's a nuanced dance between dealer and potential buyer, and to ignore that would flatten any pearl protocol, which at the time I was just beginning to pick up. Looking like I knew what I was doing was almost as important as knowing what I was doing.

The density of each pearl struck me. There was a remarkable heft to the necklace. The weight of the strand felt more like it should have come from something bigger—bullets instead of delicate pearls a woman would drape around her neck and plunge into her cleavage.

After cupping the strand for thirty seconds or so, I began to notice an almost imperceptible change. Granted, I was breathing harder, perhaps perspiring some. But something fundamental was *happening.* The pearls seemed to be pulsating in the flat of my hand. I looked at them and, for a second or two, the pearls sparkled, not just glinting light off the high-intensity bulbs above, but actually seeming to absorb the light. A luminescence appeared to be penetrating each pearl into a core deep inside.

If that weren't strange enough, as I held the strand, I could feel the pearls taking on my own body heat. The pearls had the capacity to seek and then transfer my body's warmth in a kind of natural transfusion. That was just the beginning of the exchange. Because pearls aren't nearly as hard as diamonds, gold, or platinum, they also absorb a wearer's scent, perfume, and skin oils, becoming a kind of olfactory mirror to the subtlest traces of the wearer. Women unwittingly leave telltale signs of themselves on their pearls. DNA can be swabbed off pearls just as though it had come from blood, saliva, or hair.

Finally, I rubbed one pearl against another to corroborate the obvious—that these were real. I was looking to feel a slightly gritty sensation. (I could also do this by rubbing the pearls against my teeth, but if I did that I'd really show what a quack of a doctor I was.) Just as I was about to return the strand to the dealer, I fastened their clasp. As I did that, several pearls clicked against each other, and there it was again, that clean clacking sound from a half-century earlier, the same sound I had heard when I was a little boy and my father struggled to fasten the clasp on my mother's strand. My whole exploration of the Australian necklace had taken no more than five minutes and it had brought back a memory of fifty years earlier. With regret, I handed the strand to the dealer, who returned the necklace to a stiff gray velvet form inside the display case in a manner I surmised way too blasé.

However much of a poseur I was at the time, I was swooning. How to explain it? A middle-aged college professor smitten, head over heels over *pearls*? At the time, I still wasn't sure how to explain my fixation, but there I was, beaming like a man in the throes of first love. I flashed back on my old tuxedo story and thought about how many hands had touched these gorgeous South Sea pearls—twenty, fifty, a hundred, five hundred? How long had they been separated from their oysters—they're called mother-of-pearl for a reason. What had been the path these three dozen colossal pearls had taken from Australia to Tucson? How many technicians, scrubbers, graders, sorters, stringers, traders had held these pearls in their own hands? How many other admirers had been slayed by them? Whose body heat had also turned up their temperature?

I continued walking, really gliding by now, swept along with the pearl group from vendor to vendor. I couldn't get the Australian whites out of my mind. They were freaks of nature. A host of factors had serendipitously conspired in absolute perfect harmony to produce them, then to be meticulously matched by teams of anonymous laborers. I suddenly imagined myself telescoped out of the Marc Chagall painting *Birthday*, floating off the ground. But I wasn't in snowy Belarus, where Chagall had set the painting, but in a hermetically sealed Tucson conventional hall, and the object of my affection wasn't a pretty girl holding a bouquet of flowers. What was it about pearls that was propelling me to take leave of my senses, to say good-bye to my family for months on end, to travel thousands and thousands of miles on a hopeless, wild chase? I wasn't sure, but I took my buoyancy as vindication for the journey around the corner.

I smiled.

No one on the Pearl Walk seemed to notice. They were as entranced as I was.

4

Into the Mix

The first night of the jewelry show, on the way to dinner, Bo made a wide U-turn to avoid hitting a mangy coyote that skittered across a lonely intersection. We pulled into the parking lot of a down-and-out cowpoker kind of place called Cody's Beef n' Beans. Next door was a pawnshop and a dog-grooming parlor illuminated by a neon sign in the shape of a dachshund. Cody's looked to be popular among prostitutes over forty and hobos with names like Hooter, Red, or Owlie. Our beer came in glass mugs in the shape of cowboy boots. Bo waxed rhapsodic about blasting anti-armor rocket launchers in the desert.

We got back to pearls when Bo suggested I meet some of the outlying pearl dealers at the show, the vendors camped out in Tucson's seedy Holidome and seedier Econo Lodge on Sixth Avenue on the wrong side of the freeway. I also wanted to meet the natural-pearl dealers. These vendors were perceived as renegades who eschew cultured pearls (99.9 percent of all pearls on the market today), and trade exclusively in rare pearls produced the old-fashioned way—random flukes of nature. They had a niche following; natural pearls found these days are generally small and malformed, but whenever a dealer finds a natural pearl that is anything close to large and round, it causes shockwaves in the industry. Depending on quality and pedigree, a sizable natural pearl can sell for tens of thousands of dollars.

I'd also heard about a burgeoning business in pearls sold on the Internet, and when I asked Bo about it, he said I had to meet a former Northwest Airlines flight attendant by the name of Jeremy Shepherd, who'd gotten into selling pearls through a network of Web sites he controls. "Jeremy might very well be the future of pearls," Bo said as I finished my plate of ribs. "A lot of conventional dealers hate him, and they have good reason: He can undercut their prices by half—sometimes more."

"But who'd ever buy pearls through the Internet?" I asked.

Pearls (like all jewelry) need to be examined, touched, worn, and admired. Online photographs are at best misleading, since the jewelry pictured is seldom (if ever) the same as the jewelry sold. By their very nature, most pearls have blemishes, flaws, color variations, dull and dirty sheens. When strung together, pearls must share complementary characteristics and sizes to form a unified strand, like the Australians I'd held that day. Buyers would have to be nuts to purchase pearls from a dealer like Shepherd without first examining and modeling them, no matter how inexpensive the Internet price and regardless of any money-back or exchange policy. I knew cable networks like QVC, HSN, and Jewelry Television reported tens of thousands of dollars' worth of jewelry sales every day. But I couldn't imagine anyone buying pearls that way.

Back in my hotel room, my mind conjured up image after image of those creamy, perfect Australian beauties. They floated, one by one, flawlessly matched, on strands that got longer as my dream deepened. The pearls got larger, so large that I could climb on one, and jump to another, and still another, bouncing from pearl to pearl to pearl. I was having a grand time hopping this Orient Express of pearls, not quite knowing where I'd end up.

The next morning I arrived an hour before the convention doors opened. I wanted to be among the first to walk the aisles, to meet as many dealers as possible. They'd be too busy by late morning and through the afternoon showing their wares. That's when they'd be locked in negotiating sessions with retail jewelers looking to buy stock for the coming season. The dealers were fundamental to my story. They were the nexus among a multitude of growers, middlemen, and retailers. These were the guys (at least some of them) who traveled to Asia, Micronesia, and Australia to secure the best deals from local suppliers. They were essential mile-markers on my serpentine, multi-continent route.

As I walked past the pasty guard and the brigade of patrolling off-duty cops, I realized this windowless, subterranean refuge was a kind of man-made cave filled with riches beyond the reach of everyone except a precious few. Much of the jewelry—not the pearls, but the glittery, in-your-face, knock 'em dead pieces—was designed so wealthy women could proclaim, "Look at me! I've got something you don't!" They were the kind of gaudy baubles that consisted of drippy gold and ostentatious gemstones. It was bling of the worst order. Seeing all the over-the-top outrageously expensive dreck made me realize again why I liked pearls so much.

The dealers I passed on the convention center floor ranged from Hasidim with yarmulkes and worn-thin black suits to Armani-clad, Donald J. Pliner-shod, cologne-spritzed Los Angeles sharpies. Scores of Indian families, women in saris, bindis on their foreheads, men wearing turbans operated row after row of booths, mostly selling small gems. There were three dozen pearl dealers I wanted to meet, and leading the list was Alex Vock, who owns a top-drawer wholesale business called ProVockative Gems in Manhattan. Vock is a key player in the world of pearls—he used to work for Salvador Assael, the cagey millionaire pearl dealer I'd already visited on a trip to New York. After a falling-out with Assael, Vock started his own business in the building that houses more pearl dealers than any other in the United States, 608 Fifth Avenue, a block south of Saks and St. Patrick's Cathedral.

"Alex, be careful what you say. Please," Jenine Kelly, Vock's strawberry-blonde sister-in-law and pearl trader pleaded, not making eye contact with me. "Don't get anyone angrier with us than they are already." Vock wore his own self-interest clearly.

Vock, 46, was articulate, smart, and opinionated. He speaks French, Spanish, and pretty good Japanese. At first blush, he reminded me of a compact James Gandolfini, aka Tony in *The Sopranos.*

Vock had a strange beam of light that seemed to shoot out of his right eye. Maybe that came from wearing a jeweler's loupe too often. I wanted Vock to let 'er rip, but in five minutes an early-bird customer had shown up. "Gotta go," he said, scurrying to the other side of his booth to show a strand of Australians for which he was asking thirty thousand dollars wholesale.

As I took leave of Vock, walking the convention floor, I could plainly see that at the heart of the jewelry trade was the business of schmoozing. Maybe all businesses have at their core a fundamental verbal jostling of give-and-take, but it seemed, at least in Tucson that day, all around me were tight coveys of two, a buyer and a seller, lots of hand gestures, both low-key and hyperactive, exaggerated haggling. Many in the pearl trade had parents, grandparents, great-grandparents once in the diamond district on Forty-seventh Street in New York City. Food follows palate. When pearl dealers wanted to nosh, I noticed, they headed over to Oy Vey Café, where food was prepared under the supervision of Rabbi Shemtov.

I did a little of my own schmoozing with K. C. Bell, one of the world's premier natural-pearl dealers. Bell specializes in a tiny sliver of a niche business—abalone pearls. He's a prosperous hippie in his mid-fifties, smart enough to have followed his dreams, living in San Francisco two blocks away from the ocean in the Sunset district. "I started out not knowing a cut emerald from a Heineken bottle chip. Pearls made sense to me, and the more I got into them, the more I gravitated to abalone pearls." Bell finds his pearls on the west coast of Baja, the Persian Gulf, in South America, China, anywhere he gets a lead. "When you're going after natural pearls, you end up in some very primitive places. I talk to local people, some of them the sweetest folks in the world. They generally give natural pearls to their wives or girlfriends as presents of love. I'm a businessman, but I'm also someone who's in this not really for the money. It's a way of meeting some of the nicest people in their own backyards."

I made a pass at two other natural-pearl dealers, Tish and Wes Rankin, a husband and wife team from Petaluma, California. One of their strands was causing heads to turn. It was a necklace made from natural pearls that the Rankins were asking twenty-five thousand dollars for. The pearls were small-to medium-sized, certainly no more than 8 millimeters, and while the lustre wasn't brilliant, these pearls were well matched and had a slight pinkish hue. Tish Rankin told me she had acquired the strand from an estate, but wouldn't go further. That was routine for pearl dealers. Like cocaine, you didn't ask too many questions when it came to pearls. You were pleased just to have scored such high-quality goods. Questions raised eyebrows. Whaddayou, FBI, DEA, CIA, IRS, Homeland Security? Keep your mouth shut.

The cocaine comparison with pearls was apt. Per gram, high-quality pearls sell for about the same as pure cocaine. Exceptional pearls sell for more. Both products are white, lightweight, portable, and can be hidden easily. Like cocaine, there's always a ready market for top-quality pearls.

Both commodities start out as essentially worthless, value-less products. In the case of cocaine, its origins are coca, a crop that's prized, cultivated, and guarded. Pearls today begin by design, the result of a biological action when a foreign body is inserted in an oyster, and the bivalve secretes a natural coating to protect itself, forming a pearl. Both cocaine and pearls are plentiful, command huge worldwide markets, and sell for prohibitively high prices. Both can be bought and sold twenty, thirty times before reaching the retail customer, with markups of thousands of percentage points. Seldom can anyone track the zigzag path either takes. Like cocaine, pearls are virtually untraceable. There are too many twists and turns along the way, with legions of laborers, growers, sorters, graders, couriers, and dealers spread out worldwide. Rising labor costs have pushed growers to shift production sites to developing nations with lax environmental and law enforcement. Both products require low-cost, uneducated, and plentiful labor in remote regions. Coca is grown in impoverished third world countries; an increasing percentage of the world's pearls today come from developing nations (particularly rural China, as well as Southeast Asian and Micronesian islands and atolls). In production sites for both goods, guards are armed with rapid-fire rifles to protect crops. Small, private aircraft is the preferred means to get to farms. Theft, pilferage, and raids are not uncommon at pearl- and cocaine-harvesting and production facilities.

Pearls and cocaine are free-traded, their prices based on everyday shifts in supply and demand, which makes for daily ticks up and down on an invisible yet real global stock market. The industry of both is controlled by fewer and fewer producers and distributors, buying out small, family-run farms, thereby consolidating political and economic power into fewer and fewer hands. The surviving owners today are men of means and influence.

Once production is completed, goods travel from grower to dealer to trader, each kicking up the price a notch, as the commodities are further refined, graded, sorted, and packaged for distribution through a global grid of buyers and sellers. Pearls are generally sent in sealed pouches inside FedEx boxes (or via Brink's, or a more exclusive Israeli courier, Malca-Amit); cocaine travels on private planes, inside hollowed-out cargo containers on commercial jets, in crates stored in hulls of freighters, or via condoms inside the stomachs of human mules. Compared to cocaine, international trafficking of pearls is a piece of cake.

As I was to find out, pearls are sold in lots at highly structured, invitation-only auctions, where bidders pay millions of dollars (actually, Japanese yen is the preferred currency) to buy directly from producers. Cash is the only means of payment. Both products share long, global journeys from crop to customer.

Once in the Western world, both commodities end up at an assortment of distribution points—for cocaine, the neighborhood drug dealer; for pearls, the local jewelry store.

Once at its final destination, there's no shortage of customers willing to pay dearly for top quality of each. Pearls and cocaine are luxury goods that appeal to educated first world consumers with disposable incomes. Talk to any inveterate pearl wearer, and you'll come away with the distinct impression that, although pearls aren't addictive, they're certainly habit-forming. The pearl freaks I would come to know couldn't get enough, and would go to extraordinary lengths to get more.

The biggest difference, really, between the two products is that the sale and possession of pearls is legal, and the sale and possession of cocaine (in most places) is not.

I like the cocaine-pearl comparison because it strips pearls of the cultural construct of glamour and converts them into any other precious good that comes from nature cheap and goes to consumers expensive.

That day in Tucson I trekked to several outlying jewelry expositions, and the most remarkable was in a huge, sweltering, seedy place called the Holidome, a series of connected makeshift structures and domed tents in the parking lot of a Holiday Inn. It seemed to go on forever. The Holidome looked as though it had been designed by someone who not only flunked Architecture 101, but never made it through Blocks. Almost everything was in bulk, including truckloads of freshwater Chinese pearls in every size, shape, and color of the rainbow. I spotted a nice strand of gray pearls, an obvious knockoff of Tahitian pearls.

I liked them. I rubbed the pearls against each other. I felt the gritty friction I was looking for. The pearls certainly were dyed, but they also were real.

"How much?" I asked a skinny, pimple-faced salesclerk no more than seventeen, who looked up at me, pulling earbuds from his ears.

"How many you want?"

"One, maybe two strands. Depending on the price, maybe three."

The salesclerk punched into a calculator a series of numbers. "These good. High quality. I charge you two hundred dollars per necklace."

"No way. Gimme a good price."

"I charge you five hundred dollars for all three."

"I give you seventy-five dollars per strand."

"Too cheap," the clerk said, putting his earbuds back in, then walking away insouciantly.

This was my introduction to the business of markup. I probably could have talked to the bossman, an overweight lug in a T-shirt, with greasy hair, lurking near the cash register, and pushed the price down to a hundred dollars a strand, but I wasn't in the business of buying pearls—yet. I'd be in China in two months. There, I'd see how much identical pearls go for at the source.

5

The Rana of Fresno

I

Before I went to China, where I really wanted to go was Bahrain. I wanted to sit across from a sheik in a flowing white *dishdasha* as he displayed his collection of pearls. For a thousand years, the global center of the natural pearl trade had been Bahrain. Bahraini pearls had been among the finest and most plentiful natural pearls in the world, second only to New World pearls of the sixteenth century. Gulf pearls flooded Asian and European markets for centuries. But after the Japanese pioneered pearl cultivation in the 1920s, and once oil was discovered in the Persian Gulf in 1931, oil profits drove Bahrain's economy from pearls to petroleum. Oil became the nation's extractive legacy, and Bahrain's natural pearls turned into anachronistic artifacts.

As though still protesting Mikimoto's pioneering pearl-culturing process, to this day the Bahraini government has zero tolerance when it comes to cultured pearls. Bahrain looks at cultured pearls as scourges, a blight on what once had been the nation's prized commodity. The Bahraini government today considers such pearls contraband (even inlaid in jewelry), and the penalty for trafficking in cultured pearls in Bahrain can be one year in jail. But that's nothing compared to what it used to be—the chopping off of hands or feet. At customs inside Bahrain International Airport these days, a starkly worded sign warns passengers that cultured pearls may not be brought into the country. While natural pearls of any substantial size are rarely found in the Persian Gulf any longer, they still are king in Bahrain, and wealthy sheiks are known to collect natural pearls the way American boys collect baseball cards.

When I mentioned my pearl-sheik fantasy to Jeremy Shepherd, the Internet pearl guru I'd met at the Tucson jewelry show, he laughed and told me to save my money. "It'll be a lot cheaper to go to Fresno if you want to see one of the world's largest collection of natural pearls."

Huh? Fresno?

Shepherd said that for the last several years a woman by the improbable name of Zeide Erskine had been posting on two dozen online chat rooms outrageous claims of her vast collection of natural pearls. Erskine boasted in these heavily (at least among pearl aficionados) trafficked forums that she owned a necklace of perfectly round 8-millimeter red natural pearls. *Red* natural pearls? Such a strand could fetch $100,000, maybe more, depending on the pearls' quality and how well they were matched. The price tag of the Rankins's natural pearl strand at the Tucson jewelry show had been $25,000, and that was wholesale and for a nice, but not spectacular, strand. White, black, gray, gold, blue, green pearls, yes, but *red* pearls? If they were really natural, they'd be an amazing find. It'd be like an astronomer who discovers a planet beyond the planet beyond Pluto, or a coin collector who finds a 1955 double-stamped Lincoln penny. If Erskine's claim were true, even one such natural pearl could go for thousands of dollars. I couldn't imagine what a whole strand would fetch.

The red natural pearl strand was only one of many pieces Erskine had bragged to the Internet pearl cosmos that she owned. Erskine boasted that she had an exquisite necklace of pearls cultured by Kokichi Mikimoto himself. The prized Japanese necklace, she said, was in the original red velvet Mikimoto jewelry box. Erskine broadcast online that her grandfather had bought the necklace from Léonard Rosenthal, the famous Parisian pearl dealer who in 1925 had gotten it directly from Mikimoto. There were more claims. Erskine said she owned strands and strands of natural pearls. She said she owned natural *Pteria sterna* pearls from the Gulf of California—the same oyster species Steinbeck wrote about in *The Pearl*, which so many years ago fanned my own curiosity about pearls.

Such a magnificent collection of one-of-a-kind, historic pearls ought to have made Erskine the toast of the pearl world. She'd be hotly pursued by dealers and auctioneers from Basel to London to New York. But hardly any of the dealers I asked in Tucson, except Jeremy Shepherd, had ever heard of Erskine. Bo Torrey shook his head when I mentioned her name. American's three major private dealers of natural pearls, K. C. Bell and Tish and Wes Rankin, had never heard of her.

Fresno is only a forty-minute plane flight over the Mohave Desert from Tucson, and when I called Erskine and told her that I wanted to see her collection, she seemed eager. But the day before I was to leave the Tucson gem show for Fresno, all hell broke loose (at least in the arcane world of pearl freaks). Word had reached a coterie of pearl enthusiasts on the convention floor that Zeide Erskine might be a fraud.

At a lecture given by pearl expert Elisabeth Strack, the room was filled to the rafters with pearl groupies lining up to have Strack sign her book, *Pearls*, recently translated into English. I had met Strack, one of the world's great authorities on pearls, the day before, during the Pearl Walk. She's an intense woman, a professor and gemologist, who had arrived nonstop from Germany, without any sleep, but was as cordial as could be to me. It seemed, though, that the buzz at the talk was less about Strack and more about Erskine. One of the most active contributors to the dozen or so online pearl forums buttonholed me after Strack's talk. With daggers as eyes, she told me pointblank that she had caught Erskine in a bald-faced lie. Erskine, she told me in no uncertain terms, wasn't the great collector of natural pearls she claimed to be.

"She's a fake, that's what she is," declared Caitlin Williams, a woman in her sixties with a gray shag haircut and glasses that Tootsie might have worn. There was a disconnect between Williams's kindly physiognomy and her turned-nasty countenance. Williams was so excited and agitated that her words fired from her mouth like projectiles. "She confessed to making it all up. There's no way she's gonna weasel out of this one. We got her!"

In addition to the implausible story of the red natural pearls, one of the many suspicions pearl groupies had of Erskine was her claim of the Mikimoto necklace. An original Mikimoto? I suppose it could be true. If so, though, it'd be the stuff of legend. I'd love to watch an episode of *Antiques Roadshow* when such a strand shows up, just to see the appraiser drool.

But pearl sleuth Williams wouldn't have anything of the sort. She'd be damned if Erskine's charade would be allowed to go that far. In a flurry of e-mail exchanges, Williams had thrown down the gauntlet to Erskine, writing, "When people say they have a Mikimoto on the forum, we assume you have paperwork to back it up. We expect to see a clasp or some other proof. To make such an extraordinary claim as you have done, you need some provenance. It is time to pony up, Zeide."

Jeez, these pearl freaks do take their business seriously.

Erskine responded by ponying up nothing, except more extravagant claims—which whipped everyone in the pearl blogosphere into an even greater lather.

Williams was outraged. What Erskine claimed she owned was preposterous. There's tolerance for a little bravado. Everyone's allowed to stretch the truth *a little*. But to Williams, what Erskine was doing was beyond the pale. It was a web of shameless lies meant to defraud the pearl world. To Williams, Erskine was undermining the decency that binds pearl aficionados everywhere. Had she no shame? Thieves have honor. To Williams and everyone in the everyone-knows-everyone-else world of Internet pearl collectors, Zeide Erskine had to be taken down.

Who knew what Erskine would claim next? That she had in her possession the pearl strand Queen Elizabeth I was buried in? Or Cleopatra's *other* pearl earring, the one she didn't dissolve in wine and swallow to impress Antony? The integrity of all pearl aficionados was at stake. Pearl provenance simply can't be willy-nilly made up. In the cosmos of pearl purveyors, certain things simply just aren't done. Without trust among pearl freaks, there would be grave consequences. It'd be like someone in the birder community crowing that he spotted a slender-billed curlew, when it fact it was just a curlew.

To destroy Erskine, Williams did a Google Earth search of the location of Erskine's home in Fresno, prompting Williams to rebuke Erskine online, writing to hundreds of people in pearl forums that Erskine's home was "very average, lost in a subdivision of crowded suburban homes. I was shocked, because I would have imagined that if you had the money to play high stakes games with Arabs, you wouldn't live in a subdivision. How could you protect your world class pearl collection in that house?"

And if that grenade wasn't enough, Williams lobbed more, going after Erskine's description of herself, which went something like this—"a six-foot-tall woman with a lifetime of multi-colored uncut hair, who wears big pearls and lots of them." Or, as Williams put it, Erskine claimed she had so many pearls she might as well resemble the "Rana of Dolpur."

Talk about nerve.

II

I checked into a crummy motel across the street from Cal-State University, Fresno, not far from Erskine's subdivision. My room radiated Lysol and old sneakers. When I tried to open the windows, they wouldn't budge. The air conditioner vibrated like a Subaru badly in need of a tune-up, periodically interrupted by a tap-tap-tap clunking sound as though a spelunker was desperately trying to climb out of the ductwork.

I called Erskine, who seemed a mite coquettish. Not being anything close to a football fan, I hadn't realized that this was Super Bowl Sunday. I apologized for the timing of my visit, but no matter, Erskine invited me over right away. She didn't care a whit about football. Score one for the Rana of Fresno.

Caitlin Williams had been right on one count. Erskine's house, billed as containing one of the world's great collections of rare, natural pearls, was a dump. The place was in a rundown, lower-middle-class cookie-cutter development with cars on cinderblocks in the front yards. No one had watered what once was grass, it seemed, for years. I couldn't imagine any would-be thief even thinking there might be anything of value within Erskine's house, except perhaps a nickel bag.

Zeide appeared promptly as I rang the bell. The first thing I noticed was what was hanging from her ample-sized neck: a strand of pinkish pearls the size of gumballs. You couldn't help being waylaid by them. But they were too large. Even a pearl novice like me could make them: These pearls were dyed Chinese freshwaters, cultivated to imitate astronomically priced South Sea pearls, perhaps from Indonesia. They were nice. But the color and size were wrong. They were a dead giveaway.

Their comin'-at-ya size certainly matched Zeide's stature, the second thing I noticed. Zeide was a very large, big-boned woman in her late forties. She might not have liked football, but she certainly looked like she could play the game. Her hair came all the way down to the small of her back, a mélange of chestnut to auburn strands. She wore maroon velour pants, a beige blouse, and running shoes. She was certainly prepared. We sat down in her cluttered kitchen around a small round table piled high with jewelry boxes. There had to be at least fifty. She said she had plenty more in her bedroom.

Just as she was about to open the boxes, this is what told me:

"I vanted to expose all dhe pearl Internet sites as shill zites. Jeremy Shepherd created a persona dhat *he* vas dhe greatest pearl expert in dhe vorld, a benevolent seller who'd look out for dhe consoomer," Zeide said, letting out the feckless laugh of a woman who'd been scorned and who wasn't about to resume her quiet life of bowling on Monday nights, shopping at Walmart for tube socks, and thrice-weekly sit-downs at the D-Q.

Zeide came clean from the get-go. She admitted to being a sort of Internet pearl provocateur. She copped to Williams's charges of (some) fabrication, exaggeration, and misrepresentation. "I've alvays loved pearls," Zeide said, her native German accent coming on full force. "I've alvays taut dhat every voman should have a strand. I love dhe idea of pearls for everyone. Dhat's essentially vhat Jeremy's site promised, but he turned on us." Shepherd's multiple Internet sites were cloaked as purely information-based, but, in fact, most were platforms that led to pearl-purchase sites owned, operated, or licensed by him. Zeide said she believed Shepherd had "tricked 'nd deceived us."

So *this* is what the contretemps had been about? Punishing Jeremy Shepherd, the snake-oil Anthony Robbins of pearls, who'd brought shiny orbs to thousands of middle-aged, middle-class women via the Internet?

Zeide's story leading up to her moment of love and deceit was guarded and succinct. Born in Germany and raised in Jakarta, she returned to Germany for university, where she met her American husband, a philosophy student and translator. Ten years ago, they came to the United States. Pressed for details, she demurred. This was her house and these were her pearls. "None of dhis ist relevant to pearls, and dhat's vhy you're here, is it not?"

Zeide promptly started placing multiple strands of pearls on the Formica table between us, as though to proffer proof that not all her claims were bluster. Her kitchen became a courtroom, each succeeding pearl strand another exhibit in her defense. When asked why she had taken on the Internet world of pearl fanatics, Erskine smiled like she had just popped a cherry bonbon. "Dhat can vait. Let me show you vhat I have. I tink you vill like."

Fresno was a long way from Bahrain, and Zeide didn't look much like a sheik, less like a babe in a harem. My fantasy of tawny-skinned girls fanning me with palm fronds while a guy in tailored whites and a headdress showed off his pearl collection would have to wait. Zeide looked more like Mrs. Gloop from *Willy Wonka & the Chocolate Factory*.

"What exactly do you have?" I asked, my ardor rising at the prospect of seeing her assets.

And with that, Zeide smiled in exactly the way Mrs. Gloop would have, and brought out dozens more boxes of pearl necklaces, earrings, rings, pendants, and bracelets. She started with the best. From a silk pouch, she carefully poured onto the kitchen table the touted strand of the red pearls. I couldn't help but hear their clacking sound as they made contact with the Formica.

I was flabbergasted. At first blush, these were gorgeous, shimmering red pearls, small, but nicely matched.

"I got dhe first one," Zeide said pointing to a center pearl, "in Bahrain from an old man. I'm *absolutely* certain it is natural."

It was time for me to work *my* magic, the little magic I knew. I picked up the strand in my right hand, just as I had done before the beefy pearl dealer in Tucson. I handled it delicately and elaborately, holding it with both hands; perhaps ten inches from my eyes to better examine the pearls. They weren't perfect. There were some surface blemishes, some nicks, but those actually might have gone in Erskine's favor. Natural pearls seldom were perfect. These certainly were matched well. That could have gone in Zeide's favor or not. To match natural red pearls, if they weren't dyed, could take decades, maybe longer. I rubbed one pearl against another, in the grit test. These certainly were real, but the test did nothing to distinguish a cultured pearl from a natural pearl. I examined each of the pearls, laying the strand out flat on the kitchen table, and counted how many pearls there were—fifty-three. I nodded to Zeide, who seemed to be holding her breath as though I knew what I was doing. I wondered who was more of an imposter, Zeide or me. "Nice," I said. "Extremely nice. I like these."

Elisabeth Strack had told Caitlin Williams that red natural pearls simply couldn't exist—there was no known bivalve that produces them—but when I told Zeide that, she blanched, suddenly rearing back, angrily flicking a mass of her mane over her right shoulder. "Vell, dhen Elisabeth Strack must be wrong, musn't she?" I wanted to gauge Zeide's countenance at that moment and looked at her point-blank. She held my gaze steady. Neither of us blinked.

"Where did the rest of the strand come from?" I asked, feeling like an interrogator at Gitmo who had absolutely no right to ask anything, but recklessly pushing forth nonetheless.

Zeide said assembling her strand with matching pearls had taken "forever. It's been my life's verk." She said she bought the first pearl for two gold bullion (about $1,600, she said) in 1982.

"Where'd you get gold bullion?" I asked, not wanting her to get too far.

"Dhat is another story," she replied rebuking me with what seemed like a dismissive backhanded swat.

Zeide said the other red pearls came from an assortment of places—dealers in Texas, divers on the east coast of Mexico, collectors in France. But when I pressed (who, when, where, how much?), Zeide waved me off again. Provenance specificity wasn't a characteristic central to Zeide's pearl persona, but, as I was to learn over and over again, it wasn't central to many pearl collectors, either. Why all the questions? What's it to *you*? This don't-ask, don't-tell mentality is because dealers often want to obscure where their goods come from, but also it's because they simply don't know. Like cocaine, the goods ought to speak for themselves.

But why couldn't Zeide just say the whole strand was dyed and came from a pearl market in Beijing (which is where I suspected it was from)? That'd be like a cocaine dealer saying his blow wasn't from Colombia but from Cleveland.

I loved the concept of a natural red strand of pearls, but I could see Zeide was growing restive and testy. She put the strand aside without explanation and brought out another. This one was sixty-three natural gold pearls, which Zeide said all had come from snails. These were lustrous pearls, smaller than the red pearls, perhaps 7 millimeters. I knew that snails could produce pearls, but again, to assemble so many that were so well matched was a stretch beyond belief. I let her ride with this strand.

Zeide was on a roll. Next, with requisite aplomb, she pulled out her prized Mikimoto strand. These pearls weren't in a silk pouch, but in a damn near original-looking hard case in very good condition. I pushed the case's clasp, and the red-velvet lid sprung open on two tiny gold hinges.

Inside were some of the most gorgeous pearls I had (and still have) ever set eyes on. On the inside of the top of the box, modest gold letters read:

K. Mikimoto, Inc.

Ginza, Tokyo

Like many old pearls, these had taken on a shape wholly their own. As pearls age, whether they are cultured or natural, they gradually can become more and more elongated, assuming a slightly baroque appearance. And these round pearls I could see had evolved; it was almost as though they were still living, continuing to grow into elongated contours. The necklace had thirty-eight pearls with outrageous lustre and orient. I was absolutely convinced these were the real thing. But *real* with pearls is relative. They certainly were cultured pearls, but did Mikimoto himself culture them? Of course not. Was the box in which they were displayed real? Probably. But had it always housed *this* particular strand of pearls? Could have. Had the pearls been restrung?

Perhaps. These pearls were prime examples of the first or second generation of pearls created through the insertion of a bead into an oyster, which grew nacre to produce a pearl. The strand was a stunner.

I put the strand on my palm, and damn, my hand started to perspire. I could almost feel my pores releasing droplets of sweat. The alleged history of these pearls, and the sheer beauty of them, started to make my palm shake. These pearls, beautifully misshapen into burgeoning teardrops, had weight and heft. Their grace was something to behold.

With the strand still on my vibrating hand, Zeide was off and running into the bowels of her house, and when she came back she was carrying a wooden chest. When she thumped the chest down on the kitchen table, the table groaned. Inside, she must have had sixty silk pouches, all filled with pearls.

Zeide brought out a two-strand choker of what she described as natural river pearls from China. She said a friend purchased the pearls loose near the Vietnamese border, and Zeide had matched each of them, placing at the middle a 10-millimeter pink button pearl. I was doubtful. They were pearls, that was clear, but no way were they natural. They looked like high-grade Chinese freshwater cultured pearls. They were too shiny. They seemed to have been polished with either wax or some other reflective agent. I had just seen thousands of the same pearls, strung in hank upon hank, at the Holidome.

Next, she proudly displayed a rose-colored choker with matching bracelet. "Vun lab said dhese are natural pearls, another said dhey're freshwater Chinese pearls," she said with a shrug, once again flicking a hank of her own around her shoulder. A black, mixed-breed dog started pawing at the kitchen door to the garage as Zeide brought out more, jewelry box after jewelry box filled to the gills with more pearls. Even though few, if any, I surmised, were natural pearls, they most certainly were all pearls. She could stack all of the boxes in a pile on her floor and it would reach to her shoulders. Zeide could wear pearls every day of the year and not wear the same pearl combination twice—as earrings, necklaces, brooches, rings, cufflinks, even as buttons.

Every so often, Zeide would get up and leave me alone in the kitchen with the teetering tower of pearl boxes and pearl pouches, only to bring back more. I thought, in passing, that she might have had a hidden camera recording my actions, but then I reproached myself for such a sneaky notion.

When she returned, it was time to talk turkey. "Many of these are not natural pearls," I started, marveling at my moxie.

"I'm just having a little fun," Zeide allowed. She said she buys online to tweak the pearl world and its virtual claims of provenance. "Dhey come with guarantees, vhich are not vorth de paper dhey're printed on. Dhey're all phony certificates. Vhat good is a certificate, anyvay? Vhat I'm doing is an adventure for me. I'm still vaiting to find something dhat's vhat the seller claims it to be."

In reality, Zeide finally conceded she has only four natural pearl necklaces, but I assume that it was probably closer to none. No way could the red necklace be natural.

I decided to go for broke. "Do you mind taking off the pink necklace you're wearing?" Without missing a beat, she removed the strand, and handed it to me.

The pearl gumballs, as large as 15 millimeters, were heavy in my hands. They were near perfect rounds. I could tell Zeide had been wearing the strand all day; the pearls had absorbed her body heat and thick perfume. They were hot. "Dhese," she said, "are cultured. Vhen I have cultured pearls, I don't hide dhe fact. Although probably no one in Fresno vould know dhe difference."

I handed back the strand. Zeide did not ask me to fasten the clasp. She promptly left again for somewhere in the house, again leaving me with all that covered the table, her chair, and now the surrounding linoleum floor. She returned with still more jewelry boxes and sat on what was left of the kitchen floor, knees akimbo, opening with glee each box. She moved more boxes onto the kitchen counter, and within a half hour, that, too, was covered with strands and strands of pearls. In progression, Zeide showed me what she described as her Burmese and then her Philippine necklace collections. Then came the earrings—she'd been trying to find replicas of those in the Vermeer painting *Girl with a Pearl Earring.*

Zeide had now run out of counter and floor space, so she started piling boxes on top of the stove, toaster oven, and refrigerator. She brought out her Venus earring collection—three pearl drops strung together. She showed me what she called her Rana of Bophar—a massive Teutonic breastplate she was assembling to sort of resemble what Maria Callas wore in the opera *Medea.* It was colossal: twelve concentric strands of 8- to 11-millimeter pearls. The ensemble resembled what Xena the Warrior Princess would wear to battle.

We were sailing along at a rather nice clip until I asked matter-of-factly whether Zeide ever traded or sold her pearls. She was absolutely appalled by my question.

"Most of my pearls are my friends, and you don't sell your friends," she said in a single breath. "Dhey represent everything dhat is good—for a pearl to grow it has to have a clean, healthy environment. To abandon a pearl would be like abandoning a child."

Zeide said she has nothing but scorn for pearl sellers—either on the Internet or in jewelry stores. "Dhere are no trusted sellers in dhe pearl business. No one. None. Period. Dhe more exclusive, the vorse dhey are. Tiffany's, Cartier, I have dhe most distain for. Dhey operate with a ten-thousand percent markup. *No one* can be trusted vhen it comes to pearls. You ask tree experts and you get five opinions depending on dhe time of day you ask. Buyer beware are dhe vatchvords in pearls."

I came to realize that it was out of such a fuzzy, subjective sense of what's valuable and what's not that Zeide—and other pearl collectors, in fact—derive so much pleasure.

"Pearls represent beauty out of suffering. Dhey hold vonderful intrigue, vhatever their story may be. Even as a little girl, I was mesmerized by dhem. I've alvays coveted pearls. I live pearls every day, even here in Fresno. Typically, I carry a few spares in my purse so dhat I can give avay a strand to a pearl-challenged voman vhenever I vant. I'll see someone who I tink deserves a strand and I'll go up to her. Sometimes, I'll be in church or a school. Other times, it's in a mall or a store. I have a sixth sense who might need a strand of pearls. I get pleasure out of it." A real-life Robin Hood of pearls.

An unnamed boy of about eighteen squeezed into the kitchen and started cooking ramen noodles, the Bears continued to tank, and I realized it was time to leave. I bid good-bye to Zeide and set up another meeting tomorrow. Even if none of Zeide's pearls were natural, she'd still have one of the largest private collections of pearls anywhere.

III

Day Two was time for Zeide's recantations. When I returned after a sleepless night of spelunkers, Zeide and I sat on a cluttered back porch, adjacent to a swimming pool with leaves and algae floating on the murky water's surface. She poured herself a large mug of coffee and fessed up to her antics, saying she actually owned only one or two natural pearl strands—that is, pearls not made with an inserted bead nucleus. But she remained unrepentant.

"I took on the persona of dhe Natural Pearl Queen to debunk dhe Internet. I vanted to poke holes in all dhe claims dhat pearl traders make on dhe Internet so I could show how dangerous dhat thing can be. People need to be saved from dhemselves," she railed like a Pentacostal preacher.

"Dhere are vomen who have spent dhemselves into oblivion by buying and buying pearls dhat aren't vhat dhey're advertised to be. I vant to be an advocate for pearl lovers. I vant to bring pearls back to dhe gem status dhey vonce had," she said hitting a crescendo.

Zeide told me she spends hours policing pearl Web sites, and to test her hunches between the fakes and the real pearls offered, she allots herself a pearl budget of $1,000 a month. "One of dhe gripes I hold against dhe Internet is dhat dhese dealers create language. *Tahitian Black Pearls* are different from *Black Tahitian Pearls*, vhich is a protected term. Jeremy was dhe first to use dhe term *Tahitian Black Pearls* on e-Bay. But vhat exactly is dhat? Do dhey come from Tahiti, China, or Vietnam? No one has to reveal *anything* about provenance. *Baby South Sea Pearls* has become code for off-round Chinese freshwater pearls." To confuse matters, she said, some Internet sellers advertise that their pearls are "natural" to distinguish them from being outright fakes or beads. And if terminology weren't enough of a smoke screen, there's sizing. In the industry, you always have to subtract *at least* one millimeter from what's advertised, she said.

So Zeide had found her calling—a one-woman band, an Internet pearl pitbull. But why does she continue throwing away her money on pearls she assumes will be fake?

For the same reason that pearlers continue to pry open millions of oysters in search of the perfect natural pearl. It was Kino's story in *The Pearl*. There's always the possibility of finding that perfect pearl, like hitting three 7s on a Vegas slot machine. "Buying pearls on e-Bay is like playing dhe stock market," Zeide railed, her voice gaining strength again. "Dhere's risk, but you absorb it as part of dhe cost of not knowing vhat you'll turn up." Sounding like a shill for Gamblers Anonymous, she advised you should buy only as much as you're willing to lose.

And every once in a while, you win. Zeide pulled out a strand of perfectly shaped 11-millimeter pinkish-white pearls she said she paid $120 for. No matter that they were Chinese and freshwater. These were beautiful pearls of quality that probably would fetch at least five times that amount at any retail jewelry store.

But what about her pride and joy—the strand of red pearls? I asked Zeide if I could see them again, one last time. I half-expected to get rebuked—a stranger questioning her core essence, but Zeide shrugged her shoulders, brought out the strand, and recalled the most memorable day in her life.

"I vas vith a friend, taking a tour of Arab countries in 1982." I wanted to stop her—"Which Arab countries? What's the friend's name? How could I reach her?"—but this was her show. "I had to vear lots of headgear. Ve vere sipping on sugared peppermint tea, and across the street, dhere vas a jewelry shop. It had no diamonds, just heavy gold ornaments, and a few little, inconspicuous pearls. Nothing of interest, I thought. But dhey spoke good English dhere, and at dhe time, I wasn't fully aware of how forbidden cultured pearls vere. Dhe jeweler showed me a crimson necklace of natural pearls, vhich he said vas from a local fishery. I forget dhe price, but it must have been astronomical. Right then and there, I thought if he could do it, so could I."

Thus became Zeide's mission in life: to complete her own strand of natural red pearls. So, several years after she bought a single red pearl, she set out to find fifty-two more to match it. No way would Zeide speculate on how much she'd spent on finding all the pearls.

It was getting toward midmorning. I had to catch a plane back home to pack, then leave in a few days to start my own pearl journey. I thanked Zeide, shook her hand, took one last look at those gumball pink monsters around her neck, and left.

<h1 style="text-align:center">IV</h1>

Christopher Columbus, Bo Torrey, the Opie-faced security cop, pearl dealer Alex Vock, the sausage-fingered wholesaler, Internet Pearl King Jeremy Shepherd and his cat-fighting sirens, Caitlin Williams, and the Rana of Fresno— all of them had been foreplay to the worldwide odyssey on which I was about to embark. As I kissed my wife, Iris, and our son, Mikey, good-bye, I felt like a soldier going off to war. I was confident I'd be coming back, I just didn't know when. I had bought "open-jaw" plane tickets (I liked that; it described my thoughts as I jammed notebooks, pens, T-shirts, and jeans into my bulging Flight 001 suitcase). Going to Tucson and Fresno had been one thing, but traveling halfway around the world was another. I might be gone three months, but depending on what I found (or didn't find), it might be six or eight. I planned to start in Japan, then move to Hong Kong, rural China, as well as Shanghai and Beijing, a tiny remote island in the Philippines, and ten or twelve atolls in French Polynesia. I'd work Down Under as a deckhand on a pearling vessel, and finally end up at the place where it all began, the island where Columbus first spotted those walnut-sized pearls five hundred years ago. I'm not sure Iris fully understood why I was leaving on this global journey to tell such a strange, arcane story. I'm sure our son, fifteen at the time, didn't have a clue. Both had been through this before. "Pearls?" Mikey asked offhandedly one evening. "Why pearls?"

Mikey had a point I couldn't fully answer at the time. I was in too far over my head to reconsider. I was off to see where millions of the world's pearls came from, in hindsight a particularly curious venture considering the global depression around the corner. But the lure of pearls had grabbed me, just as it had surely grabbed Zeide. Zeide's story had been a walk-up to one of my own, a story I couldn't shake. I wanted more than ever to descend among the legions of anonymous workers through whose skilled hands the great multitude of the world's pearls pass. In doing so, I wanted to give meaning to these laborers' workaday lives. Along the way, too, I'd be able to return to my mother's own pearl necklace. Late at night when I listened, I could still hear those creamy-white pearls click-clacking against each other, telegraphing to me the urgency of the journey to come.

6

Pearl City

Americans know Kobe as home to tender, succulent, über-priced beef. Sorry to dispel that myth, but little, if any, cattle is raised in Kobe. Kobe (and Osaka, thirty miles away) is merely the port where the prized Japanese beef is shipped all over the world. That's the same story, more or less, with Kobe pearls. Kobe is known worldwide as Pearl City. It's the globe's largest center for sorting, grading, and pricing wholesale pearls and, as such, is the focal point for the entire pearl industry. But no pearls have their origin in Kobe.

Most of Japan's pearls used to come from nearby Ago Bay in Mie Prefecture. That's where Kokichi Mikimoto first cultured them a hundred years ago. But because of overproduction, pollution, marine viruses, a pearl-infecting plankton known as the Red Tide, and suspected global warming, production of akoya pearls has nosedived. Those factors, along with Japan's high labor costs, as well as bigger and cheaper freshwater pearls from China, have devastated Japanese pearl production. The largest producers these days of Japanese akoyas are spread out on the western shores of Shikoku Island in Ehime Prefecture, near the fishing village of Uwajima. Japanese pearl production peaked in 1966 at two hundred and thirty tons. By 2008, it had slid to twelve tons.[1] Those twelve tons of Japanese pearls are augmented by at least eighty tons of imported pearls, and they all pass through Kobe. That made Kobe a mandatory destination for me.

To get to Kobe from Osaka's Kansai airport, you have to traverse more than twenty bridges. Elevated skyways take commuters past skyscrapers, too-many-to-count golf driving ranges, baseball diamonds, and baseball stadiums. Nestled against verdant hills with winding, narrow streets that snake like sidewinders, Kobe (pop. 1.42 million) is outrageously picturesque, a geographic anomaly of sea inlets on one side and dense forested mountains that dramatically rise from city streets on the other. A block from Shin Kobe Station, which sends bullet trains to Tokyo, is a cable car that transports visitors high into the mountains to hike manicured trails of an elaborate, aromatic herb garden. If Japan's great economic bubble has finally burst, there were few signs I could see of it in Kobe. The city appeared prosperous, evolved, and civilized. The original pearl district is concentrated in Chuo-ku, a quiet, tree-lined downtown neighborhood, in midsized buildings, where hundreds of pearl companies are located on streets such as Nakayamate-dori, Kano-Cho, and Higashi-machi. A new pearl district has cropped up in reclaimed marshland called Port Island, adjacent to downtown. The buildings in both districts were designed to face north so pearl sorters and graders get the benefit of the natural light pearlers say is unique to Kobe because of the city's proximal combination of so many inlets and verdurous hills.

The pearl trade brings tens of thousands of foreign dealers to Kobe. They pass through on the way to Hong Kong for giant international jewelry shows twice a year, as well as for two of the most famous pearl auctions in the world—one organized by Nick Paspaley, the Australian magnate who leads in production of marble-sized South Sea pearls, and the other sponsored by Robert Wan, the French Polynesian millionaire with a corner on the Tahitian pearl market. Pearl trade in Kobe is still firmly in the hands of the Japanese, with five exceptions—two Lebanese, one Spanish, and two Swiss dealers. There are several Indian traders in town, but they mostly trade in smaller quantities of lower-grade pearls.

To everyone, Japanese traders included, the most knowledgeable of dealers in Kobe is a lanky string bean of a guy who has made the city his home for almost forty years. Andy Müller, originally from the village of Belp, Switzerland, is at the center (or near it) of seemingly every pearl deal that passes through Kobe. While a student in elementary school, when asked where he wanted to live out his life, Müller surprised his fellow students and his family when he piped up one word: Asia.

He came to Kobe when he was twenty-two, married a local United Airlines flight attendant, and never looked back. Müller first worked in Kobe for the Swiss jewelry firm Golay Buchel, then for Australian pearler Rosario Autore; he now works for himself, heading his own pearl-trading company, Hinata (which means *in the sun* in Japanese). On the day I visited him, Müller, smoking miniature cigarros, had around-the-clock appointments with wholesale buyers, six from New York, two from Spain, and one from Armenia. He was a whirl of pearl showings all day long, hyping $10,000-wholesale hanks of Tahitian baroques, as well as hundreds of flawless, loose peacock-grays.

To top matters off, five government auditors, each dressed in a black suit, black tie, and white shirt, bowing so frequently that they practically knocked heads in Müller's congested fourth floor offices, had decided to audit Müller's books on the busiest week of the year. The auditors had arrived at 10:00 a.m., and by 2:00 p.m. were still going strong, questioning Müller and his three secretaries. Meanwhile, a rumpled New York pearl dealer wearing an off-center yarmulke was eyeing seven strands of midsized Tahitian blacks going for $3,000 apiece. All the while, from recessed ceiling speakers, Elvis Presley was wailing, "You ain't nothing but a hound dog."

Müller squeezed me in for a quick lunch. "I'll be waiting for you at twelve to twelve," he instructed me precisely. When I paused rather quizzically, Müller quickly responded, "I'm a Swiss in Japan," pointing out two undeniable national characteristics of punctuality.

Much of the pearl trade in Kobe is a nuanced social dance, with home base the Kobe Club, a members-only retreat minutes from the heart of the pearl district. Called by old-timers the Gaijin Club (from the word *Gaikokojin*, which literally means "outer world person," and has come to signify *foreigner*), the organization was founded more than one hundred years ago. Current rules mandate that no single nationality claim more than 20 percent of the club's membership. Here Kobe's pearl dealers wine and dine out-of-town buyers before repairing to showrooms with large (north-facing) windows, where $100,000 multiple lots of pearls are examined atop tables covered with thick white cotton cloth. The reason the cloth is white is so pearls don't reflect a color other than their own true hue.

Again, I thought, under different circumstances, the product traded on these tables could have been cocaine, with private jets of international dealers arriving around the clock, specializing in different grades, cuts, and amounts, all assembling in a central location to buy and sell, before sending the high-price commodity on its way to worldwide distribution points. As is the case with cocaine, each pearl dealer has a niche that distinguishes him from others. Müller, for example, doesn't deal with Japanese akoyas, Chinese freshwaters, Australian or Philippine South Seas, but focuses these days almost entirely on large baroque Tahitian pearls, which, depending on quality, can sell on the wholesale market for as much as $30,000 a strand. Another key player in the Kobe pearl scene is Yoshihiro Shimizu, chairman of Hosei Co. and president of the Japanese Pearl Exporters' Association. Shimizu is tanned and Hollywood-handsome, an ingratiating and suave schmoozer. His niche is medium to very large South Sea rounds and baroques. Buyers often favor dealers like Müller and Shimizu because they can purchase in much smaller quantities than at the huge auctions in Hong Kong, which are increasingly being flooded with bottom-feeders from India, who buy lesser pearl grades in bulk and then form their own distribution cartel. Most Kobe dealers' pearls are presorted, so quality is thought to be consistently higher, which makes the Japanese city a mandatory stop-off point on the pearl trail for high-quality goods.

Dealers like Müller and Shimizu are the pearl industry's middlemen, savvy, swaggering traders who favor cashmere sweaters and sport coats, Ermenegildo Zegna trousers, and tasseled Bally loafers. Both, at least during the week I shadowed them, are hyperkinetic, fast-talking nonstop multilingual dealers constantly on their global cell phones, driving BMWs up and down the city's winding streets, entertaining clients at the Kobe Club, or drinking single malt Macallan scotch in smoky, polished bars, ensconced a world away from where the goods started (on a remote Micronesian island or perhaps on a rust bucket in the Timor Sea) or where they might end up (around the Chanel No. 5-misted neck of a woman about to leave her Eastside apartment for a benefit at the Met, or dangling from the earlobes of a Parisian model readying for a photo shoot in the 16th arrondissement).

Both Müller and Shimizu grew up in non–English speaking countries, but both speak elegant and fluent English. Neither grew up in the pearl business; they came to it as young men. Each flies tens of thousands of miles a year, away from home as often as not. If you ask Müller or Shimizu, I doubt either would care about where their pearls ultimately end up. Oh, they might be vaguely curious, but their business is to sell from one rung of the pearl ladder to the next. They are extraordinarily well paid for their specialized services, and they resist any temptation to incorporate more rungs, either higher or lower, in their purvey. Wherever their pearls eventually go—to Neiman Marcus, Harrods, Barbara Bush, or Michelle Obama—is not their concern. Their motto is buy and sell as quickly as possible. Holding onto pearls is like putting a house up for sale. Each day on the market, the more the seller loses.

II

On the bed in my hotel, a folded pair of pajamas had been placed, as though my mother had laid them out for me. They were way too small for me, but I appreciated the sentiment. I slipped under the covers, slept a few hours, and early the next morning, I was greeted in the lobby by a rather curious duo: Mikio Ibuki, a studious man in his late sixties who heads the Japan Pearl Exporters' Association, and Tomokazu Nakamura, a rotund, wry older guy who had bought and sold pearls for more than fifty years. Nakamura had broken his left arm, which was in a sling and cast. He had come directly from a hospital checkup to greet me. "Oh, it's really nothing," Nakamura said, in elegant, continental English.

Months earlier, I had emailed Ibuki and Nakamura that I wanted to meet Shunsaku Tasaki, the founder and president of the huge, vertically integrated pearl company Tasaki Shinju. Tasaki is a sort of waning Japanese godfather, or *Kyoufu*, who used to lord over the national and international pearl scene. Formerly chairman of the World Pearl Organization, for years Tasaki went by the title the Emperor or the Boss.

Tasaki was *the* old guard of Kobe's pearlers a generation beyond the young (at least younger) turks now running the show—dealers like Müller and Shumizu. Tasaki's claim to fame, along with Mikimoto's, was owning everything pearl—from spat hatcheries to retail outlets, the whole pearl ladder. Until bought out for $65 million by a private equity firm in 2008, Tasaki owned and operated sixty-one Tasaki retail stores, from Tokyo to New York, and was making inroads into China, Hong Kong, and Taiwan, with more than thirty stores. These days Tasaki's pearl empire is on the skids. In 2006, his company posted a $12.49 million loss, and the Russian firm Sakha Diamond had purchased 10 percent of Tasaki Shinju's stock in a fire sale, with backing from the giant U.S. food processor Cargill. Tasaki, 78, even had to let go of his flagship store in Tokyo's high-rent, signature Ginza district.

But I wanted to meet Tasaki-san (nobody mentions his name without automatically adding the honorary *san* after it). While he may be old school, his mere presence still girds much of the pearl trade in Kobe. Tasaki-san used to sport a little goatee like Colonel Sanders. He even gave out business cards of the colonel and himself standing next to each other. Several pearl dealers had told me stories of how Tasaki-san surrounds himself with bevies of beautiful young women to wait on him hand and foot (and apparently in between, they said). Tasaki-san had a reputation as a prodigious drinker. One U.S. dealer told me he could drink in one sitting more than any three men in the world. I'd heard an apocryphal story running the pearl circuit about when Tasaki-san was visiting his pearl farm on Amami Island and decided to commandeer his yacht's controls. It's not clear whether Tasaki-san was drinking for the other three men or just for himself at the time. But none of the crew had the balls to tell Tasaki-san he was driving the yacht like a madman. Following Japanese protocol, Tasaki-san's uniformed minions had lined up in formation on the pier; after all, the bossman was arriving. But Tasaki-san was going so fast that he crashed into the dock sending dozens of servants flying helter-skelter into the air.

Born in 1929 in the port city of Nagasaki, Tasaki-san entered the Imperial Naval Academy, but Japan's surrender to Allied forces in 1945 made his dream of becoming a naval officer pretty unrealistic. He moved to Kobe, worked under a Taiwanese pearl dealer, and opened his first shop in 1954. From his retail store, he moved down the pearling ladder, taking over each rung, all the way to growing his own oysters.

The ungainly trio—the constantly bowing Ibuki, the erudite Nakamura, arm in a cast, and me—caught a cab to Port Island, where the building still bearing the bright big letters of Tasaki-san's name was located. As soon as our feet touched the pavement from the taxi, a beautiful young woman in uniform, on cue, sprinted to greet us. She bowed formally and deeply (known in Japan as *saikeirei*), not just from her neck but from her waist. It was as close to prostration as any person could perform while still standing. As we advanced into the building's glass tower, the same beautiful young woman, high heels sinking into the thick carpet ahead of us, raced to press the elevator button before we could get to it. As the elevators door spread open for us, yet another beautiful young woman ushered us into a meeting room. As we reclined into plush, over-sized chairs, a third beautiful young woman set cups of green tea in front of us.

We waited thirty seconds or so, and although there was no gong, there might very well have been when Tasaki-san strode in. Deep bows of reverence all around, cries of "Hai! Hai! Hai!" and "Eh! Eh! Eh!" and we were off and running. But could this be the same Tasaki-san who used to sport a ponytail, the renegade who had turned the pearl business inside and out? Tasaki-san this day was impeccably dressed. No string tie, no goatee. That must have been the old Emperor. This Tasaki-san had slicked-back gray-black hair. He was wearing a tailored blue business suit (with a pearl tie tack and pearl label pin). Two hearing aids, with tiny antennae coming out from each, were tucked behind his ears. The new and improved Tasaki-san was a big boxy man who amply filled out the chair. I couldn't help but notice his high-gloss shiny black shoes. Tasaki-san had bunions. They bulged out from either side of his feet, forming two asymmetrical leather lumps.

I could see that Ibuki was deeply humbled to be in the presence of such a revered industrialist; he said nothing, beatifically gazing at Tasaki-san somewhere between Tasaki-san's nose and neck. Nakamura, who doubles as a professor of English at Doshisha University and served as my translator, kept his cool. He was higher on the Kobe pearl chain. He even kibitzed with Tasaki-san.

Was Tasaki-san concerned about the onslaught of cheap Chinese pearls flooding the global market, which for more than half a century had been dominated by the Japanese? I asked.

As Nakamura translated, there was a moment of silence. Ibuki looked wide-eyed at Nakamura, his facial muscles tightening. Tasaki-san's flunkies bristled. I could see almost imperceptible frowns on their faces. But Nakamura shrugged as though to say, "Bring it on!"

Tasaki-san broke the hush in the room. "Those pearls are like JUNK diamonds," he started, raising his voice. "JUNK! That's what they are! The average person will look for good quality. In Japan, there's a saying, 'If you don't spend too much money, eventually you're going to lose money.'" Nakamura's translation aside, I had struck a nerve. Chinese pearls were Japan's No. 1 scourge. Knockoffs of Japanese akoya strands were selling retail for less than $80, likely around the block from where we were sitting. Even the Japanese were harvesting Chinese pearls, then bringing them back to Kobe for processing, and calling them Japanese pearls.

Tasaki-san paused. He gazed out the window behind me, suddenly appearing deep in thought. I thought to turn my back and look out the same window, to see just what was so riveting. But manners restrained me. We all waited for the Emperor to end his reverie. Five, ten, fifteen seconds. The room was silent. Who knew how long this could last.

"You have white, black, yellow people the world over," Tasaki-san finally said. "Yet only white people get respect. The colored people are looked down upon. White people get respect, and that's the same with Japanese pearls. Japanese akoyas have an intrinsic value that no other pearl can compete with."

Nakamura nodded, followed by Ibuki and Tasaki-san's doormats. The Emperor had spoken.

I looked toward Nakamura to make sure he was translating right. Nakamura lowered his head, nodding ever so slightly, and adjusted the sling on his arm.

When I asked Tasaki-san about the international pearlers' mania to grow larger and larger pearls, so now they're the size of gumballs, whereas akoyas by their nature can only grow to a rare maximum of 10 millimeters, Tasaki-san again paused. His assistants moved closer. Ibuki pulled at his cuffs. Nakamura leaned forward. Another fifteen-second pause.

"Our diminutive pearl size actually favors smaller people such as the Japanese, whereas American and Russian women might actually choose the larger South Sea pearls," Tasaki-san pronounced.

This seemed an honest, although simple, response. It wasn't just size that compelled women to pay tens of thousands of dollars to wrap pearl jawbreakers around their necks. It was the complicated, culturally mediated issue of status. It didn't have to be that way, but as in almost everything today, size often matters, and pearls were no exception. Australian, Tahitian, and Philippine pearls come from a much larger mollusk than the modest Japanese akoya (*Pinctada imbricata*) oyster, and the pearls extracted from those colossal bivalves dwarf traditional Japanese pearls. It's a little like looking at a Hummer next to a Mini cooper. Both are cars, both can get you to the same place, but you're never going to confuse the two. Actually, I thought Tasaki-san had it wrong: Lots of small people drive Hummers. It was the same with pearls. Status was what drove women to choose the size of pearls. Compared to South Sea honkers these days, Japanese akoyas were perceived as just too small to make a statement, not just at the presidential inaugural ball but at your kid's soccer game. They didn't pop.

I moved on. I asked Tasaki-san why pearls couldn't be graded to a uniform standard, the way diamonds and gold are. Tasaki-san again paused. The studied, dramatic pause had become his trademark. How were we to know Tasaki-san hadn't suffered a stroke?

When Tasaki-san finally spoke, everyone in the room seemed relieved. He said while there are generally accepted standards that pearl experts agree on, the elaborate and intricate nuances of differing pearl qualities usually is simply beyond consumers. "It's really a business of trust and confidence between the customer and the supplier. Customers just need to be reassured that what they are buying is appropriate for what they are paying. A mandatory grading system like in the diamond industry, I think this would be a bad idea."

The Emperor's conclusion aside, what Tasaki-san was saying was caveat emptor, buyer beware. In other words, buying pearls can be a crapshoot. Tasaki-san was blunt and to the point, but missed the integral quality of pearls that made them fundamentally different from diamonds and gold: By and large, the tricky business of pearl valuation often rests on subjective criteria determined by the seller, whose job is to convince the buyer to share those same criteria.

Tasaki-san transitioned into the political hot potato of dyeing and color-enhancing—an area of controversy, since most pearl processors can manipulate pearl hues so well it often fools even the most knowledgeable dealers. Few producers, except the Chinese, fess up to wholesale color manipulation. But Tasaki-san was the Emperor and he wasn't shy. "Sometimes, we have to get rid of a foreign obstacle that has settled on one of the layers of the pearl to enhance the natural quality of the pearl. Bleaching is one way to get rid of those impurities. The idea is not to change the color of the pearl, but merely to enhance the original color." So bleaching was okay, but dyeing was wrong.

I wanted to press Tasaki-san further on the issue of dyeing, and when I did, the Emperor made a face, then snickered.

"Women, no matter how pretty they are, have to use makeup. But colored women can't become white no matter what they do. And you can't make a black woman into a white woman, no matter how pretty she is. It's the same with pearls. Changing their colors makes what once was real into something fake."

This kind of talk wouldn't go over well in either Bedford-Stuyvesant or Grosse Pointe. It also conflicted with what most dealers in the pearl trade would bet their last yen on: that a percentage of Tasaki-san's pearls are dyed.

When I tossed Tasaki-san a lob about living in Kobe, he actually teared up. "Light is very important in the pearl business. You have to face north when dealing with pearls. North is true light, the light that allows you to see the best. On one side in Kobe, we have mountains, and on the other side, we have the sea. Both combine to make for a special light that isn't duplicated anywhere. I love Kobe. The city is in my blood." Reverential bows all around. Buddha/God bless Kobe.

My interview wouldn't have been complete without asking Tasaki-san about his innovation of vertical integration of the pearl business, and the Emperor wasn't reticent about extolling its virtues. "Most people in this business only look at one aspect—cultivation, harvesting, wholesale, or retail—but I wanted more. I was aggressive. Old-timers wanted to kick me out. They didn't like what I was doing. But you know what?"

Tasaki-san paused, I nodded, Ibuki looked down, Nakamura adjusted his sling.

"They were jealous of me. That's what it was. They didn't like me. Too aggressive. Not willing to let things stay the same. But—" Tasaki-san looked at Nakamura for help, for he must have known what he was about to say would cause even the most skilled translator trouble. "When you have wind blowing around you, it means people pay attention. They have to. If they don't, they will be caught in a typhoon."

We all nodded, a fitting way to end the interview. As we got up, another round of "Hai! Hai! Hai!" and "Eh! Eh! Eh!" Tasaki-san was spirited out of the room by a beautiful young woman. As we left the fourth floor, I tried to press the button to the elevator, but a second beautiful young woman got to it just before I could.

My session with Tasaki-san had been a great introduction to Japanese obsequiousness. I loved the supporting cast, buzzing around the Emperor. Apart from theater, though, Tasaki-san's parsed, candid statements had been newsworthy in a pearl-insider kind of way. Tasaki-san certainly hadn't given me any sense of a pearl laborer's point of view. That would have been like talking to Donald Trump and expecting to learn what maids in Trump Towers think about their jobs. By the time pearls got to Tasaki-san, they'd already been harvested, cleaned, sorted, bleached, polished (and maybe dyed), graded, strung, ready for the international ride of their life. Given the parameters of my stay in Kobe—being shown around town by dealers like Müller and Shimizu, as well as by flack Ibuki and translator Nakamura—and the fact that few pearls these days originate in Kobe, I wasn't sure I'd get too many rungs down the pearl ladder. Still, the story of how Kobe became Pearl City intrigued me, and I set out to find it.

III

At the Gaijin Club for lunch, I met Takashi Mori, another member of the old pearl guard in Kobe. Mori was as modest as Tasaki-san had been over-the-top. A slender, refined man, Mori even at seventy-eight, with little practice, still speaks fluent English, perhaps a reminder of the days when he was a skinny young hustler just after the war, hawking akoya pearl strands to hordes of curious American GIs with money to burn. Following World War II, during the occupation of Japan, American GIs flooded the nation. Within a decade, tens of thousands more would arrive on their way to and from Korea.

"I was in school and one day I showed my uncle all my books, and you know what? He laughed at me. I still remember. He said, 'How are these books going to help you in business?' At first, I discounted what my uncle said, but I listened. He had a plan."

Mori's uncle had made an observation about Americans stationed in Japan: They didn't know how to spend their money. Compared to the poor Japanese, the servicemen were loaded, but poor things, they just were lost when it came to what to do with their dollars. To help them, Mori and his uncle were to embark on something that would change fushion history.

All Mori's uncle needed was a hardworking schlepper, and smart Mori, who had taken classes in English, filled the bill. Mori remembers the date he started—Saturday, July 1, 1946. "I got myself to Yokosuka, where the American army base was, and walked to eleven souvenir stands and to the two PX stores. I had two bags full of akoya pearls, one in each hand. The bags were so heavy, each weighed me down so much that my shoulders sagged." To demonstrate, Mori rose from his chair, and walked around our table, mimicking Charlie Chaplin, both arms stiff, pantomiming lugging two satchels loaded down with bricks.

The pearls inside Mori's bags were an instant hit. U.S. soldiers couldn't get enough of them. For $20, a GI could buy a graduated choker of 7 millimeters at the center pearl and 3 millimeters at both ends. One day, a Japanese souvenir dealer, realizing the goldmine Mori was carrying around in his bags, offered the young man 45,000 yen for his entire inventory.

More than sixty years later, Mori's eyes bugged out when he recalled the amount. "I couldn't believe my ears. I thought he must have made a mistake. My entire family was living on one thousand yen *a month* at the time," Mori said, not quite believing how poor he once was.

The good times got better. From 1951 to 1955, Mori said he sold as many as 10,000 strands of akoya pearls, mostly from Japan's Ise Prefecture, and mostly from Ago Bay. Soon, Mori began exporting pearls, mostly to the United States, but also to Europe. He visited the United States and set up exclusive deals with American pearl dealers. They, in turn, came to Kobe for buying trips, often staying months.

By the early 1960s, Kobe's go-go years were in full swing. Kobe was a dream market for foreign dealers. Brokers would return home with trunks filled with as many pearls as could fit in. Soon Andy Müller arrived in town, and it was Mori from whom Müller bought his first pearls as a new dealer. Years later Mori gave a toast at Müller's wedding reception at the Kobe Club on May 11, 1979.

The Japanese pearl market, like all markets, had colossal highs and precipitous lows. At times, the market became saturated with pearls, but would naturally correct itself. By 1983, it rebounded with its greatest fury. "We couldn't get enough pearls," Mori said. He remembers Saks Fifth Avenue putting in an order with him for ten thousand strands. Mori laughed appreciatively. "Those really were the days," he said, finishing the last bite of his Cobb salad. "We were swimming in money."

IV

In those early years after World War II, Mori wasn't the only dealer of pearls in town. Soon, Kobe would become awash with foreigner dealers, all cashing in on the nacreous bounty. They all knew hugely profitable, eminently sellable goods when they saw them, and pearls were as good as gold—maybe better. Japanese pearl strands had become the latest fashion accessory to hit the shores of Europe and America. Eventually, with iconic style makers like Grace Kelly and Jacqueline Kennedy driving the Western pearl mania, every middle-class woman on both continents had to have a Japanese akoya pearl necklace (including my mother). Paradoxically, these modest strands became neon signs of prosperity.

One American who had set up shop in Kobe prior to World War II was Genaro Liguori. After the war, other Italians and Italian Americans joined him, including New York dealers Frank Mastoloni, Bart D'Elia, Victorio and Louis Borrelli, and Victor Ferrante. A young dealer by the name of Salvador Assael also came to Japan and traded Swiss Army watches to the cash-strapped Japanese for pearls. Jewish jewelry wholesalers, long active in New York's diamond trade, also began arriving in Kobe. These included Isadore Slutzky, René Schiff, Stanley Schecter, Jack Felsenfeld, and Morris Star and his father, Charles, who took up residence in Kobe for eight months every year until his death at age ninety-nine. Travel to Japan was precarious in those days, usually by Pan Am Clipper via Hawaii. Because of the distances, traders often stayed for weeks and months on end.

The Mastoloni family story foreshadows how Kobe was to be transformed by American pearl interests and, in turn, how the world was to be captivated by the escalating popularity of pearls. Frank Mastoloni came to New York at the turn of the century from Sorrento, Italy. Other Italians, including the D'Elias, Borrellis, and Cocias, came from Torre del Greco, a small town just outside of Naples. All were in the cameo and coral business. Fresh in America, they were traveling salesmen, hawking the jewelry piece every woman of the day had to have—cameos—from Atlantic City to Chicago. When they found that they couldn't any longer purchase coral in large enough quantities from their principal source, Madagascar, they traded suppliers and traveled to Japan to buy rough coral, which they sent to Italy to be processed, then to be shipped to the United States. Genaro Liguori had been among the first to move to Kobe to establish a coral export business. After the Depression, when cameos began to turn passé, dealers shifted to pearls, and the first batches of Japanese pearls slowly started coming to U.S. shores in the mid-1930s. Liguori stayed in Kobe, and because he was Italian, not American, he lived in Japan during World War II. Liguori's exports didn't just go to the United States but to Europe; the common transit point was the Swiss city of Chiasso, from which Japanese pearls fanned throughout the continent, to Italy, France, Belgium, the Netherlands, Germany, and Great Britain.

The Mastolonis started importing pearls from Kobe in 1945, as soon as the war ended. Mastoloni's first trip to Kobe was in 1953, during which he stayed with Liguori. Another foreigner in Kobe at the time was John Jerwood, a Londoner who before World War II had fallen in love with the daughter of the Japanese ambassador to Great Britain, married her, and then moved to Tokyo with her, living in a mansion next to the Okura Hotel. Jerwood was at the center of all foreign connections in the pearl business at the time. He was a guest at Andy Müller's wedding, and gave the first speech to the new bride and groom. In the 1980s, Jerwood took on English, American, and Australian apprentices to his business in Japan, and the list of those who worked for him is a Who's Who in the modern pearl industry today: Rosario Autore, David Norman, Robert Fawsett, Tony David, Paul Braunstein, Ariel Russo, and Fran Mastoloni, the grandson of Frank Mastoloni, who used to trade with Takashi Mori when they were both young men.

V

I needed to find out how Japanese pearls survived such a roller coaster of prices, as well as how they weathered Japan's environmental saga of pollution, marine disease, overfishing, and parasites, and for that I talked to pearlers at Kobe-based Otsuki Pearl, the largest buyer and exporter of pearls in Japan, and a powerful and singular player in the world pearl economy. If Tasaki-san was a proud if overbearing father to the company that bears his name, Yasuaki Mori, Otsuki's director, was a laid-back, ingratiating kind of guy whose informality made him seem more like a number cruncher for an L.A. film company than the director of a multinational pearl company. As Ibuki and I walked into the headquarters around the corner from Tasaki-san's building, pretty young girls still hovered around us, but the bows weren't as low and as oleaginous.

Otsuki is a huge operation, with rows and rows of pearl sorters, drillers, polishers, and sizers on each floor of a highrise, with enormous banks of north-facing windows. American consumers don't know Otsuki, and that's the way Mori wants it. "We sell to wholesalers in Japan and elsewhere, who in turn sell to retailers. We own our own farms and we buy from other farms. Wherever all our pearls eventually end up is anyone's guess," he told me, seemingly dumbfounded that I would ask such a question.

Otsuki's pearls do end up in high-end stores worldwide, including hundreds of jewelry emporiums in New York, Los Angeles, London, Paris, Dubai, Hong Kong, Santiago, and Sydney. In fact, while the stores' owners and managers might not know it, if they stock pearls, those pearls probably have passed through Otsuki's Kobe headquarters. The company has some 300 workers in two locations, Kobe and Tokyo. Ninety percent of Otsuki's pearls are akoyas, making the third-generation company the largest exporter of akoyas in the world, with 3.75 tons a year.

Like Tasaki-san, Mori is competing with Chinese freshwater pearls, which he, too, dismissed with the same word, "junk" (with a similar flick of the hand). Mori said that Japanese akoyas are the gold standard, and while Chinese pearls may have a much cheaper price point, women will gladly pay for the higher quality of Japanese counterparts. I wasn't sold on this last point. Even by then, in the early months of my pearl travels, I knew that few women had any idea where the pearls they proudly wrapped around their necks came from. Except for the top crust of pearl buyers, genuine, real provenance for most consumers was an element outside the pearl-buying equation. But with Chinese freshwater pearls becoming larger and better at a tenth of what Japanese akoyas go for, what else could Mori say?

I asked Mori if he'd take me on a tour of Otsuki headquarters, and in an instant Takashi Abe, a nervous sort of guy with a plane of flattened black hair, appeared. Off we went.

I had expected to be taken on a sanitized tour of the company, but Abe took me from floor to floor, in every room I wanted to visit, each with banks of women, mostly in their late teens to midtwenties, purposefully going about their tasks. The average annual salary is the equivalent of $32,700–$37,400. Workers are generally high school graduates; some come from rural areas to the big city, and for those employees, Otsuki maintains a dormitory. All wear uniforms. Soft music wafts out of speakers. In the last room, workers put together 40-centimeter hanks of matching sizes, shapes, and colors, handily manipulating thousands of shiny pearls with bamboo tweezers.

The issue of theft or pilferage, Abe said, seldom comes up. Each unit has a supervisor, but Japanese culture, Abe said, seldom allows for such ignominious crime, which would dishonor a family's name for generations. I'm quite sure there are minor instances of pilferage, but theft on a wholesale level in these pearl-processing plants probably doesn't exist. Too risky, too much at stake. Abe lifted one of many blue plastic buckets filled with thousands of pearls, and let the akoyas drop through his fingers, as though to show how many pearls his company deals with on an hourly basis, and how little concern he has safe-guarding them.

I asked him if I could take a closer look, and following Abe's lead, I felt the orbs drop through my fingers, from bucket to bucket. They made that pinging sound I loved, the north light reflecting off of each pearl, and as I poured more and more, they looked like a kind of tiny waterfall, a miniature rainbow cascading from my hands back into the blue containers. They were mesmerizing, as pearls have always been to me. Abe smiled, seeming to understand.

While walking to hail a taxi, I asked Ibuki how the Japanese can possibly compete with China's low wages and the flooding of the international market with its seemingly limitless supply of freshwater pearls. It was the first time Ibuki seemed miffed with me, for, as I was to realize, this is the central issue facing Japanese dealers today. Ibuki had not just a public-relations dilemma on his hands but a veritable crisis. "If people don't want poor goods with underpaid workers operating in poor conditions, they will not be buying pearls that come from, or are processed in, China." It sounded as though he had memorized the answer. My retort would have been, "But how will buyers know?" although, for the moment, I let that go.

VI

Not many years ago, Japan was able to produce a different breed of pearls, freshwaters from Japan's largest lake, Lake Biwa in the Shiga Prefecture, but these larger pearls are no long being produced because of pollution and other environmental factors. In the mid-1990s, another Japanese pearl produced from hybrid mussels also started appearing on the market. Cultured in Lake Kasumi-gaura, northeast of Tokyo in the Gifu Prefecture, these were large-sized pearls (11–16 millimeters), known as Kasumiga pearls, but their quantity and quality has largely eroded in recent years, and mass production is at a standstill.

So what are Japanese pearlers to do?

One alternative is transporting akoya oysters outside of Japan, where un-sullied environmental conditions would allow the Japanese oysters to flourish and, through technology, produce pearls. That's why Japanese pearl producers are going not just to China with akoya oysters but to venues as far away as Brazil and the United Arab Emirates. It was the idea behind Yuji Suto's bold plan to start a large-scale Japanese-pearl-cultivation farm, 125 miles north of Sydney, Australia, in Port Stephens, just north of New Castle.

I wanted to meet Yuji, and while I was in Kobe, he had just returned from one of his trips Down Under. Yuji, 54, is a civil engineer, although he looks more like a college professor than someone trained to build roads. Dressed in a blue blazer, khakis, an open-collar pinstripe shirt, and gray Merrell slip-ons, Yuji comes across to some as a modern-day visionary and to others as a crack-pot. His massive project could be called quixotic or Sisyphean, maybe both. Yuji has had to overcome almost insurmountable red tape and daily logistical nightmares that include multinational capital development, mollifying envi-ronmentalists and green-supporting politicians, not to mention Australian bu-reaucrats and scientists tiptoeing around the murky politics and science of a Japanese firm introducing a new organism into Australian waters and har-vesting its by-products. There's also the issue of competing with Australia's own pearl godfather, Nick Paspaley.

Yuji married into a pearl family, his father-in-law having started a farm just after World War II. Yuji grew increasingly frustrated with the topsy-turvy pearl cycles of boom and bust, as well as with the onslaught of viruses, pollution, and predators that seemed to torpedo each new promising crop. So he started traveling, trying to find where else he could grow akoyas without the problems that undercut Japanese-grown pearls. He went to Vietnam, China, Thailand, Cambodia. He exchanged letters with Venezuelan marine biolo-gists. He paid farmers to begin trial oyster cultivations. He spent five years trying to make sense out of incomprehensible geological surveys and world weather data. He checked arcane historical records of tidal conditions and rainfall. He learned oyster cultivation techniques inside and out, and in the late 1990s, he came up with a startling yet simple conclusion. How and when the oyster is nucleated is important; so is the nature and size of the bead. But what Yuji concluded was the single most crucial factor was the water in which the oyster grows.

"When seawater conditions are good, oysters are always healthy," Yuji said. The key was the delicate balance between fresh and salt water. Pearl-bearing oysters, Yuji concluded, flourished best in salt water that had a constant supply of pristine fresh water. In other words, rainfall.

Conditions like the strength and direction of water currents, and water temperature were important, too. So were the nucleating beads: He knew beads made from pearl shells from the United States seemed to work best. But Yuji wouldn't let go of what he grew to believe absolutely—that pearls needed to be nurtured with rainfall. The theory harkened back to what scholars and scientists had believed for a thousand years—that pearls were born when oysters rose to the water's surface, opened their bivalves, and got impregnated by waters from the heavens. Yuji had updated to the twenty-first century what had gone for gospel from Jesus Christ's time.

With rainfall data in hand, and hundreds of marine topographic maps spread out on his desk, Yuji came to the conclusion that Australia would be the ideal place for his experimentation, but when he went to the pearling capital of that country, Broome, he found the region didn't have enough rainfall year-round, and besides, the water temperature was too high for akoyas. He returned, deflated, to Japan, ran more calculations, and discovered an area north of Sydney, in New South Wales, that had a preponderance of rain and matched all of Yujis's criteria. He returned to Australia and started hatching oysters.

Although his first harvest was just one hundred pearls, from 6 to 8 millimeters, the results blew him away. He said he found pearl quality to be as good as it had been in Japan thirty to forty years ago. The nacre was thick and the lustre deeper than he'd seen in a long time. That's when the local opposition began. There were protests from well-organized environmentalists who pulled into their camp retired residents (the area is a haven for retirees from Sydney). "It was a classic case of NIMBY—not in my back yard," Yuji said. Elderly Australians were against the project because of a rekindled form of xenophobia, he said, adding, "some of them were still fighting against Japan in World War II." The environmental forces used the resentment to galvanize support against the project, and politicians jumped onboard. Yuji's application to turn the pilot project into a permanent one was rejected twice by the New South Wales Ministry of Planning, but when it came before the Australian Land and Environmental Courts, it was approved. Today, Yuji is trying to raise capital for the project, and he's in debt by more than he could bear to admit, but he said he hopes to get under way with full-scale operations within three years.

VII

Even though Japan was less and less a world player in pearl production, I wanted to explore the lives of pearl workers. I felt an obligation to get to Toba, where Kokichi Mikimoto had cultured the world's first pearl. The museum there is a shrine to Mikimoto, a revered figure in Japan, sort of a Henry Ford and Thomas Edison wrapped into one. Nearly every Japanese child is taught about his ingenuity and pluck.

Mikimoto was a tireless inventor, yes, but also a unrepentant self-promoter. Foreigners and Japanese alike had warned me about the touristy, gimmicky nature of what is now called Mikimoto Island—from the souvenir-stuffed gift shop to a show every hour when *amas* dressed in white uniforms dive on cue to the sea's shallow floor, disappearing for, it seems, minutes on end, then suddenly breaking the surface, holding high, to the delight of cheering crowds, an oyster. When the oyster is pried open in front of the crowds, a gleaming pearl is to be found inside. (Don't try this at home, kids; it's all a concocted show, which probably wouldn't even fly at the Japan pavilion at Epcot.)

One misty morning, Ibuki and I took the train from Kobe to Osaka to Toba. I was glad to get out of Kobe, be a part of rush-hour traffic on the subway, feeling the jostling of polite Japanese as they maneuvered their way without brushing against each other into packed trains.

The Mikimoto museum was just what I expected, and we breezed through it, not even stopping to admire the *amas*. I wanted to get to Kashikojima, in the heart of Japan's Ise-Shima National Park, which surrounds Ago Bay, where the first cultured pearls were developed a century ago. These days, there are only twelve or so small pearl farms at what once was the world epicenter of cultured pearls. The farms are members of a pearl cooperative that pools its pearls for auction. Ibuki and I went to one of them, the Kashikojima Cultivation Farm, operated by Mori's Otsuki Pearl, where I met Takuya Fujimura, a biologist, and Deguchi Takafumi, the technician who oversees bead insertion.

Once Deguchi tucks a tiny bead, along with a strip of mantle tissue, next to the oyster's gonad, the oyster is placed in a wire cage and submerged into floats in the water. This is where the art of oyster nurturing takes place, a practice more complicated than that of Napa Valley winemaking. It's a nuanced science, influenced by intuitive sense and experience. The lower the oyster is placed in the water, the colder the water. This is good, since colder temperatures can trigger a richer lustre in pearls. But Deguchi and Takuya have to be careful. If the oyster is submerged too low, the amount of oxygen the oyster gets is reduced, and that increases oyster mortality. Monitoring development is essential, too. If the oyster grows too fast, the pearl's shape won't be round.

Then there's the issue of the notorious Red Tide, an aggressive infestation of plankton, which kills oysters. Other pitfalls range from pollution to global warming, which, Takuya said, has raised the temperature of Ago Bay by as much as three degrees over the last decade.

Takuya and Deguchi are continually reinventing a system that has evolved since Mikimoto first cultured pearls in these waters. The process of inserting beads into the oysters is done by a team of women, paid about 20 cents per oyster. With practice, each can nucleate as many as 500 akoya oysters a day, working from five in the morning till seven at night, for about $95.

"It's hard work," Takuya said, adjusting his black-rimmed glasses, sipping green tea that did little to ward off the March breezes coming off the inlet. "Young girls don't want to do this kind of work any longer. Most of them have other options." The women I saw cleaning and repairing nets mostly looked to be in their fifties and sixties, all sitting on their haunches or on stools in a circle, gabbing and working their hands quickly.

The wind was picking up, and it was time to catch the train back to Kobe, transferring in Osaka. I bade good-bye to Ibuki at the main train station and climbed into a taxi. Tomorrow I'd be flying to Hong Kong to attend two invitation-only pearl auctions. The Paspaley and Wan auctions were major sources of South Sea and Tahitian pearls. Dealers from around the world would buy millions of dollars' worth of pearls, only to unload them minutes or hours later in darkened, secure corners at the Hong Kong Convention and Exhibition Centre or over dinner in pricey restaurants. Some dealers would courier their purchases thousands of miles away. Hanging onto pearls for any length of time is bad business. It's sell as fast as you can.

7

Hong Kong— Dealers' Paradise

Pearls aside, I came to Hong Kong because I wanted to see the place. Historically half Chinese, half British, today it's closer to 90 percent Chinese and 10 percent British, and the British quotient is crumbling as fast as the Chinese numbers are multiplying. Hong Kong was among the last holdings of the British Empire, surely being gobbled up bit by bit every day by a voracious Chinese economic and cultural machine. These are the last years before the total conversion of everything British to everything Chinese. The British Jack has been lowered, folded, and placed in mothballs. Hong Kong today is India during the years following independence in 1947.

Still, the city-state remains the West's traditional entry into China. It's the spigot through which billions of dollars, yen, pounds, and marks flow into China, and the city reflects that surge with towering bank buildings (with clubby restaurants inside), mega shopping malls, an escalator that scales Hong Kong's rugged hills, a packed subway system, along with requisite pollution, some of the highest urban density in the world, and impossible bumper-to-bumper traffic. Forget Manhattan. Hong Kong is fifty Manhattans rolled into one tiny gridlocked island.

But it was pearls that ultimately brought me to Hong Kong, specifically those sold at the world's two highest-priced auctions, which take place inside the city's glittering convention centre, which juts out into Victoria Harbor, where three-masted junks and super yachts vie for space. Thirty thousand dealers from forty-one countries attend the Hong Kong convention, one of the largest jewelry shows in the world. Like the Tucson show, the items for sale aren't just pearls but watches, gold, diamonds, jade, platinum, precious and semi-precious stones, silver, already-made jewelry, and raw materials—almost anything placed against the skin as adornment. The jumbo convention is a manifestation of throbbing Hong Kong. As I walked into the main glass-walled structure, futuristic synthesized gongs played. Hundreds of girls dressed in matching uniforms and hats, identical smiles plastered on their faces, stood pivoting as though they were on slowly revolving pedestals, holding signs directing conventioneers.

From Sunday through Tuesday, Australian Nick Paspaley's Darwin-based company held its auction of pearls. Then from Wednesday through Friday, Robert Wan, the millionaire Tahitian pearl magnate, held his. These are exclusive events, and it took me months to arrange access. I sent more than twenty e-mails to each pearling company. My first e-mails were ignored. When I pressed, I got tepid responses. "You have to be a qualified buyer to attend," Wan's people wrote, discouraging any further communication. Many pearl dealers can't even swing invitations. You first have to buy privately from Paspaley and Wan, and if your sales figures are acceptable, an invitation may be issued. Or it might not. "If a new company wanted to come in, they'd have to apply," Paspaley consigliere Dennis Hart told me. "We do a background check, and we'll usually suggest that the dealer start buying wholesale from us from our offices in Hong Kong or Australia. We'll then look at how much he spends, what he buys, where his pearls might go. We don't want one of our customers coming to us, telling us how badly he's been undercut by a dealer we sold to at auction. That would be a total disaster."

The timing of the auctions, one after the other, of course, is intentional. Both take place tucked away in the back of the convention centre, Paspaley's on the fifth floor and Wan's on the third floor, each with beret-wearing, private security guards toting semiautomatic rifles.

Auctions are delicate balancing acts. If Paspaley ever allowed retailers to catch a glimpse of what goes on inside an auction, their eyes would turn into saucers. They certainly wouldn't believe the prices, though they wouldn't be able to buy in the quantities required. And allowing them in would burn Paspaley's mainstays, dealers like Andy Müller, Yoshihiro Shimizu, Yasuaki Mori, Alex Vock, David Norman, and Fran Mastoloni, whose customers are those same retailers. But allowing entry to haphazard dealers also can be perilous. If dealers at auctions sell off Paspaley's pearls to other dealers who, in turn, dump the pearls at discounted prices so that they end up in the marketplace with lower prices than Paspaley's *own* retails shops, then Paspaley would get burned.

"We can't have some wholesalers buying here. That would upset too many of our loyal dealer customers, and it'd be counterproductive for the company," Hart, a jolly, red-faced Australian said. It'd be like showing the other team the playbook. So both Paspaley and Wan have created a complicated vetting system to allow access.

Dealers who get invited have the advantage of gauging the quality of the latest pearl crops and up-to-the-minute prices different quality pearls go for. It's essential intelligence in the fast-moving, minute-by-minute changing ticker of wholesale pearls. Many dealers successfully bid for pearl lots, then turn around and divide the lots, jacking up prices for certain pearls and holding back others. With their purchase, they then go onto the convention floor, selling reconfigured lots privately or, if they have booths at the convention, placing the pearls in display cases for sale to retailers or other dealers. They also string loose pearls they've bought at auction into strands, or make them into composite jewelry and turn such pieces around for specific customers back home.

The trading-floor action at both auctions wasn't what I had expected. It wasn't civilized bidding from men with Connecticut lockjaws and women with coiffed helmet hair holding up numbered paddles as an auctioneer with a gavel intoned, "Going once, twice, sold!" This was an entirely different kind of auction and its seat-of-the-pants, don't-blink rules fascinated me.

For the Paspaley auction, inside a very large room (the Grand Foyer) with a bank of two-story windows overlooking Victoria Harbour, were fifty or so round tables, each covered with a thick white tablecloth. In the middle was a rectangular configuration of twenty additional tables upon which white plastic trays were placed, inside of which were thousands of pearls. Most trays had loose pearls—anywhere from a low of eight to a high of 1,355. Several trays had hanks of large-sized pearls. Each of the trays had a number written on it, indicating a lot number, and each lot corresponded to a sparse, but exacting catalogue description. Size usually varied from 10 to 18 millimeters (the latter is extraordinarily rare, and can fetch retail prices of upward of $20,000 per pearl, depending on shape, lustre, orient, color). Most were Australian pearls in varying shades of white, but Paspaley also put up for auction pearls from the Philippines, Thailand, and Myanmar. They all came in a variety of shapes (round, near-round, button, drop, oval, and baroque), sizes, and colors (white, cream, silver, gold, even yellow). Paspaley stipulates that all pearls he puts up for auction have "natural colour and lustre," which means that he guarantees they are not dyed or color-treated.

Here's how the bidding works:

A dealer indicates that he or she wants to examine a specific lot. Paspaley caps the number of each company's bidders at the auction to four; for this Hong Kong auction, about 120 companies sent representatives. Dealers are allowed to check out one lot at a time; they also can place a request to be the first to examine any lot when it is returned by another dealer. Pearls are weighed on precision digital scales, after which the dealer affirms the weight by signing an affidavit, and then the dealer is allowed to take the lot to one of the inspection tables to examine the pearls at will.

I saw only one dealer bring out a loupe or magnifying glass, and he looked shaky and unsure of himself. He was a man in his eighties, accompanied by a fiftyish woman in a miniskirt, with bronzed skin, matching hair, and very long, French-manicured nails. Most dealers looked askance at the pair. They knew pearls so well they didn't need anything extra to assess the orbs. I did see dealers use digital calipers to verify pearl size, to check whether Paspaley's listed specifications had been inflated. Other dealers brought handy stainless steel measuring cards with a series of graduated millimeter holes. Some held up pearls against the graying light from the harbor to check orient and lustre. Many used cell phones to confer with colleagues thousands of miles away or out trolling the convention floor. Others typed furiously on laptops or thumb-typed on BlackBerries to figure out how the offered lots would complement or offset existing inventories.

Usually within fifteen minutes, the dealer would return the lot. The pearls were then weighed again on digital scales to verify weight. If there was any doubt, enforcers in suits patrolled the area, not unlike Vegas pit bosses. By entering the auction, dealers agree they can be searched, body cavities included, for unaccounted errant pearls.

Dealers place bids by blackening a bubble on a supplied computer card. Lots come as is; they can't be split or reconfigured. Dealers have to buy everything in the lot—the good and the not so good. Indeed, putting together individual pearl lots is a science. Often in each lot, there are AAA-gem-quality pearls that dealers might wrestle each other for, but those beauties are offset by lesser-quality pearls. No mixing and matching allowed. Bids are in yen. Dealers slip bids into a slot of a lockbox behind each pearl lot. Dealers can fill out additional cards to increase or decrease their previous bids. Bidding closes each day at 4:00 p.m. sharp, when Paspaley consiglieres feed the bids into a computer scanner that sifts out the winning offers, which are posted at 6:00 p.m.

Payment is in cash or cashier's check—no personal, company, or traveler's checks—and must be made before the transfer of pearls. Cost of freight is borne by the buyer, but almost always the dealer takes delivery immediately. That's why every dealer totes around omnipresent black leather cases of varying sizes. Only the amounts of the winning bids are posted for each lot, not the names of the successful bidders. This way, dealers can put up for resale the pearls they just bought, and the price paid won't be readily known.

One interesting term is a stipulation that buyers not identify the pearls as having come from Paspaley; dealers are expressly forbidden any use of Paspaley's name in conjunction with the pearls' sale. I am not sure how this was actually enforced; nonetheless, I thought it was a telling condition in an age where brand loyalty, designer labels, and product placement are at the core of most businesses. The idea, again, wasn't dissimilar to trading in cocaine. It also was a bit like money laundering—erasing provenance. The practice protects Paspaley and the dealers who buy from him. This way, every pearl, whether inferior or superior, can be sold at a subsequent free-market price, and resold as often as a dealer wants, without succeeding buyers ever being able to trace where an individual pearl came from and how much it originally fetched. The practice also allowed Paspaley to avoid undercutting his own potential retail market, with word leaking out how much the wholesale price for a particular strand was compared to what a retail customer is being asked to pay.

Another way Paspaley protects himself is by setting minimum or undisclosed minimum bids for each lot. For example, one of the lots I saw was an outrageous hank of twenty-seven perfectly matched round white South Sea pearls, ranging in size from 15 to 18 millimeters. There were six 15-millimeter, twelve 16-millimeter, and eight 17-millimeter pearls, and one 18-millimeter pearl. All were strung in a graduated fashion, so the 18-millimeter pearl was positioned in the strand's center. Paspaley had set an undisclosed minimum on this strand, which meant that bidders wouldn't know what an acceptable minimum bid was, and Paspaley could reject any and all bids under that undeclared minimum price. Dealers scoffed that the so-called minimum often was nonexistent, so Paspaley could choose whether or not to sell the necklace, depending on how much the bids were.

On the day of the auction, that particular strand didn't sell, but another one of lesser quality did. Lot No. 3 was a single hank of thirty-one pearls, ranging in size from an acceptable (but not spectacular) 14 millimeters to 15 millimeters. It sold for almost 4 million yen, about $33,000. How does this translate to the retail customer?

Something like this: The dealer will have to sell the necklace to a retailer, or another dealer, for somewhere around $50,000 to make just a one-third markup. The seller then will likely bump the price to what's known in the trade as the keystone price, or 100 percent markup, escalating the strand to a retail level of $100,000. And that strand wasn't particularly eye-popping, either. Of course, an alternative would be to break up the strand, combining the pearls with others to make several different necklaces.

That strand made up just one lot out of a total of 573 lots up for auction. Those thirty-one pearls were among thousands and thousands of pearls up for auction, amounting to a total of more than a half ton of pearls. Some of the individual lots numbered as many as 2,843 loose pearls. Lot No. 30, with 935 pearls, went for 22,777,000 yen, or $195,000. Lot No. 168, with 528 pearls (147 11-millimeter, 105 12-millimeter, and 276 13-millimeter pearls) went for 16,508,000 yen, or $141,000.

One outstanding lot (No. 285) had 124 loose pearls in it, ranging from 15 millimeters (forty-three of them) to an unheard of 19 millimeters (two of them); it went for 16,050,000 yen, or $137,100. These pearls could end up making five or six necklaces that could ultimately fetch an average of $50,000 apiece.

Robert Wan's Tahitian pearl auction was operated in a similar fashion, with several key differences. The mode of currency wasn't yen, it was euros. And Wan offered more lots with undisclosed minimums than Paspaley did, which allowed Wan not to sell if the bids didn't match what he wanted.

Of course, Wan is dealing with Tahitian pearls, unlike the Australians, which come in a variety of colors and qualities. He offered six grades of pearls—ranging from the lowest, called commercial (or, ironically, A quality), less than 30 percent clean surface, to top gem, which is "spotless and excellent lustre," with greater than a 95 percent clean surface.

There were 485 lots in the Wan auction, with the smallest just seventeen 10- to 13-millimeter loose pearls (Lot 50, tear drop shape, asking price, 5,100 euros, or $6,700) and the largest an assortment of 6,466 4- to 8-millimeter loose keshi[1] pearls (Lot 149), with a minimum bid of 41,700 euros, or $53,000. A larger lot of keshis, 4,723 pearls, from 8 to 15 millimeters, called for a minimum bid of 61,400 euros, or $80,750.

Wan's auction was hidden away from the masses trooping through the convention centre. There were several signs pointing the way, but the auction was tucked in Rooms 301–312, and unless you knew where you were going (or someone took you there), you'd surely get lost in the labyrinth mega structure, with its serpentine hallways and endless rows of booths and rooms. Tighter security seemed to pervade the Tahitian pearl auction; more dealers had electronic passes to gain admittance to the Wan auction than to the Paspaley auction. (200 vs. 140 dealers).

Paspaley and Wan hold three other auctions each year in Hong Kong, and Paspaley holds one in Kobe in the fall. All the major dealers showed up at either or both, including many I'd already met in Kobe or Tucson—Mastoloni, Shimizu, Vock, Müller, a team of representatives from Otsuki Pearl. Such auctions, though, seem to be getting less and less popular with niche top-end pearl dealers who can go directly to Paspaley or Wan to buy goods, bypassing the rigmarole of the open-bidding events.

In both auctions, when the winning bids were posted in the early evening, hardly anyone hung around to see the results. I half-expected the winners to jump up and down and shout "Yippee!" but I was one of just five people still milling around in the Grand Foyer when Paspaley's staff posted the results of the first day at precisely 6:00 p.m. The reaction was really one of no reaction.

Earlier in the day, Paspaley had seen me nosing around, and he immediately stuck out his hand. I had tried repeatedly to contact him via e-mail and phone for almost an entire year, and if I got any response, it had been from an underling who'd said Paspaley was too busy to be bothered.

Paspaley is the world's largest producer of Australian South Sea pearls and, because of that, single-handedly controls much of the global market for all pearls. After the Hong Kong auction, he planned to fly his star employees for a week of helicopter skiing in Aspen. "They've been working awfully hard these last few months. It'll be good for everyone, me-self included," Paspaley said brightly.

Paspaley was a thin, slight, wiry man of fifty-eight, with a full head of moussed mahogany hair. This day, he was wearing a conservative blue suit, open-collar shirt, and incongruously a pair of brown kangaroo-leather boots.

To see sycophants queuing up to Paspaley was an occasion to note a man at the center of power and others desperately seeking to step into that private circle, if only for a matter of seconds. Asians bowed servilely when they passed him; the Americans and Europeans waited patiently to catch his eye, and then sidled up to him, clapping him on the back with one hand and grabbing his hand with the other. Paspaley seemed a genial kind of guy, but I got the impression that, given his druthers, he'd rather be kicking back drinking a VB and fishing off Australia's Top End than hobnobbing with pearl dealers.

This was Paspaley's thirty-fourth auction. By now, he knew which kinds of pearls sold at auction and which didn't. He never offers truly one-of-a-kind pearls, particularly perfectly matched jumbos in a hank, at auction because usually they go to private buyers for top dollar (actually, top yen) in one-on-one transactions. There's always a market for such rare pearls. Dealers like Alex Vock are always looking for such gems. "The stuff that you'd call daily stuff, the stuff that goes to the processors, that's what goes at auction. In other words, the auction is a clearinghouse. But," Paspaley added, "we always like to throw in some amazing pearls just to keep everyone interested." Other than those pearls in the rough, "all of the triple-A pearls, and the finer goods, go privately. The commercial-grade stuff, the lower quality, is what goes up for auction. The important goods we keep to sell privately."

As he did with today's auction, Paspaley said he likes to put several finished hanks of pearls up for sale with undisclosed minimum bids. It's a no-risk way to offer top-end matched pearls and to see how much dealers are willing to pay. It works out nicely: Paspaley gets an idea of the strands' going price with the safeguard that he won't have to sell if it's too low.

I asked Paspaley why he doesn't have conventional auctions, like Christie's or Sotheby's, where dealers have several days to examine goods and then publicly bid against each other.

"We've tried it and it doesn't work. We get more when dealers can study the lots and, then and there, put their bids in, knowing that by the evening they'll take possession of the pearls." I got the feeling that dealers simply didn't have the patience to wait. They saw which pearls they wanted, and wanted to have them in their hands quickly, so they'd be able to flip them as fast as they'd bought them.

Paspaley shook his head when I asked him about pearl dealers, as though to say they weren't just a different breed but an entirely different genus. He readily unloaded on some of his wealthiest clients, dealers who pile their plates high, crowding around the Paspaley lunch buffet in the adjacent room to the auction (four nationalities of entrees: Chinese, American, Japanese, and Indian). He laughed when recalling how often dealers whisper in his ear to ask for special deals. "One pulls me aside and says, 'Nick, old boy, next time we give you an order, make me wife a necklace, will you?' Then the bloke tells me he wants one that's nice, but not *over-the-top* nice, not too expensive, and he wouldn't mind if I 'could take care' of him. So, I'm used to this, and I say, 'Sure, I'll give you a deal,' send it to him with his company's shipment, and put a *special price* on the invoice. That's when the bloke says to me, *'Oh, no, Nick, don't do that!* My partners will see it. Just bill me separately, and the next time I see you, I'll pay you on the side. Okay?'

"Talk about cheap! These guys are dealing with hundreds and hundreds of thousands of dollars' worth of goods and this bloke wants a deal for his wife— and one that he doesn't want his partner to know about! And, he won't even buy for his wife one of the high-quality necklaces!"

"Occupational hazard of any business," I commiserated.

"I don't know 'bout other businesses, but it sure is of mine. I can't tell you how often that happens. They must think I'm made of money."

As we talked, I could see several deer-in-headlight faces of lesser-known dealers who knew Paspaley and knew his power.

"Hiya, Nick," one man said, waving as he sprinted by.

"Meester Paspaley, how goooood to see you again," a man I took to be Italian said in an elegant, regal manner. A heavily made-up sixtyish woman with gold hair at his side fluttered her eyelashes.

"Phew!" Paspaley said to me, wincing.

I had just met Paspaley, but we seemed to get along. Maybe that's *why* we got along. Perhaps Paspaley was angling for ink in this book, but I doubted whether he needed or trusted any writer. I came to think our first meeting was simpatico simply because I was an outsider, a world apart from his cosmos of kiss-ups and pushy pearl dealers.

Two hours of prime time had gone by, and there were only ninety minutes left before the close of the second day's auction. Around the room, the dealers had picked up their collective pace. Some were using calipers, others fitted pearls through corresponding millimeter-sized holes on stainless steel guides. Some pored over laptop screens to assess potential inventory complements. Almost all had calculators and were frenetically punching in numbers as they shouted to each other in a mélange of languages.

"The auction will close in thirty minutes," Dennis Hart announced into a microphone. "Please return all lots to the display tables."

The atmosphere changed. A table of four Indians got to work in earnest, two dealers confirming the number of pearls in the lot, another dealer holding pearl after pearl against the natural light, a fourth feverishly working a calculator. Two of the dealers started arguing back and forth, as one rolled a pearl on top of the white tablecloth to check whether it ought to be classified round or merely near-round.

At 3:55 p.m., a Paspaley consigliere rolled a cart from a backroom with an oversized brown cardboard carton on it. A last-minute flurry ensued. A member of the aforementioned Indian quartet rushed to one of the bid boxes and slipped a bid in, then patted the box twice for good measure.

At 4:00 p.m., the bid boxes were placed into the large cardboard carton, and Paspaley employees begin to pour each lot of pearls into clear baggies, then the baggies were placed in the lot trays and wheeled to a backroom.

At 4:30 p.m. there was an announcement that one of the bidders had entered an incorrect bid. "Would the bidder of lot 132 please see an auction employee as soon as possible?" But the bidder had left the auction room. Meanwhile, coming from somewhere in a backroom, the soundtrack was the endless click-clack of a thousands of pearls being transferred from container to container.

I saw Paspaley off to the side, talking with Hart. "These boots are killing me," Paspaley said as much to me as to himself. "I bought 'em right before I left Darwin, and they're the only shoes I brought with me." He took off his left boot and was standing with one boot on, one boot off.

"Wanna have a look in the back, mate?" Paspaley asked me.

The backroom reminded me of a stockroom at a high-end department store. All the glitz was on the other side, the side meant for the customer. In very cramped quarters, a dozen young men, all wearing white shirts and ties, but without shoes, were sprawled on white tablecloths strewn on the floor, busily affixing thousands of pearls onto sticky strips of precise-sized circles. Each pearl had to go into a particular circle on a particular sticky strip, to be inventoried, checked, and, if sold, passed onto the salespeople for eventual dispersal to the buyer.

Paspaley and I stood over this Australian minyan of young men, scrambling on all fours, a kind of Twister game in action. "I love auctions," Paspaley said. "They're good for the boys, too. The blokes who farm the pearls and those who price them. It's judgment day for all of us. No use growing something you can't sell, is there?"

8

The Traders

As Paspaley and others had advised me, the highest-grade pearls seldom make it to auction. Those pearls are almost always picked off by traders who flip them in high-end private deals, usually wholesale, but occasionally on the retail market. Such traders occupy a lucrative niche in the pearl world. By the time a trader purchases such exceptional pearls, the jewels almost always have been presold to a specific client, or have been bought with a specific client in mind. In the event they haven't, the dealer might keep them for a matter of minutes before reselling them. Or, although unusual, the dealer might hold onto a particularly rare strand for years (even though this'll kill him) until he's found just the right buyer, usually a well-heeled private client, but occasionally it'll be another dealer who's presold the necklace to one of *his* clients. There's little honor in the high-stakes world of pearl traders. Client poaching is frowned upon but happens all the time. To make matters worse, wealthy top-of-the-line clients are notorious for shopping around, playing dealers against one another. A dealer can wake up one morning to find himself unceremoniously dumped because he's fallen out of favor within his client's ever-changing circle of glit-terati, his goods aren't what his client wants any longer, or the client simply wants to do business with Vanessa or Fiona's absolutely *fabulous* jewelry friend. Often, competitors steal clients by offering them perks of bracelets, rings, ear-rings, or strands thrown in at cost or as an outright gift as a sort of "signing bonus." Pearl producers like Nick Paspaley, Robert Wan, Jacques Branellec, and Rosario Autore sometimes inject themselves into the mix by offering out-rageous pieces to celebrities attending events such as the Oscars, Emmys, and Tony Awards, but also for high-profile private bashes (benefits for symphonies, operas, museums, hospitals, and disease cures are particularly popular). Celeb-rities, through agents, essentially rent out body parts (necks, wrists, fingers, or earlobes), and when the event is over, the celebrities return the jewelry, are of-fered it at steeply discounted prices, or for free with contractual obligations to wear the pearls at a schedule of selected functions. These public showings are advertised by reams of press releases and glossy photos of the celebrities wearing the baubles, this time with the producers' names splashed everywhere. Celebrity fashion shoots for magazines are treated similarly. Product place-ment in films, television, and theater is another negotiated business that cuts out dealers; pearl producers contract with agencies, which then negotiate di-rectly with actors' representatives.

High-end pearl traders usually buy in four varieties—matched 16-inch-long hanks, matched pairs for earrings, a spectacular single pearl suitable as a pen-dant, or loose. The hanks are threaded on silk string and aren't finished neck-laces. They have no knots between pearls, nor do they have clasps at the end. Hanks are how almost all strands are assembled for the trade, whether they're strands of walnut-sized Australian pearls bought by a dealer shopping for An-gelina Jolie, or crates of tens of thousands of commercial-grade Chinese pearls snapped up by bottom-feeders for the jewelry counter at Walmart. Dealers seldom buy finished necklaces. This way, they can create whatever pearl prod-uct they want. If the pearls end up as a necklace, it's the jeweler who has them strung and knotted.

At the Hong Kong International Jewellery Show, thousands of jewelers made purchases, but most of the exclusive jewelry retailers (places like Harry Winston, Gump's, Tiffany & Co., Van Cleef & Arpels, Bulgari, Neiman Marcus, Christie's, Sotheby's) rarely, if ever, buy directly at such shows, and never buy at auctions (Paspaley and Wan wouldn't let them in). Instead, they usually opt to purchase jewelry that, in essence, has been preselected by a cadre of well-connected, respected traders. Müller, Vock, Mastoloni, Shimizu, Assael, and

David Norman are among a handful of hundreds of such pearl middlemen worldwide. Anyone can call himself a pearl trader; some are gemologists, but certainly not all are. The most successful have been dealing pearls for a very long time, some as second- or third-generation traders, and all have worldwide connections. These are men (and they're practically all men) who with a single call can locate and purchase within seconds any pearl in the world.

In the small world of pearl traders, every established trader has a mythology swirling around him. Like any specialized profession, pearl traders carry reputations that are impossible to shake. The pearl trader with the biggest cachet in the world is, without a doubt, a suave, elegant, continental man in his mid-eighties, who speaks Italian, French, German, Portuguese, Japanese, Spanish, Turkish, and English. He has been at the center of pearl trading for more than fifty years. His name is Salvador Assael, and outrageous stories about him abound.

II

Of the dozens of pearl traders, vendors, jewelers I'd already met, not a single one didn't use the word *charmer* when I mentioned Assael's name (pronounced Ah-say-el). But along with that fulsome encomium came a caveat. The second-oft-used word was *balls*. No one left Assael unassailed. Everyone had an opinion and, at the very least, a vintage Assael story, usually one with bite marks left intact. "He has a brain like a computer," one dealer told me. "He's brilliant." Others described Assael as a tenacious bargainer, a bulldog, an egomaniac, a man with no compassion. And these were the compliments. Ultimately, in the more than 30,000 miles I was to travel, outside of laborers on the bottom three or four rungs of the giant pearl ladder, few people I talked to anywhere in the pearl business didn't know Assael, and few had much to say that was wholly complimentary. "He's a ruthless and despicable snake," said one dealer not known for storing bile in his throat. "Watch your wallet," another dealer told me, referring to negotiating with Assael. "If your hand isn't on your wallet at all times, Sal will remove it, take out your cash, then return it to your pocket without you ever realizing a thing. And he'll be smiling every second he's robbing you blind."

In response to an e-mail I'd sent Assael, I received back from his assistant, Albert Friedel, an effusive reply, informing me that Assael (whom Friedel volunteered was recognized worldwide as the Pearl King) would gladly meet me in

New York. After guards on the first-floor lobby of Assael's office at 580 Fifth Avenue photographed me and took my driver's license as a security deposit, I arrived in Assael's crowded showroom and office, only to be informed by Friedel that Assael had overlooked a family commitment and with regret couldn't make the trip to the city from his estate in the Hamptons. But Assael would gladly allow a phone interview. So, at the appointed hour, while I sat behind Assael's massive desk and peered at dozens of photographs of famous women he'd sold pearls to, all vying for wall space, we talked.

Assael *was* charming. When asked about names of his clients, he laughed in a studied kind of way, and said he absolutely couldn't and wouldn't reveal their identities, but then managed to repeatedly drop names that included Elizabeth Taylor, Margaret Thatcher, Nancy Reagan, Evelyn Lauder, and Robin Chandler Duke. "All wonderful women and wonderful people," Assael effused. I didn't think there was an equivalent of doctor-patient confidentiality when it came to pearl dealers, but if there were, Assael had tossed it out the door. For good measure, Friedel had prepared for me a typed list of thirty-five notable clients.

Assael is married to a leggy blond Swedish woman almost half his age. Christina Lang and Assael met at a dinner party on the French Rivera several years after Assael's first wife, Dorette Vock Assael, died in 1991 of cancer. The couple has an adopted sixteen-year-old daughter, Sophia; Assael has a grown daughter, Arlette, by his marriage to Dorette. The Assaels have several homes, one on the twelfth floor of a fourteen-floor, twenty-three-unit vintage co-op building at 485 Park Avenue (at Fifty-eighth Street); another a half block from Further Lane (known as Billionaire Row) in Amagansett, New York, a hamlet within East Hampton; and a third in the horse country of Dutchess County. The Assael Amagansett home is across the street from the Nature Conservancy's Double Dunes Preserve, one block from the Atlantic Ocean, and down the street from Christie Brinkley and Billy Joel's old digs, where Jerry and Jessica Seinfeld now live, the same street where Tommy Hilfiger sold his home for $26.5 million in 2007. Assael and his wife bought the 2.3-acre property in 1993 for $1.8 million and transformed the 1909 shingle cottage into a 6,478-square-foot, two-story estate with a forty-five-foot-long pool, cabana, and greenhouse. The exterior resembles an Italian villa, complete with bocce ball court; the property is landscaped with prize French and English roses. The interior is filled with eighteenth-century Swedish antiques. In 2006, the Assaels bought an eighty-one-acre estate in Washington, New York, on Route 44. They built a 7,344-square-foot seventeen-room mansion with two kitchens, two fireplaces, five bedrooms, and six baths. The couple is building three more living quarters on the property, a caretaker's cottage, guesthouse, and four-bedroom visitor's apartment. The county assessor's office puts a value of $4.5 million on the property, near Millbrook.[1]

Assael favors Carlo Palazzi suits and monogrammed shirts, and owns a vintage 1976 Mercedes. He collects art and owns paintings by François Boucher, Camille Pissarro, and Maurice Utrillo. He was an early financial supporter of Rudy Giuliani's failed presidential campaign, and has consistently donated to Republican candidates, including George W. Bush, Elizabeth Dole, and George Pataki. Christina Assael, who lists her profession as "philanthropist," gave campaign contributions to both Hillary Clinton and John McCain's 2008 presidential campaigns. She is a board member of the American-Scandinavian Foundation, as well as the World Childhood Foundation, and a member of Saint Peter's Catholic Church.

The Assaels are popular dinner guests in their high-flying circuit of friends. No wonder. One of the ways Assael courts the super-rich is by bestowing on well-heeled society women small gifts of pearl earrings the first time he meets them. It's his signature. So popular is Assael because of his pearl baubles that women fall over themselves, wangling to get invited to any affair at which Assael may be present.

But that's only the beginning of an Assael charm attack. One dealer I talked to put it this way: "When you're buying a pearl, you're really buying a piece of the seller, and *no one in the world* sells like Sal. You buy into Sal as much as you buy the pearl. Somehow, he's able to create the impression that you, and only you, *deserve* these very special pearl earrings or this necklace."

Once the client is on the hook, Assael is unrelenting, alternately turning on his charm and tenacity. A former employee told me, "Assael's philosophy is simple: Get the most from the customer, particularly elderly clients, because they might die tomorrow. It was always, 'Go, go, go!'"

Assael has a curious reputation as a hypochondriac, and on the wholesale level every dealer seems to have a story about Assael's numerous aches and pains, and how he uses such alleged ailments as gambits in negotiating. Assael drives a bargain like no one else in the business. He zigs and zags, weaves and feints, promising to pay one price, only to bear down hard on the seller, suddenly demanding less the moment he's about to sign off on the deal. By then, the seller is too exhausted to object.

"The one thing I cannot figure out is that my own company is selling more necklaces in the range of fifty thousand to a million dollars this year than ever before," he mused to *Avenue* magazine in October 1998. "Maybe it's because ours is the only company of its kind in the world to carry such merchandise. And for the very wealthy person—whether it be an Arab king, a sultan, or a billionaire from Germany or Ecuador or the United States—a million is still peanuts, even today."

Assael often refers to himself in the third person. After undergoing quintuple bypass heart surgery in the mid-1990s, Assael told a reporter, "People worry about what's going to happen when Assael dies. Well, Assael is not going to die, not for a long time."

I discovered as I began plumbing Assael's life that many of his stories were embellished, dramatized, and sanitized according to his grand sense of self, beauty, opulence, personal history, political patronage, and business advantage. With Assael, there was no telling where the truth ended and an overwhelming fabrication of reality began. From what I could gather from reliable sources this is his story:

Assael grew up in northern Italy as a Sephardic Jew, the son of James Assael, a Turkish-born diamond trader with offices in Antwerp, Cairo, and Milan. The Assael family had a villa on Lake Como. As a teenager, one afternoon Assael was at the villa playing Ping-Pong when his father drove from Milan and matter-of-factly informed the family they would immediately be leaving Italy. In May 1939, after Mussolini gained power, fourteen members of the extended Assael family fled their wealthy, insular lives, sailing from France bound for Havana on a ship teeming with Jewish refugees desperate to leave Europe. When corrupt Cuban immigration officers imposed a bond of $5,000 on each passenger, James Assael opened a leather-and-cloth satchel his wife was carrying and counted out $70,000 in bribes. Incensed, Assael's father "had the balls to demand a receipt, which he got!"[2] All fourteen Assaels were allowed to walk off the ship shortly before the oceanliner and the one next to it, *The St. Louis*, returned to Europe, where Jewish passengers were put on trains bound for concentration camps. James Assael started two businesses in Havana, a diamond-cutting factory and a jewelry store. Two years after their arrival, James Assael presented his "immigration-bond receipt" to the newly installed Cuban government and received a refund for the bribes he'd paid to save his family.

That same year, the Assaels emigrated to New York, where young Salvador found his first niche product: waterproof Swiss watches. During the war, Germany had blocked the exportation of Swiss watches to the Allies, but James Assael was able to buy shiploads of twenty different watch brands as long as they first went to Cuba. Assael then had them shipped to New York. After serving as a translator for the army's 78th Infantry Lightning Division, Sal returned to New York and joined his father's business. James Assael found himself with a mountain of Swiss Army watches and no buyers. Through an Army buddy who had relocated to Japan, Sal tried to sell the watches to American GIs stationed there. This is where Assael got into the pearl business, by witnessing a fundamental tenet of economics: World markets were not monolithic; what one market rejected, another market often welcomed. The Japanese were cash-poor after the war and could only barter for goods. They had plenty of cultured pearls and they needed portable mechanized instruments that could tell time—Swiss watches.

By 1950, Assael had unloaded all of his father's watches in exchange for some of the finest cultured pearls the Western world had ever seen. But to Assael, the Japanese pearls, though plentiful and popular, were trifling. They were dainty and modest. Assael was looking for major jewels, even half a century ago, that would make a statement. He was searching for pearls that could (literally and figuratively) knock out the eyes of anyone who took one look at them. Instead of focusing on the small akoya pearls native to Japan, Assael broadened his geography. He began seeking larger South Sea pearls that had been farmed by Japanese pearlers prior to the war off Thursday Island, northeast of Darwin, Australia. The size of these pearls was gigantic, some as large as 15 millimeters. With small caches of the largest pearls the world had ever seen, Assael started selling these gumball beauties back in the United States. American jewelers went gaga over them.

Assael was off and running. He broadened his hunt; travel was no obstacle to finding his treasures, and by the early 1960s, he had became the world's largest buyer of large Burmese pearls. At the time, the largest akoya pearls were, at most, 10 millimeters; these diminutive orbs might fetch at most $3,000 a strand wholesale. But the most spectacular Burmese pearls, at 15 to 16 millimeters, might go for as much as $50,000 per strand. Assael flew back to New York with suitcases full of these huge *Pinctada maxima* strands and made a beeline for Harry Winston and Van Cleef & Arpels, which gladly snapped up however many Assael brought them. When political instability threatened Burmese pearl production, Assael looked toward pearls that were being developed in French Polynesia. These were exotic black and gray pearls that came from the black-lipped *Pinctada margaritifera* oyster.

Dealers told me that Assael always seems to have the prescience to be at the right place at the right time—whether in Burma, French Polynesia, Australia, or New York. One of Assael's many claims to fame is that he was the only dealer in the United States who had access to rare large Tahitian pearls as far back as the mid-1970s. Assael made a fortune selling them. Jean-Claude Brouillet, a French multimillionaire developer who owned a Tahitian atoll called Marutea, found himself with a plethora of these odd black Tahitian pearls. Then, up till the late 1970s, practically all cultured pearls worldwide were various shades of white. The only black pearls were novelty items, usually small, white cultivated pearls from Japan that had been dyed, viewed by most dealers as nothing more than unconventional jewelry.

In 1973, Assael went to Tahiti and signed an exclusive agreement with Brouillet, who used to dock his yacht next to Assael's in Saint-Tropez. Assael took back to the United States a box full of black pearls and showed them to jewelers at Harry Winston, who suggested that if such pearls could be cultivated larger and rounder, Winston might be interested. Assael invested in Brouillet's farm on Marutea and returned to New York five years later with a sampling, this time large, round, and flawless. The jewelers at Winston went crazy. So did the entire New York jewelry world. Capitalizing on the buzz, Assael's company promptly came up with the advertising slogan "A New Gem Is Born." In 1976, Brouillet's harvest was eight thousand pearls, and in 1977, it was 14,000. Brouillet sold his entire crop to Assael for $1 million, and Assael offered eighteen strands exclusively to Winston, which took them all. "We thought he'd buy three, maybe four, necklaces, but no, he took everything," Assael told *Modern Jeweler* magazine. Winston displayed the best of the black pearl necklaces in its window. Each was priced at one million dollars and all of them sold almost immediately.

Other top-end New York jewelers began agitating to be included in the high-ticket Tahitian pearl frenzy. But for a period of more than five years, Assael was the sole funnel through which almost every single Tahitian black pearl came to America. He was the only dealer with access to the only Tahitian farm producing such large, high-quality black pearls. Assael gave strands on speculation to Van Cleef & Arpels, and they, too, sold out immediately. Meanwhile, Assael kept strands for himself for a coterie of private clients, and this is when he really started making money, selling the Tahitians directly to the crème de la crème of his wealthy clientele. Assael sold necklaces to women who waited in line to fork over millions of dollars for the privilege of wearing the newest species of pearl in the world. Neither they nor Assael could get enough of the world's newest had-to-have bauble.

III

So, there I was, sitting behind Assael's grand desk on the twenty-first floor of 580 Fifth Avenue, listening to Assael's smooth, mellifluous voice as he waxed rhapsodic—"the single most beautiful object nature creates is the pearl." With Assael effusing, I began studying his office walls, covered with the dozens of framed, signed photographs and testimonials. As I could plainly see, Assael (as do all prominent pearl dealers in New York) had a large circle of pampered clients. It seemed like anyone who's anyone eventually found her way to Assael's offices, and although all his clients were flush with money, the lure of buying wholesale directly from a broker—the Pearl King himself!—not from a street-level jewelry store that allows *anyone* to buy was a powerful inducement, even though Assael's prices might not have been any lower.

Assael's list of clients was the absolute, unsurpassed A-list of American and international society of the 1980s and '90s. Rosalynn Carter met Assael at a dinner party Manhattan real estate agent Alice Mason hosted in 1993, and out of the blue, Assael, on cue, gave Mrs. Carter a pair of Tahitian black pearl earrings. Former President Ronald Reagan sent Assael a letter on May 2, 1991, in which he thanked Assael for his gift of an oversized black pearl tie tack. "What a happy surprise to arrive in the office this A.M. and find your letter to Nancy and me and your magnificent Black Pearl. I assure you it will be worn and with great pride. You were most generous to do this and you have my heartfelt thanks." Another client was Robin Chandler Duke, the fourth wife of Angier Biddle Duke, the former U.S. ambassador to El Salvador, Spain, Denmark, and Morocco, and great nephew of the founder of the American Tobacco Company. Robin Duke, herself the former U.S. Ambassador to Norway, wrote Assael, "Your pearls look so wonderful I wanted you to see these pictures." Then, rather curiously, Duke wrote, "I am so grateful for your kindness in putting them in my price range!" Assael persistently courted Elizabeth Taylor by giving her Tahitian black pearl earrings. Assael says he was instrumental in the creation of Taylor's line of perfume, Black Pearls, launched in 1996.

Assael's Rolodex of pearl-buying socialites includes those who have slipped a notch or two. Susan Gutfreund, the extravagant second wife of disgraced former Salomon Brothers CEO John Gutfreund, was a client, as was Judy Taubman, the wife of imprisoned former Sotheby's chairman and shopping-mall developer A. Alfred Taubman. Another client was Lily Safra, whose fourth husband, Lebanese-born Edmond J. Safra, one of the richest men in the world, died in a suspicious 1999 fire in Monaco.

Assael boasts hundreds of clients, including Lady Evelyn Jacobs, Cecile Zilkha, Jayne Wrightsman, Lady de Rothchild, Daisy Soros, Gustavo Cisneros, Shahpari Khashoggi, Princess Michael of Kent, Duchess of York Sarah Ferguson, Nancy Kissinger, actress Linda Evans, socialite Doda Voridis, Ernestine Bradley, Princess Silvie d'Arenberg, Evelyn Lauder, Annette de la Renta, Brooke Astor, Sondra Mack, Barbara Davis, Mona Ayoub, Harriette Levine, Chantal Miller, Pia Getty, Alexandra von Furstenberg, Marie-Chantal Claire Miller, Mercedes Bass, and Karen LeFrak.

Although Assael could sell anything (he once sold a drunken and stoned Prince Johannes von Thurn und Taxis a $70,000 sapphire ring for his wife, Princess Gloria, a former waitress known as Princess TNT), his specialty was one-of-a-kind pearls. In 1990, an Assael necklace of twenty-seven Tahitian black pearls ranging from 13.5 to 17.9 millimeters sold at Sotheby's New York for almost $800,000. In 1992, an Assael necklace of twenty-three Australian pearls ranging from 16 to 20 millimeters sold at Sotheby's New York for $2.32 million.

Assael's pearl business flourished through word of mouth. Globel doyennes flocked to his offices, buying iconic large Tahitian or South Sea pearls that, it seemed, only Assael had for sale. Of course, it was Assael who pumped up the bubble, saying that these were the largest pearls ever cultured and their supply was finite (this may have been true, but larger pearls were always being cultivated). Of course, Assael's bubble could burst at any time. Dealers know the cyclical ups and downs of pearls, which aren't any different from those of gold, diamonds, oil, cocaine, and precious minerals. One hedge that Assael had was that, like all dealers, he seldom held his merchandise long, particularly in the mid-1980s. The bottom could fall out at any time. You never wanted to be stuck with merchandise you couldn't move or, worse, whose value plummets. That's what happened on October 19, 1987.

Kobe pearl dealer Andy Müller was in Assael's New York showroom that day, known as Black Monday, when stock markets around the world crashed and the Dow Jones Industrial Average lost 22 percent. Müller had just gotten off a plane at JFK Airport. He took a taxi directly to Assael's office and was in the midst of spending a million dollars of his employer Golay Buchel's money to buy pearls. Assael and Müller had a pleasant conversation, but Assael never mentioned to Müller that the world markets had just fallen off the face of the earth. Müller had no idea, and if he did, he never would have spent that kind of money. Pearls, unlike gold, ride the market.

More than two decades later, this story still makes the rounds of pearl dealers. The dealers' thinking goes something like this: You don't have to tell buyers *everything*, but news this big probably merits a mention, no? Two dealers talking about a million-dollar transaction, and not a single word of the biggest stock market collapse in modern history?

Here's another story a producer told me:

"So, Sal's in my office and he says he wants a nice gold bracelet for his wife that I happen to have, and all along, I'm thinking, 'This isn't going to be pretty, how much am I going to charge him?' but I let it go, and when it comes time to set a price, I come up with a *huge* discount. Sal nods his head, and so I figure it's all settled. But as I prepare the invoice, Sal grabs the pen out of my hand, and draws a line through the price, and says, 'All the millions of dollars we've exchanged. I want you to *give* the bracelet to my wife.'

"It was shameless—but it worked, I suppose, because I let him have the bracelet. To deal with Sal is to get a headache. He has the biggest balls of all of them. He'd buy thirty percent at an auction, then skims the best, sells the loose pearls at what he paid for the whole lot, and then gets the strands for free."

"Sal doesn't play nice in the sandbox," said another pearl wholesaler diplomatically. Almost all of the dealers I interviewed didn't want their names used, particularly since Assael, even in his late eighties, still wields so much influence. "If you get more press or attention than Sal, he doesn't like it. That's Sal's weakness, but also his strength. He's as vain as can be. But he's also one of the greatest pearl salesmen ever. He goes for your balls and once he's got them, he never lets go."

Assael, of course, didn't corner the high-end pearl market all by himself. He had help. Besides Friedel, pearl skinner* Andres Babio, and a jewelry designer who supposedly is Prince Dimitri of the former Yugoslavia, Assael employed two top salesmen, patrician Henri Masliah and then-tyro Alex Vock.

Masliah, now also in his eighties, enchanted Assael's wealthy, often neurotic, clients. He was very good at talking in a French accent, while he smoked his pipe, blowing heady smoke rings into the air. Masliah specialized in the kind of client who needed handling, who required patience. These were women who

---

* The art of peeling blemishes off a pearl.

vacillated, who just couldn't make up their minds, women who had to take pearls home and then return them because they just weren't absolutely sure yet. Masliah was Assael's Old World go-to guy, the genteel salesman who could close any deal that Assael seemingly couldn't.

Vock was fresh out of college when his uncle, Assael, hired him. Now forty-seven, Vock operates his own New York showroom, ProVockative Gems, at 608 Fifth Avenue, down the block from his old boss. Fast-talking Vock was poised to take over Assael's mantle. If pearls were golf, Assael might be Gary Player and Volk would be Tiger Woods.

At Bates College, in Lewiston, Maine, Vock majored in economics. Two years out of college, in 1983, he found himself working for Assael. Assael suggested that Vock, then twenty-three, keep a diary of his first month working in the trade. Vock recently unearthed the yellowed, dog-eared diary from the back of a desk drawer. The pocket-sized, spiral-bound notebook was a refreshing sojourn from Assael, but also from the hard-nosed dealers I'd been surrounded by at the Paspaley and Wan auctions in Hong Kong. The diary details the education of a neophyte dealer during the throes of the frenetic, frantic pearl go-go years in New York in the early 1980s. It's also a document that reveals how a pearl dealer learns the industry's ropes.

In one of his first entries, Vock scribbled his impressions of a pearl buyer at Van Cleef & Arpels, who had a "keen eye and very opinionated tastes." Vock noted the buyer was "quite capricious, moody and difficult. She is so overpowering and intimidating, even though she is the customer." Vock set out to figure how he could appease the prickly buyer, and came up with a solution: "Maybe the key to selling her is to make her feel she is great, smart, knowledgeable without openly flattering her. She is too sophisticated to be flattered blatantly."

In another entry, Vock summed up a particularly artful deal Assael had brokered with a pair of Colombians who had brought with them a cache of outrageous emeralds. (Emeralds and other stones are add-ons for pearl dealers; while not at the core of their business, there's no use sending clients out the door if they're seeking something other than pearls.) "Mr. Assael was tough as nails," Vock wrote in the diary. "During the negotiations he always bargained from a position of strength. After the sale was consummated the Colombians admitted that Mr. Assael was a real professional. What this means: He bought the stones at a very reasonable markup, just enough to give them a profit they [the Colombians] would accept but leaving Assael the opportunity to make a high profit, and still price the stones at a sellable price and not out of the market."

Vock summed up his first week by scribbling, "The strong impression I have of the business in general is the strength and charm of the personalities involved. It is not an industry of weak or mediocre people. Being confident of one's taste and the quality of one's experience looks like the key to success. One saying, which has often been repeated to me by a man who made a fortune buying and selling in art auctions, comes to mind: 'Something is only worth what someone else is willing to pay for it.'" At the end of his diary, Vock listed his sales for the month—to Tiffany, Bulgari, Harry Winston, H. Stern, and Cartier. The total came to $55,693. Not bad for a dealer's first month.

By 1990, Vock and Masliah had left Assael, tired of hearing that it was Assael who drove the business and that, without him, their client list would dry up. Each went into business for himself.

IV

Congested, densely populated Hong Kong is not a city of clean, inexpensive hotels. Prices of just about anything (except handmade suits and foot massages) are astronomical. The rents Hong Kong apartments fetch make New York real estate look like what you'd pay in Dubuque. When I started figuring out where I could afford ten days in Hong Kong, I made an observation. There were two kinds of hotels located anywhere close to where I needed to be: high-priced palaces like the Renaissance Harbor View that went for six hundred dollars a night, or budget, hot-sheet dives with roaches and cigarette burns in the sheets. I thought I'd come across an exception after a colleague who works at the *Wall Street Journal* in Hong Kong recommended a place called the Charterhouse, smack in the middle of the onetime red-light district, Wan Chai. The hotel turned out to be a dump—the kind of place where outcall massage service is advertised nonstop on a staticky room TV. The bathroom floor was sticky. I made a mental note to wear flip-flops at all times. No way was I going to meet any high-flying pearl dealers at this place.

But as I was finishing breakfast, preparing to go to day two of the Paspaley auction, Vock and his sister-in-law Jenine Kelly walked into the mezzanine restaurant. What were they doing at this hole?

It was a choice between flying New York–Hong Kong coach and staying in a palace, or flying business class and staying in a pit. Business class won. Other dealers (like Fran Mastoloni, whose family for three generations have stayed at the Peninsula on the Kowloon side) would never slum it in a place like the Charterhouse.

"You wanna hang with us today?" Vock asked, swallowing a slice of papaya as he slathered an English muffin with butter.

Like his former boss, Vock chases pearls everywhere he finds a deal. He was once arrested and put in a holding cell at a jewelry convention in Basel, Switzerland. Security guards assumed he was a thief because he had two strands of pearls on him and had left his convention I.D. badge back at his hotel.

Vock was in a rush. He wanted to get to the Paspaley auction just in case there was anything worth bidding on. I finished my French toast, and an hour later caught up with Vock, only to have him tell me what Paspaley and others had advised: There weren't enough top-end pearls to make the auction worth his while. *Maybe* there were one or two lots, but they could wait till the afternoon. We bolted out of the convention centre and caught a cab to Paspaley's Hong Kong office, at 9 Queen's Road, in the Centre district, on the thirtieth floor of a skyscraper.

To get access, we first were allowed into a holding area, and once the glass door behind us closed and a camera snapped our photos, were allowed to proceed.

"Whaddaya wanna 'ave a look at, mates?" Peter Paspaley, Nick's nephew, asked as we were buzzed in.

We went into a corner showroom, with floor-to-ceiling windows on two sides. The room had a table with a white tablecloth and calculators on either side. Paspaley brought out two trays filled with hanks of large-sized white South Sea pearls. They looked to me flawless. Jenine picked one of the hanks out right away, a matched strand of 12–15-millimeter round pearls. The price tag read 2,875,000 yen, or $24,452. The arrangement that Vock and other dealers have with Paspaley is to take 45 percent off the asking price, which brought the price down to 1,581,250 yen, or $13,449. And that was before the pearls were knotted and outfitted with a gold or platinum clasp, which would ultimately drive Vock's costs higher. It meant the wholesale price point for the strand would have to be somewhere around $30,000. Vock assured me that wouldn't be a problem. The retail price then could go to $60,000 or so. It wasn't so much price that concerned Vock, it was quality and three other factors: what his customers wanted, what he could persuade retailers would sell, and what his reserve inventory back home was.

"I like this color," Jenine said to no one, picking up the strand. "Whaddaya think, Alex? It's got a little bit of pink in it." She handed the pearls to Vock.

"But it doesn't," Vock countered, handing the strand over to me, as though I knew enough to be the final arbitrator.

Before I could say anything, Vock piped up. "They've got too much blue-green in them," he said. "I don't like 'em."

Jenine shrugged her shoulders, making a face at Vock. Jenine, a former Chicago social worker, was as calm as Vock was hyper. The feminine vision of Vock's macho eye. Her fair complexion and strawberry blond hair were the yin to Vock's olive-hue Semitic yang.

The moment that Vock had said he didn't like the strand, I knew exactly what had bothered him. If you held the hank just so against the north light of the window, there was a hint of the tiniest amount of greenish-blue. It was so subtle that if Vock hadn't mentioned it, I'd never have noticed it. The give-and-take between Jenine and Vock reminded me of what anyone who's gone to Home Depot to buy a can of white paint knows: There are many, many shades of white.

Peter Paspaley brought out more hanks, multiplying trays of increasingly large, round pearls. He kept them coming, but Vock didn't like any of them. Maybe it was cagey buyer bravado. I couldn't tell. "Lots of beige here," Vock said. "Beige doesn't have a personality. The worst thing in pearls."

"*Ugh!*" Vock suddenly exclaimed as though he was about to expectorate. "Pearls have got to have a personality. One thing they can't be, and that's bland."

"You gotta have an idea of potential buyers," Vock said, eyeing another hank. "Different buyers have different customers with different tastes. Rounds might go on the East Coast, whereas baroques might sell on the West Coast. Neiman's might be interested in these," he said, picking up a strand of semi-baroque-shaped pearls. They were slightly malformed, nowhere near round, but the shapes seemed more free form, more artsy.

"Hey, lemme look at those," Jenine said, taking the strand. The hank had twenty-nine, 12–16-millimeter pearls, and cost 2,442,825 yen. Vock punched in numbers on the calculator. With his discount, the strand came to $9,473.

"But Alex," Jenine broke in. "The center doesn't match."

The center is the pearl that hangs the lowest—in this case, the pearl that held position 14 or 15.

"They'll change it."

Jenine shook her head. "It's not just that. I have a problem with the shoulder pearl on the left," meaning the pearl to the left of the center. Jenine put the strand aside as though it had cooties.

All through this, Michael Bracher (Nick Paspaley's other nephew) or Peter Paspaley would exit the room, leaving us with tray upon tray of pearls, whose total value was well over a million dollars. He closed the door each time, and before he entered again, he knocked, returning with more hanks, which he handed to me, for some reason. "Take a look at dis 'ne, mate," Bracher said, then left again.

"Now you're talking," Alex said, stealing the necklace from my hands. "You're looking at the real thing. The real color, lustre, the shape of a top-quality strand. This is natural color, too." The necklace had twenty-nine pearls; and with Vock's 45 percent rollback, it came to $46,125, which meant that he'd put it for sale for close to $100,000. Who had that kind of money to spring for something that expensive? Didn't the recession mean anything to these buyers?

The issue for Vock really boiled down to inventory back home. "How many necklaces can we have in the higher price range that are similar? I got enough of these. I need something that isn't a round. I'd rather pay for something no one else has."

At which point, Bracher knocked and brought in a single pearl. It was a single baroque in all its glory, with irregular rivulets, gullies, peaks, and crevices. The pearl seemed the size of my thumb. It measured 20.3 millimeters. About the only thing you could do with this supernova was hang it as a pendant or, more likely, just stare at the thing.

But Bracher said it wasn't for sale. I wondered. Everything's for sale. Maybe the reason he'd brought out the eye candy was to undercut what he was about to bring out next.

When Bracher returned, he came back with a 10–13-millimeter, thirty-three-piece necklace. Vock sniffed. "They're a little small for our customers—and too silvery. These don't work well." The strand was priced a relatively reasonable 1,164,159 yen, or $9,901.

Another knock. Paspaley came back. This time with rounds, but again Vock noticed something. "Lemme spin these pearls." Jenine and I shot glances at each other.

Vock took the strand and, with the palm of his right hand, rolled the pearls toward me on the table. "They're semi-rounds. These ain't rounds! No way. Look, they wobble!"

"Dere not wobblin'," Bracher said, less defensively than declaratively.

"I've had enough Wild Turkey to know when somethin' wobbles," Vock crowed.

"Come on, mate! They don't wobble."

"My ass! There's movement. Look." Vock continued to roll the pearls under his flat, open hand.

There was sudden silence in the room, as all four of us looked on as Vock continued to roll the strand. Maybe, yes, there was a miniscule irregularity in a couple of pearls. I'm not sure if wobble was what they were doing, but two of the pearls weren't perfectly round, and we all could now plainly see that.

"They'd probably pass," Jenine said, more to break the stalemate than for anything else.

It was terrific swagger by Vock, and Bracher, embarrassed, ignominiously removed the offending strand. Kudos to Vock.

Jenine still had her eye on the baroques. "Whadda they want for 'em?" Vock asked, looking my way.

I started punching in numbers. With his discount, the necklace went for 1,513,000 yen—the equivalent of $12,866 at Vock's cost, which could go for $25,000 wholesale at home and, with the jeweler's markup, maybe close to $50,000 to the end user.

"Not bad," Vock said peeking over my shoulder at the numbers.

Another knock. Bracher came back into the room.

"We'll take this one," Vock said, holding up the baroque.

"Just one, mate?"

"Yeah, just one," Vock said. "We just *look* loaded."

There was no haggling, no bargaining. Quick and painless. Bracher placed the necklace in a padded brown envelope, which Vock put inside his briefcase. Vock signed a voucher. No money exchanged. Handshakes all around. As we left, I promised to shout a round (Aussie for buy a round of beers) for Bracher and his cousin when I got to Darwin in a couple of months. Jenine went her way and Vock and I went ours. The airlines had lost her luggage and she needed to buy some clothes.

Vock wanted to celebrate his purchase. We passed through a maze of up-scale malls to look at pearl necklaces in the windows of several high-end jewelry stores. "This guy has very nice stuff," Vock said, pointing to a strand of mammoth white South Seas. "Those are top quality. Look at 'em."

How much? I asked.

"Who knows what he can get for 'em?" Vock answered with a shrug. "Probably a hundred thousand dollars—give or take some. Depends what the market for them here is now."

The jewelry stores were just sideshows. Vock wanted to buy a cigar. We found ourselves at the Cohiba Cigar Divan, off the lobby in the Mandarin Oriental Hotel. The cigar emporium was a throwback to the 1930s—one room jam-packed with antiques, Tiffany lamps, a retro sofa, and several upholstered easy chairs upon which five men sat, puffing away on their just-bought cigars.

A small showroom next door was filled to the gills with humidors of boxes and boxes of Cuban cigars. The manager of the store, Simon Lam, seemed to know Vock and bowed reverently to us. Vock simply had to have a Bolivar and he wanted a *robusto* size. He found a torpedo-shaped one, a Belicoso Fino, maybe six inches long, that went for 147 Hong Kong dollars, or $19. "These babies are the ones George Bush will put you in jail for smoking," Vock said as he put the stogie in his jacket pocket, then patted it comfortingly. "Tonight," he said.

Vock whipped out his credit card, but just as Lam was about to swipe it, Vock shrieked, "No, wait!"

Lam and I looked at each other. Alarmed, several smokers on the divan turned our way while exhaling plumes of smoke.

"If my wife sees this, I'll be in big trouble," at which Lam smiled, then nodded, in an understanding way. Vock took out a second card, and completed the transaction.

It was getting late, and we were hungry. Vock wanted to get back to the Paspaley auction to crash the free buffet and to look at several lots he thought might be promising. We hailed a cab and were back in the convention centre's Grand Foyer within fifteen minutes, eating an assortment of sushi, Indian curry and chapattis, fettuccine with seafood, and Mongolian beef.

"This light's no damn good," Vock said in a testy tone, as we found a table closest to the wall of glass. It was the third straight cloudy day in Hong Kong. Short of bringing in portable lights, there wasn't much else to do except make the best out of the grayish glare.

Vock wanted me to keep an eye on his briefcase, which contained the baroque necklace, while he strolled over to take a closer look at the lots. He checked out Lot No. 552, whose reserve was set at 5,579,000 yen, or $47,869. This lot had 400 loose baroque-shaped pearls in it, and not just a few very nice ones. There were thirty-four 15-millimeter pearls, fourteen 16-millimeter pearls, three 17-millimeter pearls, and two glorious 18-millimeter pearls. But there were too many small 10-, 11-, 12-millimeter pearls in the lot, and Vock said his clients had no need for such minor pieces. Nor did Vock have a ready market to dump the outliers. He probably could consolidate the large baroques into two nice necklaces, and their worth to him maybe would push $30,000, and on the retail market, they'd perhaps could go for as high as $25,000 a piece, but then all of his profit would go down the drain with the 347 smaller pearls in the lot. What would he do with all of them? Vock got up and gave the lot to the smiling woman behind the table who bowed as she took back the tray.

Vock checked out Lot No. 510, made up of 184 smooth, less irregularly-sized baroques than the previous lot. Vock made three piles of different-sized pearls—a good pile, a so-so pile, and a rejection pile. He then took out the Paspaley strand he had bought to compare. "These ones," he said, pointing to the rejects in the loose lot. "They're too green, they're not creamy. No good. They're bullshit."

Vock went into his briefcase and pulled out an electronic Teclock digital calipers to check the pearls' size, just to make sure Paspaley hadn't pushed up the millimeter size. The pearls were in the ballpark, maybe a shade or two smaller. The 14-millimeter pearls, Vock said, "aren't great. If they're all like this one." As though displaying a smelly sock, he held one pearl with surface blemishes, and scrunched his nose. "No way," he said.

Vock put six large, round, sparkling, almost effervescent pearls in one pile. "These are really extraordinary. I love them. But this stuff," he said, shaking his head, pointing to the pile of rejects. "What am I gonna do with them? Look at this guy," he said, holding up the stinky sock's mate, another tear-shaped pearl with tiny brown blemishes on one side.

I was hoping Vock would place a bid on at least one lot. Two or three would be better. I wanted to have a dog in this hunt but Vock was hesitating too much. "Too many creamies, maybe for Europeans, but not white enough, too soft for me," he said.

What Vock said struck me. His customers were primarily Americans, and Americans, in South Sea pearls at least, like white pearls, not beige, not creamy, not ivory, certainly nothing with a green-blue hue to them. The Europeans go for off-whites, but Americans, Vock said, are purists. If they're going to pay $50,000 or more for a strand of white pearls, they better be a deep, lustrous white with spellbinding orient and lustre.

The auction seemed to be going like clockwork. Three Indians were punching in numbers on a calculator at a table thirty feet away, and on the other side of them four Japanese men, one of them on a cell phone talking excitedly, another emptying a lot of pearls into his own plastic strainer with holes to measure millimeter size, seemed very much in the hunt. A French dealer was lining up loose pearls in the crevice between his thumb and index finger, held close to each other, to determine how round the pearls were. He was adroitly sliding the pearls on the back of his hand, looking for imperfections.

Vock came back with Lot 538, and as he sat down, he gave the pearls a quick thumb's down. "Too many mixed shapes," he said, "these pointy things are hard to pair up, and it's difficult to match up these buttons, even for ear-rings," Vock said, pointing out a dozen flattened round pearls.

Vock returned with Lot 536. "When I grabbed this lot, I knew it was fucked." He took out one unusually shaped baroque pearl with extraordinary color. He sensed my approval (I had grown to like the baroques, thinking the symmetry of the rounds was too perfect, two conservative, too Barbara Bush). "No good. Don't be taken in by these. Too hard to set. No good for a strand, then you have to turn them into earrings. First rule of pearls: Don't fall in love. It'll cost you. And not just with pearls."

After three more lots, Alex was finished. Jet lag was catching up with him. He wanted to take a nap; we were going to meet that evening for Peking duck.

I was still going strong, so I slipped into the convention centre's VIP lounge, a two-tiered lounge with international dealers jabbering in a host of languages, from Russian to Portuguese. The so-called Dragon Lounge was a find. Plasma TV screens hung from the walls, you could get free food and al-cohol, and there was free Internet.

I sat down next to an Israeli dealer. He hadn't been at either the Paspaley or Wan auction and, I surmised, wasn't a major player. But what he was doing intrigued me.

From a digital camera, he was downloading onto e-Bay a photograph of a strand of pearls he'd ostensibly just purchased. He was trying to unload the necklace. Maybe he hadn't bought the pearls at all. Maybe he had borrowed them, leaving a deposit with the seller, or most likely, he had just snapped a photo of the strand on display. After the computer upload was complete, the dealer scrolled several ongoing pearl auctions on e-Bay, then used Skype to make a call.

When he finished his conversation, I tried to chat him up, but he got up and left in a hurry. "No time," he said. "Need to go." Another pearl dealer, per-haps five or six rungs lower than Vock and Assael, but a dealer nonetheless in the ladder of pearl buying and selling.

9

Across the Chinese Border
to the Transformatron

I

When it came to access, the Chinese pearl lords had been the toughest to crack. While wary at first, the Japanese, Philippine, Australian, even the suspicious French Polynesian producers eventually came around and begrudgingly sought to accommodate me. But when negotiating with Chinese producers, I was greeted with piles of unanswered e-mails and, when I met them, icy stares. I needed to get access to their processing centers, where millions of inexpensive freshwater pearls are turned out every year, flooding the global marketplace, undercutting the price points of every other pearl-producing nation's products. Finally, after negotiating for almost two years, executives from a conglomerate of the largest Chinese freshwater pearl firms allowed a crack. When I met with them in Hong Kong, they huddled, came back at me with questions, huddled some more, then rendered a verdict: They'd allow me to visit their factories, located in Joo-jee, in the province of Zhejiang, China's mega-pearl-production center, 100 miles southwest of Shanghai. I'd be allowed unfettered access. Or so they promised. I wasn't convinced, but the gesture was a monumental breakthrough. I felt like Nixon after Mao invited him behind the bamboo curtain.

Joo-jee (pronounced SHOE-ghee) is the epicenter of the world's freshwater pearl market. These are cultivated pearls that don't come from oysters but instead from large, oval-shaped mussels. China produces 99 percent of all such freshwater pearls in the world. The province of Zhejiang is dotted with thousands of small, family-operated pearl farms, most of them state cooperatives. Such farms are seemingly everywhere, with millions of green plastic pop bottles bobbing up and down on the surfaces of thousands of small artificial lakes, each bottle signifying another crop of fresh mussels, and each mussel containing as many as fifty pearls inside. Exactly how the Chinese have been able to cultivate mussels that produce so many pearls remains something of a mystery. These pearls don't develop around an inserted nucleus, as their counterparts in oysters do, but instead grow from multiple tiny squares of mussel mantle tissue inserted into each host mussel.

The first crop of Chinese freshwater pearls appeared in the early 1970s, and since then, pearl exports from *Hyriopsis cumingii* mussels have grown exponentially. At first, the pearls were miniscule. By the 1980s, their size had grown and they started coming in a variety of striking rainbow colors. These pearls were often labeled and sold as Lake Biwa or Lake Kasumigaura pearls from Japan, fetching higher prices because of the Japanese label.

The Chinese freshwaters were a breakthrough in the fashion marketplace. Fashion-conscious women around the world started wearing pearls that weren't just white or cream-colored, and weren't always round. Stylish younger women in particular gravitated to them. These pearls had four things going for them: they were colorful, they often weren't symmetrical (the baroque shapes appealed to nontraditional pearl wearers), they had the legitimacy of being real pearls, and they were downright cheap when compared to traditional pearls. As their size got larger, the Chinese freshwaters readily turned into trendy fashion items, accessories that fashion-forward women in their twenties and thirties from Paris to São Paulo just had to have. It didn't hurt that women like Meryl Streep, Jennifer Aniston, Nancy Pelosi, and eventually Michelle Obama started wearing them, too.

As Chinese technology got better, more and more freshwater pearls came on the global market at a fraction of the price of their international counterparts. By the late 1990s, the best of the Chinese freshwaters were virtually undetectable from increasingly scarce Japanese akoyas, and soon, the Chinese pearls were available in even larger sizes than the Japanese species would allow. Symmetrical freshwater Chinese pearls now come as large as 14 millimeters (that's as big as a marble) and are getting larger. Their skin can be flawless and comes in a multitude of colors (pink, blue, violet, orange, gold, gray, for instance), some right out of the shell, others the result of dye, chemical, and radiation treatments.[1]

The flooding of so many Chinese pearls into the world market presented a problem for producers of more expensive pearls (just about every producer outside China). It'd be akin to the De Beer's diamond syndicate discovering a competitor had come up with a new process that could create a genuine diamond, not a zirconium knockoff, but a real diamond that cost pennies to the thousands De Beers diamonds fetch. No wonder the worldwide pearl industry started screaming.

Example: A strand of medium-sized, near-perfect Chinese freshwater pearls can be bought wholesale today for under $150. Such reverse sticker shock is freaking out just about every other national producer of pearls. To make matters worse, to most consumers, such a strand is virtually identical to strands that sell for five and ten times as much (and sometimes more). Chinese freshwaters are showing up everywhere, from top-end retail jewelry boutiques like Mikimoto, Bulgari, Harry Winston, and Van Cleef & Arpels to low-end merchandizing giants, such as Walmart, JC Penney, Jeremy Shepherd's Internet sites, and cable TV's QVC. Their price point is so low and their quality can be so high that it's no surprise that some dealers intentionally mislabel Chinese strands as of a more expensive provenance (Japanese, Tahitian, even Australian). This can be by unscrupulous intention, but it's often just an uninformed mistake. Chinese pearls can look so good they fool wholesalers and retailers alike. Chinese freshwaters are often offered up as something else simply because retailers are ignorant of the nuanced differences of where the pearls came from.

Inexpensive high-quality Chinese pearls are out there, and out there in a big way, and because of their proliferation, the global pearl industry is undergoing the same cataclysmic changes it faced in the 1930s, when Japanese cultured pearls were introduced to world markets. The rapid abundance of cultured pearls devastated and soon destroyed the natural-pearl market. Some dealers say today that the same could happen with Chinese freshwaters, ultimately replacing their much more expensive seawater counterparts from around the world. I wanted to see how the Chinese were going to make this happen.

In all things Chinese, huge is good, but massive is better. Hardly anything in China seems built on a small, intimate scale, as, for instance, it is in Japan.

In keeping with that seemingly national characteristic, when I got to China, a conglomeration of government and private interests was in the midst of building a humongous complex to accommodate the cultivation, processing, and sale of Chinese freshwater pearls. CP&J (China Pearls and Jewellery) City, scheduled to be completed by 2012, is touted as the largest pearl trade center in the world, a staggering thirteen million square feet—the equivalent of something like fifty airplane hangars.

My trip to Joo-jee would get me inside China's pearl mission control and, I hoped, allow me to interview soldiers in the army of workers who readied Chinese pearls for the international market. It'd also get me to Pearl Internet King Jeremy Shepherd's partner in Joo-jee, a young U.S.-educated entrepreneur by the name of Faye Tian, a second-generation pearler, through whom I hoped to try my hand at harvesting freshwaters.

II

From modern Hangzhou, the capital of Zhejiang Province, to Joo-jee took an hour by bus, but the ride seemed more like a hundred years. Workers marched alongside dirt roads with hoes hoisted over their shoulders, others carried water in twin bamboo pails lashed to a pole. Battered, barely motorized three-wheeled go-carts loudly puttered along. Women under conical straw hats sat on haunches in fields. Men using tree branches as whips urged on tired oxen pulling carts impossibly loaded down with stacked crates. A single ox deep in a field of dirt pulled what looked like an ancient plow. The only indication that Mao's revolution had come was every once in a while a red Chinese flag with a gold star in the upper left corner waved from atop a house or government building.

Pearls are emblematic of China's rising global dominance. They're a national cash cow, but they're also a fitting metaphor. Nearly everything the world uses today comes whole or in part from China. What formerly was manufactured in the United States, Europe, and other parts of Asia now likely originates from the provinces of Guangzhou, Fujian, and Zhejiang, the workhorse engine that pulls China's economy. Refrigerators, washing machines, computers, TVs, building materials, cell phones, microwave ovens, processed foods, automobile components, toys, biotech products, clothing, shoes, baby strollers, tools, the list goes on and on. All are products assembled by Chinese peasants lured from the countryside, now toiling for a minute fraction of what their counterparts in the United States and other Western nations earn (or used to earn, before they were laid off, their factories shuttered).

Small, satellite towns surrounding Joo-jee are incubators for what is known as "lump economics," the process of specializing in one particular niche product. Nearby Datang has the distinction of being the world's largest sock maker, manufacturing more than ten billion pairs a year (more socks than there are people in the world). Diankow has become a hardware manufacturing district. Fengqiao specializes in the manufacture of shirts. Sandu makes pashminas every woman in the West seems to covet. Shanxiahu (where Faye Tian's company is, along with hundreds of others) specializes in pearls. Tens of thousands of peasants leave the countryside every year, flocking to these specialized factory districts, where jobs are waiting, along with dormitory housing and cafeteria meals.

As my bus got closer to downtown Joo-jee, I noticed more and more piles of discarded mussel shells alongside the road. The piles got taller and taller, one after another, until I realized they weren't piles any longer, but continuous mountains of used shells lining the thoroughfare. They were a welcome of sorts to where I was going. Downtown, in the middle of a traffic circle, an imposing sculpture of three silvery sea nymphs (who did not look at all Chinese, but amalgams of Nordic and German beauties) beckoned visitors. Each Brobdingnagian nymph was kneeling on her right knee, thick long luxuriant hair horizontally caught in midflight. In each nymph's palm, lofted high above her head as an offering to the gods, was—what else?—a gigantic silver-colored pearl.

Joo-jee, China, is to pearls what Hershey, Pennsylvania, is to chocolate. Atop a building that housed a scale model of what CP&J's sprawling complex would eventually look like sat another colossal faux pearl. I wanted to see pearls, I wanted to touch them, to hear their click-clacks. Tomorrow, the foreman explained. Wait for tomorrow.

III

Early the next morning, CP&J lieutenant Dave Bing drove me six miles from downtown Joo-jee. This was early March and the weather was brisk. Bing looked harried, nervously pushing back his black hair as we sped down a busy boulevard. We turned off onto a secondary street, then onto a gravel road that ran perpendicular to the first, driving four miles or so, until we stopped at a fence. Bing nodded to a sentry, who pushed open the wide gate. We traversed a muddy road filled with potholes. The ride was so bumpy that, after a particularly deep pothole, Bing's head and mine hit the van's ceiling, and as we came down, our shoulders bumped against each other, which prompted Bing to apologize. "Bumpy," he said, "Too much rain." We crossed a narrow, rickety bridge. For another mile or two, we drove on a field rutted with tire marks. Finally, we parked on a steep, pitched grade overlooking a small lake filled with dirty, almost black, water.

I could see against a backdrop of purple fog and haze scores and scores of similar lakes, cut into the patchy Yangtze River Valley countryside. The lakes seemed to go on forever. Dotting the surface of each were tens of thousands of green plastic pop bottles bobbing up and down. It was a bizarre sight. Deep in rural China, as far as possible from anything Western, it seemed a 7-Up bottling plant had unloaded millions of green, liter-sized bottles that magically found themselves floating on the surfaces of a multitude of opaque lakes.

"Follow me," Bing instructed. He took a machete from the pickup.

A small welcoming party awaited my arrival, and therein ensued all the requisite bowing that accompanies such occasions. As we finished with formalities, Bing asked me to choose whichever green bottle I fancied on the lake before us.

I did, pointing to a bottle thirty feet from the shore, which seemed off in its own world. A worker promptly got into a flat-bottom wooden boat and paddled over to the bottle.

"This one?" he shouted in Chinese. "This is the one you want?"

I nodded, getting the distinct feeling that I was being set up as the rube at a magic show far from the midway.

The worker promptly pulled up a muddy five-foot rope tethered on top by the green plastic bottle and on the bottom by a round wire basket. He cut the rope and dropped the basket onto the ribbed floor of his boat, then quickly paddled back to shore. Inside the basket were four large hard-shelled mussels, their halves shut tight. As the worker dumped out his haul, I noticed how different these mussels looked from oysters. They certainly were larger than any oyster I'd seen. And their shape. If I hadn't known these gnarly-looking mollusks were mussels, I might have thought they were some kind of crustacean, maybe an exotic hard-shelled crab whose legs had retracted into its body. Bing lined up the four bivalves on the cement apron to the lake.

He asked me which mussel I wanted him to open, and I pointed to the sec-

ond one. It looked as ugly and as unprepossessing a thing as possible, even after Bing cleaned it off with a squirt of water from a hose. A circle of onlookers
edged closer.

Bing wiggled the machete firmly inside the twin halves of the mussel. He
lifted the machete and the attached mussel chest high. Then with a whomp, he
slammed both down to the concrete, splitting apart the twin hemispheres.
The assembled around me clapped, nodded, and bowed.

What I saw first was an excess of flaccid, fleshy meat, oozing out of the
split shells. The insides were markedly different from the gray translucent
viscera of oysters. This stuff resembled pinkish-white fatty tissue, and it carried a foul odor. Bing quickly put down the machete, knelt down, and pried
open the twin halves. He grabbed the gooey innards of the mussel. Bing's blue
tie kept getting in the way, swinging back and forth, and, out of frustration, he
finally flipped the tie over his shoulder.

Within seconds, he was picking out from the mussel halves glowing ob-
long things that looked like jellybeans. They were pearls, of course—purple,
pink, lilac, white, and yellow. And they were shiny. I had never before seen
so many bright-colored, smooth-skinned nuggets come from anything. I
couldn't count how many Bing had scooped from the mussel, but he had at
least fifty, and they weren't small. More squirts from a hose to clean off his
treasures, and then Bing held out both his hands, cradling four dozen iridescent pearls.

"Wow!" I said.

The circle of onlookers seemed pleased with my reaction. "Wow!" they
mimicked, nodding to each other, smiling widely. "Wow! Wow!" "Wow!"
they joined each other in increasing volume. I guess "Wow!" was one of those
universal words like "Okay!" that needs no translation.

If the tripartite premise of a magic trick is first to present the audience with
an exhibition of the ordinary, followed by a promise to transform the ordinary
into something extraordinary, finally to be capped off by an eye-popping finale
that sweeps the audience off its feet, then Bing's Amazing Mussel and Pearl
Show had worked.

"Pick one," Bing offered majestically. I chose a pinkish-orange pearl, which
I carefully picked from his open palm. I placed the pearl in the middle of my
own flattened palm, as the sun had finally made its way through the morning
haze. I marveled at its color, shine, lustre, and density. It was, at once, hard
like a stone yet, in its own way, soft and vulnerable. Wow, indeed.

The show over, prestidigitator Bing drove me back to the center of town. Near the sea nymphs statues, Bing handed me off to a series of CP&J managers who took me on tours of six mega pearl-processing plants, which lined the main thoroughfare of Joo-jee. Each lobby was presided over by a pair of welcoming, fresh-scrubbed, young women dressed in uniforms. The lobbies were palatial, each more mammoth than the next, all with impossibly high ceilings. Suspended from the ceiling of one were gigantic flat-screen plasma screens on which luscious pearls floated in slow motion through what appeared to be a black cosmos. In another lobby, cascading water from indoor waterfalls was choreographed to strains of celestial music. Another had rows of lighting fixtures, which resembled illuminated pearls, forming a flowing canopy. The pearl lobbies looked like heavenly places where people who had led upstanding lives were greeted in the hereafter.

Upstairs were endless rooms of sorters, tens of thousands of pearls being poured onto long tables covered with taut, stretched white tablecloths. Under banks of bright fluorescent lights, scores of girls no more than sixteen sat on rows of benches, peering over interminable multitudes of pearls. Each girl used oversized bamboo tweezers, grouping the pearls according to a variety of criteria—color, shade, shape, size, surface quality, lustre, orient. Each girl wore a smock and cotton sleeves cinched at the wrist and above the elbow. Next, I went into a room with hundreds of plastic tubs and sacks, filled with thousands and thousands of categorized pearls. Other rooms had large bamboo pails filled with same-size but multicolored pearls, ready to be sorted more.

My presence caused no small amount of tittering among the girls. "Do you mind if I ask you some questions?" I asked one girl, through Sofinny Kwok, a company minder assigned to me.

She flushed ruddy cheeks and very white teeth, an unlucky recruit singled out by the middle-aged foreign man. I could see how terrified the girl was, in front of her friends, bosses, and a strange-looking, curly-haired stranger who spoke a language she had likely never heard.

She said she had worked as a pearl sorter for a year, and was one of four children who migrated from southern Anhui Province to Joo-jee. Yes, she enjoyed her work. Of course, she enjoyed her work. In fact, she loved her work. I got it. She said through Kwok that she hoped to return to her home in several years, after saving money, to get married and start a family.

Rank-and-file workers at the processing plants were almost all women from fifteen to thirty years old. Most started out at the equivalent of 1,200 RMB a month, which converted to $167. (RMB is the abbreviation for renminbi, which means "people's currency.") This compared with $2,500 a month in Kobe for the same work done by workers with the same skills.

Kwok suggested there was ample opportunity for advancement in the company. In ten years of employ, sorters who showed exceptional promise could earn as much as 3,000 RMB, or $418 a month. The job is 8:00 a.m. to 5:00 p.m., six or seven days a week (depending on the season), with two tea breaks a day.

"What's 'exceptional promise'?" I asked, trying to break through company speak.

"Reliability, dependability, a good attitude. We look for girls who are stable, have good eyes, able to concentrate," said Kwok. Indeed, after forty, he said, a sorter's vision begins to soften and her worth to the company declines. "This is job for young girls," Kwok said with no apologies. "Many far from their home. They have companionship here. Very few stay for more than ten years. This is good adventure for girl from a rural village."

Sorting was one of many jobs at the plant. Once the millions of pearls have passed through the banks of hundreds of eagle-eyed sorters, each pearl is classified into further minute categories. Then the pearls are sent to an assortment of treatment rooms.

I came to think of these rooms as a kind of transformatron, where pearls, some plain and homely, come out stunners. Kwok opened a heavy metal door lined with shiny chrome and mirrors. I stepped inside. The room was so bright, I immediately looked down to shield my eyes. Inside were hundreds of large glass apothecary-type jars filled with thousands and thousands of pearls, all sitting under bright fluorescent lights and mirrors on the walls and ceiling. Pearls would stay here for weeks to months, to be transformed into orbs with vibrant shades, sparkling shines, and effervescent orients.

In another transformatron, I saw jars filled with pearls going from various stages of white, to gray, then to black, so eventually they'd be as dark as classic Tahitians. I walked into another transformatron, and the opposite was happening: mousy off-whites were being bleached over a course of weeks and months to turn into brilliant whites in an attempt to mimic the dazzling natural shades of Australians.

This kind of wholesale enhancement and color alteration included sunlight, heat lamps, irradiation, various chemicals (silver nitrate, hydrogen sulfate, metallic silver), dyes (potassium, carotene, pomegranate extract, cobalt, and silver salts), as well as nonstop fluorescent rays. Some rooms were lit brighter than a glary day in Nome, others were sealed and kept pitch-black. There were still other rooms in which pearls were heated to infuse new color. Nearly everything could be altered about the pearl, except its size and shape, although I have no doubt Chinese technicians were working on pearl-growth hormones, too.[2]

Kwok ushered me into more than two dozen transformatrons, each for a different purpose. He freely copped to the oft-repeated charges that the Chinese treat their pearls, enhancing their lustre, deepening or altering colors. Neither Kwok nor any of the other managers trailing on my tour was in the least defensive about the business of pearl treatments. It was no big deal. Whereas to the Tahitians, Philippines, and Australians, as I was to learn, such wholesale tampering with the integrity of a pearl was akin to fraud and manipulation. Executives from all three nations angrily charged the Chinese with essentially creating fake pearls by employing these methods.

But Kwok just shrugged his shoulders when I asked. "We do it to make our pearls as competitive as we can," he said, no apology.

Kwok took me into another room where large stainless steel mixing vats sat, into which workers dumped sacks and sacks of pearls for polishing. I could hear the telltale pearl plink: the click-clack-click of the pearls bouncing off each other and the side of the vats. Pieces of cork, ground-up walnut shells and eucalyptus chips, wax, even pulverized gold or platinum dust were added to enhance the pearls' lustre. Kwok again had no qualms about such methods. "Shine is good," he said, adding, "as long as not *too* shiny, then it look fake."

There were other rooms in this mission control of pearls, in which workers further refined already matched pearls before they were classified into varying grades. The young women worked their tweezers fast. The pearls proceeded to rows of more young women, who sat before drills, placing a new pearl in a slot to be drilled every three to five seconds. Still another room was filled with more young women with the nimblest of fingers, for here was where stringing took place.

It was a continuous production line that spanned the length of a hangar-long building, all leading up to the Sales Hall, where buyers could purchase anything, from bushels of sorted pearls to completed hanks of AAA-quality ones.

That's where I begged out. I wanted to make my way to Joo-jee's public pearl marketplace, where freelance family vendors set up stalls to sell their wares. The least I could do was buy a necklace for Iris, pulling double-duty, caring for our son, Mikey. As I strolled inside the market, I immediately liked it. There was something unplanned and random, as there is about the best of farmers' markets wherever they are. Other than for pearls, I hate shopping. Here there were no vegetables, fruit, meat, chickens, fish. No fresh-baked goods. No eggs. No clothes, CD, or DVD knockoffs. No fake Louis Vuitton, Chanel, or Prada purses. No cut-rate European soccer jerseys. No gold or silver. Just pearls. My kind of market.

I walked up and down each row. My curly hair allows me to pass for a host of nationalities. I've been mistaken for Italian, Greek, Brazilian, French, Russian, and Israeli, but no one has ever mistaken me for Chinese. In rural China, I stood out like a white guy at a Louis Farrakhan prayer meeting. As such, hundreds of vendors, almost all women, all in the most vociferous and vigorous way, began hawking pearls directly to me, the sole Westerner, someone they figured to be loaded.

"Meester, lookey here!" one vendor teased, dangling multiple strands from red-lacquered fingertips, shaking the pearls so they resembled a hula dancer.

"Toop cal-le-tee!" another woman yelled. "Come. You like!"

"I make special price," another vendor cooed.

As I made a loop back again to the second aisle, a pretty woman shouted, "I luv-e you, sir!" I imagined carrying my newfound Pearl Princess through the pearl market to thunderous applause in a Chinese remake of *An Officer and a Gentleman*.

High-quality, near-perfect round 10–12-millimeters choker strands at the market were going for the equivalent of $75 to $200. That wasn't cheap, but similar strands I knew fetched as much as five times that in the States, and if the retailer called the pearls Japanese (or Australian), the price would be higher.

At first, I wanted to opt for something classic, a white Jackie Kennedy choker, but that was classic Japanese akoya pearls (like the one my mother used to wear), and today those pearls look small and dated. Besides, this was China. Why get a knockoff Japanese strand in China? What made the most sense was to buy a strand of dyed Chinese freshwaters.

I found a vendor, perhaps in her mid-forties, and started bargaining. Shaving $10 or $20 meant a lot more to her than it did to me, and we settled on $120 for a strand. I was about to pay a stranger for one necklace of 31 matched pearls more than what most workers in Joo-jee earn in an entire month. I wasn't sure if I should feel guilty or glad that I was investing so much in one family's economy.

I opted for a strand of slightly punk pinkish pearls, but after going through all the strands, I found nicks and abrasions in more than several of the pearls, so I asked to see a bag of loose pearls of a higher quality.

I sat in a corner of her stall, carefully picking out three-dozen drilled pink pearls I thought were perfect, and handed them to the vendor. She picked them up, laid them on a table (with the requisite white tablecloth) and went to work, thread and needle in hand.

Within fifteen minutes, she'd strung the pearls, tight little knots between each, and had put a small clasp on the end. I examined them, and they were as perfect a strand as I'd seen.

The vendor held the strand by the clasp, pulled a silk pouch from a drawer, loosened the black string to open the top, and then dropped the strand into the pouch. She tightened the string closure, and smiled as she handed me the pouch. We each bowed ever so slightly.

10

Faye's World

Ever since I'd met Jeremy Shepherd, the Internet pearl whiz kid who'd so scorned the Rana of Fresno, he had suggested that I absolutely had to connect with a twenty-nine-year-old woman by the name of Faye Tian when I got to the freshwater pearl region of China. Born in Joo-jee, Faye now runs a second-generation pearl business in nearby Shanxiahu. She studied in Boston and New York, speaks English, and knows the Chinese freshwater industry like no one else, Shepherd promised.

Faye promised she'd take me on a tour of a People's Pearl Cooperative, really her family's own mom-and-pop operation, thriving in the shadow of the big boys. No way was Faye part of the CP&J City mafia. She vehemently opposed Man Sang chairman Ricky Cheng's messianic plans to transform Joo-jee into the Disney World of pearls. She was an outspoken independent pearl executive fighting the monolithic Chinese pearl establishment. Faye was David, armed with a slingshot aimed at Goliath Cheng's burgeoning empire.

Faye showed up for our appointment in a shiny black Cadillac. She wore her hair in a post-Farrah long shag and had on tight Calvin Klein jeans and a tighter black sweater. Inside the Caddy were: an opened package of banana chips, three cans of power drinks, half-drunk bottles of days-old Nestea, lipstick, lip gloss, mascara, eyebrow pencils, Clinique Moisture Surge Face Spray, and a nearly empty container of massage oil. Faye had Norah Jones blasting from the Caddy's aftermarket CD player. "Let's open the windows," she suggested, turning up the sound full throttle, spinning out past the sea nymphs' statue.

"I want to move back to New York," Faye told me, yelling over a track called "Creepin' In." As she reached a crescendo, her cell phone suddenly rang.

"WHEY!" Faye shouted, the Chinese equivalent of "Hey!" "Hello!" "Sup!" She followed with a nonstop high-decibel rant of yelling, screaming, and what I inferred to be a string of Chinese profanities. After five minutes, Faye slammed shut the phone.

"What was that all about?"

"Too long story," Faye said, adding something about a former boyfriend in the midst of doing her wrong. Like disease, world hunger, and politicians on the take, the scourge of ex-boyfriends is without borders.

Faye's former boyfriend wanted to get married, but no way could she be serious about this loser, she said, peeling onto a gravel road, almost fishtailing. Faye volunteered that she harbored a huge crush on Mr. Pearl Internet, Jeremy Shepherd, and even was considering having a love baby with him. She volunteered that Shepherd had dutifully told her he was married, but that detail hadn't registered with Faye, who seemed at the moment to be alternately grinding her teeth and lip-synching.

We were tooling toward the People's Pearl Cooperative her family owns. But how could a family *own* a cooperative? Faye said it was a cooperative in name only, since the employees work for Faye and her family, and the profits from the cooperative go to Faye and her family. She said her father and uncles started the pearl farm a decade ago, renting out four hundred acres from the provincial government at a negotiated price that was under market value. During planting season, she said, her family hires four hundred workers. She has technicians cutting mantle tissue and inserting it into the mussels, which in turn are placed in net or wire baskets, dangling from green plastic pop bottles. The workers are itinerants, usually coming from the rural countryside, either Zhejiang or other adjacent provinces. They start at 1,000 RMB a month ($140), with returning employees, particularly those with technical skills, able to earn upwards of 3,000 RMB ($419) a month. "It all depends how good they are," Faye said, breaking away from a song called "Toes." The planting season goes from August to October, and in certain years, planting also takes place during the winter months. We were in between planting and harvest seasons, and Faye was taking me to visit the caretakers who live at the farm year-round.

As Dave Bing had driven two days earlier, Faye pulled off the same thoroughfare, took a series of quick turns, a right onto a dirt road that ran for two miles, then a jog to the right, a 120-degree turn to our left, down a bumpy narrow path that challenged the Cadillac's girth, not to mention its suspension system.

We approached a cement-block hut with a flat corrugated metal roof. As we got closer, I couldn't help noticing the mountains and mountains of rotting, discarded mussel shells and, this time, mountains of empty plastic bottles. Faye screeched to a stop. As we got out of the Caddy, I took in a whiff of the morning air. The aroma was a combination of stick-in-your-nostrils fertilizer and rotten fish. In Iowa, the smell of pig shit is called the smell of money. Here money smells like shit *and* decomposing fish.

Faye strode into the dilapidated block hut as though she owned the place, which, in fact, she pretty much did. I hurried to keep up with her. Faye would have been at home in the Back Bay section of Boston or Manhattan's Upper West Side, but here in rural China, I wasn't so sure. She was Western with a vengeance.

The caregiver couple inside tentatively rose to greet us. They surely accentuated the cultural and sartorial differences Faye brought full force into the primitive hut. Ju-Hua, 38, has two children, one in middle school, the other in high school. She wore a white turtleneck sweater under a ragged jacket, and navy blue cotton pants. On her feet were hand-knitted slippers the color of turquoise. She offered Faye and me tea, and we huddled close to a single burner as the water started boiling. The hut did little to break the cold, brisk wind that seeped inside, making a high-pitched whistling sound.

I asked Ju how pearls from Faye's farm could possibly compete with the big companies I'd visited the day before. "It's not easy," she said, to which Faye nodded while translating for me. Prices, Ju said, were down 50 percent from what they had been a year earlier, even though the quality and size of Chinese freshwaters keeps getting better and bigger. It can take seven years from tissue insertion to pearl harvest, and that puts small farmers at a disadvantage, tying up their investment. This gestation period was twice as long as pearls cultured from oysters. But there was a key, fundamental difference on the Chinese growers' side: a single mussel can produce dozens of pearls, while an oyster produces just a single pearl at a time. And within a single mussel, there's also a wide variety of colors, shapes, and sizes. That gave a huge advantage to the Chinese growers in their ability to overwhelm their global competition just by the sheer number of pearls produced. Factor in rock-bottom labor costs, and Chinese pearls had their international counterparts beaten hands down. One other difference: There was no nucleated bead at the center of the Chinese freshwater pearl; its growth was as close to a natural pearl as possible.

The Chinese are the world's only pearl processors to succeed at large-scale cultivation of the *Hyriopsis cumingii* mussel, but I imagined it would just be a matter of time before savvy entrepreneurs smuggled the hardy species outside of China to cultivate the mussel elsewhere. Well-compensated biologists must have already tried it, and the first batches of *Hyriopsis cumingii* mussels are now surely being harvested—or already have been harvested—even though no one was talking about it. Such an act would be akin to what the Southeast Asians did in the late 1800s, raiding the rubber-tree forests of the Brazilian Amazon, smuggling seeds out of the country, and successfully cultivating rubber plants closer to home, which subsequently destroyed the Brazilian rubber market. The Asian rubber tree boom was short-lived; when synthesized rubber eventually was pioneered, it swiftly ended the need for natural rubber sources anywhere in the world. With pearls, the chronology of such a scenario is slightly different: Mikimoto had already discovered how to culture pearls, so now the global race was on to create the largest and most perfect pearls developed from any mollusk as quickly as possible.

"It's very complex how and why we get so many pearls out of the mussels," Ju said, warming her hands around a ceramic cup of green tea. "The only thing we know for sure is that the deeper we place the oyster, the colder the water is, and that makes for more colors at a higher lustre. On average," she said, "each mussel produces about forty pearls."

I asked about the smell.

"Oh, the fertilizer," Ju said, wiggling her nose. "You get used to it. We don't even smell it any longer."

"What's in the fertilizer?"

Faye and Ju laughed. "It's the real thing," Faye said. "From goats and chickens, and we experiment to see how different fertilizers affect the mussels and the pearls inside." The lakes, Ju said, are cleaned once a year. Unlike oysters, the mussels seem to welcome the onslaught of waste pollution and the introduction of various trace elements to the water. This means that unlike the cultivation of oysters, which will not tolerate water with even minimal additives, these mussels adapt and somehow flourish within a variety of contaminants, which inevitably seep into, or are systemically introduced to, the mussels, thereby affecting pearl color and shine.

One effect of the Pearl Rush in China is a vast reallocation of land use: Many lakes used for pearl cultivation today are old rice fields, an economically viable conversion since pearls per kilo realize profits much greater than land allocated to rice production.

"The pearl harvest on the farm," Faye said, "sells wholesale for on average 1,000 RMB per kilo, about $140." Such a kilo contains hundreds of pearls of all grades, colors, and sizes. I had paid at the local pearl market a little less, for Iris's thirty-two-pearl strand—which, in part, goes to show how rare large, round, near-perfect pearls are, and, when separated from the chaff, how much such beauties go for. It also shows the markup from grower's hand to my hand to my wife's neck. It, of course, could show, too, that I got ripped off in a major way, paying way too much for the necklace. But that hadn't been a concern to me; if I chose to sell it at home, after the same necklace passed through five or six hands, its retail cost might go as high as $500 to $1,000. And if any of the dealers along the line up represented the strand as something it wasn't (for example, Japanese or Australian pearls, 100 percent natural, or untreated naturally pink pearls), the necklace could fetch more.

We took a break to sip at the tea, the four of us (Ju's husband joined us, but didn't say much) sitting in bamboo-frame chairs, listening for a moment to traditional Chinese music from a tape deck plugged into a noisy cranking generator, which also powered the sole light bulb in the couple's home. A neighbor farmer peered through a cracked glass pane and rapped on the door. He was carrying an electric hot plate—a gift, a barter of goods, or the return of the borrowed appliance. Everyone stood, and there was a certain degree of hubbub— bowing, shoulders and chest raising and lowering. For a moment, their actions reminded me of Hasidic Jews davening.

The neighbor, Jian Hao, joined us in our little circle, and Ju poured some tea for him. As farmers do wherever they are, from Spencer, Iowa, to Joo-jee, Zhejiang, they groused about the weather, crops, government interference, ruinous wholesale market prices.

Jian was a tall man who resembled less a Chinese pearl farmer and more a budding New Age executive. He wore a woolen sports jacket and black-and-gray turtleneck underneath. He looked as out of place in this rural China setting as Faye did. Perhaps Jian had dressed for the occasion. Maybe he wanted to make an impression on Faye or, less likely, on me.

Jian had three partners, and they shared two hundred acres of freshwater pearl lakes. When I asked about the CP&J complex looming on the horizon, Jian had a different viewpoint from Faye and Ju's.

"Maybe it'll be good," he said. "Maybe more people will come and there'll be a bigger market for our products," he said, sipping pensively. "As it is now, we're producing more and more pearls, and because of that, our prices are nosediving." Faye was doing the translating from Mandarin to English, but I understood what Jian's last two words meant as he raised his right hand to shoulder level, fingers straight, thumb tucked under palm, then abruptly pushed his hand down in a forty-five-degree angle. "Someone needs to be doing a better job of selling what we're producing." Jian's take sounded right out of Marketing 101.

The tea did little to take the chill off the cold. A scrim of fog had settled over the multitude of lakes dotted in the distance, and as I got up to stretch my legs, it was hard to make out anything but a hazy outline of these black pools filled with plastic pop bottles, fertilizer, mussels, and nascent pearls within. The tableau lay spread out in front of me for miles and miles. Despite the dropping temperature, I still wanted to try my hand at a pearl harvest, and Jian offered to take me.

The two of us got into a corroding flat-bottom metal boat. This was trickier than it looked. You have to crouch low, keeping your center of gravity close to the boat's floor. As I stepped into the boat, it teetered precariously, then leveled itself as soon as I hurriedly sat down. Everyone laughed. The American might know a little about pearls, but take him out on the water and watch out. I took Jian's offer of a paddle and began paddling as Jian stood in the front of the boat with a long bamboo pole, guiding us. As had happened with Dave Bing, Jian pulled up a submerged metal basket of mussels from the opaque water. He emptied out seven hard-shelled mollusks from the net. The mussels hitting the boat's aluminum floor clanked like a slot machine jackpot.

There's excitement at any harvest, no small amount of hope and expectation. Harvest is the culmination of nature's whimsy, science's promise, and farmers' nurture. Ju and her husband joined Faye, Jian, and me at the water's edge. Jian pulled out a machete and split open all seven mussels. As Bing had done, he opened the halves, laying them on the shore, and began poking around the fleshy innards. Faye crossed her arms against her chest, holding onto her upper arms as the cold sky turned grayer. Ju and her husband bent down to get a closer look.

Even though I had seen the same trick a day earlier, I was still blown away by how many pearls Jian was finding in the folds of mussel flesh. I asked Jian whether I could join in the treasure hunt, and he nodded, so I got down on one knee and started kneading the slimy meat, feeling for pearls. I found two dozen. The experience was akin to panning for gold nuggets on a Sierra Nevada riverbank. Every few seconds, I felt another pearl hiding in another fold of the slimy mussel meat.

Faye came in for a closer look. Ju brought out a strainer, and Jian started dropping pearls inside, which made that clicking sound once again. The haul this day was substantially less than Bing's, about ninety pearls for seven mussels, which made for a measly average of about fifteen pearls per mussel. But harvest season wasn't for a few more months; presumably when mature, the mussels would yield perhaps not more pearls, but larger pearls. I was impressed with what the seven mussels had given up. As in Bing's show, the colors were an astonishing rainbow assortment, most of them orange-pink, but also silvery as well as white pearls.

Faye seemed disappointed, though, as did Jian and Ju. The pearls ran from 2 millimeters to 9 millimeters—buttons, teardrops, ovals, semi-rounds, not a single perfect round. The mussels we pulled out represented five years in the water. The most valuable were the two 9-millimeter semi-rounds. Each looked nearly flawless, shiny without even going through the transformatron. They were the only close-to perfect pearls in the haul. Faye said that the mussels in this region produce pearls with the strongest lustre, but there's a price to pay for that. Joo-jee pearls take the longest to grow to maturity. Jian washed the pearls with a hose, then Ju patted them dry with a towel. Faye pulled off a baggy from a plastic roll, poured the pearls inside, and managed to tuck the bag into the pocket of her skin-tight jeans.

Faye and I said good-bye, more bows and smiles, to Ju, Jian, and the husband who didn't say much. Back in the black Caddy, Faye said over Norah Jones that even after a decade, whenever she sees a mussel being opened, it still makes her heart flutter. "You think you know what's inside, but until you actually open it, you never know for sure." I liked that. Not unlike human birth. Even with all the technology, amniocenteses, ultrasounds, and the assortment of screening tests, you never are certain exactly what you are going to get.

At a restaurant downtown for lunch, Faye took out the baggie of pearls and emptied it onto a dinner plate. More click-clack-click. "Nothing special," she said matter-of-factly, getting up for the buffet of hot dishes, which were cold.

"What do you think about children?" Faye asked out of the blue. "My biological clock is ticking." She plopped a wilted dumpling into her mouth. Maybe there was a future with Shepherd, something that could be arranged; she wasn't giving up.

"What do you think of the names Ashley, Braden, and Casey? I adore them," Faye said, launching into a discussion on how she was destined to be a mother, but how most Chinese men she met in her line of work really weren't marriage quality, certainly not with an independent Chinese woman like her.

Faye opened her purse and laid on the table a well-thumbed copy of *Getting in Touch with Your Inner Bitch.* "I'm learning a lot from this," she proclaimed. "You ever read it? Guys can pick up a lot from this book." Then after taking a sip of tea, she said, "We'll see in two weeks."

Two weeks?

Two weeks was when I planned to meet Shepherd and another one of his Chinese lieutenants, a mysterious operative Shepherd referred to only as Mr. You. We were to rendezvous in southern China at Mr. You's farms in Xuwen. Mr. You was Shepherd's seawater pearl partner, and Faye had decided she'd join us.

We moved to Faye's office, on the third floor of a building that overlooked the sea nymphs in the downtown traffic roundabout. Faye showed me the latest deal she and Shepherd had cooked up: very large, more than 13-millimeter baroque pearls, in pink, silver, and turquoise. Faye had a sack filled with them. She said she sells exclusively to Shepherd a strand of such pearls for about 800 RMB each (about $112), "sometimes more, sometimes less, it depends," and he turns them around on his Web site for about $750.

Of everything I'd seen in Joo-jee, these were the pearls I fancied the most, more than the pink rounds I'd bought for Iris. I asked Faye if I could buy two strands for the wholesale price, and she nodded.

Her cell phone suddenly rang.

"WHEY!" she yelled.

She hung up; within seconds, it rang again.

"WHEY!"

That's how the next hour went. In between multiple "WHEYS!" I began picking out from a burlap sack fifty or so large multicolored baroques. As Faye took call after call and relentlessly ordered her staff of ten around, I busied myself in a corner of the walk-up pearl factory as though I was a little boy selecting from thousands of cat's-eye marbles the ones I liked best. I made four piles, each of different colors (pink, gray, blue, orange), discarding any baroque with a flat side to it. The best baroques had multifaceted surfaces; baroques with flat surfaces were considered less valuable.

While everyone else in Faye's cluttered, smoke-filled office was busy— sorting, drilling, treating pearls, tooling on the Internet—I plunged my hands into a heavy sack of slick, shimmering pearls, letting them fall through my fingers, setting aside my favorites. It was the same activity that had so captivated Isabella of Spain five hundred years earlier, sifting through the thousands of luscious pearls Columbus's antagonists had brought back with them, or so I imagined.

11

Tammy and a (Sort of) Barbara Bush Sighting at the Hongqiao Pearl Market

What struck me about Beijing was what must strike everyone upon first arriving in China's capital: the smog, then the scale of the city. My plane glided through powder-blue skies; as it descended, the aircraft pierced a filthy air mass, which hovered over Beijing like a cancerous lid. In part because of China's dependence on coal and the proliferation of so many gasoline-powered engines, Beijing's pollution is five times that of the World Health Organization's basic standard of acceptability. Hazy, dirty Beijing is spread out through five bumper-to-bumper concentric rings (a sixth is under construction), with Tiananmen Square (the Gate of Heavenly Peace) at the center. The city's once-ubiquitous masses of bicycles have largely been replaced by an unrelenting army of small, smog-belching mini-cars in perpetual gridlock. Beijing's epic scale transforms everyone into stick figures.

I arrived just prior to Beijing's annual dust storms, which bring swirling gales of soot and grime from the northern coal-producing provinces. The dust blizzards are of biblical proportion, right out of the ten plagues of Egypt. Beijing residents pray for rain, the only respite to ease these gritty tempests that sweep into the capital each spring. As the storms get closer to Beijing, they pick up pollutant particles from outlying industrial-chemical districts, making the gusts particularly noxious. Residents take to caulking their windows with rags. Airports shut down because of low visibility. Even in mid-March, when I was in Beijing, early for the dust monsoons, I saw pedestrians scurrying around with their heads swathed in scarves, narrow slits for their eyes, a prophylactic measure against the onslaught to come. Many residents wore surgical masks.

I had an appointment the next morning at Beijing's world-famous Hongqiao (which translates to *Pearl*) Market. All the way to Beijing, and I wouldn't have time to see the Great Wall (a section, albeit overrun by tourists, lies just an hour from Beijing), something my family couldn't fathom. "That'd be like a Chinese guy going to New York and not visiting the Statue of Liberty!" Iris remonstrated during one of our infrequent phone conversations. "Dad, at least take a picture!" Mikey pleaded.

The Hongqiao Market is located in Beijing's Hongwen district, a twenty-minute walk from Chongwenmen subway station, across from the Temple of Heaven. Hongqiao used to be just a fish market ("pearls from the sea"), but today it stocks just about anything, including what appeared to be a bear claw (not the pastry kind, but the real thing) that two Tibetan men were pushing in a freelance stall outside the market. Hongqiao's first floor had knockoffs galore, clothing, electronics, kitchen goods, shoes, DVDs, fabrics, tools. Curios and assorted items were on the second floor. I headed straight for the third floor, where three hundred pearl vendors had stalls. There was a fourth floor, home to a half dozen full-fledged jewelry stores that specialized in pearls.

As I had done at the Joo-jee market, I first strolled the aisles. By now, I was totally in my element. Pearls, pearls, pearls. Necklaces, earrings, bracelets, pendants, brooches, rings, even loose pearls. It was the necklaces that for me represented the apogee of pearls. Girding a woman's collarbone, resting atop her bosom, encircling her neck, heat transferring from body to strand, this was the essence of pearls. Hongqiao had all colors, sizes, quality, and shapes. I'd gotten so accustomed to pearls at this point in my journey that it wasn't any longer just the click-clack sound I instantly recognized and homed to. I could smell pearls. They had a clean, fresh, pure scent, although here in Hongqiao, they seemed to have a slight lacquered odor—perhaps too many spins in the transformatron.

I had made plans to connect with Liu Jun, a reporter for *China Daily*, who was to be my translator for the day. We met at 10:30 a.m., when the market was empty of the throngs of foreigners that tromp through in the late afternoons. With Liu at my side, our morning stroll on the third floor caused an immediate stir. A foreigner buying a present for his Chinese girlfriend, wife, daughter? The vendors, almost all young women, wore tidy, official-issue pink smocks, which gave them the appearance of dental hygienists. But as Liu and I walked the floor, I quickly realized these women weren't at all like Lynne at Dr. Clemons's office back home.

"Come-ee here! You like!"

"Hel-LOW! Hel-LOW!"

"Look what we've for you, Meester!"

"Best plices!"

A couple of vendors leaned over their stalls, dangling strands of pearls from slender fingers. "Try ours. We have best," two girls suggested in unison, smiling provocatively.

After a couple more spins around, Liu and I decided to break the ice with a young woman who went by the name Tammy in Stall 105. I was attracted to Tammy for no other reason than a cursory look suggested she had a large inventory of what looked like high-quality pearls. She shared the stall with her mother (at least Tammy introduced the woman as her mother). Tammy, who was twenty, seemed knowledgeable, smart, and talkative. She had studied English at a vocational middle school in Taizhou, Zhejiang, a two-hour ride from Joo-jee. Tammy immediately thrust business cards into our hands. When I asked how she got such a Western name, Tammy flashed a row of white teeth.

"My real name is Cai Meimei, which means *pretty girl*," she said. "But foreign people, they never able to say my name. They always forget. They always ask for my English name and I never know what to say. I like Cai Meimei, but I need something they can remember. So they can tell their friends. Having name here that foreigner remembers is important. So, one day, a customer tell me that I look like a Tammy. That's how I became Tammy. It's now me."

Tammy's family has an interest in a pearl cooperative in Taizhou, and the pearls in her stall mostly come from there, she said. Her monthly tax/rent at Hongqiao is 3,000–4,000 RMB ($422–$562), she said, excluding an initial buy-in of 30,000 RMB (then about $3,200) in 1995.

Tammy started working at the family pearl stall when she was sixteen. While Tammy's English is pretty good, all she really needs to do business with foreign customers (few if any Chinese ever buy pearls at Hongqiao) is a universal translator—her calculator. "This time of year, we sell only a few hundred RMB a day, maybe a thousand RMB. Very slow. That way, I make you special deal," Tammy offered. "I give you deal better than I give other customers."

The tourist season, she said, runs from April to August, when Russians, Europeans, Americans, and Middle Easterners flock to the market. The Russians are the toughest bargainers, followed by Middle Easterners, she said, with Americans and Europeans the easiest.

Enough with all my questions, Tammy said. "Why don't you buy? I show you what you want. Very good prices. Special price for you. I make you good price. You trust Tammy."

But Liu had already made an appointment with the owner of one of the jewelry stores on the fourth floor, a well-known pearl boutique called Fanghua. I promised Tammy we'd return. "The prices up there, way too high," Tammy counseled, bruised that we'd pass her up for another vendor, even one with a fourth-floor pedigree. "You come back to Tammy. She take care of you. Very good price I make for you," Tammy said, winking at me.

Before leaving though, I wanted to get an idea of how much cheaper Tammy's pearls would be than those upstairs. I needed a baseline. I'd been cautioned that to take home a good deal, I should bid as much as 70 percent less than the asking price. I really was more interested in the dance of negotiation than in acquiring another strand of pearls. I wanted to understand this particular rung of the pearl ladder, the protocol of how a pearl necklace goes from market vendor to consumer, so I gave Tammy fifteen minutes to show her stuff. By now, I knew enough about pearls to calculate how much her pearls *ought* to sell for. I wanted to see how low she'd go.

Tammy started by showing Liu and me high-quality white pearls on a hank with blue tassels on each end. These were first-rate, top of the line, and offering them up first was right out of Retailing 101. Tammy or her mother could in fifteen minutes knot the pearls, put a clasp on, and we'd be ready to go. Liu wanted to buy a strand for her mother for Mother's Day. If Liu bought her mother a necklace and a strand for herself, and I bought one for Iris, we'd have three strands, and we'd be in a good negotiating position. Liu's mother and Iris would go for some white rounds, and Liu said she liked a less expensive strand of pink button shapes.

Tammy's stall was so crowded with pearl jewelry that there was little room to do any serious appraisal on the counter, so I performed the wobble test I'd learned from Alex Vock on the wooden stool I'd been sitting on. I got down on one knee on the cement floor, and started rolling a strand with my palm, looking carefully for any trace of wobble—every pearl maven's nemesis.

"These are pretty good," I said, to which Tammy nodded vigorously.

"Sure, they good! AAA quality! Tammy tell the truth!"

I rubbed two pearls from the strand against each other to make sure they passed the telltale real-pearl grit test, which they did. Then I balled the strand up and held it in my cupped hand, feeling the density and weight, slightly clicking them. The three strands carried a collective heft. I held them for ten or twenty seconds, and again as in Tucson, my hand started to perspire slightly, an auto-anatomical reaction. I felt the pearls taking on my own body heat.

"I like these," I said, handing the warmed orbs back to Tammy. "The hanks are nice. The color is consistent, so's the lustre. How much for all three—the two whites and a pink strand?"

Tammy knew that we'd be leaving for Fanghua, the jewelry store one floor up, so she knew she'd have to float a good price before us.

She punched numbers into her calculator, her red fingernails clicking against the gray keys. "Two thousand RMB for all three, the two sets of round whites and the pink strand." It was the equivalent of $278.

The dance had begun.

"Two *thousand*!" I remonstrated. "You must be kidding! And I thought you and I were friends, Tammy! Two thousand's *way* too much. No way would we EVER pay that much. What do you take us for, Tammy?"

Liu stood by, half shocked, half fascinated. I considered introducing the word *rip-off* to Liu and Tammy's English lexicon.

Granted, it was Tammy's opening salvo and her price was supposed to be over the top. I grabbed Liu by the elbow and began to steer her toward the escalator.

"Now, wait, you two. I give *special price* I give to no one else."

Ah, the *special price* gambit.

"I drop to fifteen hundred RMB." This was $212.

"Come on, Tammy! Please, no more insults. Okay?"

"That is good price. Believe me. For three necklaces!"

"What about our discount?"

"You already get discount. A big discount!"

"That's the discount you give *everyone*. What about the *special* price you promised? We are your friends, Tammy. You promised."

"That is good price for all three necklaces. Really."

"But you said we're *special* customers."

"Okay. Because you so nice, I go down an extra one hundred RMB"—$14.

"Tammy," I said disappointed.

Tammy stood shaking her head, arms crossed in front of her chest, hands on her pink-smocked elbows. We had reached a standoff.

"C'mon, Liu. Let's go. Tammy doesn't really want to do business with us. And she said we were *special* customers. *Very* special, I can see."

"Okay. Okay. I go to thirteen hundred RMB. But last price. This is steal, really. You getting three necklaces! I shouldn't even be doing this!" We were down to $183.

The old *"I shouldn't even be doing this"* ploy. If Tammy were a car salesman she'd have thrown in that if her boss found out, she'd be fired.

We had gone from $278 to $183 in ten minutes. Not close to the recommended 70 percent off, but we had established a base price for further negotiations.

Liu and I were running late for our appointment upstairs. "Let's think about it. We'll come back. We really will," I told Tammy, knowing she must hear that rejoinder every day. Tammy managed a resigned, halfhearted smile.

The best of Tammy's pearls were reasonably high quality. Fanghua may have a larger inventory of bigger Chinese freshwaters, but Tammy's midsized freshwater Chinese pearls were as good as anyone's.

Foreign shoppers freaked by the free-form negotiations and the in-your-face salesgirls below could get more personalized treatment at Fanghua and the other more traditional jewelers on the fourth floor. As soon as we walked into Fanghua, I immediately realized this was the kind of jewelry store that paradoxically puts men to sleep and makes them fidgety at the same time: banks of glass showcases filled with outrageously expensive baubles, an imperial all-women staff wearing tailored lime-green jackets, a rarefied atmosphere that makes wives and girlfriends do uncharacteristic things often culminating in very large purchases. Realizing this, Fanghua provided an alcove for men with Barcalounger-type chairs and a flat screen television set tuned to a sports channel, along with liquor served in cut crystal tumblers.

My first impressions of Fanghua I think were probably shared by the sole guy in the store's Men's Club, as he sipped on a Glenlivet scotch, watching the Houston Pistons playing the Boston Celtics, as his wife (presumably she was his wife) tried on a multitude of pearl strands. I nodded at him. The Chinese man raised his glass to me in a toast of sorts. There was no need for words.

At Fanghua, there was little of the spirited give-and-take at Tammy's stall. But that was by design. Fanghua was quiet and private, none of the riff-raff and hubbub that reigned supreme below. This was the kind of place where customers—no, clients—could learn the nuances of pearls, so the store's pearls would be transformed into *their* pearls.

Owner Bai Rufang was running late, so Liu and I pretty much had the run of the place. Behind a lime-upholstered Louis XIV couch was a photo gallery of famous Fanghua customers. And there, right before my eyes: the international doyenne of pearls, Barbara Bush, wearing a strand the size of Rainier cherries. She was flanked by a smiling George H. W. Bush and an equally beaming Bai. Alongside that photograph was a veritable Hall of Fame of clients: Margaret Thatcher, Lynn Cheney, conductor Zubin Mehta, Nancy Kissinger, Queen Sofia, Vladimir and Ludmilla Putin, Tarja Halonen (the president of Finland), and Maria Shriver Schwarzenegger (but no Arnold).

Like the Paspaley auction, Fanghua's prices were all in yen. This was part marketing ploy, part common sense. A large percentage of Bai's customers are Japanese, so prices need not be converted. But also at play was the yen price tags seemed to convey wholesale prices, somehow indicating that the client was getting prices closer to the source. (The contrary was true, of course, since almost all of Fanghua's pearls were from China.)

Bai showed up, wearing sneakers, jogging pants, and a monogrammed gray turtleneck sweater. "Hello, hello, hello," she said, breezing in, speaking in the fractured, mechanical way many educated Chinese speak English. "So sorry I am late. Whatever you like, I am here."

Bai's ascendancy in the retail pearl business neatly parallels China's rise in freshwater pearl cultivation. Born in Wenling in Zhejiang Province, the daughter of a father who was an accountant and a mother who worked at a glass factory, Bai came to Beijing in 1987 fresh out of high school. She started working for an aunt at an open-air market in front of the Temple of Heaven, selling cheap plastic goods like cups, stools, bowls, and basins. Two years later, she teamed up with a friend from Wenling, who convinced her to trade up to pearls. At that time, there were some thirty pearl dealers at the open-air street market. Bai said she and her partner pooled their savings and borrowed from family members, paying 40,000 RMB (then about $4,500) for two stalls on the third floor of the then-new enclosed market, around the corner from Tammy. Three years later, she moved her operations to the fourth floor and now rents out her two original stalls downstairs for about 10,000 RMB ($1,400) a month.

Today, Bai, 38, is a leading pearl retailer, with a small chain of stores in

Beijing and Shanghai. She said she pays her staff, mostly girls who have recently graduated from high school, a salary of 1,500 RMB a month ($211), and
houses them five to six to a dormitory room. This was just slightly more than
what the pearl-processing workers in Joo-jee earned, even though the expenses
of living in Beijing, of course, were much greater. Bai employs three hundred
salesgirls, who do not work on commission, and scatters them through her
stores. She trains them in rudimentary English, French, Italian, and Russian.

Bai had a regal appearance, with a heart-shaped face, high molded cheek-
bones, a slightly aquiline nose, light skin, and a pointy chin. The combination
created a pleasing countenance, so much so that when Bai left to attend to a
client, Liu confessed that she thought Bai was strikingly beautiful. "In China,
she has the looks people love."

Bai effused that she's a social butterfly when it comes to the embassy scene
in Beijing, wangling as many invitations as she can to state dinners and cocktail parties. "I'd never give out cards, that would be wrong, but word gets
'round, and soon everyone starts coming to you," she said. "One woman wears
a necklace from Fanghua, and says we give her good price, and then someone
else comes to us, then someone else. It's word of mouth. Best advertising."

At this point, Bai asked me whether I'd be interested in buying a strand,
and with the array before me, I couldn't say no. I wanted to get at the price
structure of Bai's operations, for she, too, was as much a part of the global
pearl assembly line, from diver's hand to woman's bosom, as Alex Vock, Andy
Müller, Nick Paspaley, Faye Tian, the Joo-jee vendor, and Tammy downstairs
were. I wanted to see the best Bai had, and when I asked her, she pulled out a
strand of white Australian semi-rounds, very nice, at 16.5 millimeters. There
were some slight imperfections, surface marks and wobble I could see without
the wobble test.

"How much?"

"We'd sell this for twenty-thousand dollars. But if interested, we can talk."

"We can talk, but I'm not interested," I countered in an amiable way. If I
sold everything I owned, except our house and car, I couldn't come up with
half that.

"But this is investment. A strand like this go for sixty-thousand dollars in
New York," Bai volleyed.

Which was baloney. When I had been with Vock in Hong Kong, I'd seen
nice Australian strands, with slightly smaller pearls, that maybe would fetch
in the mid-20s in the States.

Since I wasn't in the market for anything high-end, and Tammy had me covered for the low-end, I asked Bai what she had in Tahitian pearls. I had grown to love the blue-green-silver peacock colors of real Tahitians.

"I give you big discount. For you, I give discount much bigger than I give to my usual customers."

Bai had just met me, and she was already undercutting the prices she gives her best regulars? I wondered what Barbara and George had paid, if anything. How about the Governator's wife? These celebrity photos were worth an awful lot in advertising and good will.

Bai pulled out six Tahitians, ranging from the equivalent of $12,000 to $1,000 per strand. At least, Bai said they were Tahitians. I focused on the $1,000 strand, and placed it in my palm. First, I rubbed two pearls against each. They certainly were real. Then I brought them up to my eyes. This *had* to be a dye job. The pearls were large, maybe 13 millimeters, but nice with very few blemishes. I looked down the drill hole to see any variation of color, and couldn't see anything. These had to be unusually large Chinese freshwaters, baked in a transformatron, and matched perfectly. No way could this strand be a Tahitian for $1,000.

"You want these for free?" Bai suddenly offered.

"For free?"

"I give you these for free."

"Why?"

"Because I like you. And you tell others to come to Fanghua."

"What are these pearls? They're not Tahitians. They're Chinese freshwaters, right?"

"You want free?"

I didn't want anything for free, and I told Bai that, which seemed to surprise her. Crazy American, he *wants* to pay? Maybe she wanted to get rid of the pearls. Who knew their story? Maybe they were hot. Maybe they were unlucky.

"What you give me if you don't want me to give you for free?"

I knew what Tammy's freshwater strands go for, and I knew what I had paid for Iris's pink strand in Joo-jee. Matched dyed freshwaters this size should go for the local retail equivalent of about $250, even though their initial *special* price had been $1,000. I told Bai I'd pay $100.

In a Beijing second, Bai accepted my offer, carrying the hank to a stringer, who instantly began knotting them.

Bai wrapped up the pearls (with a plain clasp) in a red satin box. We bowed and said good-bye. By now, the man in the Men's Club drinking Glenlivet had nodded off in the lounger chair, his wife still shopping with great vigor. Bai did not ask to take my photograph. Liu and I stepped on the escalator, relieved to be out of the store.

Tammy looked surprised to see us. "I tell my mother you come back," she said smiling. "My mother say you gone forever. Tammy said no."

After exchanging pleasantries about how ridiculously expensive everything on the fourth floor was, we got down to business. Tammy's last offer had been the equivalent of $183 for the two freshwater whites for Iris and for Liu's mother, and a third strand, the pink choker, for Liu.

"Tammy," I started. "Let's save time. You're busy, we're busy. What's your absolute lowest price for the three strands?"

"Because you come back, I make *very* special price. I go down to twelve hundred RMB." It was the equivalent of $169.

I pulled out two 500 RMB notes and said, "Let's agree to one thousand." We were at $135.

Tammy shook her head, swinging her bangs. Then she leaned over to her mother, whispering. Then she went back to her calculator. Liu and I waited.

"Okay, we do business!" Tammy announced, clapping her hands.

We had gone down 50 percent from Tammy's initial offer, not the recommended 70 percent, but I didn't have the nerve to go that low anyway. Tammy's mother started working on transforming the hanks into necklaces, and we picked out clasps for the three strands, then boxes. "If it's black, my mother will never wear the pearls," Liu said, echoing a custom that older Chinese follow. We chose a blue satin box and two red satin boxes. And, so we'd leave with a smile, Tammy threw in a couple of pearl pendants. Everyone was happy.

There is a coda to this story, and it involved Liu, or really, Liu's mother. As promised, Liu proudly presented the white pearl necklace in the blue box to her mother for Mother's Day two months later. Liu wrote me that her mother was overjoyed. In fact, the pearls were so beautiful, Liu's mother said, she promised to wear them only on special occasions—once, perhaps twice, a year.

12

Miss Pearl

I had two days left in Beijing before leaving for the south to meet Jeremy Shepherd, Faye Tian, and the mysterious Mr. You. We were to converge at the Haikou airport in Hainan Province and take a ferry back to the mainland, where I planned to visit two rural seawater pearl farms Mr. You and Shepherd own. I wasn't quite sure why Faye was tagging along, other than to spend time with Shepherd and convince him to make a love baby.

My last bit of pearl business in Beijing was to get an industry overview of China's pearl economy, and for that I had arranged an interview with Shi Hong-yue, whose exact title was deputy secretary-general of the Gems & Jewelry Trade Association of China, a trade industry group that keeps statistics and lobbies the government on behalf of pearl growers and processors.

Shi was the pearl expert of the GAC. I found him in Room 4158 of Building 19, a classic Chinese government edifice girded at the front door by two cement lions on a street with the impossible name of Xiaohuangzhuang. Down a narrow, smoky hallway, I found Shi, who bowed, then offered me tea. I wanted to find out where China's 1,500 tons of pearls go each year. That was an awful lot of pearls. Shi and I chit-chatted over the tea, then he began juggling multiple spreadsheets of figures.

There seemed to be some confusion, and Shi went back and forth with a man who kept punching in numbers on an old computer between puffs from a cigarette. Shi looked over the man's shoulders, and pulled on his own cigarette. The two men argued, going back and forth for ten minutes or so. Finally Shi seemed ready to present the most recent figures that the GAC maintains.

According to the two officials, only a little more than a third of the pearls China produces, 572 tons, end up leaving the country. Of that, Hong Kong imports 70 percent, with India, the United States, and Taiwan importing almost all of the rest. Of course, Hong Kong is simply a distribution point, a city through which the Chinese pearls get to the rest of the world, with many more ending up in the United States, as well as Europe and Asia. But that still left 928 tons officially remaining in China.

Shi was vague, either fabricating, concealing, or not really knowing much. It was hard to tell which. But, if he and his chain-smoking colleague were anywhere close to accurate, the number of pearls that never leave China each year was truly staggering. It seemed likely that many of China's pearls had to be stealth-exported under government radar to destinations like Hong Kong, Japan, and the United States. Shi's figures showed, though, the vast potential of the Chinese pearl market both at home and abroad. How could the Japanese, Filipinos, French Polynesians, and Australians ever hope to compete with such a huge pearl stockpile? Such a figure meant that China's already dirt-cheap pearl prices would probably have to drop more. As Chinese pearl prices continue to plummet, and their quality continues to improve, the pearls would further undercut the international pearl market, making it even more and more difficult for other producers to compete against China's rock-bottom labor costs. All the while, the size of Chinese pearls would be getting bigger. I suppose if there was any winner in all this it'd be pearl buyers—larger, higher-quality, cheaper pearls.

Shi and I sat on two fake-leather chairs facing each other. He pulled nervously on another cigarette, his third within the last fifteen minutes. Could these numbers of his—some 900 tons of pearls stay in China—be accurate?

Shi took the cigarette out of his mouth, burped, lit another, then nodded.

What was China doing to increase its exports of pearls? "If only a third go outside of China, and the Chinese aren't buying pearls, you have a problem on your hands, no?"

Shi shrugged. Japan had Mikio Ibuki, French Polynesia had Robert Wan and (I was to find out) Martin Coeroli, the Philippines (I was to find out) had the bluster and expertise of Jacques Branellec and Manuel Cojuangco, the Australians had the raw power of Nick Paspaley (and, I was to find out, the pluck of Rosario Autore), plus a 24/7 well-lubricated global publicity machine. The future of China's global pearl empire rested on the likes of Ricky Cheng, Dave Bing, and the coterie of businessmen who'd concocted the CP&J white elephant in Joo-jee. Faye Tian and her crowd were minor players. But the job of alerting the world to China's awakening pearl giant belonged, in part, to the taciturn man sitting across from me, who took another nervous pull from his cigarette.

Would the industry fight tariffs other nations might consider imposing on cheap Chinese pearls imports? What about pearl product placement on Chinese television or in films to spur national consumption? Just what was Shi's plan to jumpstart consumption?

Shi shook his head. He didn't know about any tariffs or quotas that were depressing international sales (they seemed unlikely considering the hundreds of tons of Chinese exports of every conceivable product leaving unabated from Chinese ports every month), and regarding product placement, that was something occasionally discussed, but never implemented, Shi said.

"So," I persisted, "how, then, are you going to convince Chinese women to buy pearls?"

A light bulb went off in Shi's head. His eyebrows twitched on.

"Last year we cooperated with a television station to crown a Miss Pearl," he said.

Now we were getting somewhere. I'd arrange an interview with Miss Pearl. Pretty, pearl-clad girl valiantly skipping from shopping mall to parade to red-carpet gala to blue-ribbon factory opening, wearing glistening Chinese orbs for all to see. This I had experience with, interviewing Pork, Beef, Plum, and Strawberry Queens. A grassroots movement to stimulate national, even global, sales of Chinese pearls. Perhaps a page from Japanese showman Kokichi Mikimoto's old playbook.

How could I reach Miss Pearl? I asked.

"Oh," Shi said, shocked. "She can't be interviewed."

But her role is to spread the gospel of pearls, I countered. How could she not be available?

"Her parents are very protective and they won't let her talk to the media."

Maybe I could see her on a float in a parade, or putting in an appearance at the Beijing aquarium next to the mollusk tanks.

"No," Shi said, shaking his head, taking a last pull on his now stubby cigarette. Her next appearance wasn't for another three months.

This was worse than trying to score an interview with Snow White, who'd talk to the press, but only in character. Miss Pearl wouldn't talk at all.

13

The Way of the Internet:
A Trek from the Neighborhood
Jewelry Store to the Rural Chinese
Villages of Haian and Xuwen

I

Iris and Mikey had been my biggest boosters, but they were getting tired of going it alone in the cold, snowy Iowa winter back home. I sensed a growing frustration over cell phone calls that, without notice, went dead, I imagined, somewhere over Iceland in the starry frigid cosmos of the dark night. Iris and Mikey had both heard enough of my stories. Stories only go so far. Iris wanted her husband back, and I sensed our son wanted me home, too. Tracking pearls and the people who produced them on this global assembly line still was an addictive story I wanted to chase. But my only son would be in college in three years, and I'd have only myself to blame for missing him; perhaps more importantly, for his not missing me. And my wife of two decades?

Traipsing around the world like Tintin, was this any way to nourish our marriage? Towering gift boxes of pearls went only so far.

This global pearl adventure had been a solo trip. Pearls were giving me a chance to sneak behind the curtain, to bask in the reflection of an object that had for years captivated me. On one hand, pearls were an insignificant component in a complicated world, but given context, pearls became a lens that give meaning to how a part of the world works. Like a dog with a bone, I couldn't give up. After a marathon phone call, that probably cost a hundred dollars, Iris and Mikey halfheartedly agreed. I carried on.

II

Hainan is China's only island province. It's the farthest south in China, located directly east of Haiphong, Vietnam, across the once-contentious bay known in China as Beibu Gulf, but in the United States as the incendiary Gulf of Tonkin. I wanted to see how China's seawater pearls were cultivated and processed, and this was the center of their production. I planned to interview peasants who worked for Mr. You and Jeremy Shepherd. I wanted to get as close as possible to the first rungs of the global pearl ladder.

A trip to such an isolated region would also give me an opportunity to get to know thirty-three-year-old Shepherd, who by all accounts had become the undisputed leader in Internet pearl sales over four short years. When I met Shepherd in Tucson, he gave me a DVD about himself and his company, pearlparadise.com. Several excerpts:

• "Shepherd's real life reads like a fairy tale. Exciting enough to begin with the words 'Once upon a time,' it is an epic saga of a young man who journeyed to Asia, where he traveled far and wide, seeking Nature's most elusive Holy Grail—the perfect pearl."

• "Pearls were much more than just a financial investment for Shepherd. Ultimately, he was a true collector. And so he mastered the difficult art of discerning the worth of these opalescent prizes through trial and error, plus the sheer force of his determination to succeed."

• "By using his twin talents as a negotiator and expert appraiser, Shepherd eliminated layers of middlemen and local agents by personally visiting every farm in Asia rumored to produce quality pearls, no matter how remote."

Sure, all of it was over the top, but that last statement took the cake. The claim was flat-out preposterous, not to mention, impossible—*"every* farm in Asia." C'mon.

Without a doubt, Shepherd had become an important element in the wholesale and retail business of pearls. Whenever I mentioned Shepherd's name to anyone in the trade, I'd wait and watch their eyes widen and teeth clench. Pearl *machers* dismissed the Santa Monica, California, upstart as a poseur, a troublemaker who ought to be disciplined and thrown out of the insular club of pearl traders. In a most disagreeable manner, Shepherd had crashed the nonstop party jewelers had kept going for centuries. No one had invited him, and now he had the audacity to be bellying up to the bar, drinking the same booze as the dealers and scarfing down tray after tray of hors d'oeuvres. At none of the major jewelry shows (in Tucson, Basel, Hong Kong, Las Vegas) did Shepherd make the rounds and introduce himself to the old guard. He certainly wasn't invited to participate in the annual Pearl Walk at the Tucson show, and if he had been, he'd probably think it was beneath him. He didn't play by the same rules; he didn't play by any rules, many in the old guard harrumphed. Shepherd had stuck his thumb in the eyes of pearl dealers, it seemed, with glee. If ever there were a villain to the stability and long-term health of the global pearl industry it was upstart Shepherd.

III

Traditional (and that's what practically all of them are) retail jewelers view Jeremy Shepherd much the same way independent booksellers look at Jeff Bezos, the founder and president of Amazon. Old-school wisdom in both trades calls for selling products by establishing a fiercely loyal clientele who shop at conventional brick-and-mortar stores. Some of these stores are large, others quite small. In the jewelry business, all of them at one time had been family-owned— Tiffany's, Bulgari, Van Cleef & Arpels, Cartier, and Harry Winston were among the largest and, of course, the most well known. But today many of the nation's once-prominent jewelry retailers have either closed or been gobbled up by multinational holding companies. There are still plenty of second-, third-, and fourth-generation jewelry stores flourishing in America, most of them owned by the sons and grandsons of the original founders, many of them Jewish. Every city of over fifty thousand in America had a premier jewelry store, the place where generations of loyal shoppers would shop to buy engagement rings, wedding bands, bracelets, pearl necklaces, and brooches. These stores—

most of them begun in downtown city cores, now with branches in upscale suburbs—soon expanded to include household items, often luggage, leather goods, and later, appliances. The jewelry retailers developed wedding registries, where affianced couples following custom would create lists for what they hoped family and friends would use to buy presents to outfit their new home—matching stemware, china, flatware, vases, silver services, bowls, assorted household *tchotchkes*. In the suburban town of South Orange, New Jersey, where I grew up, Marsh's was such a store, a second-generation jewelry emporium that one of my high school classmates, Stuart Marsh, was to take over to make a third-generation store back in the early 1970s.

All things must come to an end and thus so did the traditional retail jewelry business. In the mid-1990s, along came the Internet and everything changed virtually overnight.

Online stores like Amazon and e-Bay (and hundreds of thousands of others) became vendors of everything, from books, shoes, TVs, lawn mowers, and movie tickets to prescription drugs, mortgages, homes, and online stock trading. It was just a matter of time before jewelry joined the list. Jewelry was already being hawked twenty-four hours a day on cable TV. And people were buying it.

To a large segment of the upper-middle-class jewelry-wearing public, spare time that in generations past might have gone to shopping and lunch with the girls was no more. Very yesterday. These days there weren't enough hours in the day if you were an upscale, college-educated, professional woman, having to juggle a marriage, demanding job, putting dinner on the table, maintaining a home, rearing children, staying in shape, taking well-earned vacations, and perhaps volunteering for some favorite cause.

Enter online jewelry shopping. It was hip, convenient, and, most of all, time-efficient. Younger, well-heeled customers had no loyalty to their parents' stodgy old jewelry store. The jewels these new customers coveted were different, too. Many opted for freer-form jewelry; classic sold, but baroque and retro pieces also became popular. Price became a factor, too. The new generation of consumers liked the idea of demystifying the buying process, prying open the black price box that heretofore only the jewelry-store shamans had the key to. Shopping online was fun after a hectic day at the office. negotiating with the kids to get to bed, and making time for your spouse. Online shopping was private and discreet. No one had to know what you were buying. Nicole from down the street wouldn't have to see you trying on that strand of *outrageous* Tahitians at the very public jewelry store in town. As for Nicole's husband, he could surprise Nicole with a strand he bought online for less—and he could give another strand to his cute (but increasingly demanding) secretary. And for single career women, why shouldn't they, too, have the same jewelry that Nicole had? They worked just as hard, maybe harder. Why wait for a man to come along to give you that necklace? You might even have more disposable income, too, than your married counterparts. And no one would have to know. The jewelry discreetly came like a little present, delivered to your home. The Internet allowed for efficient comparison-shopping, with full disclosure of what you were buying. Color, close-up product photographs allowed customers to view jewelry from every possible angle (even if the piece shown wasn't always the same piece delivered). With programs that allowed customers to virtually browse jewelry, even to "wear" hundreds of different pearl strands around the virtual neck of the intended recipient, why waste time at a real store when you could buy with a simple click? Outside of me, who needed to hear pearls' click-clacks or to feel the transfer of heat from body to strand before laying down a plastic card? And this was key: *If the jewelry wasn't right for any reason, reputable Internet jewelers would fully refund your money.* So there was no risk. What an invitation to try out pearls at prices that undercut traditional jewelery stores by as much as 80 percent.

IV

Jeremy Shepherd established pearlparadise.com in 1997 and now operates more than a dozen similar sites where pearls are sold at a deep discount. At last count, Shepherd told me his annual sales were $11.8 million, doubled from the previous year. I had no way of corroborating this, but whatever his sales, Shepherd's business was erupting. Not bad for a former Northwest flight attendant, who on a three-day layover in Beijing one day found himself strolling through Hongqiao Market, where he bought a pearl strand for his girlfriend. Back home, he had the necklace appraised, and what he discovered made his head spin. The strand would sell for twenty times what he'd paid for it.

On his next trip to China, Shepherd made a beeline back to Hongqiao and bought twenty more necklaces. On another trip to Beijing, he bought a hundred. Each time, he'd return to the United States and unload the strands online, within days running out of inventory. Shepherd soon cashed out his savings and began buying trunkloads of pearls on his Beijing layovers. Within five years, he quit his flight attendant job, bought into two Chinese seawater pearl farms, and structured an agreement with Faye Tian to access tens of thousands of Joo-jee freshwater pearls. Then he bought, with the mysterious Mr. You, two saltwater pearl farms. These days, Shepherd deals in all kind of pearls, selling them exclusively through the Internet. He has a small office in Santa Monica but discourages customers from visiting. Buy it on one of his Internet sites, he counsels; showing real pearls to customers in person takes up too much time.

I spotted Shepherd as soon as I got off my plane in Haikou. While waiting for me to arrive, Shepherd, Mr. You, and Faye all had gotten foot massages at the airport. They seemed giddy by the time I arrived. Faye was in high spirits. Shepherd was rolling a heavy black suitcase he told me was full of black Tahitian pearls he'd brought from the United States to be treated, processed, drilled, and polished at Mr. You's plant. These pearls must have already traveled twenty thousand miles, and would travel another ten thousand miles before Shepherd would post them on his Internet site. "To get these pearls ready for market in the States would cost a dollar a pearl," Shepherd told me as we both struggled to lift the suitcase into the trunk of a taxi. "Here it'll be maybe a dollar a strand."

We needed to get from the airport to the ferry terminal within thirty minutes to make our connection to the mainland, but with Shepherd's roller and the massive suitcase Faye had brought, we had to take two taxis. Faye snuggled next to Shepherd in one, Mr. You and I took another. Mr. You was a new breed of Chinese entrepreneur. Year by year he had acquired more and more property; he now owned a pearl-processing plant, two seawater pearl farms (along with Shepherd), his own house, and a car. He had also taught himself a smattering of English.

We had to catch a 5:45 p.m. ferry, and arrived at the terminal with just seconds to spare. With two loud, sonorous blasts, just as the ferry was about to pull away, the four of us heaved the suitcases aboard and leaped on the departing ship. Faye went outside to the deck, her shag blowing in the strong wind as we crossed the nineteen-mile-wide Qiongzhou Straits to the mainland's Leizhou Peninsula. On the enclosed top floor of the ferry, Shepherd filled me in on his global plan of selling pearls to the masses via the Internet.

"'Buy low, price low, and sell like crazy to make a very big profit.' That's my motto," Shepherd started, as our rust-bucket ferry sliced through strong swells. The son of a U.S. military officer Shepherd was born in Heidelberg, Germany, then raised by his mother, who returned to the United States and settled in Woodland, Washington. Shepherd picked up languages quickly, starting at sixteen, when he spent a year in Japan as an exchange student. Today he speaks Japanese, passable Mandarin, Spanish, and Chuukese, an obscure language of South Pacific Micronesia, where his wife is from.

Shepherd has a long, rectangular face, a broad forehead, short, wavy hair closely cropped on the sides, and a large chest, this day barely covered by an unbuttoned shirt opened wide. He had a barely visible goatee and moustache, pinkish pale skin, and a bald spot on his crown. His tall, once-lean body was developing flab and paunch. He wore a large single Tahitian pearl on a leather string snug around his neck. It looked most uncomfortable, like one Adam's apple on top of another.

It was during his stint as a flight attendant that he realized the potential of Chinese pearls. "I used to sell pearls to crew members on the flight home, and bought a mobile credit-card machine to run through their purchases. We'd have galley pearl parties, and it wasn't unusual to sell thousands of dollars on each flight. I launched my first Web site, bought more and more pearls, and soon I couldn't keep up with all the orders. It was starting to get crazy.

"At this point, I flew to South China, to Haikou, and took taxis everywhere, trying to contact as many pearl farmers, traders, and companies as I could. Back home I developed a network of Internet sites. Today, just about everything that has *pearl* in a URL address I control. It's like a franchise setup. I teach the vendor about pearls. The vendor designs the Web site however he wants, but he must buy his pearls from me. We have fourteen Web sites; two are in Germany, two in France, one in the U.K., one in Japan, and another in Korea.

"Here's how it works: The vendor builds the Web site for thirteen thousand to sixteen thousand dollars. I want every one of the sites to be successful, and each can't be a carbon copy of my own site, pearlparadise.com. The vendor can have his own company without the risk. It's their own business, but I'm their source for pearls."

As for the power of the Internet and pearls, Shepherd is a believer. "If you understand the product you want to buy, there's no risk. Let's say you want to buy a car and it's gonna cost you twenty-five thousand dollars at a traditional car dealer. But online, you see the same car for five thousand dollars—and you can buy it at that price for no risk. Why would you ever go back to the dealer? You'd be crazy. Right now, just four percent of the U.S. jewelry market is online, but it's growing *every minute*. And it'll continue to grow. Like Amazon— why pay twenty-five dollars for a book in a bookstore when you can get it for seventeen ninety-five online?

"At first, the bricks-and-mortar jewelers dismissed me. They bashed me. 'Who *is* this guy?' they kept saying. That's because they were scared. Jewelers said I didn't have the right to buy from a farm and sell directly to consumers. Too bad. Maybe they should have thought about that before *I* starting doing it. They were lazy and satisfied, sucking off the big cow's teat. Traditional bricks-and-mortar jewelry stores are all part of a system that jacks up the price of jewelry. The product they get is the result of everyone along the line with their hands out, expecting to get paid. But why not go directly to the source, and then sell the product directly to the customer? Doesn't that make more sense? It's the wave of the future—and it freaks out everyone except the customers and the vendors who work for me.

"Sometimes, a guy will bring a pearl strand he bought from me to a jeweler, and the jeweler turns up his nose at the necklace, and says no way are these worth what the guy paid me. In that case, I either refund the money, or we send the pearls to a laboratory for an independent appraisal."

Shepherd stopped momentarily as the ferry struck a large wave broadside, and we rocked in our seats. What he'd said about getting an appraisal at a laboratory brought up a touchy issue. Pearls are worth only what people are willing to pay for them—and that varies hugely. Although the Gemological Institute of America is trying to create mandatory standards, none are currently accepted by the industry. Shepherd has his own appraiser in Idaho, who generally falls in line with his prices, but the fact is, many jewelry technicians don't know pearls very well. The methods to examine pearls are by microscope, ultraviolet light, X-ray, neutron activation, spectroscopy, and cathodoluminescence. Except for the microscope, which doesn't yield much information, the other methods are costly and largely inconclusive when it comes to settling on a price for a pearl appraisal. In addition, since Chinese freshwater pearls (which don't have nuclei and are generated solely from mantle tissue insertions into the mussel) are relatively new, many jewelers are unfamiliar with them.

Shepherd's Web sites are full of information and spirited discussion. They're where the Rana of Fresno first appeared in pearl circles and, according to Shepherd, made a mint, claiming she had natural pearls for sale.

Shepherd backs his pearls with a ninety-day money-back guarantee. He said his return ratio is less than 2 percent, most of which are pearls bought by husbands for their wives who for some reason don't want them, perhaps because the wives want to select them themselves in a more conventional way, such as trying on an assortment at a traditional jewelry store.[1]

The whole enterprise, Shepherd freely confessed, "has made me a very wealthy man." He volunteered that he lives in a $2 million home, drives a Lexus, loves to travel, and "might treat a good client to a thousand dollar bottle of scotch."[2]

V

We arrived in rural Haian on the mainland, where Mr. You's silver Honda Odyssey was waiting for us. We checked into a surprisingly modern hotel, built in the throes of the region's Pearl Rush. In ten minutes, the four of us converged in Shepherd's room to see what had been in his rolling suitcase. Ceremoniously he unzipped the valise and pulled out two large plastic bags of black, gray, and peacock-colored pearls, almost eight thousand of them, which he said he paid $3 apiece for. I couldn't believe my eyes. "These are drops and circle shapes, and after I put them together, I'll be able to sell the best for seven hundred to eight hundred dollars a strand." And the higher-quality pearls, the ones with peacock coloring, he said he'd sell for $3,000 to $3,400 a strand.

Mr. You, Shepherd, Faye, and I, all of us pearl freaks, were swooning over so many pearls. For a moment, I imagined we weren't looking at pearls at all, but cocaine, a comparison bolstered by, among other things, Mr. You's right pinky finger, which had a long, manicured nail, like a dealer of blow.

That night five of us (Mr. You's aide-de-camp tagged along) went for dinner to a kind of restaurant annex located behind a parking lot with dozens of large fish tanks. Mr. You picked out two large fish swimming into each other in a small tank. He passed on a tank of thousands of tiny, crawling scorpions; too bad he said, since scorpions are a prized delicacy in this part of China.

We walked up a back staircase to a private room, outfitted with a large, round table, a brown Naugahyde couch, and a television set turned on very loud. Mr. You's aide-de-camp kept switching between a tape-delay feed of the Detroit Pistons playing the San Antonio Spurs and a Chinese soap opera with singing, crying, and temper tantrums. Faye seemed to mimic the action of the TV soap, alternately sulking, laughing, crying. Sensing her discomfort, Shepherd at one point got up and gave her a back and shoulder massage.

Shepherd and Faye went off somewhere the following morning to discuss business, and at 8:00 a.m. Mr. You picked me up at the hotel. To get to his factory you had to walk up five flights of steep, creaky stairs. At the bottom, I counted thirty-eight pairs of shoes, from baby shoes to men's shoes, belonging to people who lived in the house, as well as to the employed sorters, drillers, chemical technicians, and stringers. The fourth floor was where pearl drilling took place. The nerve center was on the fifth floor, where Mr. You was outfitted with all the transformatron accoutrements of Chinese pearl processing: drying machines, pressure cookers, polishers, air-conditioned fluorescent-lit rooms, cabinets filled with bottles of chemicals and dyes, brown-tinted bottles, beakers, colanders, and heat boxes. Sixteen young women, all dressed in blue smocks, were seated in a windowless room with low-hanging banks of fluorescent tubes over tables covered with white soft fabric. For ten hours a day, the women pored over thousands and thousands of pearls, aggregating them to size, shape, quality, lustre, and orient. They used bamboo tweezers the size of a large grasshopper.

Mr. You dealt exclusively with seawater pearls, which generally are smaller than freshwater pearls and resemble Japanese akoyas. The pearls range mostly from 6 to 9 millimeters. They can spend as much as four months in jars filled with bleach in sealed vaults at a constant 40 degrees Fahrenheit, all the while bathing in fluorescent rays to brighten the batch. After that, the pearls are stabilized in a warm water solution, then sent to the fourth floor for drilling, to be returned for polishing with a wax or cornmeal mixture, then they're sorted and strung.

Mr. You allowed me access to the laboratory rooms, even the transformatron vaults. I noticed dark bottles of sodium silicate, sodium hydrogen carbonate, benzyl alcohol, absolute ethanol. Hundreds of apothecary jars filled with various colors and sizes of pearls sat on glass shelves while high-beam bulbs shined nonstop.

Mr. You and I walked into the sorting room. Absolutely quiet, no one talking. The only sound was the plinking of pearls. I spotted one worker, Huang Jin. She looked terrified when I asked her if she'd mind my asking her questions, but after Mr. You assured her she could take a break without penalty, she sat with me and, through a translator, shared something of her life as a pearl sorter.

Jin was twenty-eight, the youngest of four siblings. A senior sorter and stringer for Mr. You, she had worked ten years for him, and earns a monthly salary of 1,200 RMB ($169). This breaks down to about 83 cents a hour. Workers start out at 550 RMB ($77) a month, then they get a raise every three months of 50 RMB, till eventually they reach a cap of 1,200 RMB. Jin estimates that she strings 120 strands a day, about 2,800 a month. This breaks down to about $1.40 per strand. Shepherd will offer the same strand, depending on size and quality for anywhere from $80 to—if the pearls are large, round, and mostly perfect—$600.

Jin wasn't married, but added with a smile that she has a boyfriend, who is a taxi driver, and she hoped they'd be married soon. She went to school in Xuwen for nine years and, upon finishing, came directly to work for Mr. You. Her parents work on a small farm, growing vegetables. She's never been to Beijing, and the farthest north she's traveled is Guangzhou, Guangdong's capital.

Between phone calls and overseeing sorting and the bleaching pearl vault, I got Mr. You's story. He was thirty-seven, married, with a ten-year-old daughter. Born in Xuwen, after high school, Mr. You studied international trade at a college, then for fifteen years he worked for a state-owned company, arranging import/export deals. All the while he saved, waiting for the opportunity to make a break on his own.

That break came when he met a pearl farmer who allowed Mr. You to invest some 400,000 RMB ($50,000) to become a partner, and eventually to take a controlling interest in the farm. (I was uncertain how Mr. You saved so much money working as a state functionary.) With Shepherd, Mr. You bought another farm, and now has a payroll on both farms of some eighty-five workers. He produces 685 pounds of pearls at both locations annually. Through their partnership, 10 percent of those pearls get exported to Shepherd, which translates to the equivalent of five thousand strands.

By now Shepherd had come back from his meeting with Faye, who had impulsively decided to leave Haikou the following morning. She was back at the hotel, sleeping, which gave Shepherd an opportunity to explain his financial arrangement with Mr. You.

The pair owns a nearby pearl farm called Xuwen Pearl Paradise. Shepherd's initial investment, in May 2006, was $40,000, for which he owns 40 percent of the farm. "For this, I get product, price, and a say. We have a million oysters on the farm, but a capacity of five million," Shepherd noted with some amount of pride.

We were planning on driving out to the farms tomorrow. The Chinese pearl business is built on casual labor, not unlike farms in the United States and elsewhere. Harvesters make 25 RMB a day ($3), and those who do bead insertions into the oyster make slightly more. (Unlike freshwater pearls, seawater pearls come one to an oyster and are the product of bead insertions around which nacre grows.) Pearl nucleators are itinerants, traveling from farm to farm, starting out as apprentices, moving up to skilled technicians making upward of $6 a day.

Meanwhile Faye bopped in, wearing #10 jeans and a V-neck pink-and-white baseball jersey that read:

PRINCESS
ALL AND ON SUNDAY

Shepherd, Mr. You, and Faye had to discuss a business deal, which gave me an opportunity to interview another pearl sorter.

Fan Mi had a long, narrow inquisitive face, framed by thinning straight black hair pulled back into a ponytail. She had long, tapered fingers that looked like those of a piano player.

Mi started three months ago working for Mr. You, and makes 500 RMB ($70) a month, about 35 cents an hour. "I think the job is really challenging," she said, tilting her head to one side. "When I came in here, I knew nothing about pearls. Every pearl was the same size and the same color and the same quality." These didn't seem like throwaway lines.

When I asked Mi what she wanted to be doing in a year (admittedly a yuppie, Western kind of question), she paused and shared two short-term dreams: work for the government and become a salesgirl in a big jewelry store. Her long-term goal was, she said, "to work hard every day, save money, and eventually open up my own jewelry store. I would love to do that!" she said, her eyes widening.

Mi said she was looking forward to going to Beijing for the first time within the next year. She lives with her parents and, because of that, is able to save almost all her salary. In her spare time, like Huang Jin, Mi said she likes to go window-shopping with girlfriends, but also enjoys watching American cartoons on TV. "I love the Copycats. I also like American movies. I loved *Back to the Future* and *Braveheart*." As for music, Mi is a major fan of Madonna. "I adore her," she said, her eyes going dreamy.

Mi has a boyfriend and hopes they'll marry next year. "I want to have one daughter and one son, but not right away. I want us to get settled financially first."

I shook Mi's hand, a Western convention I surely should have abandoned by now. I doubt too many others have grabbed Mi's hand the way I did. She didn't quite know what to do. She took my hand and held it loosely, unclear on the concept. I rescued her and my hand, and said good-bye with a more familiar bow.

I considered Mi's optimistic view of the world and wondered how far she'd go toward achieving her goals. Bai Rufang, the owner of Fanghua, the upscale jewelry store on the fourth floor of the Hongqiao Market, had started out with a similar story and she certainly seemed a commercial success. But, really, what were the chances of a peasant girl like Mi getting even close to realizing any of her dreams, except for marriage, children, and work as a sorter with Mr. You, even if she continued to perform well and got a raise to the equivalent of $169 a month? Compared to Mi, Faye Tian had been born dripping in pearl wealth, which had allowed her to go to the United States, attend college, and return to run the family business. I wasn't sanguine about Fan Mi's future. At her current salary, she'd have to save up for several hundred years to open her own jewelry store.

I was finally getting close to the source of pearls, and that was my intention from the moment I'd started my pearl journey. Shepherd, Faye, Huang Jin, and Fan Mi were perhaps the third or fourth hands that came in contact with pearls as soon as they left the sea. Tomorrow, I'd get closer to the source—the workers who place beads in the oysters, and those who harvest the bounty. That was the idea: To get to the first rung of the pearl ladder. It was a moment I'd been waiting for.

14

To the Source

I

Faye said practically nothing through the whole evening except to complain about the dinner. Her eyes were mascara-coated slits. She and Shepherd sat across from each other, as far apart as possible at the round table. *Getting in Touch with Your Inner Bitch* had not worked its charm. From the way things looked, I doubted any love baby would be forthcoming.

The Olympic trials of women's diving were on the TV, but no one seemed to notice. Mr. You's aide-de-camp flirted with the waitress and for twenty minutes the two went to a backroom. We heard giggling. I was alert to anything crunchy in my mouth.

After dinner, I said good-bye to Faye in the lobby and wished her well.

"I try," she said with a shrug.

II

We got into Mr. You's Odyssey and were on our way. There seems to be a compulsion in rural China that whenever one vehicle passes another, each driver honks wildly. Neither a greeting nor a warning, it appears to be an affirmation that someone in addition to you is behind the wheel of a moving vehicle. We were headed toward Xilian and Xujiacun, tiny towns near or along the western side of the Gulf of Tonkin. Mr. You drove from the main thoroughfare to a red-dusty road that got narrower and narrower, becoming at best a one-lane dirt path. We passed a farmer urging on his oxen-driven cart, then a furrow of piglets slogged by. Presently, we happened on two guys playing a quiet game of mahjong on the side of an overgrown path, and as Mr. You slowed down, the men looked surprised and then waved merrily. We next found ourselves behind an exhaust-spewing mini-truck hauling rough-hewn bricks, which slowed Mr. You. For a moment there was a symphony of bleating horns, a series of two-way signals that communicated to the truck driver that Mr. You wanted to pass. At a wide section of the path, both vehicles sped up in what appeared to be a game of chicken, until Mr. You prevailed, and the mini-truck driver took a trailing position to us. As though to celebrate, Mr. You beeped his horn twice. Ahead of the brick deliveryman, Mr. You eased up on the accelerator, then flipped on a CD of the Eagles singing "Hotel California."

The narrower the makeshift roadway, the faster Mr. You drove. It was a macho thing, trailblazing a jungle in Mr. You's station wagon. Mr. You took a left at an unmarked fork, and soon we found ourselves passing dozens of crudely constructed two-story brick apartments. As we reached a compound of sorts, Mr. You skidded to a halt in a sudden clearing. The Eagles were just finishing up with "The Last Resort." We piled out of the Honda and walked to a sandy field, where scores of large nets lay waiting to be repaired. The smell of shrimp hit me hard. The stench was awful.

We walked down a trail perhaps a hundred yards to a grimy open structure with a beat-in concave aluminum roof attached to two crumbling brick walls. The smell, while no longer of shrimp, was equally putrid, a revolting odor of rotting fish. This is where the oyster shuckers worked. There were as many as a hundred, almost all women, sitting on flattened emptied oyster sacks, low-slung stools, wooden boxes, or on nothing but their haunches. They sat with their legs open like Vs as high as their elbows, doing their work at arms' length, prying open shells between their thighs. There was lots of animated conversation, a multitude of voices with fast, staccato crescendos of a dialect that my translator from Haikou, just two hours away, had a difficult time following.

Shucking oysters was a messy, muddy job, with scores of shucked shells in ever-growing piles among the mud, alongside blue, orange, and pink sacks filled with more oysters to be shucked. The women wore straw hats, jackets or heavy shirts, and jeans. On their feet some had high rubber boots or rubber scuffs. All wore gloves to protect against the oysters' sharp edges. The shucker's job was to separate the meat from the oyster. It wasn't to pick out a pearl, but simply the messy task of opening as many oysters as quickly as possible. Then the meat and embedded pearls were fed into an aged, rusty machine that separated the pearls from the oyster's fleshy innards. The women operating the separation drum weren't allowed to touch the pearls. The pearls fell through rusted strainers to the bottom of the drum, clicking against the drum as it revolved round and round like a mini-Mixmaster. The ping was the sound of money. Every four or five minutes, there were enough pearls on the drum's bottom to stop the machine and empty it out.

That job, at the top of this first rung of the global assembly line, belonged to a middle-aged woman, dressed not in rubber or plastic boots but leather shoes. Her hair was not covered in a peasant's straw hat or baseball cap but by a silk scarf. The woman washed the loose pearls with water from a hose, then picked them out of the drum, placing them in bags to be transported back to Mr. You's processing center. Of the hundred or so female laborers working in the grimy, congested shucking area, she was the only one wearing a strand of pearls.

I knelt down next to one of the shuckers, Li Hung, as she wedged a knife blade into the closed edges of an oyster the size of a child's palm. Li, 45, said she averages an unbelievable 200 oysters an hour, and makes 25 RMB ($3.25) a day, or about 43 cents an hour. Another shucker, Hu Xiao Mei, worked fast, like a one-woman assembly line, not bothering to look up when I sat next to her. She was twenty-five, and sometimes brought with her to work her ten-month-old son, who sat playing across from her with shucked shells. Hu shuffled her job with another at a different oyster plant, where she said she earns 5 RMB more per day.

Next to the shucking area and the separating drum was a room where mother-of-pearl shells were dumped, to be punched out into buttons of all sizes. The drill presses were so old they had to be way pre-Cultural Revolution. The entire twenty-by-sixty-foot drilling room was thoroughly coated with mother-of-pearl dust—on the machines, tables, chairs, walls, floors, ledges, closed windows, and the still fan vanes overhead. The noise from the presses was deafening. No way to ask questions here. The five button-makers, all older women wearing dust-saturated surgical masks, reminded me of coal workers, but instead of bituminous soot covering their faces, thick layers of fine grayish-white oyster shell dust had settled on their clothes, the hollows under their eyes, their cheeks, chins, necks. Errant strands of hair not tucked in and covered by straw hats were caked in the dust. It was as though the women had been sprayed with an aerosol can of silver paint.

All told, Mr. You said, workers at the processing center open as many as 150,000 oysters a day, with a yield of 45,000 pearls, slightly less than one-third of the mollusks yielding pearls. Again, I thought of pearls as cocaine. Mr. You's operation was a cloistered labor camp, where legions of local un-skilled workers toiled to bring to market an inexpensive and abundant organic product, which would be marked up dramatically each step along the way to the final consumer, an affluent buyer on a different continent. Labor in these open-air worksites was as cheap as anywhere in the world. The pearls' produc-tion markup was high, and the end-consumer's price, of course, much, much higher. To safeguard such valuable raw products, armed sentries in primitive bamboo shacks patrolled the labor camp, guarding against poachers, particu-larly at night, when most pirating takes place.

We headed for Xillan, closer to the Gulf of Tonkin, where oysters were embedded with beads by technicians, and then placed in the gulf to mature and grow their pearls. Again, back in Mr. You's Honda, "Hotel California" serenaded us as we bounced down narrow paths cut through overgrown ba-nana trees.

Mr. You pulled up next to two guys, lazing in black-rope hammocks, Xie Hong Wu, 54, and Xie Hong Chong, 60 (no relation, they insisted). It was by now midafternoon, and both men were taking a break. Each made 30 RMB per day, about 50 cents an hour. As the two stretched out, their torsos weigh-ing down the loose rope netting, the hammocks barely cleared the assorted oyster shells scattered under them and everywhere else.

"Our fathers were fishermen from the time we both were little boys," Xie Hong Chong said. "We grew up over there," he said, pointing north. "Our fa-thers fished these waters. So did their fathers, and *their* fathers. For as far back as anyone knows."

Xie Hong Wu said pearl cultivation had taken over fishing as a more eco-nomically viable industry in the village twenty years ago. "We can make a steady income doing this. It's not much, but it's steady. Steady is good. Fishing was what we could catch and nothing more." (It dawned on me that what Xie Hong Wu was saying was the literal English expression "Catch as catch can.")

These guys were the village habitués. For entertainment, they sang folk songs, using oysters shells as a kind of Chinese calypso accompaniment. Xie Hong Chong had practically no teeth, and Xie Hong Wu's mouth was full of crudely fashioned metal and not much else. Mr. You wanted to take in the local color, and as he joked with both men, I could see the marked social class difference between them and Mr. You. The guys lolling in the hammocks were rural country peasants. Mr. You, younger by fifteen years, was modern China, the entrepreneurial bossman in tailored suit (but no tie). As Mr. You approached, Xie Hong Chong and Xie Hong Wu in unison swiveled their legs to the ground, got out of the hammocks, slowly straightened their backs upright, and then solemnly bowed to greet Mr. You. An awkward moment as much for Mr. You as for Xie Hong Chong and Xie Hong Wu. The rank-and-file were being called on to meet the plantation owner. The occasion was akin to a general palling around with two noncom soldiers for the amusement of an observer.

We left the Xies and walked to dozens of shacks built on bamboo stilts at the water's edge. This is where the pearl technicians worked. With the sun beating down, billowing striped cotton sheets had been stretched over the open rooftops to shield the workers from bright, reflective rays. Technicians were seeding oysters; in a little more than a year's time, they'd be harvesting pearls from the same oysters. For the seeding process, the technicians affixed each oyster to a small, tilted wooden board. Then the technician pried open the oyster about a half an inch with a wooden wedge. With two metal instruments (that resembled what a 1950s dentist might use), the technicians slid inside the oyster's gonad a tiny round bead, followed by a small, cut square of oyster mantle tissue. The process took less than a minute, and most workers were able to embed as many as a hundred oysters per hour. The oysters were placed in nets and left in cement tubs of saltwater to recuperate from the surgery.

The technicians, almost all girls and women in their late teens or early twenties, worked side by side, ten or twelve to each hut hugging the perimeter of the water. They were casually dressed in T-shirts and jackets, wearing elastic coverings over their sleeves, their hair in ponytails. The job was an open-air assembly line; workers traded gossip, conversation, jokes as they opened an oyster, poked and probed inside, inserted bead and tissue, then moved on to the next.

Xioa Ling, 20, has worked inserting beads in oysters and harvesting pearls since she was sixteen. She left primary school in the sixth grade. The job, she readily admitted, is boring. Once you get the hang of it, it's routine, she said, never once taking her eyes off the pried-open oyster in front of her. "I make myself like it," she said in between insertions. "What else really is there? This gives me something to do."

I asked Ling whether she had any idea where the pearls she was helping to create would eventually end up. Did Ling have any concept, any notion of who the end customer of her labor might be? Did she ever imagine where that woman might live or for what special occasion she might wear the pearls Ling helped create? A crazy thought flashed before me: The pearls Ling had coaxed into existence perhaps might one day be shown on TV, worn by the elegant wife of a politician, standing next to her husband, who was making a confession about an extramarital affair. Or they'd be worn by a woman in Paris about to board a plane to join her husband in Geneva for a weekend of museum-going, ballet, and elegant dinners. Or maybe they'd be worn by a bride walking down the aisle, arm in arm with her father, in a church in Philadelphia.

"Do you ever think the pearls from these oysters may eventually be worn by a woman in another country?" I asked. The question was absurd and I knew it.

Ling volunteered that she had never left the village three miles from the hut in which she was working. She was born in that village, and, although she never thought too much about it, that's where she'd likely die. Ling had never been on the ferry I'd taken with Shepherd, Mr. You, and Faye three days earlier. She'd never visited Haikou, the capital of Hainan Province, ninety minutes away.

"Would you like to go to Haikou?" I asked.

"I think so, but I'd be scared. Many thieves there."

That there was a world outside Ling's village was a concept she accepted, but one about which she seemed to understand little. The idea that towns, cities, countries outside China might exist was an abstraction. The notion of a pearl that Ling helped create being worn by a woman in the United States, France, or Switzerland was a concept fantastic to consider. These fresh, radiant pearls that came from the skill of Ling were widgets. A way to pass the time, to work alongside her girlfriends, and, in the process, earn the prevailing wage of 38 cents an hour.

Ling looked up briefly between insertions, the skinny long toes of her bare feet curled around an orange plastic tub filled with discarded oyster shells beneath her. For a moment, I could see she was speculating on where the pearls might someday end up, but then she shook her head and giggled. What happens to the pearls was irrelevant to Ling's life. She said she never for a moment had thought about it. "I don't know anything about what happens to them," she said, pausing for a few seconds and reflecting. "I'm not sure when or where they're processed. I just know what is here and now and what I do with the pearls in this hut. This is my job."

One of Ling's co-workers two stations down, Xie Xian Hua, 25, piped up. "I know the pearls go to Hong Kong, but after that I'm not so sure. Maybe they come back to Haikou. But I don't know."

What about the final price? Did anyone have any idea how much a finished pearl strand could and does sell for?

The six girls in a row shook their heads.

Ling seemed the most pensive. I knew I was pushing. Her friends were starting to laugh in a good-natured kind of way, but my presence was calling attention to her.

"Do you have any dreams?"

Another silly question—a cultural construct asked by someone from a far-off land. I wasn't sure whether the translator would even be able to convey the meaning of the word *dreams*, at least in the way I had intended it. I was afraid *dreams* would come out literarlly, as in "do you dream at night?" What I meant, of course, was, "Do you have hopes or aspirations?"

Ling looked at me, then shifted her eyes right and left to gauge her friends and their reaction to her, to me, to what she'd already said and what she was about to say. She put down one of the metal instruments, touched her right temple for a second or two with her hand. Then she flipped her ponytail from in front of her left shoulder to behind it.

"I don't have a boyfriend yet, and I'm not really thinking about a family. All I want to do is do my job. It's my dream to do this job. It's what I want to do for the rest of my life."

The exchange piqued my curiosity about whether Mr. You or Shepherd had any thoughts about what these first-line global assembly workers had told me. It is the workers' labor that creates the product that both men sell all over the world, via the Internet, for huge profits these workers could hardly register. On our way back to Haian, I asked.

Mr. You was in businessman's mode and responded as such. "I have many workers at the farms and in the office. Very big payroll, sometimes, I think, too big. But as I get more and more successful, I hope to add more. The more I add, the more I help the local economy. I make money, they make money. We produce a good product together. We sell it globally. This is good, no?"

I suppose it was—building a community of workers that a generation ago did not exist. Their labor created a product that consumers around the world were willing to pay handsomely for and would cherish.

No stranger to what I was driving at, Shepherd, though, wouldn't take the bait. "It's the capitalist system," he said as we made our way back to town. "The way I look at it, these people have jobs we've created. Having a job isn't an entitlement. They're earning what the going wage is. We wouldn't pay them any more. What we do with the product they're paid to produce is our business. That's the way it works."

15

Karaoke-Krazy

Mr. You wanted to do it. Shepherd couldn't have cared less. Mr. You's aide-de-camp would have followed Mr. You to the end of the world. I certainly didn't want to sit in my room back at the hotel and watch Chinese TV or go out for another pick-your-own dinner. Faye had left in a huff. What was left for four guys to do in rural China?

Earlier in the day, Mr. You had suggested that we all go to a cockfight, but I put the kibosh on that idea. So when Mr. You boomed, "Let's go to karaoke!" I hardly was in a position to say no. Four dudes on the prowl, reading lyrics off a monitor, and singing Chinese and American songs at the top of their lungs couldn't be all that bad.

Over the last two days, when we had driven through Xuwen, I noticed more than a dozen karaoke bars, places with names like Polygra, Beauty Palace, Monarch, and Moonlight City. The Chinese call karaoke KTV, at least in Xuwen they did, and it seemed the village's residents were karaoke-krazy. I needed a respite from all the pearl talk. It was time to cut out.

A karaoke aficionado, Mr. You's favorite KTV bar was on a side street in Xuwen. As we got out of Mr. You's car, the parking attendant shook our hands as though we were long-lost friends, then merrily waved us toward a two-story building. The four of us walked up a very dark staircase. On each step, my shoes stuck to some kind of goo, which I later determined was layer upon layer of dried beer. We got to a darker second floor, illuminated by a series of naked red light bulbs.

There, we were greeted by a stubby bossman, wearing a black ribbed T-shirt and shiny nylon black pants. Like the parking lot attendant, the boss-man vigorously shook our hands, and when he was through, he patted each of us on the back, for what I wasn't sure. I didn't know where this was going, but I had suspicions. I was with three guys in what by all appearances resembled a filthy whorehouse.

The bossman introduced us to a large madam-like woman with a robust laugh, teetering on high-heeled mules with fake ostrich feathers on the front, who escorted us into a windowless room filled with girls in their late teens. Some were watching TV, others played cards. A group in the corner was talk-ing in an animated fashion, gossiping in what sounded like a Chinese version of Valley Girl talk. But the room was so dark and smoky, and with just those red lights illuminating the grunge, I couldn't get much of a glimpse of much of anything.

"Hey, what *is* this?" I whispered to Shepherd, who responded with a smile. "You'll see."

Shepherd said he had to take a pee, and just as he was about to leave, he whispered to me, "I hate this part. Pick one out for me."

Meanwhile, Mr. You and his aide-de-camp were all smiles as the madam barked something out, which resulted in the girls quickly forming a line. They looked and acted like teenagers, which was what they were. Some of the girls were dressed in shorts and tank tops, others in jeans and T-shirts.

"Which one you want?" Mr. You asked me.

I was in one of those moral quandaries, and Shepherd had already bested me by opting out. I shrugged my shoulders, indicating to Mr. You that I was abdicating all choices to him. In the smoky haze, Mr. You seemed to give me an understanding cross-cultural nod.

Mr. You picked three girls for us, with Mr You's aide-de-camp choosing his own. The eight of us rather awkwardly proceeded to a private room with two Naugahyde La-Z-Boy couches, a broken-down coffee table, and a televi-sion setup of two screens and a remote-control clicker. A crooked sign hung over the doorway: VIP Lounge.

Almost immediately, even before we sat down, Mr. You started singing with amazing gusto. Mr. You was deeply serious about his basso profundo. The bossman came in, smiled in a knowing way, set down a tray of twenty-four cans of beer and eight shot glasses, and we were all soon crooning at the top of our lungs.

Mr. You belted out song after song into a tinny microphone, and Mr. You's aide-de-camp tried without success to neck with his karaoke partner, a very petite girl in shorts and a skimpy halter top, as we played a Chinese game of dice in a tumbler that you slam down on the table, not unlike Yahtzee.

It was too loud to talk, much less engage in the most minimal of conversation, so to keep things going, I took a turn with "Hey Jude" followed by "Somewhere Over the Rainbow." When I finished, I wanted to find out the girls' names, probe their lives, the usual journalistic drill, but then I realized: This was their *job*—to sit and sing with middle-aged guys getting drunk. To ask their names would have been like asking a cocktail waitress in a bowling alley hers. It'd be an insult. Be civilized. Play by the rules. I retreated.

The girls took small sips of their beers each time they lost in the dice game. Each time Mr. You or his aide-de-camp lost, the girls promptly filled our glasses with more beer.

We continued like this, song after song, until we had gone through all two dozen cans. There really wasn't much untoward behavior, not counting the aide-de-camp's rather pathetic attempts at affection, just everyone blowing out his or her lungs. I'm quite sure the whole evening was just another dreary night of business for these karaoke workers. I never found out their stories or their names. They certainly weren't wearing pearls, and probably never would. Some of them might have been sex workers, given the right confluence of opportunity or desperation. Surely when you mix large quantities of alcohol, men with money, and rooms full of underage girls, there is a gross lopsided power tilt.

By one in the morning, it was time to leave. We smiled and thanked the girls, who smiled back on cue. We stumbled down the sticky stairs into Mr. You's Odyssey.

Shepherd left, hung over, the next morning; more business deals in Hong Kong. I had one more day in Xuwen. After interviewing more of Mr. You's employees at his processing plant, we faced a similar dilemma: What to do in the evening? One night at the karaoke bar had been enough, cockfighting was out, and when I suggested to Mr. You the possibility of foot massages, he lit up. I'd had two foot massages so far on my travels, one in Hong Kong and another in Beijing, and both had been out-of-body experiences. "I know just the place," Mr. You said.

Mr. You and I made our way to an even raunchier place than the KTV bar. We walked through a hair salon, up the stairs to a grimy massage area, where side-by-side Mr. You and I sat in malodorous recliners covered with plastic slipcovers, while masseurs worked on our feet. All the while, we watched women's synchronized swimming from Sydney on television. My masseur had something up his sleeve. He did something I'd never experienced before—an ambidextrous massage. He worked on both my feet simultaneously. Perhaps this was a convention particular to Xuwen, although when I stole a peak at Mr. You's masseur, he was following the more traditional two-hands, one-foot approach.

Early the next morning, I went back to Mr. You's plant and picked out one hundred loose pearls for two seawater necklaces I wanted to buy Iris. Mr. You quoted me a price of $100 for each strand. After all we'd been through, he was highballing me, but business was business, I suppose. I probably could have gotten each for $50 (or less), but I didn't bargain. Shame on me, I know, but they were more souvenirs of my stay in Xuwen than anything else. Both sets were unusual baroques, one silvery, the other an assortment of off-whites.

I had a special request: I wanted each strand strung by Fan Mi, the girl whose dream had been to open up a jewelry store. She smiled when I asked her to string and knot them, and when she presented me both necklaces, we each bowed and said good-bye.

I needed to catch the ferry back to Hainan to catch a plane to Manila that afternoon. I was about to embark on another pearl journey, this time to a distant pearl farm on a small island off the island of Palawan in the southern Philippines. Mr. You drove me to the pier, again with "Hotel California" rocking the car. As I boarded the ferry, I could hear the Eagles' lyrics as Mr. You stood in the car's doorway, one foot on the ground, waving good-bye.

From Xuwen I made my way from the Chinese mainland on the ferry's bottom deck, where a salesman for ninety minutes tried without success to hawk indestructible black socks and laminated maps of China to an impassive crowd. From Haikow, Hainan, I was to fly to Hong Kong, then to Manila, where I was to take a four-hour helicopter trip into the Philippine jungle.

16

A Dog in My Crotch

I

The Philippines is synonymous with Imelda Marcos's shoes, nonstop political tumult, and pearls. In the annals of pearl history, Palawan, a long, narrow island in the southern Philippines, is legendary: On May 7, 1934, a Muslim diver, swimming off Brooke's Point, found what he called the Pearl of Allah, the world's largest pearl—9.4 inches long, 14 pounds, and valued at $40 million.[1] Palawan is still considered one of the world's primo pearl regions, so when I got an opportunity to spend a week on the island of Bugsuk, off the southern tip of Palawan, not far from where the Pearl of Allah was found, I couldn't wait to pack my bag.

Bugsuk Island is where the oldest pearl farm of Jacques Branellec and Manuel Cojuangco's company, Jewelmer, is located. Jewelmer, which employs nine hundred workers, is celebrated in the pearl world as producing a rarity among rare South Sea pearls—naturally gold-colored pearls. The pearls come from the *Pinctada maxima* oyster, which at harvest time can grow as large as a man's outstretched hand. The outer lip of the *Pinctada maxima* in the Philippines and Indonesia is gold-colored, which matches the color of the amazing pearls the prized oysters produce. Jewelmer owns six farms on Palawan and Busuanga, all extreme, remote outposts pretty much accessible only by helicopter or sea-plane. The company, started in 1979, is a partnership between Branellec and Cojuangco, a scion of one of the wealthiest families in the Philippines. The Co-juangcos are a national lightning rod of controversy. Depending on whom you talk to, they're either Philippine saviors or villains rivaled by Ferdinand and Imelda Marcos, with whom the Cojuangco family were business associates.

The invitation to visit Jewelmer's holdings put me in a quandary. Just as I had done with the CP&J suits, I demanded from Jewelmer's co-owner Branellec that there'd be no strings attached to my visit, that I'd have unfettered access to everything and everyone. Branellec assured me that I'd be free to roam as I pleased, that I'd able to talk to anyone. There are a handful of smaller pearl farms in the Philippines not owned by Jewelmer, but they are not key players on the international pearl scene, and as such, Branellec and Cojuangco reigned as the indisputable kingpins of Philippine pearl cultivators.

"You have a call from Sir Branellec," the hotel operator informed me, just as I finished unpacking my suitcase near Manila's traffic-snarled Makati Center. I didn't know if it was Philippines custom to call every man over a certain age "Sir," like Mr. in the United States, or whether in fact Branellec was an actual Sir. Did they even have knighted sirs in the Philippines? The operator seemed to recognize the name Branellec, and uttered it with the utmost of reverence.

"I trust your trip was good," Branellec said, and when I answered in the affirmative, he said he'd pick me up at 6:30 that evening. "This will be very informal," he said. "Drinks and dinner."

II

But first things first. My trip from Haikou, China, had not been good. The flight had been fine; it was my arrival that set off alarms. As soon as we landed at Ninoy Aquino International Airport, I was ensnarled in the highest level of security protocol I'd ever experienced. If the U.S. Department of Homeland Se-curity has five stages of warnings, from who-cares green to screaming, take-cover red, the Manila airport was nuclear crimson. Japan, Hong Kong, and China had their equivalents of airport-screening guards, but they were hang-loose guys who went about their sinecures with a shrugged-shoulder, what-the-hell irreverence. They seemed to be in on the same joke, that airport security was a waste of time and money, but it provided them with jobs, so they had to do *something.* Passengers weren't required to take off their shoes when going through metal-detector gates. Passengers who forgot to remove coins from their pockets were politely admonished and sent on their way with a forgiving nod. None of that silly three-ounce liquid or gel rule. All this changed when I arrived in Manila.

On the ferry ride back to Hainan, I started running a fever. Perhaps it had to do with the ambidextrous foot masseur, the grime of the massage parlor, or the general carousing at the KTV bar. By midday I had the chills, and six cups of chamomile tea had done nothing except greatly increase the necessity to pee. By the time I landed in Manila, my face was the color of watermelon flesh. Rivulets of sweat oozed from each and every one of my heaving pores.

As I joined the beleaguered, wrinkled masses of travelers queued up before Philippines customs, a small, compact man wearing an untucked plaid shirt and khaki pants tapped me on the shoulder. I assumed he was hustling me for something.

"Sir, you must come with me," he pronounced.

Countless situations had taught me never to yield ground when confronted with such requests. "Sir, you must come with me. *Now,*" he insisted.

"I'm not going anywhere with you or anyone else."

"Sir, I can force you to come with me."

The dude was grating on my nerves. "Leave me alone," I said as quietly as I could.

My response proved to be unfortunate.

Within a split second, the man jumped to a spread-eagle commando position, and aimed at my head a gun with a long clear tube attached to it. He held the gun with both hands. Actually, the gun looked more like a device that fires Ping-Pong balls or marshmallows. Whatever he was holding, the guy's sudden action got my attention (and made for a wide berth of the other incoming passengers).

"Sir, you have a temperature," the man said, motioning with his chin downward to an official I.D. hanging from his neck.

Wielding the Ping-Pong marshmellow gun like it was a .357 Magnum, the enforcer said: "I will not let you proceed. I will call the police and they will arrest you. Let us make this easier. Let us not make a scene."

I surmised the enforcer's gun, pointed at my forehead, scanned body temperature and I was in the danger zone. The enforcer grabbed my arm and steered me to a cramped, stuffy, windowless room for interrogation.

Perhaps the enforcer figured I had AIDS, avian flu, tuberculosis, a relapse of SARS. Maybe I was a stealth carrier of the Human Virus Bomb, about to unleash a deadly strain on Manila's eleven million residents.

My confinement would mean dealing with the U.S. Embassy—never a pleasant prospect, especially in these times. And it was Saturday night. Until I got someone's attention (and until my temperature dropped), it could mean a lock-down government hospital stay. I had visions of hacking, malaria-infected patients—or, worse, the obese guard in *Midnight Express*.

The enforcer gruffly pointed to a couch and informed me I was running a 39.1-degree temperature. I tried to compute what that was in Fahrenheit. But the fever, not to mention my limited math skills, had turned my mind into mush.

"Were you drinking alcohol?" the enforcer asked in an accusing tone I did not like.

Ordinarily whenever anyone (a cop, my boss, my wife) asks that question, my response is to deny any and all consumption. But this time might be an exception. Maybe it would explain my red-light face.

"I did have a couple of drinks," I stammered, hoping for the best.

"But that would not explain your temperature!" the enforcer exploded. He had set a trap for me, and I had been stupid to buzz right in and be swatted. "You have a fever and I have the right to send you back!"

"What was your port of debarkation?" he asked in a loud and annoyed manner, pacing back and forth.

The enforcer's question posed a series of delicate issues. If I said Hainan, the gateway to vast rural South China, that might translate to all kinds of trouble (meningitis, hepatitis, tuberculosis, the World Health Organization fold-out chart of infectious diseases). If I left it at Hong Kong, where I had transferred planes, that would be safer, but upon further checking, the enforcer would eventually realize that I'd concealed my real point of departure.

I decided to play the professor card.

I reached (very slowly) into my briefcase and obsequiously handed the enforcer, with both hands Japanese-style, my business card. I bowed my head as reverentially as my fever allowed, and peered up with the whites of my eyes.

The enforcer snatched the card from my hands. He examined it for several seconds, glanced toward me, then down at the card again. He turned the card over and, for some reason, examined the back side, holding it up against the ceiling light bulb. He said nothing. The only sound was the muffled voices of incoming passengers jostling to get through customs.

The enforcer stared at me for a full ten seconds. Was he waiting for a bribe?

"Ah, professor," he finally said. The once-snarling enforcer suddenly had turned into a pussycat. Just my business card (sans a wad of bills) had taken care of my global temperature. The enforcer appeared to be an honest albeit impressionable bureaucrat.

He smiled and suggested that I might want to see a doctor in the next several days. No hurry, but something I might want to do. If I could take time out of my busy schedule.

In the meantime, he produced a little green pill and a paper cup of water. "Take this," he offered.

No way was I going to fall for that one, and when I hesitated the enforcer assured me the pill would make me feel better, "like aspirin," he smiled.

"Take it," he commanded.

I swallowed a gulp of water and popped the pill, carefully lodging it under my tongue, then between my teeth and gums.

The enforcer led me to the head of the customs queue, where an agent stamped my passport and motioned me to proceed. I waved to the enforcer and he waved back. Around the corner, out of his sight, I spit the pill into a potted plant near the baggage carousel.

The enforcer, the temperature gun, and the interrogation room underscored the exaggerated, often nonsensical security I was to experience during my stay in the Philippines. An hour later, when the taxi turned into the driveway to my hotel, a guard with a mirror at the end of a broomstick checked the undercarriage of the cab for bombs. Another guard searched my suitcase, even feeling for a false bottom. No building seemed immune to patrolling armed guards. At every entrance to Manila's profligate shopping malls, guards with semiautomatic rifles monitored all who entered. I have no doubt that these rent-a-cops were ill-equipped to handle a shoplifter, let alone a terrorist, but their presence was a reminder of a nation the government wanted everyone to think was under siege. National elections were in a month, scores of dissidents had been jailed, and an insurgency was flourishing (or so the newspapers warned), with Muslim rebels seizing control of several island outposts in the south of the country. Political kidnappings were common for good reason: Anyone who could afford the ransom paid it since the municipal and federal police, as well as some in the judicial system, were suspected to be corrupt. Payoff money was used by rebels to buy more weapons. All this was the reason Branellec had told me in our communications that he'd guarantee my safety as long as I promised not to travel solo. It seemed the rebels, many with alleged links to al Qaeda, had embedded themselves in the overgrown jungles in southern Palawan, not far from where I was headed.

III

Branellec picked me up at my hotel, and as we inched through Manila traffic to a gated enclave known as Forbes Park, I began to get my first glimpse at the charmed life Bo Torrey and other pearl afficionados had told me that Branellec leads.

"First, to explain things," Branellec said in precise English, with a clipped French accent, abruptly dismissing me in midsentence. "My girlfriend is quite young. She will be joining us for dinner, and she has brought a friend. I don't want you to get either of them confused with my daughter, who is sixteen."

Branellec slid his car into a U of a driveway, and as we walked into his house, I noticed golden shafts of light coming from oyster-shell chandeliers. In the foyer were a concert grand piano, a collection of antique saxophones, and an upright double bass, all surrounding a squiggly bladder-shaped Japanese sand-tranquillity garden built into the floor. *Deux Tahitiennes*, the Gauguin print of two bare-breasted Tahitian women, one holding a tray of red fruit a couple of millimeters from her nipples, hung on the wall.

Branellec introduced me to Chloe, the live-in girlfriend (who actually was closer to twenty-five), to Celeste, who turned out to be Chloe's high school friend, and to his daughter, who studies modern dance, and was wearing a very short dress, and had just gotten out of the shower.

Branellec is a self-confessed cell phone freak, and almost immediately as we sat down for a round of Cokes and Johnny Walker Black Label, his cell phone went off. The ring was a synthesized voice that announced, "Master, you have a call! Master, you have a call!" Chloe giggled, boasting that the ringtone had been her choice. "It's perfect for him, don't you think?"

Chloe and Branellec met when Branellec was brushing up on his piano-playing skills and hired Chloe as a tutor. "I could hardly concentrate on the keys. I kept looking at you. I couldn't take my eyes off of you," Branellec purred to Chloe, who fluttered while Branellec's dog, a miniature Doberman, busily burrowed her head into Chloe's crotch.

Which may or may not have been the reason that Branellec at that moment segued into a story about a jealous pet monkey by the name of Desdemona at one of his pearl farms. Desdemona survived a cerebral hemorrhage after a worker somehow mistook her head for a coconut and sliced it open. She was expertly sewed up by the farm's cook, a sybaritic expatriate Italian who subsequently disappeared to Australia. Desdemona lived a full and complete life after the mishap, Branellec explained, although she had occasional dizzy spells.

Such was my introduction to Jacques Branellec's vaunted world of pearls, girls, sunken treasure, and deserted isles.

Branellec's company, Jewelmer, is among the five largest pearl producers and exporters in the world. Branellec is a commercial pilot and often takes the helm of the two French-made helicopters he and Cojuangco own. The company the pair owns has become a model in the pearl industry for efficiency and technological expertise. Each of their farms is a veritable nature preserve. Branellec is an outspoken environmental activist and so are his employees. Through Jewelmer, the pair owns Flower Island, which has been transformed into a lush environmental resort, where Branellec and Cojuangco own hillside homes, and where they wine and dine clients and intimates. When he's not presiding over the Manila headquarters or his pearl preserves, Branellec flies around the world. A jazz aficionado, Branellec started the Manila Jazz Festival in 2002, in part to advance Jewelmer's brand, but also because he genuinely loves jazz. In 1993, one of Branellec's employees was diving off Pandanan Island, south of Palawan, and snorkeled onto a fifteenth-century junk, which ultimately was excavated in a joint partnership between Jewelmer and the National Museum of the Philippines, yielding five thousand artifacts. Branellec himself dove and brought up much of the ship's bounty. The find remains the most important precolonial maritime discovery in Philippine history.

No wonder almost everyone calls Branellec "Sir," except his senior advisors, who refer to him as Mr. B, or JB. Bald and bespectacled, barking orders, Branellec is a micromanager, hovering over everything and everyone in his purview. "You're always on tiptoes when you work for him," one of his oldest friends told me. "A gun in his hands would be very dangerous."

Branellec's reputation is something of an aging Lothario, and several pearlers warned me, chuckling, not to be surprised by his lifestyle. At the house this night, Branellec was auditioning three cooks vying for a single position, and each was more beautiful than the other. Petite with wavy, thick black hair, wearing uniforms of white miniskirts, black T-shirts, and flip-flops, the women were nervous and showed it, which seemed to please Branellec. It could have been a reality TV show, with Branellec serving as judge and jury. After dinner,

Chloe delighted Branellec when she played a piece by Chopin and another by Gershwin, her hands flying across the keyboard.

"Bravo, bravo!" Branellec shouted, clapping wildly. Chloe got up and did a victory stroll around the serenity garden, lithely springing from leg to leg.

I wasn't quite sure what to make of Branellec. He had an imperial and prickly streak, perhaps the French in him coming out in force. He seemed to bristle at the slightest imperfection. (Perhaps that's why Chloe seemed so glad when she'd finished.) He also had a ribald sense of humor. Just about everything he said had sexual undertones.

Branellec told Celeste she most certainly could stay at the house, but only "if you are frisky at night." The comment was so outrageous that the only thing Chloe, Celeste, and I could do was laugh.

"What's wrong?" Branellec said, feigning surprise. "Celeste looks like she might be frisky. Being frisky these days is considered *bad*?"

Meanwhile, Branellec's miniature Doberman jumped up on the couch, now burrowing her head into my crotch. "She likes you," Branellec suggested. "Maybe you can sleep with her, and I'll sleep with Chloe and Celeste."

Branellec this night, was wearing a tight orange T-shirt, tapered green pants, and nouveau running shoes. He reminded me of an aging Henry Miller, a comparison Branellec no doubt would enjoy. There's a famous Bradley Smith photograph of Miller in his eighties, dressed in trousers, shirt, ascot, and leather vest, playing Ping-Pong with a beautiful buxom blonde who is completely nude. This was perfect Branellec.

Neither Chloe nor Celeste seemed really taken aback by Branellec's bawdy humor. They certainly could have been indulging him because of his over-the-top wealth and influence. You never knew when Branellec might toss your way a $10,000 pearl or two. And if you were good, maybe it'd be a whole strand. The capricious exercise of power has always been an aphrodisiac, and Branellec wielded it like a club strapped to his loins.

Branellec seemed to call the shots for Jewelmer. I later got the impression that Cojuangco was there to serve as a silent partner, the local fixer whose pedigree served to deflect blowback should politicians raise the issue of what a Frenchman was doing running a Filipino company, exploiting the nation's most prized national resource—pearls. If anyone had the chops to start up and operate one of the most evolved pearl farming, processing, wholesaling, and retail operations in the world, it seemed it would be Branellec.

17

On JB's Farm

Sitting at the dual controls of his red Aerospecial chopper, wearing a French Foreign Legion-type hat and a white pilot's shirt with gold stripes on its shoulders, Jacques Branellec whirled off into the air. The Philippines is a series of archipelagoes, with more than seven thousand islands, only a fifth of them inhabited. The nation is at the apex of the so-called Coral Triangle (Indonesia and Malaysia are at the other two vertices), which marine biologists say contains the richest array of underwater animals and plants in the world. As the chopper prepared to set down on the tiny island of Bugsuk, the clean blue water began to ripple. I noticed hundreds of cylindrical buoys marking the location of thousands of meters of lines from which baskets of maturing oysters were suspended. The bobbing buoys, spaced evenly and geometrically, formed fertile aquafields, not too different from rich, fecund cornfields. These floating markers, lined up in perfect, straight lines, reminded me of row after row of cornstalks I'd grown to love in the fertile

Iowa soil. As our helicopter dipped lower, I could see as deep as forty feet in the translucent water. Fish swam everywhere.

We hovered over a small colony of well-tended huts with corrugated roof-tops, and proceeded to touch ground precisely on the white crosshairs of a landing pad as a welcoming committee gathered, their blouses, shirts, pants, dresses filling up with air, billowing.

The clatter of the chopper's blades signaled to everyone on land to drop whatever he or she was doing and race to greet us. "Daddy's Home" could have been playing on the pearl farm's loudspeakers. Branellec stepped down from the chopper and traded his Legionnaire hat for one that read JB, as he strode toward the farm's control facility. Nymphs might well have fluttered rose petals on the path before Branellec's purposeful stride. Camou-clad guards very well could have fired their M-16s in the air to welcome our trailing entourage.

Ultimately, I visited five of the farms Branellec and Manuel Cojuangco own. Branellec had to take care of some unspecified business, so I was able to explore the island outside his purview, which was something of a relief. I interviewed more than sixty employees. I lived among scores of workers at the 20,000-hectare nature preserve that surrounds the pearl farm on Bugsuk Island. Branellec's hands-on, meticulous expertise had translated to the production of more than a million pearls a year, almost all of them the color of golden honey. The island is almost completely self-sustaining, with practically all food raised or produced on Bugsuk. What Branellec and Cojuangco have succeeded in accomplishing is to create nature-friendly outposts, hiring Filipinos seemingly convinced they're among the vanguard in maintaining environmental-safe havens, the last bulwark against polluters despoiling some of the world's most pristine frontiers. Both men pride themselves on conducting the final interview of each job applicant, regardless of rank or position. Many of the workers I met reminded me of back-to-earth environmentalists I knew from four decades earlier, who had chosen to live in places like Mendocino or Santa Cruz to work on organic farms.

Pearl-farm jobs require hefty employee commitment without huge remuneration, and many Jewelmer employees had left their children with parents or spouses back in Manila or Cebu, the oldest and one of the most developed provinces. Only one of Branellec's farms has a school, in Bugsuk, and that school's curriculum is based on an American program called Accelerated Christian Education. The religion-heavy leanings are a nod to Cojuangco, a born-again Christian bachelor. Every six months, employees get a fifteen-day paid vacation, with the company footing the bill for transportation to and from the worker's home. Accommodations are included in most workers' salaries, but meals are deducted from their paychecks (although this varies, depending on the employee's classification). Many workers start at Philippines' minimum wage—about $2.75 a day—a pittance considering that a *single* Jewelmer pearl can fetch as much as $10,000 in a retail store. One question I asked dozens of employees was whether they or anyone in their family had ever owned pearls, and despite the nation's motto (Pearl of the Orient), no one answered yes.

Each farm compound is under twenty-four-hour armed guard watch. Whenever anyone arrives, whether by chopper, boat, pickup, jeep, or foot, guards toting semiautomatic rifles greet the visitor. Guards also keep watch on sentry posts far from the shore, in the water. Communist rebels with alleged al Qaeda links are congregated in the inacessible mountainous jungles on the Zamboanga Peninsula on the island of Mindanao, but many rebel groups have evacuated that region in response to an increased presence of government troops and U.S. military advisors stationed there. The rebels have responded by hopscotching to islands in northern Malaysia and the southern Philippines, moving closer and closer to the inaccessible forests of Palawan. Bugsuk Island is located across the Sulu Sea, some two hundred miles northwest of Zamboanga, a prime destination for guerrillas. Entry to the pearl farms is through a series of gates, separated by one hundred meters, which form a sort of contained DMZ should intruders breach the first barrier.

None of the farms has thus far been compromised, although political protests and outside agitation are not uncommon. One of Jewelmer's tactical officers is biologist Melinda Zinampan-de Luna, who started with Branellec in 1994. She oversees the touchy business of negotiating with politicians and government regulators, as well as overseeing much of the science that underscores how Jewelmer's pearl farming affects local habitats. Talking to me over breakfast, Mel, as her colleagues call her, said she had originally wanted to become a physician, but that when she got to college, she shifted her interests to the sea. As a child, she had heard phantasmagoric seafaring yarns from her grandfather, who worked as a fisherman, and every night, she'd have recurring dreams. "They were scenes of total and complete serenity. There were always lots and lots of fish, and I was among them, in the middle of all this rich marine life. The dreams took over me."

The most serious environmental issues facing her these days is what quick-profit freelance entrepreneurs are doing illegally around Palawan Island. Branellec and his team of biologists have reason to worry that the pollution created by the region's runaway fires will undermine the water and air quality that provide the environment necessary to produce Jewelmer's prized pearls. While flying from Manila to the southern tip of Palawan in Branellec's helicopter, we passed over more than forty separate forest fires. Towering plumes of putrid black smoke filled the air; soot particles floated upward in the clear blue sky, and below, fires raged on the slopes of some of the most lush, verdant mountainsides I'd ever seen. I took out a handkerchief to cover my nose from the acrid stench. These were illegal fires set by enterprising loggers, who slash and burn tens of thousands of hectares of forests, hauling away truckloads of timber to sell to the highest bidder. Besides destroying indigenous tree species, the fires lead to the elimination of animal species extant only in this region of the world. As we continued flying south, I saw huge swaths of naked, deforested land. The *Washington Post* in 2007 investigated similar slash-and-burn fires in other parts of Asia, and reported that timber illegally procured in central China eventually ended up in retail stores such as Ikea, Home Depot, and Lowe's as furniture and floorboards.[1] In the Philippines, forest poachers are particularly interested in mangroves for both lumber and bark (which holds ingredients for native coconut wine, as well as dyes for tanning). Mangroves prevent erosion; their elimination has speeded the destabilization of fresh- and seawater inlets. Mangrove forests in the Philippines are home to scores of species of fish, crustaceans, and gastropods. They serve as a sort of delivery and incubation room before newborn marine animals venture out to the open sea. Manila, in fact, was originally named Maynilad, which translates to "there is nilad," a reference to the mangrove species known as nilad.

If pollution caused by rampant fires weren't enough of a threat, Branellec's farms are being hit by another peril. For more than a decade, fishing vessels have come to the warm waters of Palawan to capture exotic marine delicacies. High-priced Hong Kong restaurants proudly display tanks of such fish, where diners pick out their entrees. Coral fish and humphead wrasse (also known as Napoleon wrasse) command up to $200 per kilo at wholesale fish markets, and wrasses can grow two meters long. Poachers in Palawan capture the prized fish two ways: by dynamite or cyanide poisoning. The Philippines has strict laws prohibiting such methods, but there is little enforcement and illegal fishing continues unabated. The dynamite kills some fish, but stuns more, which are then collected in nets and sold to wholesalers; cyanide fishing does much the same, with poachers squirting the toxin in the water.

In 2002 at Branellec's farm in Bugsuk, nightly face-offs between the pearling staff and fishermen were a common occurrence, with dynamite explosions nightly. At times, as many as seventy boats, with upward of 500 persons on board, many dressed in indigenous clothing, would converge in the waters surrounding the island. Even today, it's not unusual to hear dynamite explosions in Palawan waters, says Glenn Lovitos, a manager at one of Branellec's farms. "We hear, 'Wham!' and we can see a geyser of water shooting up in the distance." In addition to the fish, damage to coral reefs is substantial. The Philippine fishermen contend that Branellec and Cojuangco have taken away their ancestral fishing waters, but Jewelmer's Zinampan-de Luna maintains that those involved aren't, in fact, members of the region's indigenous Molbog or Palawan tribes, but outside agitators with no ancestral rights to the waters.

To get an idea of the impact of dynamite- and cyanide-fishing, I took a boat out into the waters surrounding the farm, and, adjusting my snorkel, mask, and flippers, I slipped over the boat's portside in an area that had been a site for poaching. A thousand yards from shore, I dropped into the warmest water I'd ever swum in—more than 80 degrees.

The depth of the water was no more than forty feet, and it didn't take long to find a dynamited crater perhaps twenty-five feet across. While snorkeling, what struck me was what I *wasn't* seeing.

One square kilometer of healthy coral can sustain as much as 37 metric tons of fish, and the Philippines is home to 488 coral species out of a known 500 coral species worldwide.[2] Yet as I swam, there was absolutely no live coral. Most coral is brightly colored—pinks, reds, oranges, greens, in a variety of shapes—but here all I could see were broken, lifeless, dead coral sticks. The place was a graveyard, with piles of brittle dead coral on the seafloor. All around me was a sort of real international symbol for poison: cross sticks. There was no luscious, supple brain coral, no soft coral, which sways with the sea's current. Assorted fish scurried by dead coral sticks, but no schools, just solitary fish poking around, then darting away as fast as they could since there was little upon which to feed.

To see the difference, I guided my launch a half-mile away, and as soon as I dropped into the water, I was greeted by a vibrant, abundant ecosystem teeming with all kinds of plant and marine life. Stripped parrotfish, as always, looked exuberant. Some bumped into my mask, looking as startled as I was. A large turtle contentedly flapped by in front of me, not in the slightest perturbed by my presence. I held my breath as a leopard ray glided fifteen feet to my left, followed by a small school of triggerfish, then what seemed like hundreds of silvery trevallies, double-barred rabbitfish, and mean-mouthed coral cods. The area was teeming with coral I'd never seen before. I spotted sea anemones, filigree coral fans that were red, yellow, and blue, and red whip coral that seemed to undulate. The abundance of coral made me bug-eyed. I spotted cauliflower coral, brain coral, mushroom coral, and a coral that looked like a wild bird's nest.

I glanced down on the seafloor twenty feet below, and my heart skipped a beat. There seemed to be scores of prickly spiny animals, which at first glance looked like balled-up baby porcupines. They were a colony of sea urchins, and I wanted nothing to do with them. I kicked with my flippers, pushing my hands outward, and motored past a happy-go-lucky pair of squiggly bigfin squid.

I looked down again, and this time I spotted dozens of purple-lipped giant clams, *Tridacna crocea*, some buried in coral, others brazenly resting on the seafloor. These clams were huge, almost a yard long and two feet wide. And they were old; some had been on the seafloor for more than a hundred years. Other gigantic clams had brown or green flesh that protruded from truly massive shells encasing delicate innards. When my flipper innocently brushed against one shell, the bivalve snapped shut, gulping gallons of water and sending gurgling bubbles to the water's surface. I headed for more of these colossal clams, and began doing a dance of sorts on their shells, lightly touching each with my flippers. Within seconds, each clam promptly clamped shut, sending effervescent bubbles upward. I felt a little like Sebastian in *The Little Mermaid*.

II

The key to understanding the day-to-day operations at the pearl farm was Cyril Brossard, the facility's operations manager. Brossard had a way of looking straight at you, and when he was about to say something important, his eyes would start fluttering, his eyebrows jumping excitedly. Sipping milk from a machete-whacked, shaved coconut, Brossard told me about life for the last thirteen years on the secluded island, far from his home in Brittany, France. Brossard came to the pearl farm single, met his wife here, and now the couple has two young children, Gwenaelle and Theophile.

Brossard took me into the nucleation room, the nerve center of any pearl farm, where the delicate operation that begins the process of pearl creation takes place. Twenty oysters were stacked in a black plastic tray, awaiting a technician's placing a wooden peg between the oysters' two sides to force open their insides. The grayish-green oysters, their surfaces rough and briny, had been plucked an hour earlier from nets in the surrounding waters. These oysters certainly didn't look alive to me, but as I moved my hand several inches from their bivalve openings, each oyster suddenly and abruptly closed, some snapping their sides shut with a thump. The encounter reminded me of my tapdancing on the giant oysters. I played a little game with these oysters, waiting for them to open again, then passing my hand over them, only to see them snap abruptly.

Branellec employs ten nucleators, who rotate among Jewelmer's six farms. Originally all were Japanese, but their knowledge has been passed on to Filipino workers, and now only two nucleators are Japanese nationals. One is Nobuhiro Kano (he goes by the honorific Kano-san), who wore a ragged T-shirt and pajama bottoms when I met him. With an oyster held by a metal clamp at eye level, Kano wrapped each bead with mantle tissue and then, with a metal surgical instrument, carefully inserted the bead, tucked in behind the oyster's gonad. Kano inserts some five hundred beads into oysters per day. The process wasn't too much different from what I had seen at Mr. You and Jeremy Shepherd's farms in Xillan.

The resulting pearls will be extracted two to three years later, depending on a variety of conditions. Some oysters will be re-nucleated with another bead and mantle tissue, so they'll be able to produce a second round of pearls. The pearls' optimum size can range from 12 to 17 millimeters, about the diameter of a large-sized marble.

At harvest, Kano used tweezers to tease the golden pearls from deep within the oysters. *Ping* was the sound each pearl made as Kano dropped it into a plastic bowl. "Ah," he said, holding up a particularly large golden-hue pearl to the light, "this one very good."

Brossard took me into the farm's library, around the corner from the nucleation laboratory, and pointed to eight shelves of neatly arranged *Pinctada maxima* shells, all with black-ink squiggly notations written on them. "These are our books," Brossard said, fanning his hand at the rows of polished shells. I took one of them off the rack and saw it was numbered and dated; the degree of angle where the bead was inserted was also noted. The size of the inserted bead was marked, along with the number of months between nucleation and harvest, the initials of the technician who placed the bead inside the oyster, and the initials of the worker who prepared the mantle tissue. It all made for a genealogy of almost every pearl produced at the farm. Through Excel spreadsheets, Brossard can track the life of every oyster the farm cultivates.

All the oysters are cultivated in nets within three miles from the farm. The science begins in hatching spat (baby oysters) and then nurturing them. Once born, the spat likely will be in the charge of April Niones, a mother in her early thirties who has worked for Branellec for nine years. One look at April and anyone would understand why she's in charge of this nursery of newborns. Niones is a large woman who radiates an unmistakable sense of nurturing. Earth Mother comes to mind, but, in Niones's case, she's more a Sea Mother.

Niones, whose salary is the equivalent of $425 a month and who has a ten-year contract to work for Jewelmer, meticulously hand-places each of three hundred tiny baby oysters in a white net, then submerges the net in seawater. Every month, she'll check in on her growing charges, sorting them as they get larger. To spur growth, she'll divide the original lot of oysters into different nets; as the oysters grow there'll be just fifteen of her aquatic babies per net, then eight, then six.

On cleaning stations that float in the bay, Brossard says the company prefers women, not men, to do the delicate job of bathing the young oysters. Using an old-fashioned fingernail brush, a woman tenderly scraped off algae and other gunk accumulated on the fragile shells one by one, then gingerly tucked them back in a net, eight oysters evenly spaced, to be submerged again in the sea. "We've determined that the women are gentler than the men," Brossard said, noting that pearl cultivation isn't about political correctness, but about growing the biggest, most flawless pearls.

A plant manager at another Jewelmer farm told me she sees her job as identical to that of a day-care worker. "These babies can't cry. They can't tell us what they need, so we have to anticipate their every need," she said, adding that she prays and sings for their well-being. "We believe that if the shells are cared for by good hands with a happy heart, they will grow healthy."

Such techniques may or may not help; science is what ultimately determines a perfect pearl. Figuring out how deep the nets are submerged in the bay is critical since it, in turn, determines water temperature, plankton interaction, salinity level, freshwater absorption, natural-light availability, and the strength of the current, all critical factors in determining the pearl's outcome. So does the gentle rotation of the oyster shell, so the pearl bead inside grows round. Branellec's staff transports via helicopter oyster spat among farms, testing whether certain baby oysters conceived, for example, at Farm Three will produce a better pearl if nurtured in the seawater of Farm Two.

Oysters at a Jewelmer facility get better treatment, nutrition, and love than many human babies, and not just in Manila's downtrodden *barangays*, but pretty much anywhere in the world. These maritime animals are pampered, protected, and primped for one reason: to produce pearls that will fetch as high a price as the market will bear. Maintaining the environment may be the right thing to do, but it's also the way to make "the perfect pearl" or the "dream pearl" (phrases Branellec mercilessly drills into his employees). Brossard is under no illusion about Branellec's goal. No one I talked to at Jewelmer would ever confuse Branellec's motive. It most certainly is not to create pearls for the People (as the Chinese are hoping with their seemingly endless quantities of dyed and treated freshwater pearls). "We provide pearls to people who can afford only the very best," Brossard told me without a drop of guilt. "If you're making a dream pearl, you have to make sure everything is done perfectly. If only the richest women in the world will have these pearls, then the quality of the shell and the quality of the environment must be absolutely pristine."

All characteristics being equal—color, size, shape, surface purity, orient, and lustre—size and shape are probably the greatest determinants when it comes to the price pearls will command in the global marketplace. Whether it is because of their relative novelty in the United States or because the gold orbs (at least to some observers) don't seem to complement fair, white skin, Branellec says his pearls generally sell best in Asia, the Middle East, South America, and southern Europe. Branellec's pearls might be buffed and polished, but none is dyed (at least none I saw).

Since all pearls that Branellec's farms grow and harvest come from the *Pinctada maxima* oysters, pearl size is ultimately determined by the depth of the oyster's cavity, which holds the developing pearl. A six-month *Pinctada maxima* oyster can grow forty times its size in just eighteen months, and the pearl inside will correspondingly grow as the shell gets to its full adult size. Twelve-millimeter pearls are not so much a problem to grow, but pearls reaching upwards of 18 millimeters become exceedingly rare for the normal size of the *Pinctada maxima* oyster and, as such, can bring extraordinary prices.

Which brought me back to what I had seen in China. The bead nuclei inserted into Mr. You's akoya pearls were as large as 7 millimeters, which meant that his pearls (as well as pearls from many producers, and not just Chinese) really have very little actual nacre. What consumers then are paying for is a bead, lightly coated by calcium carbonate and aragonite crystals the oyster secretes to cover it. Technically, it's a pearl. To everyone who sees it, it's a pearl. But really, it's a bead with a thin veneer, which over time might peel or chip.

Unlike what I saw in China, which was a go-go-go assembly line of production, Brossard told me he wants his workers to slow down, to work methodically and with purpose. At least that's the company mantra. I suppose too much slowdown and a worker would lose his or her job. But Branellec's message is for his workers to act deliberately.

As Brossard and I got back to the farm's main office, the headquarters re-minded me of a low-tech version of the *Starship Enterprise*, with Brossard playing the role of Captain Kirk, surrounded by a bevy of assistant officers. Brossard's desk was elevated and in the front, facing other stations fanned out around him—administrative officer Anabel Rivera and assistant Lucia Masendo; farm monitors Christine Marie Dagohoy, Michelle Salazar, and April Niones; biolo-gists Emma Romano, Lilibeth Asay, and Nena Dotillus. Next to Brossard was his wife, Vianney, the resident manager. Brossard could tap on a laptop Apple computer to pull up spreadsheets to examine the history of any oyster.

III

Five days after I arrived at Bugsuk, Branellec returned, bringing with him two friends. One was Italian-born Australian Bruno Savron, one of the original workers at Bugsuk when Branellec started the pearl farm in 1983 (and the cook who sewed up Desdemona's head); the other was Andy Bowers, an American health-food entrepreneur, who'd recently moved from New Zealand to the Philippines to buy an island next to the Jewelmer resort Flower Island. Bowers had made a fortune in the States when he co-founded a health-supplement com-pany called Coral, Inc., the largest supplier of, Bowers insisted, "above-water" coral in the United States. Bowers sold out his shares to his partner, Clint De-Witt, moved halfway around the world, picked up a girlfriend a third his age, and was in the midst of colonizing his own private island.

We all went for a tour of three of Jewelmer's pearl farms. For lunch, two employees had the task of methodically raising and lowering long wooden sticks with fluffy pompoms on the ends to shoo away errant flies. At one island, Branellec assembled his staff for an impromptu lecture, standing in front of a dry-erase board, quizzing employees. It was painful to watch.

Branellec started by drawing concentric circles, with a bead nucleus at the center, followed by ever-larger circles in which he wrote "pearl," "oyster," "sea," and "environment."

"What is our objective at all our farms?" Branellec shouted to the thirty workers seated in a semicircle around him.

"To make a Dream Pearl!" burly farm manager Rogelio Bas shouted, hit-ting the jackpot.

Branellec nodded sternly, and allowed Bas to go on. No-nonsense Bas was a veteran of Jewelmer's operations. He had been a communist rebel, lured out of the jungle more than fifteen years earlier by an offer of amnesty from the Philippine government.

When another employee chirped that the goal was to create the *perfect* pearl, Branellec got ornery. "And how exactly does that happen?" he asked in a testy way.

The worker stammered. Silence in the room. Five seconds, ten seconds, twenty seconds. By now, the half-circle of employees was staring at their flip-flops.

Branellec resumed in his crisp, French-accented diction. "There are fourteen hundred interactions between birth and turnout—places where our concept of the Dream Pearl can be interrupted. Any one of these interactions, if not performed *perfectly*, can spell imperfection.

"If a basket is thrown, instead of placed, back in the water—that can prevent the perfect pearl. Any small trauma can create a disturbance that will result in an imperfect pearl." Branellec snarled the word *imperfect*, spitting it with a hiss.

"If the pearl doesn't rotate freely, then you do have a circle pearl. Everything we do has to be *perfect*. Is this understood?" All heads nodded automatically.

The dressing-down complete, I recalled a pearl producer I talked to who marveled at how efficient Branellec's operations were. When he asked Branellec how he maintained such high efficiency, Branellec replied deadpan, "If any of them give me trouble, I shoot them."

With the training session concluded, Branellec, Savron, Bowers, and I took a motorboat across the bay to Flower Island, where Branellec and Cojuangco were building bungalows high on a hillside. With soft, foamy waves lapping against the shore fifty yards away, and Branellec sipping on a Coke and Black Label, he told me his swashbuckler's tale of how a French tailor's son grew up to be one of the world's great purveyors of pearls.

Branellec pins much of his drive on the death of his older brother, who, along with three friends, was killed in a boating accident. The night before the eighteen-year-old died, he gave twelve-year-old Jacques a Fats Domino album, which Branellec still holds as a shrine to his childhood.

During the tumultuous student movement in Paris in 1968, Branellec was at constant odds with his left-wing classmates. He opted out of his philosophy classes, left the university, and learned to fly airplanes. He spent a summer traveling the United States, flying from New York to New Orleans, hitchhiking to Los Angeles and San Francisco, then Vancouver and Alaska.

Back in France, he signed on to fly small planes so that bathers at the beach could see advertising streamers trailing behind the airplanes' tails. He hired on as a pilot for Air Tahiti, and was immediately smitten by what he saw in the South Pacific. "The women had the faces of Eve at the first instance of creation," Branellec wrote in an unpublished autobiography. "And I promised myself that I'd be their Adam." His first child, a boy, was born in Papeete. Branellec's daughter was born on the atoll of Takapoto.

Branellec befriended a Japanese pearl technician who used to work for the famed French jewelry family scion Rosenthal to explore the possibilities of creating a pearl farm. At the time, relatively few Tahitian pearls from the oyster *Pinctada margaritifera* had been cultured. Branellec spent time in Japan, trying to wrest grafting and implantation methods from technicians. In 1971, he set up a farm on Takapoto, where his first black pearl was cultivated, then on another atoll, Arutua. Nearly bankrupt, on a trip to Papeete, Branellec met an eccentric millionaire Jean-Claude Brouillet, who became his business partner. The two bought land and built a runway on another atoll, South Marutea, and began cultivating black pearls at a time when such pearls were viewed by jewelers as nothing more than curios. There was absolutely no market for them. Up until then, pearls were one thing—white creamy orbs. At the ripe age of twenty-seven, Branellec may have been onto something, but a row ensued between him and Brouillet, resulting in Branellec selling his shares to Brouillet, who in turn sold two pearl farms on the atoll to Robert Wan. Wan was to become a multimillionaire as the largest producer of black pearls in the world.

IV

When I got back to Manila, I interviewed Manuel Cojuangco, hoping to get his side of Jewelmer. Cojuangco and Branellec share a surprisingly nondescript office, desks facing each other on the seventh floor of the National Life Insurance Building. The partners surrounded themselves with stunning young Philippine women, who seemed to parade in and out of the executives suites, swiveling their hips, batting their eye lashes, and laughing at will at the lamest jokes Branellec could summon. I wasn't quite sure why Branellec and Cojuangco had such close quarters, other than to keep an eye on each other.

With neatly combed hair, Cojuangco, in his mid-forties, is as subdued as Branellec is kinetic. Cojuangco started his career in one of his family's multi-tentacle banking businesses, apprenticing in New York, but he said he found the work boring. He came back to the Philippines and found himself working at a coconut-processing farm his family had started in Bugsuk (it was designed to be the largest such facility in the world), but when that venture failed, Cojuangco had just taken up scuba diving and Branellec was looking for a local partner to start a pearl farm.

While we were talking, every three or four minutes Branellec came into the office, ostensibly to get something, but it was apparent he was there to eavesdrop on what Cojuangco was saying. The scene was straight out of a bad sitcom.

Just as we were getting somewhere, Cojuangco said he had to leave, something about an appointment with a banker. Jewelmer's third-in-command, Pierre Fallourd, walked in filling in for his bosses.

Fallourd showed me a flawless, thirty-two-inch pearl necklace, graduated from 13 to 15 millimeters, which he crowed was designed for a Russian retailer and would sell for $100,000. Fallourd boasted that it took 35,000 nucleations to make this one outrageous strand. I didn't for a second believe him. Perfect gold-pearl necklaces like this one are rare; still, not many would pay that kind of money for them. Pearl producers, like dealers, need to manage an extraordinary game to succeed.

Fallourd said that one of Jewelmer's biggest clients is a Chinese dealer who buys thousands of loose gold pearls in a variety of grades each year from Jewelmer. "We sell him very large lots, but he uses only 60 percent of what he buys. The rest he sells off," said Fallourd, a man in his early thirties with a robust head of hair who was expecting his first child any day. The Chinese dealer unloads the rest of the pearls to an assortment of traders, with the largest single shipment going to Japanese brokers in Hong Kong. The Japanese, in turn, sell the pearls to a network of smaller dealers, some of whom make necklaces out of the pearls, and to others, who flip the pearls to traders in Asia, Europe, and the United States. Jewelmer, of course, has no control over the prices any of the traders charge.

The upside to such an arrangement is that Jewelmer can efficiently sell huge quantities of various grades of pearls to a single dealer for a single cash payment. The downside is the dilemma that Fallourd was facing the day we met.

On his way to work that morning, Fallourd had passed an upscale jewelry store down the block from Jewelmer's offices, when he noticed a dazzling strand of gold pearls in the window. The necklace stopped Fallourd in his tracks. He knew immediately that the pearls had been produced at Jewelmer's Bugsuk farm. Pearls are untraceable, and to the casual shopper, the strand might have been stunning and opulent, but to an expert like Fallourd the pearls had the unmistakable lustre and orient distinctive to the warm waters surrounding the southern tip of Palawan. They also were near-rounds, pushing 15 millimeters. They had to be Jewelmer's.

Fallourd could only surmise their journey. He knew they'd been helicoptered from Palawan to Manila, then couriered to Jewelmer's offices in Makati Center, where they'd been sorted, graded, and eventually sold. After that, it was anyone's guess. The pearls probably had been flown to China, then to Hong Kong, then perhaps to Japan, perhaps back to Hong Kong, and after untold other transactions, they were back in Manila—selling for 40 percent less than the original wholesale dealer had paid Jewelmer.

If that weren't enough to cause any pearl producer a migraine, Fallourd had another headache about to rip. He was juggling two clients this afternoon at Jewelmer's offices—a retailer and a wholesaler, both there to buy the same grade pearls, which Fallourd would be offering to each at vastly different prices. Woe to Fallourd should the two bump into each other. "If they even see each other, it'll be a disaster," Fallourd said, quickly leaving to head off any chance encounter.

18

Sold!

I

Planning my pearl odyssey had taken two years, and by now, I'd been traveling nonstop for almost four months. I'd fully descended into the arcane world of pearls and the people whose lives revolved around them. Pearls were all I thought about. They floated through my head, still occasionally colliding into each other, beckoning me to sleep each evening. The next morning, I'd practically leap out of another lumpy hotel bed, eager to meet yet another pearl worker, anticipating his smile—and mine—as he showed off his offerings. I was as determined as ever to connect the entire serpentine string of global workers who, unknown to each other, every day pushed pearls along one giant planetary assembly line.

Somewhere along that production line, I was losing touch with my life back home. During my infrequent conversations with Iris and Mikey via e-mail and telephone, I concealed my glee at the story unfolding. I missed my wife and son, yes, but I was too obsessed following pearls around the world to have too many pangs of regret.

Iris and Mikey continued their routine of teeth-chattering normalcy back home in Iowa. Once I had returned to Manila from Branellec's sunny lair on Flower Island, on an uncertain phone connection with a ten-second delayed echo, Iris read me the Riot Act. "Come home," my wife said quietly. "Go back in the summer. The story will wait. We're fine, but Mikey and I need you at home. Please." My offer of six pearl necklaces did not dissuade Iris, which I took as a positive sign of our marriage.

The day after Holy Week in the Philippines, I flew back to the thawing upper midwest. As I sleepwalked off the plane into the tiny Eastern Iowa Airport, in Cedar Rapids, twenty-two hours and two airplane transfers after leaving Manila, I became husband and father again, at least the kind of husband and father my wife and son could see every day, eat dinner with every night, and watch *The Office* with on Thursday evenings. I'd been in perpetual motion for months. I was glad to be back.

Back home, I'd have time to noodle my pearl journey, what it meant, where it was leading. I had saved three of the most significant pearl destinations for the last: French Polynesia, Australia, and Cubagua, the tiny island off Venezuela where Columbus had first traded for pearls. I needed to go to all three places. I couldn't pass them up. Iris agreed. Take a month to type up your notes, set up more interviews, then do the remainder of your traveling in the summer, she said. Mikey seemed to agree. Everything was set.

Until ten days later.

That's when Daphne Lingon, the senior specialist for jewelry at Christie's in New York, called.

I had met Lingon at her office in Rockefeller Center two years earlier. She had promised that should Christie's acquire a major pearl heirloom in the next year or two, she'd immediately contact me. It was one thing to trace contemporary cultured pearls, quite another to witness the resurrection of a one-of-a-kind historic strand. Such necklaces were extraordinary, rare natural pearls that usually had been stashed away in bank vaults or jewelry boxes for decades. To bring a strand to light didn't happen often. To see and touch a legendary strand would be a once-in-a-lifetime opportunity. And to attend an auction to witness the frenzy surrounding its sale would be remarkable.

"I wanted to call you the *moment* I found out about these pieces," Lingon said in a hushed voice. "I knew you'd want to know about these strands. They are nothing short of amazing."

Lingon was right.

Up for sale at Christie's were the historic Baroda Pearls, two strands of sixty-eight matched, graduated gumball-sized natural pearls that the auction house touted as "the most important natural pearl necklace to ever be seen at auction." Auction houses always hype items to go on the block, but the hoopla surrounding the April 25, 2007, sale of the Baroda Pearls surpassed even the most extreme hyperbole. Here's Christie's catalogue description:

MAGNIFICENCE, ROYALTY AND SPLENDOR:
THE BARODA PEARLS

Christie's is honored to present the magnificent and legendary natural pearl necklace, symbolic of a bygone era of Indian splendor. The necklace has been coveted throughout history, and its appearance at auction represents a monumental event for jewelry collections and connoisseurs worldwide. Worn through the centuries and across generations by the Indian Maharajas of Baroda, this necklace has been documented endlessly, as the epitome of elegance, extravagance and rarity.[1]

Lingon said Christie's expected the pearls to go in the range of $7 to $9 million.

That was an awful lot. Granted, they were natural pearls and they were huge. They also had a checkered past, always a plus when selling estate jewelry. But if these strands went for even half of what Christie's estimated, they'd fetch a world record for the most ever spent for any gem at auction.

Baroda is a former state in western India that, like much of India, had been ruled for hundreds of years by a family of supremely wealthy maharajas dedicated to sloth, debauchery, and consumption of the most conspicuous kind. Wealthy Indians have had a 3,500-year love affair with pearls. The word for pearl in Sanskrit is *sasi-ratna*, or "gem of the moon." Maharajas coveted pearls, weaving them into their clothing, as well as into carpets, screens, pillars, and doorways. But the most common use of pearls was then what it is now—jewelry. Between 1275 and 1290, Marco Polo described going to India and meeting the king of Malabar, who wore a rosary of 104 large pearls, as well as pearl ankle bracelets and pearl toe rings. "Every year the King issues a proclamation throughout the land to the effect that any subject bringing pearls or precious stones to the court will be paid twice their value for them. . . . This practice is always honoured so the merchants bring huge quantities of large and beautiful pearls," Polo wrote in his travelogue of discoveries, *The Travels of Marco Polo*.[2]

Over generations, the Nawabs of Rampur, a small state in North India, amassed one of the finest pearl collections in the world, and the Maharaja of Dholpur was said to possess the finest pearls in India.[3] Fortunately for the maharajas, a plentiful source of lustrous natural pearls was off the Gulf of Mannar, in the southeastern part of the nation. That, along with the Persian Gulf, provided the maharajas with all the pearls they ever possibly could wear. But the maharajas' tastes were lavish and their desire for pearls without bounds. For the largest, most spectacular, and colossal pearls, the maharajas would have to go farther, much farther, away.

There is a common (and useful) expression in auction literature, and as I was researching the Baroda Pearls I noticed its use more than ever before: *came to possess*. The declaration makes use of the passive and, in the case of the rulers of Baroda, thus obviates whether the maharajas ever actually bought or traded for these magnificent pearl strands. It's as though these singular pearls just happened to sail one day into the maharajas' vast palaces on a magic carpet and take up residence. More possibly and more likely, they could have been stolen in the dead of night, seized from an unfortunate prince whose head was about to be lopped off, or acquired as dowry for a particularly homely daughter of a fellow maharaja.

No one seems to know exactly where the Baroda Pearls came from or how they were acquired. Here's how Christie's finessed the provenance conundrum:

> It is believed that the Khande Rao came to possess an extraordinary necklace composed of seven strands of perfectly matched and graduated natural pearls. Referred to as The Baroda Pearls, each luminous strand radiated elegance, wealth and power, and would be the prized possession of Royal Gaekwars of later generations.[4]

The first Maharaja of Baroda, Khande Rao Gaekwar, who ruled from 1856 to 1870, had a passion for flaunting outrageous pearl strands, as well as commissioning works of opulence, one of which was a carpet made of pearls, designed as a chador for the prophet Mohammed's grave. An Englishman, Edward St. Clair Weeden, who spent a year with the Gaekwar in 1909, saw the magnificent seven-strand Baroda Pearls, and wrote that at that time they were worth 50 lakhs of rupees, or £500,000.[5] After Pratapsingh Gaekwar took control of the state of Baroda in 1939, his most noteworthy achievement seemed to be a scandalous second marriage to Sita Devi, a raven-haired beauty often referred to as "The Indian Wallis Simpson," and known for an avaricious passion for jewels. Interest in the Baroda Pearls was fanned with an often-republished Henri Cartier-Bresson photograph, showing a smiling Sita Devi fastening the clasp to all seven strands on the neck of her husband, the Maharaja. I studied reproductions of the Cartier-Bresson photo and could see that these massive pearls projected an historic majesty and luminescent brilliance I'd never seen before nor would likely ever see again.[6]

I had to get myself to New York.

I somehow convinced my very accommodating family that I needed to witness the auction of these most remarkable objects. I'd be gone for at most a week, I promised. New York was more manageable than Japan, Hong Kong, rural China, or the Philippines. I'd be a three-hour plane ride away. New York was practically next door. I'd be back before Iris and Mikey would realize that I'd gone.

II

Since 1994, Christie's record in selling jewelry has been unsurpassed by any other auction house in the world, including its New York crosstown rival, Sotheby's. Christie's jewelry sales in 2006 were $355 million; in 2007, they topped $395 million; and in 2008, they amounted to $383 million.[7] Both Christie's and Sotheby's maintain offices around the world, and both schedule auctions of just about anything rare—books, photographs, paintings, furniture, rugs, classic toys, clocks, really anything rich people buy. Both houses don't auction off just antiques. If the item is of high enough quality and perceived as one of a kind, Christie's and Sotheby's will gladly auction that off, too.

Christie's is located around the corner from where the *Today* show is aired. For an elite auction house, it's not too snooty, and as soon as I arrived, I warmed to Lingon once again. A veteran appraiser on the PBS television show *Antiques Roadshow*, Lingon has handled the estate jewelry of Lauren Bacall, Louise Crane (heiress of the Crane Paper Company fortune), and Doris Duke (daughter of the tobacco tycoon). She has a job most women (and not a few men) would kill for. She shops the world for one-of-a-kind jewelry on someone else's dime.

Lingon grew up in Ann Arbor, Michigan, the daughter of a dentist who was fascinated with gemstones and jewelry design. "I always loved jewelry, ever since I was little," she told me from her office in the bowels of the auction house. "As a teenager, I used to mow lawns to buy books on jewelry." For her sixteenth birthday, two neighborhood boys pooled their savings to buy her a strand of imitation pearls. "I used to wear them all the time. And I mean *all* the time." She cashed in her lawn-mowing profits to buy a gem set from Sharper Image. Lingon was so captivated by the sparkling stones, she'd carry the set around with her all the time and at night she'd sleep with it. "Some girls like Barbie dolls. I liked jewelry," she said without a trace of guilt.

Lingon studied history and East Asian culture at Denison University in Granville, Ohio, then enrolled in the Gemological Institute of America, where she studied to become a gemologist. She moved to Europe and appendiced in Italy under Amanda Triossi, an historian who had worked for years for famed Italian jeweler Bulgari. The main course of study was going to London museums to analyze portrait after portrait, zeroing in on period jewelry.

When Lingon came back to the States, she knew she wanted to work at an auction house, but such jobs were (and still are) nearly impossible to come by. Her first job was as a "diamond picker," sorting through cans of diamond chips, searching for the right ones for tie tacks and cufflinks, freebies given away when a shopper buys a suit at JC Penny's. Picking out diamond chips didn't last long. "I wanted to deal with *real* jewelry, and what I really wanted to do was hold it. That's the thing for me. I have to touch it." Within a year, she was hired as a junior specialist at Christie's.

There are singular moments to Lingon's job that make for unbeatable cocktail chatter. "Last week, a family called from a central California farm. A mother and daughter were going though their attic and came across a collector's piece of jewelry, a brooch. It sounded interesting, so I asked them to come in if they ever got to New York. I never expected to hear from them again, but yesterday, they came to town. I looked over the piece, and saw that it was signed by Louis Tiffany! It took my breath away," Lingon said, still rather breathlessly.

While she adores all jewelry, it's pearls that Lingon covets most. Both cultured and natural pearls make her heart flutter, but natural pearls make it go fastest. "I see more natural pearls than any jeweler sees in a lifetime. I'd estimate I've probably seen three hundred natural pearl pieces." On her desk the morning I met her she had five amazing pearl necklaces, as well as a brooch with a bevy of natural pearls. "Come on, feel them," Lingon said, taunting me. "That's that only way to understand pearls. You must touch them." A woman after my own heart.

Every business has a hierarchy where those on the top look down with pity and scorn at those on the bottom, and elite auctioneers are no exception. Although jewelry brings in hundreds of millions to Christie's every year, there are specialists at the house who shake their heads at the jewelry division's runaway success. "They look at jewelry as a personal adornment," Lingon said, frowning in a how-could-they! way. "People at auction houses view paintings as the highest form of all art. They look at jewelry as something personal, not pure, elegant, or worthy of their interests. They find it too commercial."

With the extravagent Baroda Pearls under the auction hammer, Lingon could prove her colleagues wrong—or right. Seven to nine million dollars is pretty commercial.

III

Christie's Magnificent Jewels Auction was scheduled for a Wednesday, one day following Sotheby's Magnificent Jewels Auction. The houses coordinate their auctions so that prospective buyers can attend both events. Each house maintains a five-day preview schedule so would-be customers can examine the jewelry outside the glare and tumult of the auction. I had scheduled a meeting with Lingon on Monday to get an up-close look at the Baroda Pearls, but since I'd arrived in New York late Saturday night, I also had time to see what rival auctioneer Sotheby's would put up for its jewelry auction.

Sotheby's is located in a new, large, glass-wrapped building on York Avenue, on Manhattan's Upper East Side. As I entered, hundreds of people were milling around. The jewels were on the tenth floor, but on each of the other floors there were thousands of items being readied for auction, everything from eighteenth-century fountain pens and Revolutionary War beds to signed Edward Steichen and Richard Avedon photographs. It dawned on me that since admission was free, going to an auction house really was a much better deal than walking up several blocks to the Guggenheim Museum. Certainly there was more to see here, the venue was larger and more comfortable, and here, you could even (literally) check out a piece for several hours to get a closer look at it. No one asked anyone whether they were buyers. Perhaps all auction-goers wanted was to spend an afternoon indoors looking at rare collectibles. Sotheby's and Christie's had become museums for the twenty-first century—vast warehouses of one-of-a-kind objets d'art, open to everyone for free.

I'd made arrangements to meet pearl dealer Alex Vock, back for several months from his buying trip in Hong Kong, who wanted to preview the jewelry at Sotheby's. When I'd talked to Vock on the phone, he told me he wasn't in the least interested in the Baroda Pearls. "Six million bucks? Yeah, right!" Vock said. "Like who's gonna buy 'em? Who's got that kind of dough? Maybe some sultan, but no one I know. You know any sultans?"

I'd already talked to pearl dealer Fran Mastoloni, who had seen the Baroda Pearls on display at Christie's Friday. "They looked to me like they come from Broome," he said. "Natural pearls that big have to come from Australia. Maybe some of them are from Burma. As a collector's item, they are off the charts."

Was Mastoloni interested in bidding for them?

"You kidding? Try to unload them. It'd be next to impossible. The person who buys them wants to keep them. Gotta be some Arab. They're the only ones with that kind of money."

As I glided past a phalanx of Sotheby security guards, I noticed Vock's bald pate in the dealers' room. He was sitting next to the window (north light) at a table covered with a white tablecloth (of course). There were fifty or so dealers examining jewelry pieces to be auctioned off in two days. Some dealers had loupes stuck in their eyes, others brought out magnifying glasses. Most were Indians; there was a smattering of Hasidic and WASP dealers. Almost all were men. It was a congenial group that kibitzed nonstop ("Too rich for your blood, Lenny. Better put it down," one dealer shouted to another). Vock had his head down and, with a hand-held 10x magnifying glass, was examining a diamond bracelet. As I got closer, Vock barely acknowledged me, but motioned me to take the seat next to him.

"You got a twenty-dollar bill?" Vock asked, not looking up.

"I only carry hundred-dollar bills. Small bills, way too much trouble," I replied.

"A C-note'll work. Gimme one. Make it quick!"

"Oops, I *do* have a twenty," I said, opening my wallet.

"C'mon, lemme have it. Whaddaya think, I got all day?" Vock still hadn't looked up. I handed him a wrinkled Jackson.

He laid out my twenty, then smoothed it with the back of his palm, alongside the bracelet on the table. "Just as I thought," Vock said, sounding like Maxwell Smart. "This baby's short. Twenties are six inches long, and a bracelet—any bracelet, if it's gonna be comfortable—has gotta be seven inches or longer. You see this?" Vock asked, nodding his nose at the bill and bracelet. "Too short. Those sons of bitches."

Just as I was about to ask Vock for my twenty back, it occurred to me:

Why a *twenty*? All U.S. bills are the same length. I could have given him a single.

But by this time, Vock had pivoted from the table and was looking around, scanning the room.

"May I borrow your wrist, dear?" he asked a Sotheby's clerk, a woman in her seventies with lacquered apricot-colored hair.

"Certainly, sweetheart," she chirped.

Vock fastened the bracelet around her boney wrist, to which she trilled, "OH, it's stunning!"

"But it's tight," Vock cut in.

"Not really," the helmet-hair lady responded, trying to jingle the bracelet, which steadfastly clung to her wrist like very expensive Scotch tape. "It's gorgeous! Women like bracelets like this. It doesn't twist around so much."

"Twist? It fits like a hospital wristband!" Vock said.

Then to me, "It saves the manufacturer a dozen diamonds. That's a lot of money. It's shortchanging the customer. This bracelet doesn't work—at least it doesn't work for me," and in one motion, Vock unclasped the bracelet from the Sotheby's clerk, and dropped it back into the velvet display tray as though it were a dead snake.

"Wanna see something beautiful?"

"Sure," I said. "But what about my twenty?"

"What about it?"

"How about, 'Where is it?'"

"Smart. Some guys would've forgotten. You gotta future."

Vock returned my twenty just as a clerk placed in front of us another bracelet, this one Lot No. 92, a glittery platinum and gold strap with round and cushion-shaped rubies and 238 baguette diamonds that had once belonged to Helena Rubenstein. The asking price was $40,000–$60,000.

"*Way* overpriced," Vock said, making a whistling sound by exhaling through pursed lips. "And one of the rubies is fake. Look, *anyone* can see that. But it's nice, no?"

And so it went, piece after piece.

"Hey, check this one out," Vock said, nudging me with his elbow.

He held up in his right hand Lot No. 182, a signed Van Cleef & Arpels diamond Maltese cross. At its center was a single pear-shaped yellow diamond, flanked by 44 baguette and 114 round diamonds, mounted in platinum, supported by a necklace with 93 more diamonds. The asking price was $55,000–$60,000.

"This is a *major* piece," Vock announced, "and it's not priced too badly. Whaddaya think?"

But before I could answer, Vock chimed, "But who's gonna buy it? I can't buy pieces just because they're *major.* I need to have a buyer in mind before I take something on like this. Whaddaya think, I'm made of money? This is *crazy!*"

Vock was particularly interested in Lot 148, a David Webb-designed baroque cultured pearl ring at $7,000–$9,000, which he put on his "maybe" list. Practically all Sotheby's was auctioning was stone (diamonds, emeralds, rubies, sapphires, onyx) or metal (platinum and gold), and because of that, it held little interest for me. The essential element of pearls—why I liked them so much—came to mind once again. Pearls were wholly different gems. They weren't gaudy, sharp-edged, flashy, as this parade of glittery jewelry in front of me was. These pieces up for sale had been faceted, cut, melted, and formed. Pearls come out of their shells perfect (forgetting, for a minute, the transformatron). They were as simple an adornment as possible.

While Vock was pondering a pair of emerald and diamond earclips for $18,000–$20,000, I walked from the dealers' area to the public showroom, where more than 150 customers and hangers-on were milling around. Thin, long-legged *Breakfast at Tiffany's* Audrey Hepburn look-alikes, wearing pixie hair bands, oversized Chanel sunglasses pushed up on their heads, tight straight skirts with exaggerated slits up the back, Kate Spade slippers on petite feet, showing toe cleavage. Some were canoodling with partners in their sixties. One middle-aged woman had on a tight black blouse, but at the bottom it suddenly flared to reveal a pierced belly button with a diamond drop. Young marrieds, pushing Emmaljunga strollers with sleeping infants outfitted in Kate Quinn organic baby clothes. Another contingent was hyper-thin ladies-who-lunch. I spotted several couples in their seventies or eighties, walking arm in arm, occasionally stopping to admire a piece here and there; these were not buyers, just regulars out for a Sunday stroll.

In the showroom I chatted up David Bennett, Sotheby's chairman for jewelry in Europe and the Middle East, who was in town to hype the upcoming Magnificent Jewels Auction to be held in Geneva. I wanted to get a taste of the Christie's competition.

"We like to think we at Sotheby's are more erudite," sniffed Bennett, an Englishman impeccably dressed in a suit with a pattern of small gray and blue squares. "We're certainly more published. It's a *very* different group of people."

One thing that Bennett and a colleague, Alexandra Rhodes, Sotheby's senior director of jewelry in Europe, said had changed in the auction business was who attends auctions these days. Auctions used to be top-heavy with dealers and wholesalers like Vock. No more. Today auctions are made up of mostly private clients. Dealers certainly are welcomed, but more and more, even with discretionary money tight, auctions have become free-for-alls, where amateurs bid for baubles. Chalk that up to *Antiques Roadshow.*

I caught up with Vock, who was asking the Sotheby apricot-haired clerk to model Lot No. 349, a pair of huge 5.2- and 5.47-carat emerald earclips, signed by Van Cleef & Arpels, and priced at $150,000–$200,000. "These are as good as it gets," Vock pronounced, holding the pair twenty inches from his eyes, rotating them ever so slightly so they caught the waning afternoon light from the window. "They've got the name, the size. They're perfect. And you know what? They'll end up in hedge-fund land—even with the recession, a broker will buy 'em for his wife or girlfriend. Probably his girlfriend."

IV

The next day I had another appointment with Lingon, who had promised she'd show me the Baroda Pearls. On my way to Christie's, as I rounded Rockefeller Center, I passed Al Roker sticking a microphone into the crowd outside the *Today* studio, but I scurried along. I was excited about seeing the Baroda Pearls, and as soon as Lingon greeted me, I knew she was, too. This was her week. If she and her colleague Rahul Kadakia played their cards right, they'd be sitting on a record. Lingon had refused all my entreaties to reveal where the Baroda Pearls came from. I had pleaded with her to contact the seller and ask whether he or she would talk, but Lingon would have none of it. Just who contacted Christie's, and who stood to make the $7–$9 million (minus Christie's floating commission of 15 percent)? She refused to say.

I asked Lingon how she and Kadakia had determined the selling price. There aren't exactly any comps out there for these pearls. "It has a lot to do with what the client wanted, but realistically you never know until the piece goes," Lingon said.

But where did the estimate come from? I persisted. How do you know what a dealer, or anyone, really, is willing to pay? Were the Baroda Pearls just a publicity stunt to get headlines for Christie's? Was there even a real seller? Would there be a real buyer?

"I can assure you there is a legitimate seller and the seller expects us to sell these pearls for as much as we possibly can."

"Why the $6 million floor? And who's going to bid that kind of money?" I asked, echoing Vock and Mastoloni.

"We have a $40 million Warhol for sale and I'm certain that will go," Lingon replied somewhat testily. "How do you set a price on that?"

The Warhol was easy. "It might very well be overpriced, but there are precedents for what Warhols fetch in the marketplace," I replied. "But for these jewels, there's never been anything like them that's ever come up for auction."

Lingon begrudgingly allowed the point. "The highest prices we've ever sold jewelry for have been in the three- to four-million-dollar range, and these pearls are completely different than the jewelry we ordinarily deal with. We'll see Wednesday, I guess."

When I asked Lingon about the six other original Baroda strands, she said they conceivably might still be out there, but she doubted it. "We think these are the only two complete strands left.

How would she know? Lingon asked. "Would you like to see the pearls or just talk?"

We walked over to a showroom where the pearls were on display. Rose petals were scattered all around. A gauzy pink fabric hung suspended over the display case. With the help of two guards, Lingon removed the strands.

Back in her office, she dropped the necklace into my open, slightly cupped palms. "They're all yours. Feel 'em."

As I knew they would, my hands started to sweat.

The pearls were dense and heavy, and when I bounced a couple against each other, the sound was different from what I'd grown accustomed to hearing with cultured pearls. The sound of these natural pearls was more substantial— almost like what I'd imagine small lead balls would make colliding. It wasn't a click. It was more like a gong.

The pearls were a creamy white, with very good lustre. There were minor flaws, but by God, these were genuine natural pearls, assembled and matched probably over the course of a century. They had a slightly hammered, textured, look to them, the way I'd read that large natural pearls generally appear, particularly if they're antiques.

I asked Lingon to model the strands, and she did not demur. After all, what are pearls unless they hang from a woman's neck? As Lingon fastened the clasp to the strands, her whole carriage changed. She instantly morphed from attractive to glamorous. Lingon stood up straighter, wiggling her shoulders a bit. In an instant, an unmistakable demeanor seemed to have descended and overtaken her. It wasn't the pearls, it was Lingon. Her persona seemed to radiate supreme confidence. That's what pearls do. It's a cultural construct, of course, but one I'd seen many times before. When I spent a day shadowing Eve Alfillé in her jewelry store in Evanston, Illinois, I witnessed how a single strand of medium-sized Tahitian pearls had transformed a mousy, sixty-five-year-old matron into an uncommonly beautiful woman, radiating strength and beauty.

"Oh, they do feel nice," Lingon swooned, almost in a whisper. "I do love them. I feel elegant beyond belief."

Sure, Lingon's business was to hype the pearls, but I knew what she was talking about. *I* was having trouble breathing. I staggered out of Christie's that morning, tired and spent. If I were a cigarette smoker, I'd have gone through a pack.

V

In preparation for Christie's Baroda Pearls lollapalooza, I wanted to get a pre-view of what a primo jewelry auction would be like, so I made my way to Sotheby's that afternoon and found Vock alone in the ninth row, catalogue and bidding paddle (No. 239) in hand. He was wearing a gold sports coat, blue shirt opened at the collar, and gray slacks. Again the image of a slender James Gandolfini, a k a Tony Soprano, came to mind. There were forty bidders in the auction room; on either side were elevated tables at which Sotheby's employees tended phone banks to connect with out-of-town dealers or clients calling in their bids. Bids were flashed on a screen with simultaneous conversion into euros, pounds, Swiss francs, and yen. Vock was still interested in the emerald and diamond pendant earclips (No. 169), whose reserve was listed at $18,000–$22,000. The bidding started at $15,000 but quickly escalated to $20,000. Vock nonchalantly held up his paddle at $21,000, but as soon as the auctioneer noted the bid, there seemed to be a flurry of activity from the phone banks, with another bid coming in almost instantly at $23,000. Vock raised his paddle and upped to $25,000. The offer spurred a battle between two phone bidders duking it out, pushing the proffers to $29,000, then $30,000, $31,000, and finally $32,000. Vock shook his head. He had maxed out.

"Is that it?" asked auctioneer Gary Schuler.

Five seconds went by.

"Fair warning," Schuler announced.

"Down it goes," Schuler said, tapping the auction hammer. "Sold!"

Vock was itching to bid on another set of Van Cleef & Arpels diamond pendant earclips, this one with flowerhead tops, 18 round and 48 baguette diamonds, anchored by two pear-shaped diamonds, mounted in platinum. The reserve bid was $20,000–$30,000. Vock jumped in at $25,000 and steadily stayed with the action, which came from two eager telephone bidders, hitting $35,000 before pulling out. At $47,500, the bidding finally slowed.

"Are we all done?" Schuler asked.

"Fair warning."

Then Schuler brought the hammer down.

Vock and I left the floor, and as we rounded a corner, Vock cornered Johanna Hardy, a Sotheby's jewelry buyer from the London office. Hardy said she was interested in offering up for sale pricey wearable art. Hardy looked the part. She could have been an avant-garde jeweler herself, wearing a wide black belt, oversized white blouse, lumpy taupe sweater, and flouncy floral skirt.

Vock pulled out from a small briefcase a Tiffany brooch and was working fast to convince Hardy to put it up for auction. She studied the piece for three, maybe five seconds, and then looked up. "I could be interested," she said in a noncommittal kind of way.

With that crowning affirmation, Vock was ready for his big gun. He went for broke: "I'm gonna cut to the chase here. I don't want to sound arrogant, but if you care about getting pearls that are unique—if you really care about what you are taking in and selling—then I'd like to show you something."

Hardy nodded, Vock hesitated, savoring the suspense. He slowly pulled out of his briefcase one of the most remarkable strands of South Sea pearls I'd ever seen. It was a graduated strand of very large creamy whites, some as large as 18 millimeters. He handled the necklace as though it were alive, trained to respond only to his commands.

"Look at this!" He paused then, and in almost a whisper, said, "There's just a touch of pink, a hint. But no green. Absolutely none."

Hardy's eyes widened. She picked up the pearls, feeling their heft in her right hand. Vock knew he had her. "Yes," she said, "these are nice. Very nice. I am interested." No use overplaying her hand.

But Vock pushed. "It's really a magnificent necklace," he said, waiting for an affirmative nod, which he got. "I need to know earlier rather than later if this is something you're keen on. There are others if you're not." Bravado, I'm sure.

Vock and Hardy exchanged business cards, then handshakes. "Don't do anything until you hear from me," Hardy cautioned. With that, a slight smile crept onto Vock's otherwise poker face.

VI

The next day was why I had come to New York. I arrived at Christie's in the early afternoon. The Baroda Pearls were to be the last item to go up for auction, and that wouldn't be until 5:00 p.m. or so. This was Lingon's big day, and she was dressed in a cerulean jacket, black pants, and slipper flats. There were several characters out of Central Casting in the crowd, congregating in the foyer for stop-and-chats. I spotted a Mr. Clean look-alike with matching pink ascot and handkerchief, impossibly large sunglasses perched on the crown of his shiny head. A dozen women clutched their pashminas, a reaction to effusive air conditioning. An Hasidic Jew with his wife, wearing a wig, commandeered seats. On the fringes of the room was a contingent of onlookers. Relatively few in the room had bidding paddles, which meant there wouldn't be much action from the floor for the Baroda Pearls or, for that matter, any of the items on the auction block. Most would come from telephone bidders.

More and more people took seats, and by 2:35 p.m. the auction room was packed, with standing room only. The auctioneer for the first half of the auction was patrician Kadakia, Lingon's colleague, speaking in a crisp, authoritative British accent, warming up the hundred or so people in the room by entertaining bids for a series of antique art deco vanity cases. Kadakia wore a double-breasted, double-vented suit, and, just as he was mounting the stage to the podium, I caught a glimpse of a pair of bright red socks. Must be a boarding school thing, or maybe they were for good luck.

An amber, jadeite, and diamond case by Cartier went for $11,000, followed by an art nouveau agate and enamel cigarette case by Boucheron, with an asking price of $8,000–$12,000, which went for a whopping $38,000. After a lapis lazuli and diamond vanity case with a reserve of $2,000–$4,000 went for $10,000, the dealer next to me leaned over to me. "This is crazy. I have the same compact I bought at Doyle's for $300, and I can't sell it for $500." There was something in the air.

At Lot No. 188, Kadakia stepped down, and Christie's biggest gun, its top auctioneer, François Curiel, the international director of Christie's Jewelry Department, took the hammer. He spoke with an accent, but also with a slight lisp. As we got closer to the Baroda Pearls (Lot No. 262), I sensed a faster pace of bidding. Eighty percent of the bids were coming from the phone banks on either side of the auction room. An eight point three one-carat marquise-cut Van Cleef & Arpels diamond ring (Lot No. 206) went for $420,000 after a vigorous parry between two phone bidders. Lot 222 was a monster 24.65-carat rectangular-cut Bulgari-signed diamond ring. As soon as Curiel offered up the ring, Mr. Clean held up his paddle and shouted, "One million!"

The bid hushed the crowd. Then another bidder in the back, a small, dark-haired man, nodded. Curiel went to $1.2 million. Mr. Clean was out by now, but soon the dark-haired man bowed out, too. Two bidders from the telephone banks began bashing each other, edging up the price, $100,000 at a time. This was far from a record for a diamond ring, yet everyone seemed to be holding his or her breath, till finally Curiel slammed down his hammer at a little over $2 million, at which point everyone simultaneously broke out in applause.

Exactly whom were they applauding for? Curiel, Christie's, the unnamed successful bidder, the unnamed seller, I wasn't quite sure.

The heavy bidding continued for an assortment of other pieces, almost all through telephone bids. A 25-carat rectangular-cut Cartier yellow diamond ring went for $700,000. A set of Asscher-cut diamond ear pendants, also 25 carats, went for $870,000 after a duel between two telephone bidders. A pair of diamond 7-carat studs went for $270,000. By now, there was a certain rhythm to the bidding, and Curiel picked up the pace. A quick rally ensued among four phone bidders for a grayish blue diamond ring of 9 carats, which started at $1 million and, going back and forth, ended at $2.1 million. Tension was building in anticipation of the Baroda Pearls; murmurs and whispers among the crowd got louder. After Lot No. 256, a diamond and pearl pendant necklace, went for $820,000, the crowd again broke out in applause. Curiel sped up his pace.

"Fair warning," he announced after some wild and wooly bidding pushed an unmounted pear-shaped diamond of 40 carats from $600,000 to $1.45 million within three minutes. Curiel tapped his hammer with a triumphant "Sold!" Once again the crowd broke out in applause.

The ordering of the lots, of course, is part of the strategy of any auction, and Christie's has turned that strategy into science. Lot No. 261 was the last before the Baroda Pearls came up, and it was a doozy: a 23-carat cushion-cut Kashmir sapphire that once belonged to industrialist James J. Hill, the builder of what today is the Burlington Northern Santa Fe Railway. The Christie's catalogue copy, employing expected hyperbole, said the stone was "one of the most important sapphires currently on the market and is unsurpassed in richness and life." Curiel started the bidding at $1 million, and within ninety seconds, bidders had frenetically escalated to $2 million. That's when Mr. Clean jumped into the fray, going back and forth with a telephone bidder, pushing up the price in $100,000 increments every twenty seconds. Again, the room became hushed. The frenzy slowed down at $2.5 million with a bid from the telephone bank. The proffer had been laid at Mr. Clean's feet, and Curiel asked, "To you, at two point five million dollars."

Mr. Clean was hurriedly talking into a cell phone, taking instructions, and Curiel seemed to understand, nodding. The conversation continued, but in ten seconds, Curiel seemed to have had enough.

"Fair warning," Curiel said, pausing.

The dealer next to me couldn't stand the tension and urged under his breath, "Hammer it, already!"

But just a second before Curiel whacked his hammer, Mr. Clean shouted, "Two-point-six!" to the gasps and delight of seemingly everyone did. The room erupted in thunderous applause.

The elation was short lived. That bid did not hold as the mystery phone bidder pushed the price to $2.7 million. Then it was back to Mr. Clean, who shook his head dejectedly, waving off Curiel.

If a better tease could have been staged for the Baroda Pearls act, I'm uncertain what it could have been. "Now we come to the Baroda pearls," Curiel said, grinning ear to ear.

Kadakia, with phone to his ear, promptly shouted out "Five million!" to assorted nods in the crowd. There was an uncertain moment when no one else bid, not from either the phone banks or from the crowd, until a man behind me, a tall, slender, gray-haired guy who looked Indian, held up his paddle and nervously piped up, "Five point two." Everyone turned around to note the stranger. This was the first I had noticed him. He must have arrived late, and was standing amid a covey of swarthy shorter men who appeared to be from the Middle East, one of whom stood whispering nonstop into the bidder's ear.

Kadakia quickly returned the volley with $5.5 million, jumping the bid in one round by $300,000. The tall man in the back returned with $5.8, only to be quickly matched again by Kadakia's buyer at $6 million.

The room was suddenly silent. This was mano a mano battle between the mystery man standing behind me and the anonymous phone bidder tethered to Kadakia's ear.

The floor bidder returned the bid, after some hesitation, and then pushed again, this time to $6.2 million.

Kadakia promptly countered with $6.3 million.

Silence from the bidder behind me.

"Fair warning," Curiel intoned, waiting a full ten seconds.

I didn't have a pin to drop, but the floor was carpeted anyway.

Then suddenly, Curiel slammed his hammer, followed by thunderous applause. It was as though we all had truly witnessed something—Tiger Woods winning the U.S. Open or Barry Bonds breaking Hank Aaron's home run record.

The mystery bidder behind me was surrounded by what now appeared to be a large circle of friends, business associates, and assorted hangers-on, so I first made a beeline to Lingon and Kadakia, hoping to learn the identity of the purchaser, but neither would give up anything. They looked like a pair of Cheshire cats.

I went back to the mystery bidder, but by then he seemed to have disappeared.

I walked out to the foyer. A steady drizzle threatened to turn into a full-throttle downpour. Without an umbrella, I stood stalled inside. I mused how irretrievably deep I'd gotten myself into the nature of not just these extraordinary Baroda Pearls but all pearls. My mother's affection for her modest strand of pearls had launched me on a journey she never could have imagined.

A group of talky men joined me in the foyer, joking, half in English, half in a language I didn't recognize. They were standing in a semi-circle, preparing to brave the rain. I immediately recognized one of them, the tall, graying Indian, the man who'd placed the losing bid for the Baroda Pearls.

I introduced myself and we exchanged cards. He was Salih Maricar, a dealer in natural pearls with offices in New York and Hatton Gardens, London. When I asked whether he had bid for himself or for a client, he paused, then said, "We have a customer who authorized me to bid six million."

"But you went up to $6.2 million."

"And it was like pulling teeth to do so," Maricar responded regally. "We were pipped. But we had a limit. I'd have liked to go further, but my client was unprepared to do so."

"Where are the pearls going to end up?" I asked.

"They'll probably go to an Arab family, and they'll end up in an Arab museum. Middle Easterners love natural pearls."

"Who was your client?" I persisted.

Maricar shook his head and smiled. "Of course, I can't reveal that."

Just then, though, Maricar introduced me to a small, compact man with a pockmarked face. This was the same man who had stood next to Maricar during the auction, whispering instructions into Maricar's ear throughout the roller-coaster bidding. "Here is the Bahraini ambassador. He certainly was interested." As I reached to shake the ambassador's hand, the man waved me off, and moved out of the lobby into the rain. It seemed plausible that Maricar had been bidding for the Bahraini government, with the ambassador acting as its representative.

The next day, a Christie's press release stated that the buyer of the Baroda Pearls had been an Asian collector, no name or nationality. Perhaps an Asian broker had been bidding for a sheik or sultan, as Vock has predicted. But when I pressed Lingon one last time about the buyer's identity, all she allowed was this: "Wasn't the auction fantastic?"

19

French Polynesia: The Pearl that Got Away

I

By the time June rolled around, I was itching to return to the pearl trail. My pearl dreams had returned. I wanted back, especially with French Polynesia my next stop. When I had first discovered that the islands of French Polynesia were home to black pearls, I swallowed hard, not quite believing my fortune. Tahitian pearls had little in common with Barbara Bush creamy whites. Tahitians are metallic, almost iridescent, shades that sparkle. They're not all black; varieties of green, gray, turquoise, blue, eggplant are the most common. As with all oysters, the color of the pearl is the same color as the fleshy lip of the oyster just under the outer edge of the shell.

Iowa had thawed by now, and summer was about to commence. The specter of warm weather leavened Iris's spirits, and the end of tenth grade was all that it took to lift Mikey's. The three of us started out together, on a vacation to San Francisco, where Iris and I used to live and where Mikey had been born. It was a celebration of our little family. We drove to our favorite place in the world,

Point Reyes, and hiked to the ocean. The three of us mugged for photos to accompany shots we'd taken at the same spot when Mikey had been an infant and toddler. After a week of family festivities, I was to fly to Papeete, Tahiti; Mikey was to enroll in a debate program at Berkeley; and Iris was to stay with an old friend who lived at the foot of the crookedest street in the world. We were feeling good about the upcoming summer; we'd be separated, but we'd reunite as soon as I returned from pearling trips to Tahiti and, after that, Australia.

II

As soon as I arrived in the French Polynesian capital of Papeete, what struck me was the morning light—a shimmering illumination like nothing I'd ever experienced before. French Polynesia, an archipelago of 118 islands and atolls that occupies more area than Europe, is surrounded by calm, bluish limpid water that reflects like a mirror. The intensity of azure light grows as the sun gets higher and higher in the sky. I pulled out my sunglasses.

Polynesia means "many islands" in Greek, and Tahiti is the largest and most famous in the country, but Moorea (a seven-minute plane trip or forty-minute ferry ride from Papeete) is the more dramatic of the two major islands, with near-vertical mountains rising from the sea. The chain of islands lies at the same longitude as Hawaii, 2,600 miles south. Tahiti is halfway between California and Australia, making it for more than a century a port of call for steamers plying the seas between continents. The islands are also a rest stop for an amazing variety of birds, relaxing before carrying on the business of long-haul flying. Everywhere I went I heard an arpeggio of euphoric chirping.

Ever since Samuel Wallis claimed Tahiti for Britain in 1767 (to be seized by the French in 1846), word has circulated far and wide of Tahitian beauty. Thick long black hair, voluptuous bodies, tawny skin, bemused smiles, and an uninhibited sense of pungent sexuality have made for a reputation of Venus-like goddesses in Tahiti. And it's not just the women. The men historically have been portrayed as singularly handsome, dark, muscular warriors. Today, indigenous dances like the *aparima* and *hivinau* still emphasize a rapid swiveling and bouncing of the hips, along with a sensual wavelike motion of the arms and hands. Like Brazilian samba or Argentine tango, the motions are so sexual that it's difficult not to get wrapped up in Tahitian mythology of South Pacific mermaids. Paul Gauguin's vision had not been much off the mark.

Tahitian pearls somehow reflect this sensuality. Of all pearls, Tahitians are among my favorites. They invert the American concept of the traditional white or ivory pearl. These are pearls, yes, but they are also amulets that are among the most exotic of all jewelry. There's something naughty about them.

As soon as I landed at the airport in Papeete's Faaa district, I flew out again to meet legendary pearl farmer and spearfisherman Jean Tapu, who lives on the tiny atoll of Apataki. The puddle-jumper I took was a one-stop flight, with an hour-long layover on another atoll in the Tuamotus chain. As we landed on steamy Aratua, we flew through a ring of mist that hovered atop the atoll like a gauzy halo. As I sat at the "airport," actually just a concrete airstrip, I got the feeling that I was floating on the turquoise waters of the South Pacific. In a sense I was.

That was my first sensation, along with the aroma. I inhaled a combination of gardenias, roses, orchids, hibiscus, and bougainvillea. Fragrant *Gardenia taitensis* is French Polynesia's national symbol, worn tucked behind the ears of women (and men) or woven together in leis and head crowns.

The final leg of my trip to Apataki was fifteen minutes via a nine-seater Air Tahiti Nui Beechcraft plane. The door between the cockpit and the passenger section was wide open, so the co-pilot could carry on a conversation with a pretty girl in seat 1B. As we were about to land, a woman wearing a yellow dress and a head wreath of gardenias, and carrying multiple shopping bags stuffed with food, crossed herself. We skidded left and right, and precariously came to a tentative stop.

I immediately recognized Jean Tapu from a reproduction of a newspaper photograph I'd seen of him after he'd won the World Spearfishing Competition in Cuba in 1958. Almost everyone in Tahiti whose business is either pearls or fish knows Tapu, and if they don't know him personally, they know of him. Tapu has a claim few can top: A species of fish (*Pareu tapiu*) is named after him.

We joined Estelle, Tapu's wife of fifty-five years, sitting in the flatbed of a beat-up red Renault two-seater with a cracked windshield, as the three of us bounced back to the Tapu house five minutes away. Three barking dogs led our way.

When we got to the house, Tapu motioned me toward a shack near the water. He didn't bother with flip-flops and traversed pebbles and sharp stones with grace, the soles of his feet so calloused they resembled doubled-over, thick sandpaper. With a quick flick of a machete, Tapu sliced off the tops of two coconuts, and, sitting inside a straw-and-bamboo hut, he began his story.

Born in 1929 on the Polynesian island of Rangiroa and adopted by a family that moved to Apataki, Tapu grew up as the son of a local pearl diver and fisherman. When Tapu was eight, he worked for François Mais Hervé, the French government administrator for the Tuamotus Islands. It was a propitious beginning for the young, would-be pearl farmer. In the 1930s, Hervé had started the first cultured-pearl farm in French Polynesia on the atoll of Nuutina, a twenty-minute boat trip from Apataki. Hervé's method was to drill a hole in the oyster shell, insert a foreign object, patch the hole with cement, and plug it back up with a piece of the original shell. Young Tapu's job was to place the oysters back in the warm lagoons surrounding Nuutina. Hervé's experiment yielded some irregularly shaped pearls, but not many. What it showed Tapu was that Tahitian pearls could be cultivated.

As World War II began, Tapu's family moved to Papeete, where Tapu trained as a nurse specializing in tropical diseases. Tapu learned English when he spent two years in Honolulu working for an infectious-disease specialist as a researcher, then returned home and worked for the Department of Fisheries. That's when he met Jean-Claude Brouillet and Jacques Branellec, who were trying to start a pearl farm on South Marutea. Brouillet, as I had learned from Branellec, was a mercurial entrepreneur. He had made a fortune by starting and operating an airline for the nation of Gabon, and then selling his network of planes to the African state government, which turned the service into Air Gabon. As a government worker, Tapu helped Brouillet and Branellec establish their nascent pearl farm. Prickly Branellec had a falling-out with Brouillet, and Brouillet promptly bought out Branellec's interest. Brouillet offered to double Tapu's government salary, a proposition Tapu couldn't refuse, and Tapu stayed with Brouillet for three years, overseeing five Japanese grafters and ten divers for the operation. In the early 1980s, Tapu quit when he opted to start his own pearl farm. As the technicians' knowledge improved, Tahitian pearls were becoming a lucrative commodity, which for the time being only Brouillet's farm was cultivating in large enough numbers to export. That's when Brouillet connected with New York pearl broker Salvador Assael, who introduced much of the world to the tantalizing dark pearls, and made a fortune doing so. Just as the pearls were making a splash internationally, Tahitian businessman Robert Wan started his own farm in the Gambier Islands, another chain of Polynesian atolls, and six months later, Brouillet sold his operations to Wan. Tapu continued in the pearl business himself for some time, but returned to his love, sport fishing, a profession that earned him international accolades but little money.

Wearing a Nike cap, silver shorts, and a yellow Quiksilver T-shirt, Tapu was telling me all this as we sipped from our coconuts, the blue water gleaming behind him. At seventy-six, Tapu was still a strapping, healthy guy, a handsome, rough-hewn, deeply tanned, and scraggy version of Yves Montand. Every once in a while, local boys paddling dugout canoes and holding spearfishing guns glided by and merrily waved.

These days, few independent farmers in French Polynesia can make much of a living producing pearls. Tapu said the going price per average pearl ten years ago was 700 Tahitian francs, or $8. Now, the price local dealers are willing to pay is closer to 70 francs, or 80 cents. I found this impossible to believe, but said nothing at the time. "There are just too many pearls out there. That, combined with a drop in demand, makes the pearl business almost impossible for the small farmer," Tapu said in accented English, shaking his head.

The powerhouse pearl farms are concentrated in the hands of just a handful of Tahitian, notably Tahitian-Chinese, including the world's megaproducer of Tahitian pearls, multimillionaire Robert Wan. Tapu didn't have much good to say about any of them. "It's impossible to compete with them," Tapu said, tucking in his chin toward his chest, the swoosh of his Nike cap dipping. "The Chinese are always thinking about money, and because of that, they own a disproportionate amount of the islands' wealth," Tapu said, putting down his coconut.

I found his ethnic characterization revealing, since the Tahitian-Chinese producers such as Robert Wan were just as Tahitian as Tapu. The Chinese started immigrating to Tahiti in the mid- to late-1800s to work cotton fields that had been established by European colonists. Yet today, these fourth-generation Tahitians are still considered Chinese by many locals. Tapu's islander attitude had undercurrents of racism driven by the disproportionate explosion of wealth in French Polynesia of so many descendants of Chinese immigrants and their families. When asked him about this, Tapu shrugged his shoulders. "Tahitians will give you anything. We have an expression, 'Aita pea'pea,' which means 'No problem, don't worry.' That's the Tahitian motto. That's how we live. But the Chinese come and take advantage of us. They rob us blind."

Tapu expressed a similar sentiment when he talked about the French, using pearler Jacques Branellec as an example. "Branellec used to let me know all the time that he was French. He always needed to show how wealthy he was, that he was superior, that his heritage was somehow greater than mine. His driver, his house, all his money. He made me feel like he was twenty meters higher than me. And he was twenty years younger than me!" This indignant sense of natives as honest, kindhearted people exploited by shrewd outsiders was not a new concept for islanders anywhere, and it persisted as I interviewed more and more locals.

Wan controls at least 50 percent of all pearl farming in French Polynesia, and because of that, his influence is felt by just about everyone on the islands, and not just those in the pearl business. Pearls are by far the islands' biggest export, totaling $147 million. Wan produces two million pearls a year, upwards of five tons. It was a variation of the old saw that *used* to be said about American capitalism: When General Motors sneezed, everyone caught a cold. In French Polynesia, when Robert Wan trips, the nation has a concussion. Wan was the single most powerful person in French Polynesia, certainly more important than the revolving door of the nation's presidents.

I'd be visiting Wan's farms on South Marutea for three days, and I was to accompany him on his private jet plane. I'd have an opportunity to see up close how Wan wielded so much power, and the impact it had on both him and the tropical nation of 260,000 residents.

As the honey-colored sun drizzled below the horizon. Estelle joined us. She had fixed a dinner of fish-and-noodle stew and a homemade cake of dates and walnuts for dessert. We sat over coffee and talked as dusk turned to evening and several stars appeared in the clear sky. Tapu took Estelle's hand. "Fifty-five years. And we still love each other. We have arguments here and there, but we still love each other." I got the impression this was more proclamation than confession. Estelle looked at her husband and squeezed his hand. The three of us paused, sitting in the glow from the hurricane lamps Estelle had lit.

My hours of plane travel were getting the best of me; a day earlier I'd been eating dim sum in San Francisco with Iris and Mikey. I said good night to Estelle and Tapu, and climbed the steps to my lodgings, an A-frame cabin Tapu and his grandson had built on stilts jutting out over the sandy shore. Before I could take my clothes off, I had fallen asleep.

It was a good thing I kept my clothes on. Even in paradise, some circumstances remain constant. Dive-bombing mosquitoes buzzed around my ears all night. I got up to light the mosquito coils Tapu had graciously left out for me. The smoky scent seemed to work, or maybe the mosquitoes just got tired of me. There was a slapping sound to the ocean, and when I got up at 4:00 a.m. to investigate, shining my flashlight down toward the water, I could see thousands of glittery silver fish swirling, some jumping a foot or so out of the ocean. I scratched my head, considering whether this was a dream. At 5:00 a.m., the local Catholic church bells pealed.

The next morning, I asked Tapu about Apataki, the island he's called home almost his entire life. There is one elementary school, no high school. No physicians. Other than scratchy reception from a single TV station in Papeete, the only connection with the rest of the world is four Air Tahiti Nui prop planes a week to Aratua.

Tapu's rich life is the result of such isolation. In 1988, ichthyologists were baffled when an unnamed fish found at three hundred meters was caught in the waters around Apataki. Marine biologists brought the specimen to Tapu, who said, "What's the big deal? I've seen the fish my whole life." In response, the biologists gave the fish the name *Alonthias tapui*. Tapu used to be a competitive fisherman, and was a two-time spearfishing, free-dive champion in French Polynesia. At the world championship in Cuba in 1957, he caught 250 fish over a five-hour period in two days with two other team members. His prize was a trophy and a meter-long Cuban cigar, which Tapu said was a nice gesture but, since he didn't smoke, didn't really mean all that much to him. His record is a massive 138-kilo grouper. He still can hold his breath for a full minute and a half, and dives with no underwater breathing apparatus.

Tapu was my entrée to the lives of pearl farmers on the island. A decade ago there were fifteen in Apataki, but today just six survived, all struggling mightily. Tapu introduced me to two farmers, Daniel Tavere and his son, Jean Yves. Daniel, 65, was born in Arutua, but moved to Apataki to fish in 1975. He started a pearl farm in 1995 with his wife, son, and two daughters. They harvest twice each year some six thousand pearls, ranging from 8 to 14 millimeters.

We sat on white plastic chairs on a dock Tavere and his son had built five hundred yards from the shore. Tavere was a large, deeply tanned man, with watery, bloodshot blue eyes, a deeply creased face, and a gold-capped front tooth that seemed to protrude from his mouth everytime he laughed. He wore a faded red T-shirt, blue striped shorts, and a pink cap that only partially covered his unruly salt-and-pepper hair. A bulge of a belly seemed to offer evidence of a life, which if not opulent, was well lived. Tavere went back and forth between French and Tahitian, talking softly. By all appearances, he was as local and as genuine as pearl farmers come. The farthest he'd ever been from the island was the nation's capital, Papeete, and whenever he went there, he itched to get back home.

Tavere said the largest pearl his oysters had ever produced was an impossibly huge 22 millimeters, and when I asked him if I could see it, he readily said yes. When he spoke of this colossal pearl, I couldn't help but think of Kino, whose life so dramatically changes after he discovers a similar-sized pearl. Tavere had found the pearl on the ocean floor. He surmised that the pearl must have fallen out of one of the oysters he'd cultured, and had lain for several years on the porous, silty sand as schools of fish swam by. The pearl wasn't round, but an oddly shaped baroque pearl that had given back to the sea most of its sheen. But the pearl was magnificent, Tavere said. He kept it not only as a reminder of the bounty the sea creates but also as a reward the sea returns to those whose lives are so inextricably connected to it.

I was eager to understand how Tavere went about selling his pearls, and when I broached the subject, he didn't shy away from my questions. I got the impression that he rarely talked about pearling finances, and here I was a stranger, not just from the big city, but from the other side of the world, who didn't speak his language, asking him a raft of business questions. But Tavere answered thoughtfully and in a straightforward manner. At times, he'd hesitate, looking upward, adding up numbers out loud in Tahitian, nodding, then coming up with an answer.

"For my best pearls," he said, "I go directly to the jewelry stores. They'll comb through the whole lot and choose forty, fifty, maybe sixty. They'll buy only the best of what I have."

How much do the jewelers pay?

For top quality 14-millimeter pearls, he said, the going rate from retail jewelers is 3,000 to 5,000 Tahitian francs ($35 to $54) per pearl. The rest of his harvest he takes to dealers, who carefully pick and choose, with the average price coming to 1,000 to 1,500 Tahitian francs ($11 to $16) per pearl. The pearls the dealers pass on, Tavere tries to dump, if he's lucky, for 700 Tahitian francs ($8) per pearl. That last category makes up the majority of his harvest. The rejects, the majority of his crop, he keeps at home.

I held back a gasp. My initial reaction was that Tavere was getting ripped off in the worse way. I hadn't seen the quality of his pearls, but if indeed they were anywhere close to Grade AAA, AA, A, or B, and truly as large as 14 millimeters, these local Tahitian retail dealers were stringing (or mounting) his pearls and realizing huge profits. I'd seen nice—but not spectacular—Black Tahitian pearl necklaces in Hong Kong sell for as much as $7,500 wholesale, only to be doubled by retailers before the strands got to the customer. With a pedigree clasp, the necklace would go for more than $20,000. Figuring thirty-two 14-millimeter pearls for a nongraduated 16-inch choker strand, Tavere would receive an average price of $1,424 for all thirty-two top-quality pearls (if he had them), making the wholesale markup for such a necklace seven times what Tavere would get paid. Of course, dealers or jewelers would have to size, match, and string the pearls, as well as wait till they'd accumulate thirty-two similar pearls that could go on the same strand. And then they'd have to find a buyer.

My initial reaction of outrage lessened when I thought about the economics at hand. Price escalation is at the heart of the business of pearls as commodities, as it is with any raw product, whether it's diamonds, cocaine, crude oil, or coffee beans. True, these pearls didn't have to be processed as the other commodities did. Pearls come out pretty close to the finished product, and coming directly from the farmer, they were at the very bottom of a long economic ladder of price hikes. Everyone perched on each rung upward takes as large a bite as possible, just as long as the product still remains competitively priced to the next rung's buyer, all the way to the top—the end consumer. Tavere's concern wasn't what the woman in New York, Paris, or London (or her husband) paid for his pearls. As with the technicians I had met in China, those cities could very well be on the moon for all Tavere cared. That wasn't Tavere's concern. His business was growing pearls and selling them for the best price. It was plain and simple. He was not any different from the coffee bean or cocaine farmer in Columbia. That a Chicago secretary forks over $3.75 for a grande espresso at Starbucks or a Wall Street junk bond dealer antes up $2,300 for an ounce of cocaine doesn't enter into the local farmer's mind when he haggles a price with a dealer for his beans or coca leaves. The thing that mattered to Tavere was the next rung, and how much he'd get.

When I asked about Tahiti's eight-hundred-pound gorilla, Robert Wan, Tavere first hesitated, then vented. "We tried to sell to Wan, but he told us it'd be better to sell our pearls in the public market in downtown Papeete," Tavere said. I got the feeling that was like recommending to an artist that he ought to hawk his canvases in a Walmart parking lot. "Wan is trying to squeeze us out. We can't compete with someone who has so many resources," Tavere said, squinting into the sun. And to make matters worse, Tavere said, the price of black pearls has gone down each year, from their all-time high in 1996–97, when Tavere could get 6,000 francs ($65) per commercial-grade pearl.

"Too many black pearls out there," Tavere said with a halfhearted frown. Tapu nodded in agreement. When they started, Tapu and Tavere routinely sold everything they farmed. The worldwide market was so hot for these then new and exotic pearls that dealers gobbled up everything farmers could supply. "Now, all they'll buy is the best. The pearls that sell today have to be large and round," Tavere said. "The rest we pretty much keep for ourselves or just throw away."

The finances of setting up a Tahitian pearl farm also were becoming more and more daunting. Farmers lease from the government the farming area in the water surrounding the island, based on how many two-hundred-meter-long spat lines they lay. Tapu and Tavere estimated annual outlay for a small family farm, without any labor costs, could top out at $18,000. But the start-up fees were astronomical; equipment, buoys, lines, a boat, a water-based grafting station, could run as high as a half-million dollars. What young farmer could get his hands on so much money? Something else: Pearl farmers have to wait at least two years for their first harvest, which, as with all crops, whether coffee or cocaine, is dependent on a host of environmental, market, and political factors. And as with cocaine, pearl dealers had to factor in poaching as an additional expense.

Even in a tight-knit community like Apataki, stealing is common, from gasoline out of boat engines, to maturing oysters, to pearl-bearing oysters. Some farmers resort to going high-tech to thwart poachers by opting not to use traditional buoys that bounce atop the water, holding pearl lines, announcing to everyone what lies below. Instead, they use expensive GPS systems that bury the location of the pearl lines underwater, but such high-tech equipment adds cost to a farmer's already strained budget.

Looking at his son, Jacques Yves, a brooding guy of twenty-five wearing a blue T-shirt that read *Gauloises*, Tavere said, "I don't think my son will be in the pearl business in twenty years. I don't see *how*. It'll be even harder then than it is today, and I can't imagine it more difficult than it *already* is." Jacques Yves is one of a set of twins; his brother left Apataki three years ago to enroll in a science program at the university in Papeete and has little desire to return to the island.

When I asked about the national pearl cooperative of farmers, both Tavere and Tapu laughed. It was as though I had cracked a funny joke. The cooperative had about 125 farmer-members throughout French Polynesia, and acts as a go-between for the farmer and dealers. The cooperative pays for a technician to work with farmers, supplies expertise to the farmers, and arranges four pearl auctions a year in Hong Kong. In return, the co-op says it takes six percent of profits.

Tavere used to be a member for three years, but pulled out because the prices offered were too low, below what Tavere and Tapu said they could get on their own. "There was no negotiating," Tavere said. "They tell you what they will pay you. Period. You drop your pearls off with them, and they give you a number. They don't give you an explanation. It's take it or leave it."

Both Tavere and Tapu went as far as to say that they believed the head of the cooperative, M. Alfred Martin, was pocketing members' money. Neither said they understood how Martin could keep straight which pearls come from which farms and how he could figure fair and accurate prices to pay the farmers for their goods, since the auctions take place months after the farmers give Martin their pearls.

I wanted to see Tavere's large pearl, and when I asked him about it, he promised to come by Jean Tapu's house by midday with it. It seems, as with Kino, that no matter how bleak matters were, there always was the opportunity for a pearl farmer to strike it big—that in one oyster out of a hundred million lies the perfect pearl, a huge pearl that would take your breath away and make all of life's troubles disappear. The sentiment wasn't any different from the hardscrabble factory worker in Flint or Cleveland, desperately hanging on to his job, who faithfully plays the lottery each week, hoping beyond hope to hit the Powerball. Only in Tavere's case, he actually did. Or so it seemed.

Two hours later, Tapu and I were sipping coconut juice and eating last night's leftovers at the hut when Tapu made to me what I thought was a surprising confession. He didn't even like the black, gray, or other dark pearls that have become Tahiti's trademark. "They make me think of death. Too much like mourning. I like white pearls," Tapu said, looking up from the date-and-walnut cake Estelle had baked us.

Before Tapu could go any further, Tavere had motored up to our picnic in a little red scooter. He had with him his grandson, no more than three, standing on a wooden box on the floor of the scooter, holding on to the handlebars. The little boy was wearing a T-shirt and nothing else. Tavere looked somewhat forlorn, but nonetheless contented and reassured by his grandson's presence. Tavere said that when he had gotten home and asked his wife about the big pearl, she told him she had sold it!

"It's been a long time since I last saw the pearl," he said, "and when I asked my wife about it, she said someone had wanted to buy it and she'd accepted his offer. She had forgotten to tell me." Tavere shrugged his shoulders apologetically.

The explanation seemed awfully sketchy. If it was true, I didn't want to compound any familial conflict by asking how much she'd gotten for the pearl—if indeed she had ever sold it, or, for that matter, whether Tavere had ever found it. If Tavere was telling the truth, I'd think that in most relationships, such an action would be a breach of confidence of the first order. Of course, Tavere's story might not have been the whole truth. Maybe he didn't want to show me the pearl. Maybe someone had stolen it and he was embarrassed to admit it. Whatever the real story, there was no mega pearl forthcoming. Judging from Tavere's sanguine appearance, I think I was more disappointed with the news than he was.

We talked more, Tavere's grandson, Dilon, sitting on Tavere's lap, eyeing me rather suspiciously. Dilon kept busy by playing with the curly white hairs on his grandfather's muscular forearms as Tavere cradled the boy. Tapu and Tavere switched from French into Tahitian, and what little recognition I had of what they were saying was now lost on me, as surely it was on Tavere's grandson, who presently was dozing in Tavere's arms. Estelle began cooking dinner. She had put in a cassette player of Ella Fitzgerald, who serenaded us with "How Long Has This Been Going On?" Tavere stoked his grandson's head as he and Tapu talked, their voices soft. I had not seen such a quiet display of affection between a grandfather and grandson for a long time. Tapu must have said something funny to Tavere, and both men suddenly laughed, Tavere careful, though, not to wake the boy. Tavere's gold tooth caught the late-after noon light, which made it shine.

Tavere started up the scooter, all the while cradling Dilon with those large forearms of his. They putt-putted together, zigzagging out of Tapu's yard, at first precariously, then more certain. Tavere's missing pearl had gotten Tapu thinking, and when I noticed him looking into the aquamarine waters off in the distance, a pensive moment in quietude, I asked him about the largest pearl he'd ever found. As the words slipped from my mouth, I realized that by zeroing in on the superlative (journalists love stories about the largest, oldest, newest), I had minimized the heft and substance of Tavere and Tapu's long, productive lives. With some guilt, I plundered ahead nonetheless.

Tapu lowered his voice, smiling in a dreamy kind of way. "I remember the pearl. It was twenty-one-and-a-half millimeters, and mine was perfectly round. This pearl was so large, it'd been difficult to take out of the oyster. We all gathered around to see it. And when it finally came out, it was close to perfect." Tapu paused, looking out to the sea for a good ten seconds before resuming.

Tapu gave the pearl to a friend in Papeete who had an interested buyer, a foreign dealer. The would-be buyer examined the pearl, rolling it on a table, holding it up to the light to see its orient and lustre. Yes, he said, this indeed was a magnificent pearl. He was eager to proceed, but needed to have the pearl properly appraised. Then, he'd return with the pearl and an offer, he was certain, of a great sum of money, more than Tapu could ever imagine. The dealer assured Tapu's friend that the pearl was worth many, many thousands of dollars. It was, after all, one of a kind. The two men shook hands. When the friend informed Tapu about the meeting, Tapu and Estelle talked about how their lives would change, how they'd be able to buy land, how they'd assure their grandchildren's futures.

Alas, as with Daniel Tavere's pearl, fate or human fallibility intervened. As promised, the dealer returned with both a lucrative offer and the pearl. That night, though, Tapu's friend either lost the great pearl or it was stolen. At least that's what the friend told Tapu, and that's what Tapu told me. "He was my friend," Tapu explained in a genuine and plaintive way. "There was nothing I could do. I believed my friend. I trusted him. I knew that he didn't have the money to pay me for the pearl, so there was nothing I could do." As with Tavere, at face value, the story seemed preposterous, but judging from the look on Tapu's face, his forelorn sincerity, I was certain that what he told me was exactly how his friend had explained to him the missing pearl.

III

The next day, Tapu and I got into his motorboat and headed to Nuutina, the atoll where Tapu as a boy had worked when François Mais Hervé cultured the first pearls in French Polynesia in the 1930s. In 1987, Tapu had scraped together enough money to buy the island from Hervé's granddaughter, thus closing a half-century circle of sorts. Tapu and his grandson, Tyrone, have begun their own pearl farm on the atoll. They hadn't harvested any pearls yet, but hope to when the twenty thousand oysters they spawned mature in two years. Tyrone had a makeshift house on the island where he and his family often go. But mostly the atoll was deserted, with little left of Hervé's presence. Some years back, Tapu had imported a dozen pigs to Nuutina, and today their numbers have grown to sixty. The original idea was to create a piggery and then butcher the hogs as ancillary income, but the pigs had gotten too tame and Tapu had made the fundamental mistake of getting to know them. Just as Tapu was about to swing an ax down on a green coconut shell, he shouted at the top of his lungs in a low-pitched guttural sound that rose with his breath, and soon two fat hogs wobbled our way. "That's the grandmother, and she looks pregnant," Tapu said as the sow paid no heed to us and began to root the coconut, slurping its watery milk. "I can't butcher these guys now," Tapu said bringing down the ax, smiling apologetically.

Estelle made us dinner, a fish and noodle stew. Evenings were short at this time of year, and darkness fell no later than 7:00 p.m. With a match, I lit two of the remaining mosquito coils in an attempt to persuade the island insects to ravage elsewhere. The halo plume of smoke seemed to work, but did nothing about the island dogs. At midnight, I was startled awake when a skinny tan dog came into my room, stood a couple feet from my bed, and barked at the top of his lungs, uncertain about who I was.

I was scheduled to leave the next morning, and over the last of the walnut-and-date cake Estelle had baked, I asked my last questions. What had been the impact of depressed pearl prices on the island? Yes, the slowed economy had affected families on the island, but Tyrone, Tapu's grandson was optimistic about the family's fledgling farm on Nuutina. Tyrone had learned grafting, or nucleating, pearls, and his wife, Marlene, was an able cutter of mantle tissue. Tapu would help.

But for the island's other pearl farmers, the outlook wasn't promising. Many on the island had turned to drink and drugs (marijuana has been on the island for years, but crack has now made an appearance), and when Tapu said in an offhanded way that last year six residents had committed suicide, I asked him again about the numbers. Yes, six people in their twenties, over the course of several months, had hanged themselves in succession, Tapu said, as the result of jealousy stemming from island infidelities. That number was shockingly high, considering an island population of just four hundred, and Tapu said the bleak pearl market had thrown some residents into despair and when alcohol and drugs accelerated the gloomy economic prognosis, the outcome had turned deadly. It was an ironic coda to my visit to paradise.

Estelle placed two leis of white-and-tan shells around my neck and kissed me good-bye on both cheeks. We got in the Renault, and just as day was breaking, Tapu stopped at a neighbor's house that on Sundays doubles as a bakery specializing in the Tahitian delicacy of soft sticky braided rolls. Despite the early hour, little girls and dogs ran alongside us on our way to the island's airstrip. As Tapu and I pulled at the hot rolls, trying not to burn our tongues, the girls shouted, "Bonjour! Bonjour!"

At the airstrip, a quarter of the island had shown up. As a nine-seater plane skidded to a stop, the buzz of the crowd grew louder. A boy of six or seven jumped, clapping his hands in delight as his father from the plane strided toward him, lifting him high in the air. As I walked down the tarmac with the other passengers, I realized few people at the airport had little, if any, connection with either the incoming or outgoing passengers. They just wanted to be where the action was on this early Sunday morning.

IV

If what Tapu and Tavere had told me about pricing was correct, then what family farmer in Tahiti could ever hope to make a living harvesting pearls? Back in Papeete, to get at this fundamental question, I met Martin Coeroli, then the general manager of Perles de Tahiti.[1] The group was the main international trade organization for Tahitian pearls and acted as a lobbyist for its members. Coeroli's association arranged everything from cooperative advertising in such upscale magazines as *Architectural Digest*, *Town & Country*, and *W* to product placement of Tahitian pearls around the necks of Hollywood movie stars. As with all consumer goods, customers are swayed by who uses or wears the same goods. That's why Coeroli's office had just hired a Hollywood company, Norm Marshall & Associates, to negotiate product placements with television and film companies, as well as with individual actors. Coeroli had been successful in getting Tahitian pearls worn on *The Sopranos* and on *Desperate Housewives*. Contracted stars included Angelina Jolie, Debra Messing, Oprah Winfrey, Halle Berry, and Penélope Cruz. Coeroli scored a coup of sorts when Laurence Fishburne appeared in *The Matrix* wearing a single Tahitian black pearl around his neck (just as Jeremy Shepherd had done). He had just gotten word that Matthew McConaughey would be wearing a similar man pearl in a movie called *Surfer, Dude*. Pearls make up only 1 to 3 percent of U.S. jewelry sales. "So we have a lot of room for growth," Coeroli said. Which was as positive a spin as I could imagine on such low-market penetration.

The chairman of the board of Coeroli's trade organization was M. Alfred Martin, the head of Poe Ravi Nui, the country's cooperative of pearl farmers, the group Tapu and Tavere had so thoroughly dismissed as corrupt and inefficient. Coeroli and Martin were sure to have facts and figures to refute what Tapu and Tavere had claimed. At the nexus of the millions of pearls French Polynesia exports each year, Coeroli knows every significant pearl player worldwide. He travels to most of the pearl auctions and jewelry shows each year, and sits on the boards of several world governing bodies of gem producers and dealers. M. Alfred Martin also is a key player, bringing to market pearls produced by Tahitian family farms. When I'd been in Tucson to attend the Jewelry Show, I had tried to set up a time to talk to Coeroli and Martin, but both had so many dealers lined up to see them they were too busy to squeeze me in.

We were in Coeroli's third floor office, off crowded Boulevard Pomare in downtown Papeete. Just as the three of us started talking, Coeroli's secretary beeped. The French Polynesian vice president, Temauri Foster, was on the line. Sure. American author in for an interview and the nation's vice president just happens to call? But judging from the careful tone of Coeroli's responses, I came to think that indeed the vice president probably was on the other end of the conversation. Pearls are French Polynesia's cash cow, after all, and Coeroli was one of the few people who had the keys to the barn. He and Foster talked as though they were old friends, and since President Gaston Tong Sang was in France on official business this week, Foster was the acting president.

There are some 600 small-family pearl farmers in French Polynesia, and the cooperative Martin heads represents at any given time between 100 and 150 of them. Wan produces at least 50 percent of all pearls in the nation, with the cooperative accounting for another 10 percent, and independent farmers making up the rest. Of the independents, four pearling companies make up the largest bloc—Vaiatika Perles, Gauguin Perles, Pacific Pearls, and Yu Perles. In short, small pearlers like Tavere are producing less and less and have effectively been squeezed out of the nation's number-one cash crop. When I asked Martin and Coeroli about Tavere's prices, neither could believe any farmer would sell pearls so low. But then they shrugged, as though to say the market for pearls is fickle and the going rate is whatever anyone is willing to pay on any given day (a replay of Alex Vock's maxim).

I wanted to learn more about the cooperative Martin led, in part because I wanted to understand how family pearlers like Tapu and Tavere could ever hope to compete against pearling farms the size of Robert Wan's. Tapu and Tavere's chief beef was that farmers had absolutely no negotiating price; that the prices they were offered were arbitrary, and that the cooperative's opaque pricing structure was stacked against family pearl farmers.

I must admit I couldn't follow Martin's description of how the cooperative worked. His explanation sounded like lot mumbo jumbo. Coeroli suggested one reason some farmers were reticent to participate was because all sales were recorded and then reported to the government, which imposed taxes on farmers' income derived from pearl revenue. Martin and Coeroli both insisted that top-grade pearls at auction that were 12 millimeters could sell for 50,000 Tahitian francs, or $545 per pearl, almost tenfold what Tavere and Tapu said they were getting on their own. These figures sounded awfully high, and when I said so, Coeroli and Tavere insisted they were accurate. Later, when I called Jean Tapu and told him what Coeroli and Martin had said, all he did was laugh.

V

For the better part of a year, I had gone back and forth with Robert Wan's consiglieres to arrange a tour of his Tahitian pearl farms, and our negotiations lasted up till I was to leave the United States for French Polynesia. Through more than two-dozen e-mails, I got the impression that Wan was a sort of Pearlfinger character, a mysterious and powerful figure who pushed and pulled levers that controlled the world pearl markets.

Wan's name was synonymous with Tahitian pearls; that, of course, was the strategy behind his global marketing. At his world headquarters in Papeete, a huge black sign with white lettering read, simply, Robert Wan. No mention of pearls, jewelry, or anything else. Just the name. I ducked inside and strolled through what was billed as The Robert Wan Museum, really a cover for a retail store, and was struck by the eponymous branding throughout. It wasn't any different from what automobile, jewelry, clothing, or leather manufacturers had done for decades and decades, whether they were Ford, Tiffany, Harry Winston, Mikimoto, Mercedes-Benz, Gucci, Chanel, Hermès, Ralph Lauren, Tommy Hilfiger, DKNY, or the Australian pearl lords I was soon to meet, Paspaley and Autore. It's the name people want. The name is what sells. Customers were buying into the persona of a stylemaker's name as a guarantee of quality and fashion.

I got to the Papeete airport by 7:00 a.m. for the flight on Wan's sixteen-seater. The sun had just begun to rise, that luminescent light again, and as I arrived at the private hangar, I immediately spotted Wan talking on his cell phone, the morning-blue sky brightening by the minute. He looked my way, nodded, and shook my hand as he hung up. We made small talk, and for all the buildup of a nefarious Pearlfinger, Wan seemed disappointingly cordial and straightforward. He was dressed in green sweatpants and a cashmere sweatshirt. He clomped around in matching Crocs.

As we taxied down the runway, there were fourteen onboard: two of Wan's three sons, Bruno, 51, and eight-year-old Tomás; girlfriend Leila, 27, who is Tomás's mother; Tomás's nanny; three Chileans who represented Wan's pearls in Santiago; a gorgeous Tahitian mother and her equally gorgeous daughter from Paris; and a coterie of Wan's staff, including the mandatory aide-de-camp. We were to go to the five atolls where Wan has pearling interests, Nengo Nengo, South Marutea, Mangareva, Aukena, and Anuraro. As I had experienced in the Philippines, the islands were some of the most remote in the world, dots in the azure South Pacific. Four hours of flying time, 1,500 kilometers away, we landed on a makeshift runway in South Marutea, the same island where Branellec had joined with Brouillet to begin culturing Tahitian pearls in the 1970s. Wan had bought the 25-by-15-kilometer island from Brouillet in 1984. Not much was here except two pearl farms, two rustic cottages, and seven tiny guesthouses.

Wan was a pensive guy of few words. What comes out of his mouth often sounds like either Buddhist aphorisms or fortune cookie fortunes. His story is as rags-to-riches as it gets. Born in Papeete of Chinese parents in 1934, he speaks Chinese, French, Tahitian, and English. He was the seventh of thirteen siblings. His father, Wang Fong, came to Tahiti when he was nineteen from the Chinese province of Guangdong. Wan grew up in a dilapidated house that his father maintained by selling mother-of-pearl shells, vanilla, and coconuts, all the while devoting his free time to writing and painting. Wan spent his first seven years in his parents' house before studying at the Chinese School in Papeete. He learned French late, during secondary school at the age of thirteen. At nineteen, Wan's father died, and three years later, his stepmother died. Wan took a job as a bookkeeper for a French accountant, got married at twenty-two, and had two boys and a girl. The couple divorced in 1969, and Wan never married again.

In 1956, he landed a menial job working for Alfred Poroi, an importer/exporter in Papeete. Wan became Poroi's driver, then the firm's deliveryman, debt collector, and accountant. Young Wan started importing mopeds from Germany as an alternative to scooters, then introduced Fiat cars and trucks to Tahiti.

In 1963, French Polynesia found itself the site for French nuclear testing on the Mururoa atoll. The dubious distinction led to a national economic boom, with more than five thousand workers arriving on the island. Wan responded by opening a successful restaurant and nightclub, and engineering deals to import Bosch appliances from Germany. Then he hit upon a wild and crazy idea: Sherbet was already popular on the island, but nowhere could Tahitians buy fresh ice cream. Tahiti was hot, ice cream was cold. What Tahitian wouldn't scream for ice cream?

Wan imported dairy cows from New Zealand and established the nation's first dairy farm on the Taravao Plateau, which allowed him to manufacture and sell ice cream, over which, of course, the Tahitians went wild. He became the exclusive supplier of Foremost dairy products, obtained rights to distribute Yoplait on the islands, and today owns the largest dairy in the nation, Sachet.

With several of his brothers, he became an importer of canned meat. He bought a flip-flop company and started selling tens of thousands of the universal foot coverings. As he accumulated more wealth, Wan created the only private commercial airline in French Polynesia, Wan Air. He closed down the airline several years ago, but still owns two white-and-blue-striped Beechcraft 1900D planes, replete with the insignia RW on both wings.

In the early 1970s, Wan joined Australian biologist Bill Reed and several Japanese partners who wanted to start a pearl farm on Taku Island. Wan went with one of his partners to Toba, Japan, and met a grandson of Kokichi Mikimoto, who told Wan that black pearls weren't in demand, but that if Wan could produce a successful harvest, he'd be interested in taking a look. Wan returned home, and with a brother bought the pearl farm from Reed and the other investors. Wan's first harvest was 1,700 pearls. He returned to Japan in 1978 and showed the cache to Mikimoto over lunch on the Ginza at an elegant French restaurant called Éclair. The two negotiated a price for the entire lot. "But it wasn't as much as what I wanted," Wan recalled. "I thought I'd get three times as much, maybe more." But the men bowed and sealed the deal.

The next year, Wan doubled his harvest and met with Mikimoto once again, but this time, Wan refused Mikimoto's offer. Instead, Wan made his way to Kobe to see Andy Müller, who at the time was working for the Swiss jewelry consortium Golay Buchel, and Müller bought Wan's entire lot. Five years later, Wan bought his second pearl farm, the one on South Marutea, from Brouillet, and in 1986, Wan met Salvador Assael, who became his exclusive dealer of Black Tahitian pearls in the United States. Assael's head salesman, Henri Masliah, then came up with the slogan "A New Jewel is Born," and soon both Assael and Wan were flying high. At that time, Wan controlled 85 percent of the Tahitian black pearl market, and he was selling to just a handful of dealers outside Assael, including Müller, Tasaki, and Shimizu in Kobe.

On South Marutea, before the sun set, Wan wanted to show me his farms, and off we went on a tractorlike truck, which reminded me of what Iowans use for hayrack rides. The operation seemed more relaxed than what I had seen on Branellec's farms. When Wan walked through the grafting stations (he hires technicians from his father's home town in China, Qingxi), he broke into Chinese and hardily shook hands with the workers.

Workers at the farm start out at the minimum monthly wage in French Polynesia, the equivalent of $1,600. Grafters who perform well can double their salary within a year. The job include accommodations; food is deducted from workers' salaries, although workers are encouraged to fish and everything they catch is free. All registered workers in French Polynesia are covered by national health insurance, and they receive a month-long paid holiday.

We got in Wan's boat, Wan at the controls, the wind blowing wildly this afternoon, to yet another one of his farms, where eighty workers were busy scraping, cleaning, positioning, and grafting oysters. I trailed away from Wan and found the deputy manager of the farm, a forty-two-year-old Frenchman by the name of Nicholas Mace, from a small town near Avignon. He had sad blue eyes and a cautious demeanor. Mace said the job was an unparalleled opportunity to bank a lot of money, but he was lonely without his family. "When I go home, there are so many people I feel drunk," he said, with the dreamy look I had seen on some of the workers' faces at Branellec's farm off Palawan. I asked Mace about the nonstop smell of oysters, and he answered, "Smell? What smell? The smell stops, the longing doesn't."

Back at a rustic dining room pavilion, Wan talked expansively about his commercial plans. He was wearing a gray T-shirt and swim trunks, and sitting barefoot, occasionally taking a call on his cell phone, speaking first French, then Tahitian, back to French. He said he is moving to market high-end watches, as well as a line of ultra-expensive cosmetics that use extract of mother-of-pearl. Wan owns part of a Chilean winery and plans to offer a premium label of Cabernet Sauvignon and Merlot to be called Black Pearl. He also plans to open retail jewelry stores in Paris, Abu Dhabi, and Las Vegas, so he'll be able to reach the end consumer directly, instead of going through dealers like Vock, Shimizu, and Müller. When I asked why not New York, Wan hesitated. "New York would be tough with all the dealers located there. I'll wait on that one."

Asked about small family pearl farmers like Tapu and Tavere, Wan shook his head, as though remembering his own days as a struggling entrepreneur. He characterized the head of the farmers' cooperative as "very difficult," adding, "I don't want to fight with him. We're one big family in this country, producing ninety-five percent of the black pearls in the world." But like Tapu and Tavere, neither was Wan able to understand exactly how Martin computed the pricing structure of the cooperative. As for the ostensible objective of the cooperative—to make money for small family-run pearlers—Wan was doubtful. "Someone is making a lot of profit and it's not the small farmers." Wan, Tapu, and Tavere agreed on that point.

A project Wan said he wants to start soon will be his most ambitious. "I'm building a millionaire's paradise on Nengo Nengo, one of my atolls. It'll be the most exclusive resort in the world." I waited, just to make sure Wan wasn't pulling my leg, but he wasn't. Wan was planning a golf course, "not because these men play golf, but because they expect a golf course wherever they go." Wan planned to call the Polynesian crème de la crème resort Billionaire's Club, which will have fifty residential enclaves. "Bill Gates would be a good client. I know he went to Bora Bora, looking for something to buy, but couldn't find anything. These superrich guys don't want to mix with others. My resort will be totally private." To achieve that, Wan said he's negotiating with the government to open a separate immigration office on Nengo Nengo so private jets would be able to fly there directly without first stopping in Papeete. A pause, during which Wan seemed to be conjuring visions of the island paradise. "Can you imagine these guys on my island? Princes, kings, industrialists. They're so rich they don't know how to spend their money. They don't have a clue how much money they have! Ha, ha, ha, ha, ha!"

VI

Jean Tapu's grandson, Tyrone, is the next generation of family pearl farmers in French Polynesia. Thirty-three and the father of two children, Tyrone looked the part of a hungry pearl entrepreneur. With black hair combed straight back, he was a handsome man with a medium build, strong arms, and a quick, inquisitive smile.

He started working in his grandfather's pearl farm when he was sixteen, and since then has learned the essential art of embedding a bead inside the oyster's flesh. Like his grandfather, he won't participate in the national cooperative, and told me the prices that Martin quoted me were way out of whack. "No one will pay anything close to that. I don't know what Martin and Coeroli are thinking. To say that farmers get those prices for pearls is simply not true. You give them your pearls and you have no guarantee of anything. You just have to wait and wait, and whatever they say the price is, you just have to accept."

Like all farming, whether it's corn or soybeans, the nature of the business requires that farmers lay out money before they reap any return. If Tyrone is lucky, his first grafts will produce pearls, but they likely will be no more than 9 millimeters. The second grafts should produce larger pearls, which will fetch more at market. But when—and if—that happens, it'll be at least three years down the road. Tyrone will have to wait out two harvests, hoping that everything (the weather, the grafting, enough plankton production, no predators, no poachers, a serendipitous combination of scores of uncontrollable variables) conspires to create a bumper crop.

So why would Tyrone, a bright, personable guy whose wife graduated from college and is a teacher, choose to bet against those odds?

Because he loves the quietude of the far-flung French Polynesian islands, particularly Apataki, where he grew up. "Life is crazy here," Tyrone said, referring to the capital city of Papeete, where we had met. "In Apataki, our lives are simple. We have no pollution. Marlene and I can sit out every night and look at the stars and the moon. We just have bicycles. Two days in Papeete, it's too much for us. We get sick here," Tyrone said, wheezing, pulling from his pocket a handkerchief, nursing a sinus infection.

For the last four years, Tyrone spent three months on Nukuoro, a speck of an island in Micronesia, working on a pearl farm as a grafter. Last year, Marlene and their two children joined him. Tyrone earned two dollars per oyster he grafted, and over three months, he inserted nuclei in as many as ten thousand oysters, making twenty thousand dollars tax-free. The island, part of the Federated States of Micronesia, has no electricity, no mail, no lights. Two boats a year stop there. It's an idyllic life, Marlene told me. In fact, the only thing she missed, Marlene confessed, was toilet paper. "The natives use leaves and then go into the water to rinse off," she said, giving me an impromptu demonstration of sorts, bending at her knees, crouching, wiggling a little and then pantomiming swooshing water with her hands. This year when they go, her only concession to modernity will be to bring two cases of Charmin.

I asked Tyrone what he thought of Robert Wan, and his answer was surprising. "He's the symbol of the pearl for us. He can afford to do what he wants. I don't think he's a bad guy. Maybe he should help the small farmer, but why? It's a business. If I were Wan I'd do exactly what he's doing."

VII

There was another piece of the Tahitian pearl puzzle I needed to get, and that was from the French Polynesian national legislature, and I struck gold when I connected with politician Eléanor Parker, a representative who sits in the French Polynesian Assembly and is also a small pearl farmer herself, on the island of Takaroa. Parker's farm produces some twenty thousand pearls a year. She told me she had gotten into politics because she wanted to offer protection and incentives to small family pearl farmers. Elected in 2004, her platform centers on the creation of a Pearl House for French Polynesian pearlers. Here's how it would work: The Pearl House would serve as a central selling association. Every farmer, from the smallest producer to the largest (presumably Robert Wan), would be required to join the house, which would organize auctions of producers' pearls. *All* pearls produced in the nation would be sold in this manner. To start up a pearl farm today is cost-prohibitive for any small farmer, and to defray those costs, Parker's Pearl House would offer government-guaranteed low-interest loans.

I wasn't sure such a plan would work. No way would Wan go for any part of it. But Parker was adamant. She said only a small percentage of family farmers participate in the cooperative, and for the Pearl House to work, it would be mandatory that every producer join. "It's the only way to have some control over the big producers," she said.

Parker was forceful and passionate. She was a lapsed Mormon, and I could see the fiery righteousness in her cause. As Parker spoke, bobbing her head, jabbing her index finger at me, the pearl earrings she wore swung back and forth. "The big farmers won't want it. But if the government had any"—at this point, she forget the English word, and said *couille*, which translates to *balls*—"that's what would happen. We've been debating this for a long time." When I asked whether she was afraid, for her ideas had to give her cause to consider her own safety in the high-stakes world of million-dollar pearl dealing, Parker shook her head, again making her earrings swing. "Absolutely not. This is why I got into politics. For the smaller and medium-sized farmers, it's the only way."

It was clear that Parker knew the odds of creating such a program were miniscule. "In the past, everyone said about the Pearl House, 'It's a dream, it'll never happen,' but if you don't dream, nothing's ever going to change."

A day before I was to leave Tahiti for Australia, I wanted to get still another viewpoint, that of neither the largest farmer nor the smallest farmer, and for that I went to another family-run company, this one called Vaiatika Perles, which plays second to Wan's empire, producing a little more than one million pearls a year. Vaiatika maintains seven farms on five islands, Takaroa, Ahe, Fakarava, Alatika, and Kalleito. I took a chance and walked in unannounced at the company's second-floor headquarters, not far from the Tahiti airport. The whole family was in the office, and immediately I was ushered into the boardroom to hear what it was like to battle Robert Wan's global operations.

Vaiatika was started in 1994 by a Tahitian, Franck Tehaamatai, who used to own the local Volvo and Kia dealerships in town. "Really, it's pretty simple,"

Tehaamatai told me, after rounding up his three adult children, all in the business. "I got fed up with cars."

"But why pearls? Did you know anything about them?"

"Not much," the fifty-three-year-old Tehaamatai admitted. Tehaamatai, who resembled a life-sized teddy bear, started by collecting spat, and in eighteen months he had enough oysters to sell to farmers. He wised up, and, instead of selling spat, he kept them, and hired Japanese technicians who operated on the oysters, inserting the beads that would eventually turn into pearls. Tehaamatai struck a deal with a Hong Kong broker, Kent Li, who buys the entire inventory of Vaiatika's pearls from six of his farms. Tehaamatai said Li sells most of his pearls to dealers in Kobe (like Müller and Shimizu), who then broker deals with wholesalers around the world.

We sat around a big oval table with Tehaamatai's children, Glenn, Halidjka, and Vainana joining us. Glenn, 35, a telecommunications engineer, was schooled in France; Halidjka, 31, studied marketing at San Jose State; and Vainana, 26, is a former professional golfer who now heads the company's research and development division. Each had a cell phone, and over the course of an hour, the phones rang at least twenty times. The air-conditioning in the room was turned high. I got the impression that in steamy Papeete, air-conditioning was a status symbol, and to leave it on frigid was the ultimate in I-can-afford-it excess. Halidjka shivered and tugged at her cerise pashmina, pulling it tighter around her shoulders. Glenn rubbed his hands together as though he was warming them on a winter night.

None of the family had anything negative to say about Wan, and I got the impression that their viewpoint wasn't just a matter of polite politics. "Wan is a pioneer," Tehaamatai said. "He had the guts to start the business. He started out big and continues to be big. I take my hat off to him."

I asked the family about Representative Parker's idea of the mandatory Pearl House, and when I did, Glenn and Franck raised their eyebrows. "It's an old idea. But it'll never work. It's utopia," said Glenn.

Later that afternoon, I stopped by to see Robert Wan one last time. When I asked about Parker's Pearl House, Wan nodded and paused, that Buddha gaze of his coming on full force. "This is a sincere idea. But I don't ever see it—how do you say?—coming to pass. I wish Mrs. Parker luck."

20

●

Snakes & Crocs

I

Let me start with a confession. I spent almost two months in the Australian back country and didn't see a single kangaroo. I didn't come to Australia to see wildlife, at least the kind that hops, but all the way to this faraway continent and not a single roo? If not to satisfy my own curiosity, I knew that when I got home the first thing Iris and Mikey would ask would be: "So, what were the kangaroos like?" The closest I got were four wallabies springing across a dirt road in the outback somewhere in the Northern Territory.

The reason I came to Australia, of course, was because the nation produces the largest and some of the best pearls in the world. Almost all of these South Sea pearls come from oysters plucked from the floor of the Timor Sea one by one by intrepid divers off the nation's Top End, somewhere along a 1,400-mile swath of water, between the port cities of Broome and Darwin. The coveted oyster is the *Pinctada maxima*, and, as befits the name, it's huge—about the size of an ample salad plate. The oyster remains submerged for several years in a wire panel. During that time, divers will periodically rotate the panels, so that the inserted bead gets evenly coated with the oysters' rich, thick nacre. If all goes according to plan, the oyster will produce a gorgeous round pearl. Australian pearls are almost always a variation of white, pink, or silver, and generally have the thickest nacre of any cultured pearl in the world. They can grow huge. A 15-millimeter South Sea pearl is not unusual. That's the size of a hefty marble. Because Australian pearls are so large and because there's so much nacre around the bead, they're among the heaviest and most expensive pearls. A single round Australian pearl of exceptional quality, with extraordinary size, orient, and lustre, can retail for as much as $25,000. Not for a strand. For one pearl.

The cultivation of Australian pearls is tightly regulated by the Australian government through the letting of oyster-farming leases. The industry is now controlled by two major, fiercely competitive pearlers—Nicholas Paspaley and Rosario Autore. Paspaley's holdings make up some 70 percent of Australia's pearl production, but Autore is a hard-driving, Italian-born businessman who's as aggressive and scrappy as he is charming, and who's fast on Paspaley's heels. Both men maintain a healthy hatred for each other, as I was to discover over the course of several days-long interviews with each.

By the time I got to Australia, I had seen and held more than a hundred thousand pearls on three continents. My entrancement with pearls had, if anything, grown exponentially. I was pearl-obsessed 24/7. Whenever I'd arrive in a new city, I'd make a beeline for the best pearl dealers. No stops for lunch, must-see tourist destinations. Who cared about all that mundane stuff when there were caseloads of pearls awaiting me? I wouldn't call home to my family (who'd been wondering more and more when this pearl adventure thing of mine was going to come to an end). I would be salivating, just waiting for the moment until another dealer would pull out his cache of premium pearls, and I could place the best of his offerings in the palm of my hand and marvel at their perfection.

I certainly had come to the right place. Australia is the mother lode of large pearls. Just as the best chocolate comes from Switzerland and the best cashmere comes from Inner Mongolia, so do the biggest and arguably the best pearls come from Australia. How could I not become smitten with Australia? If you fall in love with a woman who takes your breath away, you seek to learn everything possible about where she comes from. Such was the case with Australia.

After a sleepless night in Sydney counting pearls (even that didn't work), I left Australia's cosmopolitan southeast and flew three thousand miles northwest to Darwin, the gateway to the sparse outback and the capital of the Northern Territory, a state as large as France, Italy, and Spain combined. Aussies seem to get a dreamy look whenever they talk about the remote Top End or Western Australia. Making a trip to Darwin and Broome is akin to going to the frontier, perhaps how Americans after World War II packed their car and moved to California.

There are two seasons in the Top End. The Australians keep it simple— The Wet and The Dry. I was in town for The Dry, so the humidity wasn't 100 percent, there were no monsoonal rains or cyclones, and the high just got to 85 degrees Fahrenheit. The Dry (May to October) is prime tourist season, and when I was there, Darwin was packed with thousands of pale Australian tourists, all of them, it seemed, tromping around in camouflage-green hats, baggy hiking shorts, and hiking sandals. They all seemed to be carrying and frequently consulting city maps, stopping only to smear more sunblock on their very white noses.

Darwin, of course, is named after the geologist Charles Darwin, who first came up with the theory of evolution by natural selection. Darwin wrote *The Voyage of the Beagle*, *On the Origin of Species*, and *The Descent of Man*, and served as a naturalist on the HMS *Beagle* from 1831 to 1836, where he collected much of the data that went into his theories of evolution. By the time the *Beagle* first made it to the north coast of Australia on its third voyage in 1839, Darwin was no longer onboard. But the ship's captain, John Clements Wickham, a friend of Darwin's, named the port city after his former shipmate anyway. Darwin has the distinction of being one of the few cities in the world named after a scientist. It made me feel good to be in a place that had such respect for knowledge.

I was in Darwin because I was to work as a deckhand on a pearling vessel. I was cleared to set sail on a Sunday, timed to coincide with what pearlers affectionately call "the neap," a critical moment during the first and third quarters of the moon when there's the least difference between high and low tide, which results in ideal pearling conditions. Neap tides occur twice a month when the sun and moon are at right angles to the earth, exerting the least gravitational pull on the earth's water. Nick Paspaley had guaranteed me unlimited access to see firsthand what pearling treasures his fleet would haul in. I had already gone behind the scenes with two of the world's great pearl lords—Jacques Branellec and Robert Wan—and now I was to do the same with the third.

II

One day before we were set to sail, though, it was time to forget about pearls for a couple hours. I needed an afternoon away from the shiny orbs that had overtaken my life. I found myself 120 kilometers south of Darwin, in genuine outback country. None of that shrimp-on-the-barbie, G'day bullshit. This was the real deal. I was on my way to see the world's largest concentration of salt-water crocodiles, or, as the Aussies call them, salties.

We motored past signs with names like Parap, Winnellie, Larrakeyah, Humpty Doo, Coonawarra, Yarrawonga, Jabiru, Berrimah, Karama, Knuckey Lagoon, Noonamah, Kakadu, Djukbinj, and Nitmiluk. These places sounded as though they were spun out of *Alice in Wonderland.*

When we finally got to our destination, Melaleuca Station, three hours south of Darwin, a gnarly guy by the name of Tony Searle greeted us. We got into his beat-up mud-white Land Cruiser, and Tony got to talking about snakes.

"'oo git bitin by 'ne of dah big 'nes, don't ev'n thank a gettin' en 'oor truk and headin' to a docto'. Eye reckin, 'oo'd be dead before 'oo'd git there."

Say what?

Bushman Tony spoke an entirely different English than I'd ever heard before. He was equal parts Steve Irwin, Crocodile Dundee, NASCAR driver Peter Brock, and tag team wrestlers Roy Heffernan and Al Costello of the Fabulous Kangaroos. I could barely make out Tony's individual words, and when they came flying at me, it was a weird and bizarre variant of English gargled by someone with half a larynx. Best to let the torrent rip and try to catch what little I could.

Turned out that Tony was talking about how to deal with a common bush predicament—when a nasty snake wants to get to know you better.

Forget about snakebite kits. They're for Boy Scouts and sissies. Snakebite kits won't do shit, Tony advised.

What about a tourniquet and razor blade, then sucking out the poison?

Tony shook his head, a grim smile coming over his parched, leathery skin. "Dat'll kill 'oo fastah than a run'whay truk barrelin' do'n a slick dert rohd in dah Kimb'rlees."

Talk about turning my whole world upside down. What was Tony going to say next? That when a rabid dingo charges you at sixty kilometers per hour, the only way to survive is to split open his belly with a jackknife, then roast the innards to a crisp in a hollowed-out boab tree?

Tony didn't address that particular scenario. Outback snakes, that's what bushman Tony was talking about, and the only way to stay alive after getting bitten by one, he advised is to get your buddy to take a swing at your noggin that'll knock you out cold.

"Dat's a bloody fack, mate," Tony said, nodding as though he had just taken a half-pint swig of XXXX Bitter lager in one gulp. That's the only way to stop the fast-acting venom from pumping through your arteries and thumping your heart dead, Tony said. "'oo gotta slow down 'or me-ta-bo-is-im, mate. Or 'oo'll be dead witin 'n 'our. Gahr-en-teed. Eye seen 'at happin wit me 'wn eyes, and it ain't preddy."

"But Tony, what happens if you're *alone* in the bush? Then what do you do?"

"'en eye figger 'or best corse of acshun wud be ta knock 'ooself out 'ooself. 'Oo take a rock and give a 'it to 'or 'ead. An' 'oo make sure 'oo hit 'ooself 'ard. 'At's dah key, mate. To *'lmost* kill 'ooself."

These remedies seemed awfully severe, and when I said so, Tony shrugged in a kind of do-what-you-will kind of way. "Suit 'ooself, mate. Eye'm jus tellin' 'oo wat 'oo shoud and wat 'oo shun't doo."

Tony allowed for one exception: if you're the type of person who can exercise self-control in a Zen Master kind of way. Once when an ornery adder bit Tony, instead of the rock-to-the-head scenario, Tony said he *very* slowly lay down and relaxed under a tree. That's really the best way to slow down your heart from pumping fast, he said (not to mention saving your skull from the rock). Tony said that through years alone in the bush, he'd developed enough control over his body that he was actually able to train himself to sleep after being bitten by a snake. Mind over matter, Tony said. "Ain't 'othin' to it."

Then what happened?

"Eye'm 'ere, mate, ain't eye?"

Snakes, though, while not trifling, are nothing compared to crocs, Tony said. "Eye seen 'em as long as five meetahs, and deh hour da meanes' animahs on da face of da 'arth. Bar none, me friend." Tony swore up and down that crocs have been known to climb aboard tinnies (aluminum rowboats), drag screaming fishermen into the muddy, brackish waters of a billabong, and rip them apart in seconds. "Eye seen it wit ma 'wn eyes," Tony said.

The only way to contend with these god-awful salties, Tony recommended, is to stay clear of them in the first place.

"But Tony, what would be the best course of action *if* a croc were to grab you by the leg and start chomping?" I asked.

Tony thought for several seconds. "Eye'd take mah pistah. 'oo never go 'nywheer near crocs widout a pistah. 'Oo doo and 'oo're just askin' fer trooble, guvner."

"And you'd aim the pistol between the croc's eyes?"

That's when Tony's own eyes went bugaboo. "Furget 'bout the croc, mate! Eye'd shoot me self! 'oo ain't evah gonnah kill a croc eatin' 'is dinner. 'nyone knows dhat! 'at's why yoo carry dah pistah. Betta to go at 'oo own 'and, than be 'orn intah shreds by 'ose 'eeth. Jah evah see a croc's 'eeth? Nast-ey. Dhey'll make a believah out of 'oo. Eye'll tell 'oo 'at, mate."

As we were walking back to Tony's Land Cruiser, I noticed four or five hopping toads on the road, and more came from the scrub alongside the road to see what the commotion was all about, and soon six dozen more toads seemed to be hopping in a circle around us. It was an infestation. They were everywhere. They looked like little brown kermits, and I made the mistake of saying something to that effect.

"Dhose hour cane toads, mate and eye 'ate 'em. Eye stomp as many as eye can. Dah hour a menace, and dah keep on mul-ta-plyin'. Stomp 'em 'here evah you see 'ne. 'ou be doin Australya a favah."

And sure enough, Tony started doing a sort of a jig, jumping up and down, trying to squish as many of these horned toads as he could with the toe and heel of his lizard-skin boots. The toads started hopping all over, like at a Calaveras County Fair.

Turns out that cane toads were brought Down Under in the 1930s from Hawaii to ward off a beetle infestation on sugarcane crops. Their importation was one of Australia's biggest eco-disasters. The toads multiplied and multiplied, and today, they're wreaking havoc, eating everything in sight, with no natural predators to stop them.

Tony shook his head, it seemed, still thinking about these insidious invaders when we drove to a brackish river where meter-long barramundi fish swam alongside the crocs Tony had the misfortune to know. And sure enough, on the opposite shore, slouching in silty, slimy mud, were more than a dozen of them. As soon as they saw us, as though on cue, they slithered down the bank into the murky water and propelled themselves downriver, glassy peepers just above the surface. "Dah're mean crittahs—if 'oo give 'em an oppor'unity, dhat is," Tony said ruefully, shuddering his torso. "Dhey open der mouths, and 'oo can smell da rot, par-tic-er-a-ly just aftah a feedin'."

Thus was my introduction to Australia's Top End, where off the north coast almost all of the country's splendid pearls come from. Tony was the minder of a huge cattle ranch owned by millionaire pearler Nick Paspaley. I was to get to know Paspaley and his operations firsthand at sea in the coming weeks. My walkabout with Bushman Tony had just been a sideshow to the main event.

21

Australia's First Family of Pearls

I

The colossal scale of the Paspaley family's pearling operations is staggering. The scope of how the company seeds, grows, and harvests pearl oysters was more technologically advanced than anything I'd seen. By far. Some of the coves and inlets where the Paspaley ships cruise are so isolated that they don't even have gazetteer monikers yet. The bobbing labs are manned by technicians, in white surgical coats and blue gauze hats, who methodically embed oyster after oyster, as many as 13,000 insertions a day. During harvest season, the same technicians extract thousands of extraordinary pearls daily. The wholesale take easily tops $5 million a day. And that's on just one ship. The Paspaley Pearling Company operates 13 capital ships of more than 20 meters (almost all of them named after someone in Paspaley's family), and at least 120 vessels of varying sizes. The company's armada is second only to the Australian Navy.

It's an amazing operation in both breadth and audacity. If there ever were a potential backdrop for a Tom Clancy or Ian Fleming novel, Nick Paspaley and his elegant, luxurious fleet of high-tech vessels, filled with scores of Japanese technicians working in top-secret laboratories in uncharted waters at the bottom of the world, would be it. What drives Paspaley is an almost maniacal obsession to cultivate the globe's best and largest pearls. That, and to make more for his pearls than any other pearl lord in the world.

If Paspaley had pioneered just the advanced technology of at-sea pearl cultivation and harvest, his contribution to the world of pearling would be a singular feat. But, like Branellec and Wan, Paspaley is also now in the midst of trying to change the way pearls have been distributed and sold for more than a century. Paspaley's operations are at the convergence of old-time capitalism and cutting-edge science. He wants to control everything about his pearls—truly from diver's hand to woman's bosom. Like Branellec and Wan, Paspaley is in a battle to grind out the middleman—dealers like Fran Mastoloni, Andy Müller, Alex Vock, Salvador Assael, Yoshihiro Shimizu. The future, as one Paspaley associate told me, is for Paspaley to own the pearl all the way until the very moment a woman purchases it. The strategy is to keep the pearl under Paspaley control; once it goes to a trader, broker, or retailer, it ceases to make more money for Paspaley. That's why producers like Paspaley are moving to create their own retail stores. It's the goal of any producer: not having to share profits with an assortment of middlemen. Paspaley wants it all.

Vertical integration certainly isn't a new economic model; it's the dream of widget makers everywhere. It's what Tasaki-san in Japan had pioneered years earlier. But while Branellac, Wan, and Paspaley are all pursuing the same goal to varying degrees, neither Branellec nor Wan seems to have stirred the visceral reaction of greed that Paspaley had spawned among so many traders. This may be because Paspaley is a bigger player than the other two. It also may be because of envy—Paspaley undeniably has a corner on the largest and most expensive pearls in the world, but also because he has spent more than the other producers to cultivate such outrageous pearls. Whatever the reason, he seems to evoke a kind of raw hostility among many pearl dealers. One longtime associate compared Paspaley to Russian Prime Minister Vladimir Putin as an oligarch who hates sharing power. "Nick finds it intolerable that other people make so much money from his products. It drives him crazy. He doesn't want to build the standard business pyramid, where others under him make what *they* should, and those under *them* make what *they* should. Nick wants everything for himself. He's a control freak; he's obsessed with lording over his pearls all the way down the line."

In Darwin, whenever I'd ask one of Paspaley's minions about financial or personal aspects of the family, I'd be greeted with a cold stare and the curt suggestion that all such questions must first be cleared by Nick, the name everyone—from deckhand to captain—calls Paspaley. There was too much risk in talking about the family that had created, and now controls, the modern Australian pearl industry and, by extension, the global business of pearls.

Wan and Branellec brazenly shouted details of their pearling operations. Their personal lives were an open book, too. Wan and Branellec had relished telling me ribald stories, perhaps out of machismo, perhaps out of aging Lothario complexes, maybe because their tales complemented the larger-than-life personas both had nurtured. Their stories fit in with the cultural viscera and construct of the product they create.

But dealing with Paspaley was wholly different. One reason was because Nick jointly owns the company with his sisters, Roslynne Bracher and Marilynne Paspaley. The three own an elaborate, interlocking and often Byzantine network of privately held companies with holdings around the globe. The company maintains a well-oiled publicity machine that cranks out reams of glowing accounts of successes and innovations. But beneath the global glitz and glamour of modern Australian pearls, which the Paspaley family wholly fosters, there are bitter rivalries and acrimonious power struggles. The international world of pearlers studies the Paspaleys the way British royalty-watchers scrutinize Prince William's and Prince Harry's every move.

Part of the intrigue has to do with the structure of the company and the natural tensions it breeds: Paspaley Pearls is controlled by a sibling troika. I met and interviewed each sibling while I was in Australia. Scratching beneath the family's public persona was made all the more difficult by lax reporting requirements when it comes to Australia's privately held companies (which the family's matrix of holdings is). That, and the Australian press's love affair with the Paspaleys, didn't leave much. I wasn't expecting much more than pleasantries and some intense pearl talk from the trio. But the family opened up to me, not all the way, though more than a crack, allowing me to view everything—from pearl sorting to employee grousing. It was something the Paspaleys had never allowed before. I came to believe it was because both Branellec and Wan had given me unprecedented access. And the last thing any magnate wants is for his competition to offer something the other won't give up.

Paspaley and his family certainly have the financial wherewithal to drive their pearling empire. Here's a boilerplate of the Paspaley panoply of holdings:

The Paspaley Pearling Company owns eleven pearl farms or leases in Australia, out of a total sixteen currently let by the government in northern and western Australia. The family controls in excess of 60 percent of all Australian pearls; one competitor called it the Paspaley Juggernaut. In addition, the company maintains interests in pearl farms in Indonesia and the Philippines. Increasingly, though, the key to the family's accumulation of wealth has been a diversification from sea to land, with rural holdings throughout Australia, including land that produces minerals, pork, beef, wool, cereal crops, and grapes.[1]

Outside of pearling, the Paspaleys own Melaleuca Station, the aforementioned 185-square mile crocodile preserve and cattle farm run by Bushman Tony. They own Kurrajong Park, a 6,500-hectare Poll Hereford stud farm west of Scone in the Upper Hunter district, 12,000 acres of wheat-farming and cattle-grazing land in nearby Coolah, and another expansive property in Thornthwaite. The family paid in excess of $10 million for these megaestates. Then there's the family's ship subsidiary, Darwin Ship Repair and Engineering, with six dry repair berths and five wet berths. One of its clients is none other than the U.S. Navy, and Paspaley engineers even work on ships of the Seventh Fleet. The family owns three airlines: Pearl Aviation, a private aviation firm; Aeropearl, a joint venture that provides flight testing, aerial photography, pollution monitoring, and civil maritime surveillance; and Pearl Flight Centre, a charter and medivac service. The company has ventured into winemaking, becoming a major player in the Central Ranges of Australia, turning into one of the nation's largest vintners. Paspaley bought 480 hectares at Eurunderee in 1995, along with 2,040 hectares in Bathurst and Oberon, for its Bunnamagoo wine label. The family bought Bunnamagoo and surrounding property in 1991 for $3.5 million.[2] In addition, the family has an interest in an Australian cruise ship line, Orion, as well as a furniture manufacturing plant. In 2006, Paspaley acquired a controlling interest in its longtime pearling competitor, Kailis Pearls. In 2009, Paspaley bought a 2,650-hectare livestock-grazing property, with a 14-bedroom home, at a place called Wagga Wagga; in New South Wales. The asking price was $30 million (AUD).[3]

The company sponsors a professional sports team (the Territory Pearls) in Australia's national women's field hockey association. It created the Paspaley VIP Host Room at Queensland's Gold Coast Turf Club, one of Australia's primo racetracks; mention of the facility and international movie stars seemingly feted there every weekend is popular fodder for Australian gossip pages. The company hosts the popular Paspaley Pearls Handicap at the same track. In Perth in 2007, the firm sponsored an inaugural Paspaley Polo match, as part of Australia's national polo circuit. In May 2008, Nick Paspaley, a fan of Elton John, anted up enough money to bring the British singer to Darwin for a concert, during which the performer announced to the crowd, "I want to thank Nick Paspaley and his family for helping us out."[4] The Paspaley company logo—an aqua outline of an oversized oyster with a P in the center—appears on the family's many holdings.

Not surprisingly, Paspaley has donated his share to the campaigns of Australian political candidates, as well as their parties. The Paspaley Group donated $265,000 to the Liberal and National parties over a six-year period; the Liberal Party government led by former Australian President John Howard awarded the Paspaley company's air rescue subsidiary almost $197 million in contracts in 2004–5.[5]

Through a wholly owned subsidiary, the family owns U.S. office buildings in lower Manhattan at 80 and 82 Wall Street and 120 Water Street, assessed at $13 million, as well as properties in Portsmouth, Virginia, assessed in excess of $7.5 million. One of the Virginia properties is the commercial headquarters for Zanetti Coffee, makers of Chase & Sanborn, Hills Bros., Chock Full o'Nuts, and MJB.[6]

The Australian version of *Forbes* magazine, *BRW*, in 2007 conservatively noted the Paspaleys had $350 million in assets, placing it in the top half of the richest families in the nation. A year later, the magazine recanted its previous estimate of the family's worth, recalculating it to be $620 million, writing, "The family's wealth rises this year due to a better understanding of the company's operations." This put only fifteen other families in Australia ahead of the Paspaleys in weath.[7]

But even the magazine's recalculation undervalued the family's worth. In an interview, Nick Paspaley flatly told me, "Our assets are over a billion dollars and we have practically no debt."

Nick Paspaley is the fifth largest shareholder in Jubilee Mines N.L., a nickel mining company in Western Australia, owning almost 5 percent. He owns 3 percent of another nickel mining company in Western Australia, Falcon Minerals, making him that company's second largest shareholder.[8] He is the fourth largest owner, at 6 percent, in a Tasmanian gold extraction company, Lefroy Resources Limited.[9] Paspaley also is a substantial owner of shares in a Perth-based gold exploration company called Sandfire Resources.[10]

As a hedge against the vicissitudes of the pearl trade, Paspaley also invests in diamonds. In 2006, he was granted five million unlisted options of Kimberley Diamond Company, valued at $9 million. Kimberley Diamond Company, underwritten by NM Rothschild & Sons in 1993, operates active diamond mines at Ellendale, about 100 kilometers east of the Australian costal town of Derby. Through 2006, the company had processed more than 545,000 carats of diamonds; its annual production of diamonds was projected to be more than 600,000 carats.[11]

Pearls, though, are at the center of the Paspaley empire, and to get to them the company owns three Grumman Mallard seaplanes that shuttle workers, supplies, executives, and VIPs to and from the company's at-sea laboratories. Only fifty-nine of these vintage planes were ever built, and fewer than twenty-four are still in existence. One of the Paspaley Mallards was once owned by Christian Dior, another by the *New York Times* (and dubbed Miss Daily News), and the third, Paspaley's archives indicate, was a flying bordello in the backwoods logging and mining regions of Canada. Sixteen full-time Paspaley engineers maintain the aircraft.

The company operates retail outlets in Dubai and Abu Dhabi, as well as stores in Hong Kong, Darwin, Broome, and Sydney. In 2008, Paspaley entered into an agreement with Sheik Ahmed bin Sulayem to create a massive offshore entertainment and retail center, along with a pearl museum, in Dubai to be called Pearls of Arabia. The 6,000-square-meter attraction will be located at a mammoth theme park called The World on a manufactured island designed to (sort of) resemble Antarctica, and is scheduled to begin operations in 2010, alongside the Dubai Pearl Exchange.

For now, though, it's the family's flagship store in Sydney, opened in 2006, that's the jaw-dropper. Located in an historic district on George Street at 2 Martin Place, a city-center plaza that reminded me of an upscale but more elegant version of Manhattan's Rockefeller Center, the Paspaley building, made from a volcanic red rock called trachyte, was originally designed as the Bank of Australia in 1896 by American architect Edward Raht. The store's important, since it's the harbinger of other Paspaley retail outlets, as Paspaley moves to open pearl boutiques in Europe and in the United States.

The present-day web of Paspaley companies is the complicated product of an archetypal Australian immigrant family business, started in the early mid-twentieth century by Nick's father, Nikolas, who came to Darwin from Greece when he was four, and became a diver for mother-of-pearl shells as a teenager. From his earliest days, Nick Jr. knew what the future had in store for him, and today he runs the company's day-to-day operations like a personal fiefdom. Paspaley was educated at the exclusive King's boarding school, the oldest independent school in Australia, located at Parramatta, in the heart of Sydney. In 1967, he graduated with a degree in economics from the nation's oldest college, St. Paul's, within the University of Sydney. He joined the family business in Darwin in 1969. Since then, Paspaley has worked in just about every position in the company. Today, he's a hands-on boss—a scrappy health fanatic who doesn't take shit from anyone, including his co-owners, his two sisters. Paspaley is a master of Japanese Aikido; he practices the martial arts form at least three times a week wherever he is. He and his first wife were divorced in the mid-1990s after twenty years of marriage and two children. Paspaley then married his children's nanny, Mylissa, a woman half his age, with whom he also has two children.

As would befit a philanthropic family, Paspaley and his sisters hold all the requisite appointments on national boards and commissions. Paspaley's older sister, Roslynne Bracher, is a member of the National Gallery Council, as well as the museum's acquisition committee. An accomplished violinist, for many years Roslynne was first violinist for the Broome Symphony Orchestra. She is Japan's honorary consul in Darwin. For more than seventeen years, Paspaley's younger sister, Marilynne, played Dr. Tessa Korkidas, a Greek physician, in one of Australia's longest-running television soap operas, *GP.* She also had a walk-on role in the 1988 Meryl Streep thriller *A Cry in the Dark* (entitled *Evil Angels* in Australia), the story of Australian Lindy Chamberlain and her husband, who maintained that a wild dingo had killed their baby girl, although police thought otherwise. Although no longer a professional actor, Marilynne retains her theatricality, and still talks with a throaty voice full of inflection. Marilynne started MP Personal Hotels and Resorts, which includes a Broome guesthouse that charges $1,000 a night, a hotel in Kununurra, in the heart of the Australian outback country, and a spa on Broome's spectacular Cable Beach (where camels trek the sand). Marilynne was named by Australian Prime Minister Kevin Rudd to the Australia 2020 Summit, representing what Rudd described as the thousand "best and brightest people to help shape the nation's future." In 2008, both sisters were appointed Members of the Order of Australia; Nick Paspaley was named Companion of the Order of Australia, the nation's highest civilian honor, in 1999.

The family shares a jet-set lifestyle, with impromptu ski trips to Aspen, private boarding schools in Sydney and Switzerland for their children, getaway homes on the bay in Sydney, very fast cars (Aston-Martins), and a $7 million two-engine Lear jet. Nick, Marilynne, and Roslynne are literate and opinionated, thoroughly conversant in everything from Barack Obama, superdelegates, and the U.S. Electoral College to Salman Rushdie, Darfur, and who wore what to the Academy Awards.

The three Paspaleys are in their mid-fifties and early sixties, and their children are now poised to take over the multitentacled company. Nick's title is executive chairman; his eldest son, James, is general manager in charge of all pearling interests, with other heirs battling for what's left. It all makes for a survival-of-the-fittest challenge to the new generation of Paspaleys as they seek control. The ensuing saga could be an Australian version of *Dallas*.

Historically, adventurers came to Australia's Top End or western territories to find fortune. The go-go towns of Darwin and Broome were Australia's versions of gold rush California. But instead of gold, it was mother-of-pearl shells, followed by pearls, that attracted tens of thousands of fortune seekers. Eighty percent of the world's buttons came from Australian mother-of-pearl shells, and almost all of those shells were located off the shores of Broome.

The first pearling camps were established in the 1860s off Roebuck Bay, but soon the backwater town of Broome became the Australian center of mother-of-pearl trade, and life there, as in the American West, reverberated with bounty and promise. There was a sudden and seemingly endless influx of get-rich schemers and schemes, and a concomitant share of profligate spending, prostitution, venereal disease, drinking, and gambling. Perhaps because of Broome's proximity to Asia and the surfeit of Asian itinerants, opium dens flourished in boomtown Broome. Mickeys slipped into bar drinks weren't uncommon; neither was murder. Broome was a classic frontier outpost in which men earned, then lost, fortunes overnight. It was an international city, with Australians, Japanese, Chinese, Brits, Malays, and Aboriginals jostling in the congested, tight quarters downtown that hugged the city's harbor, packed with pearl luggers vying for spaces to dock. At its heyday in the early twentieth century, more than four hundred luggers docked at Broome harbor, leaving early each morning for outlying pearl beds of thick oyster shells to be turned into buttons, cufflinks, jewelry, gun and knife handles, and inlays for furniture and guitars. If divers or shellers found pearls, it was a fluke and a bonus. Any pearl reverted to the owner of the lugger, unless, of course, a diver could secrete the pearl in a body crevice. Hauling up oyster shells from the deep was dangerous—divers lasting more than a half dozen years were unusual; thousands succumbed to drowning, sharks, the bends, or the poisonous sting of jellyfish. In Broome's tight, crowded, compact living quarters, pearling workers died of typhoid, measles, influenza, smallpox, some from leprosy.

Into the mix came the Paspaley family on a tramp steamer from the tiny Greek Island of Kastellorizo via Egypt in 1919, joining some 1,400 others Greeks who had arrived on the northwest coast of western Australia over the previous five years.[12] Kastellorizo is only nine square kilometers, just a few hundred yards off the Turkish coast, and today counts only 200 residents.

Once in Australia, Nick's paternal grandfather, a tobacco merchant by the name of Theodosis, opened a grocery store and bought a share in a pearl lugger, but died within five years of his arrival. To support her family of five, his widow began trading bags of mother-of-pearl shells in western Australia's Port Hedland. Nick's father, Nikolas Paspaley was a toddler when his parents arrived, but as a teenager, he became a pearler, going out daily on luggers. By the time he was eighteen, Nikolas had built his own lugger and started hauling in shells off Turtle Island, northwest of Port Hedland. He joined his brother Michael in 1937 in Darwin, eventually becoming a pearling master. Michael, known to everyone as Mick, kept the family's original name, Paspalis, and ultimately invested heavily in hotels, retail and property development, prospering as Darwin prospered, building the major retail landmarks of central Darwin. Nikolas and Mick were major donors to the building of Darwin's Greek Orthodox Church, completed in 1959. Mick died in 1972, and Nikolas in 1984.[13]

In any real-life representation of the Paspaley family, Nick's mother, Vivienne Lavinia Barry Paspaley, would play the Paspaley clan's matriarch—the Miss Ellie in this Down Under version of *Dallas*. Born in Brisbane, and reared in the cradle of Sydney establishment near Centennial Park, Vivienne attended the proper Sydney Church of England Grammar School at Darlinghurst. She met Nikolas Paspaley while working for what was then known as Qantas Empire Airways. Vivienne was secretary to the airline's first chairman, Sir Hudson Fysh, who introduced the two. By all accounts, the dark Greek adventurer Paspaley from the uncivilized Top End swept Vivienne off her feet. They were married in 1944, and within two years moved to backwoods Darwin with their first child, Roslynne. During the war, the Australian government requisitioned all pearling luggers; with no ship to haul in pearl shells, Nikolas drove a taxi and became a bookie.

To live in Darwin must have been an adjustment for the Sydney society-bred Vivienne. Soon, she bore two more children, Nick and Marilynne. Darwin at the time had no indoor plumbing, hot water had to be heated on a stove, and Aboriginal Australians cared for middle- and upper-class white children. Whenever she walked the streets of rough-and-tumble Darwin, Vivienne strolled with white gloves and a parasol. She wore a picture hat, stockings, and high heels, even during the humid wet season, when the temperature would climb to 105 Fahrenheit and the air was thick with mosquitoes. Vivienne took up gardening and golf. She was known for baking sausage rolls, scones, and cakes, but especially for her famous pavlova, a dessert of meringue, fresh whipped cream, and fruit. Since pearl masters traditionally wore all white, Vivienne took to polishing Nikolas's shoes before he went downtown every day.[14]

In the early 1940s, the bottom had started to fall out of Australia's mother-of-pearl market—plastic buttons had been invented, all but killing demand for the more expensive mother-of-pearl. So, instead of the shell, Nikolas Paspaley and other pearlers began focusing on what could be produced within the oyster: the cultivating of pearls from Australia's seemingly limitless supply of *Pinctada maxima* oysters. Nikolas incorporated his company in 1952 and joined forces with a Japanese producer, who began importing pearl-grafting techniques to Australia.

II

I was eager to get started at sea as a pearling deckhand. First, though, there were preliminaries—a dinner at Roslynne's house, then one at Marilynne's, a second interview with Nick—before I'd be flown on one of the company's seaplanes to a pearling ship.

Roslynne lives in a large, glass-paneled home perched on a hillock overlooking Darwin's Cullen Bay. The guests this night were an assortment of socialites, notably the ex-wife of an Australian politician from Melbourne and her seventeen-year-old daughter, as well as the female scion of Australia's largest coffee importer and supplier. The trio had been invited on a junket, a way to court wealthy clients to buy Paspaley's high-end pearls. The practice wasn't all that different from flying in high-stakes gamblers to Las Vegas for all-expense-paid trips. On this evening I heard a nonstop string of superlatives like *extraordinary, sensational, amazing, stupendous, fantastic,* mixed in with dozens of *dahlings* and *lovelys.* We nibbled on hors d'oeuvres of grilled oyster meat, proceded and followed by a multitude of air kisses, a seemingly universal trait in high society circles.

My interview with Paspaley the next morning was scheduled for an outdoor café in the downtown pedestrian mall in Darwin. I quickly realized this was a little like interviewing Donald Trump in the lobby of Trump Towers, since Paspaley owns much of the real estate in the mall and knew everyone passing by. Paspaley, 59, is a small, rugged, wiry Robert De Niro scrappy kind of guy, no more than five foot seven or so, with a slightly menacing "You talkin' to me?" kind of stare. He was dressed in designer jeans and an open-collar striped blue dress shirt with a black T-shirt underneath. His hair was combed back from his forehead at an angle. He munched a grilled cheese and tomato sandwich, washed down with a vanilla milkshake.

"I was my father's boy," he started. "I spent all my free time with him. I went everywhere with him. When I was a teenager, I was thinking of becoming a builder or a miner. I was fascinated by big structures, particularly big structures in cities. I wanted to build those things; my uncle had been very successful at building shopping centers, and that's what I thought I'd do."

All the while Paspaley was talking, I noticed how deliberate he was. Paspaley chose his words carefully. It was as though he was concentrating to bring himself back thirty years, only to be interrupted every minute or two by someone walking by, who'd chirp, "Mornin', Nick!"

"Darwin was a tiny town. It was all I knew. The first time I ever saw television was in a Sydney department store window when I was in college. My world changed when I went with my father to Japan to settle some accounts. It was an eye-openin' experience. I was an Australian kid from a small town, and suddenly there I was in Japan. My eyes turned into saucers. When we got back home, I said to him, 'Let me take on a lugger. I'll try some new divers. Let me see if there are any new pearl beds out there.' The pearlers then didn't go out very far, and I said to my father, 'Why not go out further, much further, and see what we find. There must be more oysters out there.'

"So, I put a boat together, got some abalone divers, and we went prospectin'. We spent a year doing this. And it turned out to be a complete waste of time. We couldn't find a pearl shell, and we couldn't drift a boat [the traditional way Australian pearl drivers cover an underwater oyster field]. We came home with nothin'."

After the fifth person came up to our table for a stop-and-chat, Paspaley suggested we go to his office a hundred meters away.

"We got ourselves closer to Broome and rejiggered the lugger, and started divin', and suddenly we were catchin' thousands of shells," he said, sipping on a glass of green tea. "We brought in Japanese technicians and offered them twenty percent of our profits, and we started again. By nineteen seventy-nine, I worked out a system, and by nineteen eighty-five, it'd revolutionize the industry. I developed everything myself, from the cages we used to how we transported them onto the ships. Two years later, when we harvested, the results were terrific. We had only a ten-percent mortality rate, and we found we had a much higher quality of pearls. I was on to somethin'.

"So I invested in new vessels, and the results were spectacular. We revolutionized the industry by bringin' technicians to the shells instead of vice-versa.

I had so much revenue at the time, I was able to buy out my competition, the Otto Gerdau Company, based in New York, and eventually, I was gettin' fifteen- or sixteen-millimeter pearls. Even today, no one really knows what I do. No one understands the whole chain of our process.

"People look at me and say, 'You're rich!' But I didn't have any money when I was working for my father. My father never said to me, 'Nick, you're doing a good job.' We argued so much that my relationship with my siblings became strained. After an argument, my father went to his lawyer and wrote me out of the will. When he died, he left *everything* to my mother and sisters. The only thing I got was his Omega watch. I only owned the part of the business that I had developed, so when he died, I owned a very small business. Everything else went to the women of the family. I only started makin' money in around nineteen eighty-six. My sisters were cared for, but not me. It's somethin' I think about, and I've never ever forgotten."

What I saw in Paspaley jibed with what I'd seen in other pearl lords—a consummate grasp of a megavision of his product in relation to the world, a sense of minute detail combined with a restlessness that goes with such detail, and an almost pathological compulsion to compete and win. He couldn't forget those who'd crossed him, even if it had been his own father. He harbored resentment that festered for years and years. He couldn't let go of the notion of being wronged. Paspaley's obsessive sense of control was a way to protect himself, a way to gird against what was merely expected of him and to surprise even his closest family members with brilliant innovation.

Paspaley, like Branellec and Wan, played for keeps. They were ruthless in their business dealings. They didn't like anyone with the audacity to challenge them or their businesses—which were one and the same. There was a begrudging sense of accomplishment these men would allow others. But the scale of Paspaley's operations made him different. He was in the business to crush anyone who wouldn't play the game the way he wanted it played. This was a billion-dollar business, and Paspaley wanted to stay on top of it now and for years to come.

22

Fight for Pearl Supremacy: The Strange Case of the Otto Gerdau Co.

I

Nick Paspaley worked hard to get where his vast pearling empire is today. His pioneering pearl-cultivation technology, his armada of specially outfitted ships, and his international auctions have translated into a global supremacy and some of the finest pearls the world has ever known. But Paspaley's fame and wealth on and off the sea today pivot on a curious connection he fostered in 1989 when he purchased an unconventional, century-old New York-based export/import business called the Otto Gerdau Co., run by Otto Gerdau's wildly eccentric son, Allan Gerdau. Without the Gerdau Co., Paspaley today might be just another Down Under pearler. The contentious Gerdau acquisition propelled Paspaley into becoming the most significant pearl producer in the world.

The Paspaley takeover of the American Gerdau import/export company is a complicated chronicle of bluster and skullduggery, one that has never been written about. No one seems to know the whole story, just bits and pieces here and there. But next to Cleopatra's fabled swallowing of a priceless pearl to boast to Marc Antony of the immense wealth of her empire, the Paspaley purchase of the Gerdau Co. and its Australian holdings, Kuri Bay, is one of the great coups in pearling history. Underscoring that narrative is a cautionary parable of how a genteel American family-run company got gobbled up by a fast-talking wheeler-dealer employed by a stealth Australian mogul halfway around the world.

When American pearl exporter/importer Allan Gerdau died in Danbury, Connecticut, in 1986 at age eighty-seven, his unorthodox will stipulated that assets from his global company be distributed to "three of the great religions of the world." Specifically, the will called for the firm's holdings to be divided among representatives of the Catholic, Episcopal, and Jewish religions. Once dispersed, Paspaley went after the Gerdau assets, and made a successful offer to purchase the company through a hard-driving Florida businessman who acted as Paspaley's bidder. Today, Paspaley owns outright what remains of the Otto Gerdau Company, once a celebrated importer of goods from Europe, Africa, Asia, South America, and Australia. Among Gerdau's largest holdings—now Paspaley's—was Kuri Bay, on the northwest coast of Australia, the world's premier location for South Sea pearls. Other assets secured in the preemptive takeover included a ragtag assortment of international properties such as an Indonesian rattan-furniture factory, an Australian piggery, and more than four thousand undeveloped acres in Polk County, North Carolina. As part of his acquisition of the Otto Gerdau Co., Paspaley also ended up owning several historic, prime-location office buildings in lower Manhattan.

Here's the story of a critical turn in how Nick Paspaley transformed himself into the world's supreme pearl monarch. It's a convoluted saga with hard-to-follow twists and turns, perhaps an excursion for some, but the account is essential to understanding how Paspaley got where he is today.

II

At the turn of the twentieth century, Allan Gerdau's father, Otto, was the American agent for a prominent Hamburg firm named Heinrich Adolf Meyer, which imported and exported great quantities of ivory. Born in Hamburg in 1853, Otto Gerdau emigrated to New York when he was nineteen, and founded his eponymous firm, which represented Meyer, but also sold a host of other imported goods snapped up by eager, nouveau riche Americans entering a new century.

The company headquarters was located in a classic twelve-story highrise at 82 Wall Street, known as the Tontine Building.[1] Although owned outright today by Paspaley, the building is smack in the middle of the cradle of American democracy—a stone's throw from Federal Hall, where George Washington took the presidential oath of office; where John Peter Zenger was jailed, tried, and acquitted of libel; down the block from where the U.S. Congress assembled in October 1765 to protest "taxation without representation," and several hundred yards from the citadel of capitalism: the New York Stock Exchange.[2]

By the time Otto Gerdau bought the building, he had become a prominent New York businessman. Forfeiting his German citizenship and becoming a naturalized American, Gerdau married Missouri-born Clara Ehlermann in 1895, and by all accounts, the couple became a mainstay in New York society. As newlyweds, the Gerdaus attended the ball of the Bachelor Circle of the Liederkranz, which the *New York Times* called "one of the most notable events in German society of the season."[3] Clara Gerdau was a founder and first president of the Lenox Hill Hospital Nurses Aid Society, a philanthropic association made up of the wives of benefactors. The Gerdaus had two sons, Carl and Allan, and a daughter, Marguerite,[4] and the family lived at 146 West Seventy-fifth Street in Manhattan. Just as his company was rising to prominence, Otto Gerdau died, at sixty-nine, on August 26, 1920.

Otto Gerdau left his holdings to his two sons at 49 percent equity each, and 2 percent to his widow to oversee any disputes the brothers might have in running the firm, said Carlson Gerdau, 75, Carl Gerdau's son. Brothers Carl and Allan were total opposites. Carl was a vaunted scholar who graduated from Harvard, while Allan was thought by his father to be slow, not academically inclined. Allan attended the Hackley School, a boarding school in Tarrytown, New York, but when he was sixteen, one year short of graduating, Otto pulled Allen out of school to apprentice at a Havana import/export firm, M. Paetzold & Co., where he worked for two years as an office boy, file clerk, cable clerk, and "occasional emptier of spittoons," he was to write years later. Allan never returned to school. In business together, the brothers argued bitterly. "Allan was always talking philosophy; my father didn't see that as having anything to do with running a company," said Carlson Gerdau, today a retired priest and canon in the Episcopal Church. In 1937, to the relief of both brothers and their worried mother, Allan bought out Carl's shares and assumed control of the family business.

As sole director, Allan expanded the export/import lines with gusto. To the surprise of some, he became an uncanny, savvy dealmaker. As ivory became more and more scarce, Gerdau diversified into Australian mother-of-pearl. It was a natural commercial step: ivory and mother-of-pearl shells possessed similar properties, and both were primary sources for dress-clothing buttons. Australia was the leading supplier of mother-of-pearl in the world (it still is), and Gerdau became the nation's primary exporter of oyster shells. To hedge his investment, Gerdau also discovered that tagua nutshells from Ecuador also could be made into durable buttons, and soon the Gerdau Company became the general agent for all Ecuadorean exports to the United States. Raw materials for button manufacturers wasn't the only commodity Gerdau traded. The firm became significant importers of pepper from India; vanilla beans from Madagascar; oregano from Turkey; and cassia bark from Indonesia, the raw product from which cinnamon is derived. While engaged in the spice trade in India, Gerdau diversified into jute furniture and later into rattan. Other products the Gerdau Co. imported included Indian rugs, Colombian textiles, and raw and processed cocoa, which the company sold to Nestlé, Hershey, and Mars. Gerdau branched out into ownership of a Brazilian mica mine, as well as importing readymade furniture from Italy, Yugoslavia, Bulgaria, and Hong Kong. The firm raised eyebrows by introducing an entire room of furnishings based on the villa of notorious Roman emperor Caligula, complete with marble urns, obelisks, spheres, and boxes.[5] Many of the company's imported goods were sold through retail giants at the time, such as Marshall Field & Co. in Chicago and the J. L. Hudson Company in Detroit. At its peak, Gerdau employed two hundred worldwide workers, with seventy at its Wall Street headquarters, along with laborers at a warehouse in Belleville, New Jersey.

The company flourished, allowing Allan Gerdau to lead a charmed life. Gerdau, tall and handsome, with sandy-colored hair and blue eyes, was elected a member of the New York Coffee and Sugar Exchange, as well as of the India House Club in Manhattan. He joined the Church Club of New York, an influential lay Episcopal organization. In 1937, he married Florence Ruperti, the daughter of a fellow import/export executive and a descendant of an early mayor of New York. The couple lived in a series of apartments on New York's swanky East Seventy-second Street, including a twelve-room penthouse.[6] Florence Gerdau joined the exclusive women's social association, The Colony Club.

In the mid-1940s, afraid that India's coming independence might mean an interruption of his exports, which included tea, jute, hemp, and goatskins,

Gerdau left his wife and four daughters and moved overseas, spending two years overseeing the Gerdau Co.'s interests in India. After World War II, he was among the first group of 102 American businessmen approved by the U.S. Commerce Department to travel to Japan to trade with the Japanese.[7]

But it was Gerdau's steady acquisition of Australian mother-of-pearl shells that became the signature of his company. For years, Gerdau was the world's primary buyer of mother-of-pearl from Broome, Australia. Back as far as 1930, the Otto Gerdau Company is listed as the majority buyer of 576 tons of oyster shells from Broome pearlers. A report of the city of Broome at that time indicated that Gerdau's purchase "stabilized the industry in Broome."[8] Often Gerdau bought out practically the entire production of mother-of-pearl shells divers pulled from the seas off Australia's northwest coast. This happened in 1949, 1950, and 1951, when Australia pearlers were sitting on huge warehouse inventories of mother-of-pearl in the wake of the invention of inexpensive man-made plastic buttons that ultimately undercut and practically eliminated the need for natural pearl shell as the base material for buttons. In 1950, for instance, Gerdau bought more than three-quarters of the 330 tons of mother-of-pearl from Broome, and paid on average £435 per ton.[9] Mother-of-pearl still had a small place in the manufacture of high-end buttons, combs, fans, jewelry, guitar inlays, and cufflinks, but plastic overwhelmingly had become the material of choice for buttons following World War II. During those years, Gerdau negotiated to pay half the plummeting prices that mother-of-pearl shells had fetched in previous years. Some say Gerdau took on the inventory because of loyalty to his Australian suppliers, but just as likely, his acquisitions were a cagey move to corner what little was left of the shell market.[10] In doing so, Gerdau effectively eliminated competition, and might have even hastened the demise of mother-of-pearl trade in order to promote the coming of a new luxury product about to be introduced to the world: the cultured South Sea pearl.[11]

Mother-of-pearl was one thing, pearls were quite another. The few large and round *Pinctada maxima* pearls discovered up to then had been natural. Such pearls were exceedingly rare flukes of nature, collector's items truly worthy of royalty—the only people who could afford the prices such pearls commanded. In the aftermath of World War II, the pearl-consuming world had to be content with Japanese akoya pearls, small in comparison with the colossal orbs that would come from Australian *Pinctada maxima* oysters. If only technicians could figure out a way to culture the Australian pearls, employing methods derived from Kokichi Mikimoto's patented process, the Australian pearls, some three times the size of akoyas, would fetch extraordinary prices.

The economic incentive was enormous. Traders would pay obscene prices for gumball-sized pearls the world had never seen produced by man (and almost never by Mother Nature). The race was on.

As World War II ended, savvy Japanese pearlers started looking toward Australian waters to cultivate these huge South Sea beauties. In 1947, Tokuichi Kuribayashi, the president of a firm called Pearl Shell Fishing Co., began readying a team of Japanese technicians to take to the waters off Broome for the purpose of setting up a pearl-cultivation venture. By 1953, Kuribayashi had organized a fleet of pearl vessels and was ready to sail. "Kuribayashi knew the coast, the sea and the shells that were there," wrote Andy Müller, in a book entitled *Cultured Pearls: The First Hundred Years,* privately published by the Swiss jewelry company Golay Buchel.[12] Kuribayashi also was familiar with the Japanese technique of bead nucleation to cultivate pearls, something no Australian at the time knew with any degree of experience or success. But before Kuribayashi could set sail, he hit a snag: his nationality.

Eight years after the end of World War II, the Australian government wasn't about to allow a wholly owned Japanese company to sail the waters off the Australian coast, particularly near Darwin, plucking the nation's most valuable resources off the ocean floor and cultivating from them priceless pearls. Japanese warplanes had strafed Darwin 64 times during the war, and 243 Australians had been killed in bombings; Darwin was the only Australian city to endure such prolonged, punishing air attacks. During the war, Japanese nationals from Australia's Top End had been interned. After the war's cessation, the Australians harbored a deep antipathy toward any and all things Japanese. Anti-Japanese fervor burgeoned in Australia, perhaps even more so than in the United States, since Darwin was only 3,000 miles from Japanese shores. The Japanese were prohibited by Australian law from holding ownership rights in any company in Australia.

This is where plucky U.S. entrepreneur Allan Gerdau stepped in and became a godfather of sorts. Kuribayashi approached Gerdau about a commercial plan to cultivate Australian pearls, and Gerdau signaled a commitment to create a joint venture. It wasn't until the summer of 1956 when Gerdau was able to form a business entity called Pearl Proprietary Ltd (PPL). The company was a complicated partnership that involved owners from the United States and Australia, but Gerdau owned the majority of shares. A corresponding entity based in Tokyo, Nippo Pearl Co. Ltd., was to be the wholesaler for South Sea pearls cultivated by the venture. The Australian side of PPL included Broome businessmen Keith Dureau and Sam Male.

A fifty-ton vessel, the *Otama Maru,* soon set sail from Yokkaichi, Japan, to Broome, with thirteen Japanese PPL crew members and enough equipment to establish a pearl-culturing operation in Australia. After weeks of exploration along the northwestern coast, Kuribayashi's crew first anchored at Augusta Island, then permanently settled on a distant bay of calmer waters 420 kilometers northeast of Broome. They named the inlet Kuri Bay, short for Kuribayashi. While the Japanese technicians were experts at cultivating the smaller akoya pearl oyster, they were neophytes when it came to cultivating pearls from these monster Australian bivalves. Boris Norman, a pearl dealer from London, and his partner, Pierre Morand, bought the small first crop from Kuri Bay in 1951, paying in the neighborhood of $300,000.[13] It wasn't until 1958 when the first sizeable crop of 651 South Sea pearls was produced.[14]

Although the Gerdau Co. had a majority interest, Kuri Bay was for all purposes a Japanese outpost, run by the Japanese with a crew of Japanese that included ship captains, engineers, divers, technicians, shell openers and cleaners—even though Japanese property ownership at the time was outlawed in Australia. In 1961, the Australian Broadcasting Corporation aired a television documentary called *The Pearling Game,* about a struggling local pearl farmer in Cygnet Bay (just north of Broome) by the name of Lyndon Brown, competing against an army of Japanese pearlers at Kuri Bay, which at the time was the work site for some eighty workers. Two smiling Japanese managers were shown laying out bag after bag of enormous, lustrous pearls on a series of tables. There was an astonishing array of thousands of round, glistening pearls stacked in the bags and on trays. Responding to an interviewer's question, one of the Japanese managers estimated the pearls to be one tenth of PPL's yearly output, in excess of $4 million a year wholesale. The very best of those pearls, the Kuri Bay manager said, would sell for $5,000–$6,000 apiece retail.[15]

By 1962, Nick Paspaley's father had started his first cultured-pearl farm in Knocker Bay in the Northern Territory's Cobourg Peninsula, but his success was limited. The Australians at the time didn't have the pearl-culturing expertise that the Japanese had mastered. Within a decade, PPL's dominance of South Sea pearls grew to greater than 50 percent of the entire Australian pearl market, and eccentric Allan Gerdau had become the American point man for all of PPL's large, flawless pearls—sitting more than ten thousand miles away in his ninth-floor executive suite on Wall Street. At the time, young Nick Paspaley was one of a dozen or so pearlers on the northern coast of Australia fighting each other for the spoils of the wholesale pearl market in the wake of PPL's flourishing operations.

Although Gerdau's structuring of PPL made him the undisputed American connection to the Australian pearl market at the time, Gerdau, curiously, wasn't all that interested in the pearl business. Actually, he wasn't all that interested in the nuts and bolts of any business. While Gerdau sat with a majority share ownership connecting him to the largest collection of the largest pearls the world had ever known, Gerdau found wealth accumulation dull. He was more cultural raconteur than hard-as-nails businessman, and as he got older, he became increasingly bored by commerce and more interested in novel, some would say, eccentric, ways to improve society. Gerdau bought scores of copies of a 1970 book called *The Servant as Leader*, by former AT&T executive Robert K. Greenleaf. Gerdau gave the book to all his management employees and urged them to read it. He struck up a correspondence with Greenleaf to exchange ideas of how businessmen could better serve humanity.

Gerdau became increasingly captivated not by the economic worth of the goods he imported but by their aesthetic appeal. In 1966, he created a quaint art gallery on the mezzanine of his firm's Manhattan headquarters, which he called the Tontine Emporium. Like its owner, the gallery was eclectic and hard to pigeonhole. Gerdau packed the salon with African masks, French floral prints, Chinese vases, Tiffany lamps, crystal goblets, duck decoys, and antique English wardrobes. He served sherry and gin-and-orange at 11:30 a.m. every weekday free to anyone who happened by. When asked by a *New York Times* reporter about his show-and-tell emporium in the middle of New York's financial district, Gerdau said wistfully: "People are coming in at the rate of 25 to 40 a day. But I'll tell you something a little bit sad. Some people are shy about it, they think there's a trick somewhere."[16]

Gerdau had an uncanny habit of popping up in the news, in both pivotal and inconsequential roles. It isn't too much of a stretch to compare him to such latter-day film characters as Forrest Gump or Leonard Zelig, the protagonist of the 1983 Woody Allen film. In 1963, Allan Gerdau was the New York grand jury foreman in a blockbuster trial that resulted in the indictment of former Joseph McCarthy aide and racketeer Roy Cohn for bribery, perjury, and conspiracy. Gerdau was the first government witness called to testify in a subsequent trial in which Cohn charged that a U.S. Attorney had been bribed in the case.[17]

But it was through another public persona that Gerdau perhaps became best known. An inveterate nonstop talker, Gerdau sensed a need to share his opinions with more than his family, friends, and business associates. In 1967 he started taking out dozens of half-page political advertisements in the *New York*

Times, which became recurring platforms for Gerdau's discourses and ramblings on politics and life. By all accounts, Gerdau's first ad was a curious proclamation. In response to a political advertisement the newspaper had published earlier in the week urging President Lyndon Johnson not to seek the Democratic renomination because of the war in Vietnam, Gerdau's $3,400 ad read, in part, "We credit our opponents with a sincere belief in ideals they consider noble." Gerdau added there "are no simple superficial solutions" to the problems of international relations. "We are in battle. On with the job!"[18] More of Gerdau's incomprehensible ads appeared in the coming months and years. In 1981, he exhorted striking air traffic controllers to return to work. In 1985, he urged South Africans to show love toward each other. That same year, he published a seven-point list of beliefs, including, "We are not so stupid as to think we can have the blessings we want without sacrifice and work." Asked why he resorted to such public proclamations, Gerdau told an interviewer, "I'm not a flag-waving person, but sometimes one just has to stand up."[19]

A compulsive reader, Gerdau took to making voluminous notes of his favorite books in small leather-bound notebooks he always carried with him. In December 1943, after reading a collection of essays, speeches, letters, and judicial opinions by Supreme Court Justice Oliver Wendell Holmes, Gerdau wrote, "Powerfully constructive thoughts. Beautifully expressed. My mind and heart feel humbly and reverently thankful for becoming at least slightly acquainted with such a great human. Life is wonderful—every day an opportunity for great joy—a new knowledge."[20]

Gerdau took to writing pages and pages of philosophical tracts, filled with counsel as well as whimsy. A ten-page typed letter was not an unusual missive that one day would sail over a business partner's transom halfway around the world. In a questionnaire he once filled out for his own company, when asked his career goals, Gerdau responded, "Become less stupid." When prompted to list his interests, he scribbled "few words," but when asked to enumerate his accomplishments, he wrote "verbosity."[21]

By his fiftieth birthday, Gerdau's interests had turned to the world's religions, a fascination that would stay with him for the remainder of his life. He'd often stop business meetings without notice to survey his colleagues about their religious and philosophical grounding. Once a year, he traveled to Broome for PPL board meetings, where he wrote pages and pages of poetry during meetings, and then asked the assembled for interpretations of his verse. "He was most remarkable, but I can also say by no small degree he was a rather strange chap," said Kim Male, whom I met in Broome. Male attended board meetings with Gerdau while working with Male's father, Sam, for the family firm, Streeter & Male.

Hearing Kim Male's genial assessment of idiosyncratic Gerdau was telling. Male himself wasn't your typical corporate bean counter, either. His nautical office in Broome resembled a film set untouched from the 1940s, complemented by Male's own pearl master's garb: white oxfords, white kneesocks, white Bermudas, and white cotton button-down shirt, all topped off by a white pith helmet. "Gerdau, I can tell you, was quite an original," Male told me.

Gerdau seldom expressed interest in money, never declared or received dividends from his company, and took as profit only $15,000 a year, said one of his four daughters, Joan Rogers.[22] Still, he reveled in playing the role of a mysterious benefactor wherever he went. He once took a liking to a waiter at Manhattan's India House and paid for the young man to visit his ailing parents in India. Several times while dining alone at his favorite Connecticut restaurant, Stonehenge, he had waiters deliver bottles of champagne to lovebirds across the room. He routinely gave taxi drivers large tips with the exhortation that with the money they should buy flowers for their wives. "He was a passionate, romantic man," Rogers told me, adding that if he ever saw a woman standing on a train, he'd immediately offer his seat. It wasn't beyond Gerdau to write poetry to young women on the train, and upon arrival, he'd deliver the epistle with an impish smile. At home on weekends, Gerdau and wife Florence took summer evening drives in a vintage black Lincoln convertible with the top down, their four daughters squished in the banquette backseat, all of them singing "You Are My Sunshine" at the top of their lungs. The family played riotous matches of croquet on the hundred-acre wooded West Redding, Connecticut, estate they called Hidden Springs, filled with cascading streams, trails, and vegetable and rock gardens that the indefatigable Gerdau had built and maintained himself. In the afternoons, the family would nap in hammocks. Afterward, classical music sprang forth from outdoor speakers during which Gerdau would indulge in a glass of Pinch scotch. Every December, Gerdau would string and light a towering Christmas tree outside the family home, which became an annual local attraction and event. In his later years, he took to ending telephone conversations not with "Good-bye" but "Celebrate!"

As his health began failing, Gerdau moved his Wall Street gallery of bric-a-brac closer to his home, in Branchville, Connecticut. It was also during these twilight years that he became a patron in the world of museum art. "Beauty was a big part of his life," said Joan Rogers, and in keeping with such an aesthetic, Gerdau donated paintings and sculptures to a number of museums across the United States. Reflecting his eclectic interests in almost everything, Gerdau specialized in no genre, donating Chinese, Indonesian, African, Spanish, and nineteenth-century American pieces to museums that included the Art Institute of Chicago, Detroit Institute of Arts, Indiana University Art Museum, Bob Jones University Art Gallery and Museum, University of Missouri Museum of Art and Archeology, Tougaloo College, University of Kansas's Spencer Museum of Art, Lowe Art Museum at the University of Miami, Samuel Dorsky Museum of Art at the State University of New York at New Paltz, and Haffenreffer Museum of Anthropology at Brown University.

Florence died in 1981, and as Gerdau passed his eightieth birthday, his behavior grew increasingly erratic, son-in-law Dick Rogers told me. He'd be on the train to Manhattan and suddenly he'd lose all sense of where he was. A letter sent to Gerdau in 1979 from London pearl dealer Boris Norman went unanswered for three years. When Gerdau finally responded, he wrote: "Dawn, 2 cups of tea out of an 18th century tea-pot and enjoyable memories of you caused this outburst. These thoughts were inspired by your kind letter. Upon re-reading same, due to my poor memory, I had no idea what it was all about."[23]

Several relatives I interviewed suggested that Gerdau did not trust his sons-in-law to run the business. When Gerdau once asked Dick Rogers, a businessman who had attended Philadelphia's Wharton School of Finance and Commerce, to become president, Rogers said he lasted two weeks.[24] One day Gerdau struck up a conversation with an affable taxi driver who had picked him up at Grand Central Terminal. In the course of their conversation to Wall Street, the driver told Gerdau that he'd been educated and trained as a businessman. By the time the taxi pulled up to 82 Wall Street, Gerdau had offered the man a job as the company's vice president for export sales. The next day, the driver showed up in a jacket and tie for work.

Gerdau suffered a stroke in the early 1980s, and as his health continued to deteriorate, his daughters moved him to a convalescent hospital in Danbury. He died the day after his eighty-seventh birthday, during which Joan Rogers helped him celebrate with one last draught of Pinch.

Since Gerdau only had daughters, there were no sons to whom he could turn over the company to complete a third generation. For a man of Gerdau's generation, leaving a company to his daughters would have been unusual, and his decision, considering his eclectic interests, to instruct his attorney, James W. Venman, to create such an unconventional will was in keeping with much of his life. The will called for one of his daughters, Alane, to receive his Redding,

Connecticut, home, while all his personal property was to be distributed equally among his daughters. That part was textbook.

The disposition of the Otto Gerdau Co., though, was anything but conventional. The will stipulated that all company assets be divided among three religious institutions: 1) the United States Catholic Conference, in Washington, D.C.; 2) Hebrew Union College's Jewish Institute of Religion, in New York; and 3) the Domestic and Foreign Missionary Society of the Protestant Episcopal Church, in New York. In explaining his decision, Gerdau wrote, "It is my hope that each religious institution which receives benefits hereunder will use such benefits for the purpose of educating and training the priests, rabbis, clergymen and other leaders of its particular faith so that more of my fellow men may enjoy the benefits which I have derived from my religious experiences."[25]

Gerdau's decision to leave the global company to the religious institutions did not come as a surprise to the family, although some members voiced concern that Gerdau wasn't of sound enough mind to know what he was doing when he had attorney Venman draw up the will in 1981. "When he died, the newspapers should have run the headline 'Kook Dies,'" one Gerdau relative told me. "The family thought he was nuts," nephew Carlson Gerdau told me.

Loyal Joan Rogers disagrees with that assessment. "Both my father and mother were rather thrilled to think they could be of assistance in developing religious leaders. My father was not a formal member of any religious institution, but had a deep but rather humbly acknowledged belief in God." Gerdau had had numerous meetings with representatives of the religions organizations he'd selected as beneficiaries, and Joan Rogers had accompanied her father to at least two such meetings.

The holdings of the Otto Gerdau Co. at the time of Gerdau's death were labyrinthine, far-flung, and at times, baffling, a reflection of Gerdau himself. Much was encumbered by onerous mortgages. To no one's surprise, the bequeathal of such an unwieldy international company to a triumvirate of three distinct religious orders was, in practice, unworkable. "A national church isn't in the business of running a pearl business," Carlson Gerdau flatly told me, and within two years, the Otto Gerdau Co. was on the auction block.

Three groups of bidders quickly emerged: daughter and son-in-law Joan and Dick Rogers; Neville Crane, an Australian pearl dealer who represented a consortium that included Broome pearler Kim Male (who still owned a minority share of PPL through his father's investment in the company); and a mystery Florida businessman by the name of George G. Levin, whom almost no one in pearling had ever heard of. Another Australian pearler, M. G. Kailis, made a late trip to the United States to place a bid, but was shut out of the proceedings.

Representatives for the religious groups instructed their attorneys that the entire Otto Gerdau Co was to be sold in toto, not in bits and pieces. The attorneys guaranteed that all bids and bidders' identities would be held in confidence. They placed no floor at which the bidding might start.

Joan and Dick Rogers put on the table a bid of $6.5 million with flexible terms of payment. "We wanted to run the company, but didn't have the money to pull it off," Joan Roger says. "We knew we didn't have enough to buy all the pieces of the company," a condition the religious groups had agreed they would not entertain.

Neville Crane and Kim Male placed a provisional bid of some $8 million on the table, but it was only for the pearl-farming interests in the Gerdau Co., namely Kuri Bay and its magnificent pearls. Crane and Male had lined up buyers for other Gerdau assets, but attorneys for the religious groups balked at that, too. Crane had been the Australian CEO of the Gerdau Co., and when the Rogerses found out he was a bidding against them, they were furious. They viewed Crane's tender as a betrayal of confidence and as hostile.

It was at this time that George Levin (pronounced le-VIN) preemptively flew to New York from South Florida, and promptly convened a private meeting with leaders of the three religious groups and their attorneys. Levin, who had no connection to either pearls or the import/export business, wanted to get the principals in the same room and make them an offer they couldn't refuse.

"We sat and negotiated for four or five hours, and we finally came to an agreed-upon price," Levin told me. "I then insisted that the attorneys give me an absolute binding letter of intent. I put up half a million dollars to bind the agreement at the price we set. We signed a contract, which in part said that neither the attorneys nor the religious leaders could speak to the other bidders. The price we agreed upon was the price the religious organizations would let the company go for. I made everyone sign a gag order, which prevented any further discussion."[26]

Unknown to almost everyone, Levin was acting on Australian Nick Paspaley's behalf. Paspaley had hired Levin to do his bidding. "When we were done that night, I called Paspaley and he was ecstatic," Levin told me. "It was a done deal by the time I left that evening."

What Levin had offered was almost double what anyone else had put on the table. The religious groups had no option other than to sell to Levin, who said he didn't recall his exact bid, but remembers it to be in the "neighborhood of $16 million." In reality, the bid was $14.7 million, according to one of the principals.[27]

"We knew Levin had a silent partner, we just didn't know who it was," said Joan Rogers. Crane and Male probably had a suspicion that Paspaley was involved in the bidding, but certainly hadn't heard of Levin. In fact, no one involved in the deal knew anything about Levin.

Levin is the son of a Philadelphia shoe salesman. He attended two years of night school at Temple University before dropping out. He first crossed paths with Paspaley after Paspaley had contracted with the Niishi Zosen Shipyard in Ise, Japan, to build his first two pearling vessels in 1971 and 1981. By 1984, Levin, through a host of real estate transactions, had acquired the shipbuilding company after it had gone bankrupt, and convinced Paspaley at the time to build a "superyacht" rather than follow the commercial designs of his first two vessels. The fiberglass ship was christened the *Paspaley III* by 1989, and became the most elegant vessel in the Paspaley fleet.

As Levin described the genesis of the Gerdau acquisition, it started with a transpacific call he received one day on his cell phone from Paspaley while driving on Interstate 95 near his home in Fort Lauderdale. "The phone rings and it's Nick, who tells me he's trying to buy this company. He tells me the whole story, and says he's only interested in the property that would help him with his pearl business. All the rest he doesn't want. Nick realized what the pearl farm was worth and wanted me to help him buy it.

"Four months later, Nick calls again, and says he wants me to go forward. He says he'll put up all the money, and wants me to negotiate for him. We'd be fifty-fifty partners."

Paspaley authorized Levin to bid 10 percent more than whatever any of the other groups had bid for the Otto Gerdau Co., a person involved in the negotiations told me. Paspaley figured the assets of the entire company might be worth as much as $25 million. But that was a pie-in-the-sky estimate. Neither the religious leaders nor their attorneys had anything close to an accurate estimate of what the entire firm might be worth. They certainly had no idea what the pearl farm at Kuri Bay was potentially worth.

Levin's preemptive bid did not sit well with either the Rogerses or Neville Crane and Kim Male. Before Crane and Male found out that Levin was, in fact, bidding on behalf of Paspaley, the Australians feared that this blustery American, who knew nothing about pearls, would swoop down in their own backyard and seize one of the most sought-after pearl farms in the world.

When they found out that it was Paspaley who had in effect bought Kuri Bay, they were even more furious.

Paspaley was viewed in Western Australia as an opportunistic poacher, an outsider from Darwin. As in all nations, state and territorial rivalries flourish in Australia. Paspaley had largely centered his pearling operations in and around Darwin, in the Northern Territory; Kuri Bay is located in the adjacent state of Western Australia. An intimate of Paspaley told me that Paspaley was worried that he'd be viewed as a "'foreigner from the Northern Territory trying to take over the Western Australian pearling industry" if word leaked that he was in the bidding for PPL and Kuri Bay. Local pearlers had seen Paspaley gobble up another local property, Roebuck Bay Pearls, in 1987, and many were determined to stop him from furthering his widening swath of pearling acquisitions, which they saw as destroying competition from local pearlers. Such was the political blowback that Paspaley couldn't snuff out. To many in Broome it made sense that local bloke Kim Male (even with backing from Perth resident Crane) ought to take over Kuri Bay.

There was little anyone could do to stop the venerable Otto Gerdau Co. sale to Levin, although after the deal went through, Joan Rogers was so disgusted that she petitioned to buy the company's name, so that she could keep it from transferring to Levin. "If we couldn't get control of the company, I thought at least I'd try to save my family's name," she said. But the attorneys for the religious triumvirate rejected her appeal.

The transfer of the two-generation Otto Gerdau Company to Levin and then to Paspaley meant an end to the bygone era of Gerdau's genteel, if not a wee bit odd, export/import firm. Before Paspaley took over the company a year later, Levin and an associate, Jeff Binder, were introduced to Gerdau workers at the New York office, and employers were struck by how different they were from their former boss. "They were crude and callous," Joan Rogers recalled. "They couldn't have cared what human beings they shredded in their paths. To call them immoral would be too charitable." Within a year, almost all Gerdau employees had either been fired or left.

For his deal-making efforts, Levin acquired half of the Gerdau Co., and when he sold out his shares to Paspaley, two years later, he was handsomely paid by asset spin-off valued in the millions. Levin assumed sole ownership of the Polk County, North Carolina, property, holding on to it till 2004, when he sold the wooded acreage to a developer who made a golf course on it. Levin said he received almost $17 million for the land.

The only fly in the ointment for Paspaley was that the Gerdau Company owned 76 percent of PPL, with the rest belonging to Kim Male. Paspaley took care of that, buying out Male's 24 percent interest in 1991 by transferring to Male a pearl-farming lease and a pearling vessel, as well as an undisclosed amount of cash. With Male out of the way, Paspaley could finally claim Kuri Bay as his own.

"We both knew that acquisition of the Gerdau Co. would do what Nick wanted it to do, and that was to make him a megaplayer," Levin told me.

By all accounts, Levin was the ultimate fast-talking salesman. "He was a spin merchant extraordinaire," one person involved in the negotiations told me. Another present at the bidding labeled Levin, "a sleaze—flashy, fast-talking and untrustworthy. He could smell money! I found him to be the caricature gold-chain carpetbagger. But Nick liked gadgets and flashiness and George had both." Joan Rogers has only the most disagreeable memories of Levin. She remembers sitting with Levin in a coffee shop on the ground floor of 82 Wall Street during the close of what once was her father's company. "He pulled out a *huge* roll of money to pay our bill, and I pushed the wad back into his pocket as much out of embarrassment as I thought we might get mugged." Rogers said Levin made a move to kiss her, but she pushed him away. Whether the action was conciliatory or not, it was behavior that thoroughly repulsed Rogers. "I took a shower as soon as I possibly could," she said.

All did not go well subsequently between Levin and Paspaley. The two had a falling-out, with Paspaley suing Levin for failure to make mortgage payments on the North Carolina land. There also were allegations that Levin had finagled with the Gerdau company's pension fund. "After the sale, we got distress calls from former employees who had discovered, to their shock, that they weren't receiving their retirement payments," said Joan Rogers.

In his defense, Levin said, "We did borrow money from the plan, but our attorneys counseled us that we had every right to do so."

This, in particular, did not sit well with the Paspaleys, especially Roslynne, whom Levin characterized as "one tough lady who watches over the business like a hawk." Originally, Levin said he had thought that he and Paspaley might both go into the pearling business together, but after several trips to Australia to familiarize himself with the operations and to meet the Paspaley family, he thought differently. "Their family is their family. No one gets in business with them who's not part of the family. They don't trust you. I saw that from the beginning."

There may have been something in Levin's brashness that appealed to Paspaley. "Nick was impressed that Levin had the right level of chutzpah and impudence to pull it off," said another former associate. During negotiation, no one could make the connection between Paspaley and Levin because Levin had only been to Australia a handful of times, and their relationship had been cemented in Japan when Paspaley had bought the *Paspaley III* from the shipbuilding company Levin took over.

Since brokering the Gerdau deal for Paspaley, Levin has been involved in a host of contentious real estate developments in New Jersey, New York, Pennsylvania, North Carolina, and Florida, including the purchase of historic Madison House Hotel in Atlantic City and the Bradley House Hotel in Palm Beach, as well as a large mobile home park in New York State.

When I talked to him in July 2008, Levin, 68, had just signed a deal to create a joint enterprise between a company he owns, Sterling Yachts, and a Monaco company, Vega, to build in Japan what he termed "giga-yachts," seafaring vessels as long as 127 meters that appeal primarily to wealthy Russians and Middle Easterners. He owns a Gulfstream jet and is an aficionado of helicopters. He also owns two prize French bulldogs.

In recent years, Levin was a financial backer of Rudolph Giuliani's bid for the 2008 Republican nomination for president and the 2004 Gore-Lieberman presidential campaign, as well as a donor to the Democratic National Committee and the National Jewish Democratic Council. Through a variety of political organizations, he said he donated almost $70,000 to the campaign of former Republican presidential candidate John McCain. "I'm not a political animal, but I found someone I like," Levin said.

Asked to summarize his role in the acquisition of the Otto Gerdau Co., Levin said, "It was a deal. I do lots of deals."

But this particular deal made pearling history. By the time Paspaley set foot on the shores anchoring fecund Kuri Bay, the outpost was a shambles. But it was the pearls for which Paspaley came; and the pearls Paspaley found at Kuri Bay were large, luminescent, and numerous. After five years of renovation, the pearls of Kuri Bay were a remarkable novelty few had ever seen before, and because of that, they eventually were to fetch on the international market some of the highest prices the world had ever known for cultured pearls.

23

Life as a Deckhand

I

While in Darwin, early one sticky, humid morning, I took a taxi to a deserted hangar in the industrial cargo section of the airport, far from where the big commercial jets take off and land. I was to be flown and dropped somewhere in the Timor Sea to work as a deckhand—in pearling argot, a deckie. Enough of the deal makers and the pearl lords. This was my opportunity to live among rank-and-file workers who get their hands dirty, slimy, and wet.

An early morning rat-tat-tat downpour had made the streets slick and shiny. The temperature was already 80 degrees and the humidity 100 percent. I felt as though I had just entered a giant steam room, and it wasn't even 6:00 a.m. yet. Darwin was empty save for a few Aboriginal Australians with no place to go, sleeping alongside roadways, stick legs and arms against the wet, red-orange clay earth. Stars hung low in the still-dark sky, illuminated by a moon sliver. There was something humbling about being so far south in the world illuminated by the glint of crepuscular light, accented by flashes of red and green streaks from the Australian aurora. The sudden staccato illumination measured how far my pearl expedition had taken me.

As soon as I walked into the hot, cavernous hangar, I spotted the Paspaley seaplane. It had softly rounded curves molded from bluish-gray fiberglass and metal. The *Mallard* looked like a dreamy version of the airplane in the mist at the end of *Casablanca* when Rick does the right thing by sending Ilsa with Victor and the letters of transit. The hangar's floodlights hit the seaplane at all the right angles, and I couldn't help but think I'd walked onto a 1940s movie set, and Bogie himself, dressed in bomber jacket and fedora, would be striding toward me to shake my hand and welcome me aboard, perhaps with a caution to "Watch your head, kid."

Alas, as I moved to the fluorescent-drenched waiting area, the only greeting I got was a grunt from one of four deckhands sprawled out on orange vinyl chairs and the scuffed linoleum floor. These deckies had spent their shore leave in Darwin and were waiting to be airlifted into the swells of the open sea for more pearling work. They looked worse for the wear, bedraggled and wasted, perhaps too many bar closings and round-shouts earlier that morning. One guy with a ponytail was snoring, stretched out over three chairs—his butt plopped in the middle chair, head cupped in the first, feet draped over the last. A woman with a nasty pierced lip and eyebrow was conked out in the corner, a balled-up knapsack sandwiched between her legs. Another deckie, his eyes closed, appeared to be sleep-strumming a guitar, and a woman with neon-red hair slept upright, breathing steadily and deeply, her head bobbing. She wore a knit cap pulled tight over her ears, ripped low-slung jeans, and Converse All-Stars.

The atmosphere transported me decades back to when I had worked at a Del Monte fruit cannery in Emeryville, California, sitting and occasionally nodding off in a similar roomful of laborers, waiting for the foreman to bellow out our names, directing us to take up residence along a clanking assembly line. That job was no more than keeping watch over mechanical knives slicing and dicing pears, cherries, grapes, apricots, and peaches, turning whole fruit into syrupy cubes to be vacuum-packed in cans. On this early morning ten thousand miles away and thirty years later, I mused about the similarities between fruit cocktail and pearls. I'd be picking off yet another one of Mother Nature's many products, helping it along its way to the final consumer. In both cases, I was a bottom-rung processing worker, a participant in how man coaxes nature into creating economic widgets that end up with the highest bidder. The pearls in themselves had little intrinsic worth. They were purely ornamental, radiating a culturally constructed sense of beauty, satisfaction, and well-being. The fruit cocktail, on the other hand, could actually sustain a person (for awhile). Yet the cost of the pearls to the consumer was thousands times more than what a can of fruit cocktail sells for. On a basic, primal level, it didn't make sense. But like diamonds, gold, and front-row tickets for a Lakers game, most commodities' economic worth has nothing to do with their inherent value, but rather with how many people want them and how scarce they are. Large, perfect Australian pearls are extraordinarily rare, but their value depends wholly on demand. Paspaley's job is to drive that demand to ever-higher levels by transforming what were essentially calcium-coated beads into exotic, enchanting, mesmerizing status symbols, positioning them at the top of millions of women's must-have wish lists even during an economic recession.

To get these astronomically priced pearls to those women, producers in Darwin and Broome rely on backpacking twenty-somethings who've just graduated high school or university and are up for adventure, perhaps some romance, on their way to making pretty good money. One-third are women. Most are Australian, but there is a sizable percentage from around the world, particularly Canada, Germany, France, England, and Japan. Relatively few pearling deckhands are American. Maybe it's the distance or the expense to get to and from Australia, or just that news of these daring jobs on the high seas hasn't yet reached U.S. shores. In part because there is such a shortage of laborers in Australia, the Australian government readily gives out yearlong work permits to foreigners engaged in the pearling industry. Paspaley pays on the high end of the nonunion scale for deckies—about 180 Australian dollars per day to start, with room and board thrown in, and an extra $30 per day while on shore leave. The work can be long, tedious, and grueling, deckhands on shore had warned me, but there was plenty of camaraderie and an occasional whale breaching to be seen off in the distance. How bad could it be?

In the corner of the dreary departure lounge early this morning, a TV was tuned to a repeating infomercial on which Jessica Simpson hawked acne cream. No one paid the least attention to the perky blonde American selling her goods. She had the departure lounge all to herself. All the way to Australia and I still couldn't get away from America's reach into the world's pores. Soon, Simpson's pitch (*Guaranteed or your money back!*) was blotted out by the rising roar of the seaplane. Groggily, the four pearl workers rubbed their eyes, struggled to stand, and queued up at the Grumman's door. Each ducked, stepping into the plane, which was stripped down bare inside except for seats. The propellers spun faster and faster, going from three blades to a blur of one. The whir of the engine reverberated in the hollow hangar, sounding like a hellacious cyclone gaining power and authority.

"Poot yer 'ir ploogs en," the pierced-lipped girl who'd been sleeping in the lounge yelled at me across the aisle.

I squished two Day-Glo red-rubber cushiony pills and shoved them into my ears, which dropped the decibel level by not much. "Dere 'edphoones, too, if 'ou wan 'em," the girl shouted as we banked steeply, veering west into the sky over awakening Darwin. The engine was full throttle, rendering more conversation impossible.

Soon we were flying over crystal blue-green inlets alongside the rugged, scrubby cliffs of the Kimberleys west of Darwin. The sky was strikingly clear, so clear that I surely thought I'd (finally!) be able to spot a kangaroo bounding along these high palisades, maybe even a mob of them. Alas, the only thing out there were more scrubland mesas and precipitous cliffs that vertically fell to the sea. What I saw were huge, remote expanses, but nary a sign of animals, not even birds, and no people or settlements seemingly anywhere. Vast wasn't the word for what lay spread out below. For hundreds and hundreds of miles, there seemed no indication that a human had ever walked about these desolate lands. Certainly, no human had ever set up permanent residence there—at least none I could surmise from three thousand feet above. This was some of the most desolate land in the world. Soon, we veered north, to the expanse of the open sea.

I wasn't sure where we were to land, but I was ready to start my stint as a deckie. I knew the Australian pearl industry operated fundamentally differently from other pearling operations in at least three significant ways:

• The first is that the Australian government let a limited number of sought-after pearl licenses for specific yearly terms. Currently there are sixteen such licenses in NW Australia. In order to farm oysters that will produce pearls on a commercial basis, companies must own or lease one of these licenses. The government allows 600,000 to 1,000,000 wild oysters to be harvested by all lessees from the seafloor each year. Along with those oysters, another 350,000 hatchery oysters may be produced by license holders. These numbers fluctuate yearly subject to lobbying efforts and maritime surveys of the existing wild oyster stock.

• The second difference is that Australia is the only country in the world where large-scale commercial pearlers continue to pick wild oysters off the seafloor. Paspaley and other companies grow some of their oysters from spat, but—and this depends on the year and the company—the vast majority of pearls come from mature oysters already on the seafloor.

• The third difference is that almost all work takes place at sea, aboard float-ing laboratories (where we were headed). There are some small pearl farms where open-sea oysters are brought to shore, but those few land-based farms are the exception. In almost all cases, divers gather live oysters at sea and deliver them to floating mother ships, where technicians insert round beads in them. The oysters are then tagged and dumped back into the sea in nets to grow the lustrous nacre that coats the beads and turns them into pearls. All this takes place miles from the Australian shore.

Ninety minutes into the flight, without any alert, we began our descent. The pilot lowered the seaplane's landing pods, and, sooner that I'd expected, we were flying parallel to the calm, bluish water, perhaps fifteen, then five feet above, then skimming, the surface, and finally skidding onto a fjordlike inlet, twin horizontal geysers gushing from the force of the water landing. An awaiting motorboat sped our way. There was some cargo unloading to do, and we formed a fire line, handing off boxes of food and supplies that had been stored in the plane's hull. Then we motored to the *Paspaley IV.*

II

"G'day, mate!" Phil Mark, the ship's first officer, yelled, grabbing my hand, pulling me up aboard.

Within minutes, I was able to see why the *Paspaley IV* was the queen of the fleet. It was a regal ship, and on every turn I was struck by the immense riches pearls had created to allow a profit-driven company like Paspaley's to justify such a luxurious at-sea station and laboratory. We walked down a flight to the operations room, where twenty-one grafting, seeding, and harvesting stations were located. These amounted to twenty-one individual operating theaters, with adjustable lighting fixtures at each and a continuous stream of filtered water running to each station. They were nothing like what I'd seen at Wan or Branellec's farms. The Australian protocol was more elaborate and complex. The laboratory was spotless.

The 75-meter-long ship (built in 2000 by the Norwegian company Flekke-fjord Slipp & Maskinfabrikk) was the most luxurious in the industry—from the library (soundproof, glass doors, scores of DVDs, hundreds of books, four re-clining leather chairs and a couch) to the deckhands' shiny, polished-wood bedrooms. On the rear deck, there was exercise equipment, including station-ary bikes and free weights. All food, as much as you could eat, was part of the deckhand's contract. Even deckhands' clothes got washed, dried, and folded by the ship's domestic, a fifty-six-year-old guy by the name of Johnny Kaye. Considering that deckhands didn't have to dip into their own pockets while aboard for anything (except for an occasional beer), the whole arrangement didn't seem shabby in the least.

Lunch soon was served, and I quickly was surrounded by three dozen deckies converging in the dining room. It wasn't too different from a college dormitory cafeteria, except that this restaurant floated and was in the middle of nowhere—and the food was excellent. Over roast pork and couscous with curried fish, I talked to seven workers, who seemed as curious about me as I was about them. Why had I come all this way? To do *what*? Surely I hadn't traveled to the bottom of the world just to ask questions.

One of the deckies was Elodie Colas, 27, a backpacker from Provence, France, who struck me as smart and literate. She was one of several non-Australians aboard. "To see what I've seen, wow!" Elodie said. She opened her aqueous, clear-blue eyes wide. "I mean, I'm *toe-tal-lee* in Australia in *ev-er-ee* way. Look," she said, sweeping her right hand toward the ship's windows, which had a panoramic view of the sea.

What was it like to be a deckhand? What was Elodie's job onboard?

"The work, it's hard. Ve get up at five a.m. and ve go to bed by nine p.m. I'm pooped [*poooohped*, she said] at the end of the day. There are, how do you say des, *cliques*—is at de word?—but by and large, everyone gets along. Sometimes, I find myself hanging out with de Japanese technicians, maybe because deer also foreigners as much as I am." Elodie's job was to wear a white lab coat, put her hair in a blue shower cap, and go back and forth to the ops (operations) room, transporting oysters in black plastic trays to and from the technicians on the deck beneath us.

The newest deckhand was Tommy Kelly, 24, from Ireland. He seemed full of swagger, but perhaps the bravado was because this day was his first aboard. Tommy had a college degree in biomedical engineering and, like many of the deckies, came for fun, travel, friendship, and to make "'ome 'erious goood mon-eh" as he put it. In a strong brogue, he explained, "Aye git bored easily. Aye worked fer Johnson 'n Johnson in da contact lens divishun back 'ome, den ah worked 'n Malta fer 'n electronics com-pan-y. Ah came to Australia because da work visa t'was so easy ta git. Ah landed en Sydney, floo ta Perth, 'nd got meself a job en fifteen minutes drew da Intanet. A bloke 'ired me 'ight away, seedin' a wheat farm. Ah worked fer ten weeks at twenty dollahs an 'our, puttin' in eighty to a 'undred 'ours a week and made meself thirteen thousand dollahs. Ah quit, bought me a car fur fifteen hundred dollars, and drove da 'hole west coast of Australia—not much 'ut dere, mate—and arrived in Broome tree weeks ago. Ah presented meself at da Paspaley office. Day gave me a fitness test (to seeh how much ah could 'ift), checked mah poleese record, gave me a blood test, and den day 'ired me. It seems like a mighty goood job, dudn't it?"

Lunch was breaking up, and I immediately noticed a division between the Japanese technicians and the deckhands. The twenty-two Japanese men ate among themselves on the ship's port side while everyone else ate on the starboard. There were two separate kitchens, not, I passingly thought, unlike a kosher household. The Japanese crew did its own cooking and serving, with its own foods, spices, pots, pans, plates, glasses, and utensils. Four rice cookers lined up on the counter. I smelled the aroma of miso soup. The separation extended beyond the kitchen. The Japanese crew also had a separate entertainment room, stocked to the gills with Japanese books, magazines, videos of old quiz shows (for some reason), and movies, some of them, not surprisingly, porn. "You want to see?" one technician asked me, nodding his head, eyebrows arched. "Verry good-loo-oking women," he promised.

The technicians generally work the entire harvest season, five months, from May through September. Some can make as much as $80,000, others haul in more depending on how productive they are. This year, Minoru Tominaga, a sixty-two-year-old technician from the suburbs of Tokyo, who'd been working for Paspaley for twenty years, told me the technicians on board requested that management hire two Japanese girls as deckhands, a suggestion heeded. "We get lonely. It work out nicely," the shaved-head Minoru told me. I didn't take this to imply that these girls were anything but affable companions who spoke the same language.

I shared a tidy room with one of the *Paspaley IV*'s divers, a twenty-seven-year-old New Zealander by the name of Sam Morton. In the hierarchy of at-sea pearl workers, divers were close to the top. "Best thing about divin' is dat youh're 'nderwater and all youh see 're fish, so many, day're bumpin' into yourh mask. It's not too long before youh realize you've got day best job in day world," Sam said, smiling. Divers wear wet suits, but they don't use scuba tanks. They rely on a hookah breathing system, long yellow air tubes attached to compressors onboard, which allows them to be less encumbered. Teams descend together, and the quick, nimble divers can grab as many as four hundred *Pinctada maxima* oysters off the seafloor a day. It's fiercely competitive.

"Some divahs shark on other divahs' territories, poachin'. It's evry man fer himself 'own there," Sam said. "Youh gotta 'ave good concentration, youh gotta stay focused, and youh need to be nimble and 'eally fit." The treasure hunt is strenuous but also lucrative. The routine generally calls for divers to work nine consecutive days; then they get four days off. Divers submerge for fifty minutes, then spend twenty minutes back on deck, time to sip a cup of tea. Then it's back to the seafloor. They normally descend nine times per day, from sunrise to sunset. Depending on the month, they get paid $4.25 to $4.50 per oyster they pick up, so some can take home as much as $1,800 on an especially good day. Their season runs March to June, and some divers end up with as much as $65,000 in three months. (Note these values are all in Australian dollars, which, depending on the fluctuating exchange rate, when I was in Broome, was about 80 cents to the U.S. dollar.) Of the hundreds of divers who hire themselves out to Paspaley and other pearling companies, none are women. Females are said to absorb nitrogen faster than men since they have more body fat, making them a high risk for the job (this may have simply been a convenient cover to maintain an Aussie old boy's club). For the off-season, Sam said he'd just bought a three-month, around-the-world airline ticket, which he hoped to start using in December.

Despite all the technological advances, the diver's job isn't without peril, as it's always been. Thriving and deadly off the coast of northern Australia is a venomous jellyfish that's been the bane of divers for hundreds of years. Called the Irukandji (named after an Aboriginal tribe), its toxins quickly attack the diver's nervous system, bringing on debilitating cramps and nonstop vomiting. Irukandji look like tiny transparent parachutes; they're difficult to spot. A sting from an Irukandji is a dreaded event. The only parts of the diver's body not covered by the wet suit—around the mouth, mask, and wrists—become prime targets for the jellyfish. Thousands of microscopic, spring-loaded poison darts discharge into the victim's skin. The initial sting is relatively painless, but divers know that they'll have to steel themselves for the agony that follows in five to thirty minutes. Symptoms include nausea, muscular pain, profuse sweating, cramps, and a sense of impending doom. "'ou feel as dho a rope's been tightened 'round your chest," diver Rory Denniss told me. There are treatments, but not antidotes. One is a shot that combines the drug legectal and morphine. Ten or so Paspaley divers a season get stung by Irukandji.

Outside the Irukandji, other species of jellyfish produce varying maladies, including one from the Whitsundays, in the heart of Australia's Great Barrier Reef, that causes a prolonged erection in the men it stings, while pushing up blood pressure to astronomical levels, as high as 280/180. Even without the poisonous jellyfish, divers' descents are dangerous. Dreamfish have poisonous spines. Sea snakes like to look at themselves in your mask and then sting you. And then there are stingrays, the kind that killed Steve Irwin in 2006.

When I asked Sam Morton whether he'd ever been stung by an Irukandji, his whole demeanor changed from happy-go-lucky, globetrotting diver to serious, vigilant believer. "Ah seen divahs who 'ave, and day look like day're gonna die. Day git da shakes, and some of 'em roll on da deck like day're 'aving epileptic fits. Yoo don't mess with Irukandji. Aye been lucky so far 'at is."

My lecture on *Pinctada maxima* diving was interrupted when First Mate Phil Mark tapped me on my shoulder. "Yoo need ta git too da bridge," he said, sounding very official. "We need ta go drough ship's rules and procedures. Required. On da double."

Phil's job was ship supervisor, cheerleader, morale captain, social director, therapist, judge, jury, executioner, all rolled into one. He had the authority to fire any of the fifty-four deckhands who weren't pulling their weight. "If you're not performin', aye'll git rid of yoo," Phil told the three new deckhands (including me) gathered on the bridge to learn what lay before us. For me, it was a two-week ride. For the others—Tommy Kelly and a Japanese girl named Nabu who didn't speak a word of English—it was three months of twelve-hour days at sea.

There really weren't many rules to follow, and Phil, a tall, thirty-two-year-old Malay with retro black glasses and a crew cut that gave him the look of a hip math teacher, seemed like a pleasant enough guy to work for.

"As yoo start workin' dis afternoon, and yoo start handlin' shell, aye don't want to see anyone throw 'em. 'at's why we're here. Da shell's da thing. Everything comes from it—dis ship, da food, yoor cabins, yoor salary. Respect da shell. Treat 'em like a woman—nice 'n gentle. Understood?"

Tommy and I nodded our heads. Nabu followed our lead.

"Don't give me reason ta search 'our cabin. No drugs. 'at goes witout saying. Aye don't mind beer or alcohol as long as yoo keep it under control. Any posseschon of comp'ny property—aye won't say *pearls*—and aye'll get rid of yoo 'at moment. We'll git yoo off da ship pronto. Understood?"

Tommy and I nodded, then Nabu.

"Look afta da boat, and she'll look afta yoo. Care for it more than yoo care for yoor room at home. It costs a 'ot more.

"We git 'p at five a.m. Make sure yoo're on da deck ready to work by five-thirty.

"Breaky is served before we start da day, depending on what we do dat day, and by ten-thirty we have Smoko (I could figure out what *Breaky* was, but what in the world was *Smoko?*) on da 'ear deck. Da food's good. Food is morale. Eat as much as yoo want, but eat what yoo take. Lunch is at twelve-thirty, dinner at five-thirty.

"'ave a shower before dinner. As long as yoo don't smell, it's allgood. But no Hollywood showers, please. We make nineteen tons of water a day onboard, but 'at's not it. Be con-sid-e-rate. 'ther people 'ill be 'aitin'.

"Yoor rooms 're to be kept clean. Dis is not a hotel. Yoo might not be 'sed to such tight quartahs. But da ship's roomy. Dere's enough space fer ev-ery-one. Work it out, or aye'll git rid of yoo.

"If someone's lazy, dan someone else 'as to do twice as much work. Sort it out amongst yooselves. Don't let it git to me. Undastood?"

24

On Board

When I first met Leigh Harding, a mild-mannered man in his midfifties with large tortoiseshell glasses and not much hair except a few chestnut strands that he tried to cover his balding crown with, he was wearing black checkered cook's pants and a snazzy white chef's coat embroidered with his name in red script. By 10:30 the next morning, the fog hadn't lifted, but Leigh gazed out at his offerings for the day's Smoko, placed on four long tables on the rear deck, and appeared to be a thoroughly contented man. It's not much of an exaggeration to say that Leigh's spread would rival the Sunday brunch at Las Vegas's Bellagio Hotel (minus the caviar, nova, eggs Benedict, and champagne). He'd baked three lamingtons (a kind of sponge cake in a cube with gooey fudge and coconut sprinkles) and two dense chocolate cakes. He had bagels, egg rolls, fried squid, sushi, little meat pies, schnitzel, pigs in a blanket, lit'l smokies, mountains of sliced turkey, ham, and roast beef, trays of fresh fruit, and probably fifteen other dishes. "Day're like gulls," Lee said of the ship's crew. "Day demolish ev'rything."

Leigh and I started talking kangaroo. I asked if what Australians called joeys were a delicacy in his culinary repertoire. He thoughtfully touched his hand to his chin, then nodded. "Da Aborigines used to eat it, but we never did." A pause. "Dhese days, dough, kangaroo tails 'ave become somethin' of a delicacy. Aye've cooked a lot of walkabout meals, and kangaroo usually appears somewhere on da menu—dishes like kangaroo-tail pasta wit akudgera (bush tomatoes) or meringue and waddle-seed soup wit witetchy grubs which taste like peanut butter. 'ots of people eat kangaroo steaks, kangaroo hamburger, kangaroo stir-fry. Dere are millions of 'em up and about, and day're not a protected species. So, dare out dere to be had. One 'hing 'bout kangaroo, 'hough: Can't cook it well done. Not dat kinda meat. It'll toughen up."

Leigh said that if I hadn't seen a live kangaroo in my travels in Australia, I couldn't very well leave without eating a dead one. I felt a little squeamish about chewing on an Australian version of our Bambi, but food is part and parcel of travel, whether you're venturing to New Orleans, Mozambique, or the uncharted seas off the northern coast of Australia. "How 'bout aye make you 'ome kangaroo stew while yoou're 'ere? Aye have some frozen tail in da freezer, and aye'll whip sump-in up. It'll be me pleasure." I thanked Leigh for his gracious offer.

I wandered down a flight toward the ops room, which was the nerve center not just of the ship but of the whole pearling operation. It was in this surgical, sterile laboratory at sea that cutting-edge technology and astronomical capital investment came together. This was the place where pearls were born and where they'd be harvested. It was the money room.

I stopped at one of the technician's stations, hovering over his hunched-over shoulders. This was deeply serious business—no kibitzing, no chitchat among the technicians or from the deckies. Twenty-two Japanese technicians, lined up in four rows, each man wearing a white lab coat, his hair covered in blue netting, working in complete silence, peering into the fleshy insides of a hard-shelled organism as we floated somewhere on the open Timor Sea. The technician quickly performed a series of cuts and insertions on an oyster as large as a dinner plate. He barely acknowledged my presence, except to slightly bow his head and then continue working. When I saw Elodie carrying a tray of oysters, she smiled at me but said nothing.

The technician was performing a "first graft," as I had seen in China, the Philippines, and French Polynesia. With a scalpel, the technician quickly cut slivers from the mantle tissue of a donor oyster, and laid out seven three-inch strips on a glass tray. He then picked out one of the three dozen *Pinctada maxima* oysters, three to six years old, from a plastic-coated wire tray that Elodie had just delivered and placed to his left. The technician placed the wedged-open oyster in a canted stainless-steel frame, which afforded him a direct view of the oyster's innards. He adjusted a light beam to illuminate the dark interior of the mollusk. With a penlike metal probe that had a squiggly wire end, the technician picked from the glass tray a strip of oyster tissue, inserting it first. He then picked up another tool, this one a scalpel to make an incision inside the oyster. He followed this with a third metal probe, this one with tiny cup at the end, to insert a white, round, 9-millimeter bead deep inside. I could see the technician rotating, then swiveling his right hand and wrist to lodge the bead at just the right place.

Then, as I had seen at the Jewelmer labs in Palawan, the oyster slowly closed its surprisingly heavy twin sides, and seemed to breath a sigh of relief. Enough already, the oyster seemed to be saying. The technician placed the loaded oyster into another tray. Each tray had a plastic tag affixed to it to denote the technician's name, date of insertion, and size of bead, as well as a host of other data. The entire procedure for each oyster was amazingly fast, no more than forty-five seconds, and for the entire tray of oysters about thirty minutes. Just as the technician was through, within seconds, like clockwork, Elodie appeared at his side to whisk away the tray of inseminated oysters, ready to be submerged back into the nutritious sea, then to be turned by divers every week or so to ensure the pearl's symmetrical shape. An efficient technician could inseminate 450 oysters in one day. With twenty-two technicians, that meant that almost 10,000 oysters could be prepared with bead insertions daily.

All their meticulous labor would be put to the test in several days, when the technicians would get to open oysters they'd inseminated with beads one, two, three years ago. Would there be a $50,000 perfectly round 20-millimeter luminescent pearl with breathtaking lustre and orient—or a shriveled, blacked dud that looked like a raisin? I'd find out.

First Mate Phil was working one level below the ops room, in a wet, dank hole, sticking black wedges in the bivalves, prying open their sides, then stacking the oysters into slots on trays, readying them for deckhands like Elodie to carry them to the ops room. He was sloshing around in seawater up to his ankles. Phil, who'd worked for Paspaley for ten years, was so practiced at the routine that he reminded me of a card dealer, fanning out the oysters like playing cards, then dropping each of them expertly into a different slot. It was a thing of beauty to see how fast and efficiently he handled three, four, five oysters at once. "Da less you touch da oyster, da better. Minimal invasion into deir lives," Phil said, heaving a black slotted tray to a stainless steel counter, then sliding it through to the other side. "So, day don't even know day're 'ere."

Like the card dealer's job, the repetitive nature of the work gets monotonous. "Yoo mix it up and yoo don't get bored. Don't know if ayd'd wana be doin' it fer da rest of me life, but it's all right fer now. Lots of jobs onboard, yoo learn ta do 'em all." As I pitched in, I asked whether he'd ever come across a natural pearl while prying open an oyster. Phil feigned shock. "Yoo wanna git me fired, mate?"

It doesn't happen very often, hardly ever, considering how many oysters come through here every season, he said. "But ev-er-y 'nce in a while we do find a pearl. But day're really nothin', cert-in-lee nothin' to write 'ome 'bout, and cert-in-lee nothin' worth pinchin' fer. Day're usually tiny, iddy-biddy keshi pearls, lit'le beads." Phil held his thumb close to his index finger, almost touching, to show how small these minuscule pearls were.

"But da Japanese technicians like to use 'em," Phil continued, a smile coming over his face.

"For what?" I asked, perplexed.

"C'mon, yoo been around."

I drew a blank.

"Yoo know," Phil said. "Day use keshies to increase—*sensation*." I wasn't quite sure why he was whispering, since we were quite alone in this waterhole sloshing in rubber boots. "Yoo eva heard of 'at?

"Day put tiny keshi pearls under da skin of deir penises, some even get dem sewed in. Deir girlfriends like it."

Was Phil trying to put one over on the Yank? I looked doubtful. "Go ask da technis-shuns, day'll tell you." I let that question go.

Phil announced that after lunch, we were cutting out from work. The crew had worked ten straight days, and Phil figured that everyone needed some R & R, so we were on our way to a deserted sandy atoll called Dingo Island for a fierce game of cricket between deckhands for the *Paspaley IV* and another Paspaley ship that'd meet us on the makeshift field (or whatever the Australians call where they play cricket).

I'd heard the deckhands talk during Smoko about the upcoming match. Bri, a brassy and muscular Canadian, had said she alone could "whip anyone's ass in cricket, and I don't know shit about the game." A couple of Aussies looked at each other and smothered a laugh.

Phil clanged a bell, officially calling an end to the workday, a decision greeted with a raucous round of cheers. As we sailed closer to Dingo Island, the deckhands donned fluorescent-green T-shirts, personalized with nicknames:

Random
Mon
Vet
Nipples
Lancho
FNG (Fucking New Guy)
Stabber
Woody
Diddy
Captain Black
Arse
Cudda
Mr. Black
Schmidty
Piranha
The Serb
Zima
Wog Boy

The competition was the Mullets & Mohawks vs. the Greens. The winner would claim an oyster shell trophy, dubbed The Love Muscle. As we pulled up to the beach of Dingo Island, deckies The Serb and Cudda hauled from the ship a car battery, tape deck, and makeshift speakers fashioned out of ten-gallon plastic food drums. A convoy of brawny deckhands hauled coolers of beer on their shoulders. We scrambled onto the beach, then to an elevated bluff five hundred yards away. As The Serb and Cudda tried to get the sound machine cranking, the Greens arrived, about three dozen of them, tearing onto the beach. The guys were topless, the girls in halter tops, and many were wearing orange wigs or furry hats.

"BULLSHIT!" Random shouted, triggering a nonstop chorus of "BULLSHIT! BULLSHIT! BULLSHIT!"

Someone had brought what I was told were called wickets, a kind of three-post catcher's stop, and bats that looked like long-handled wooden blades. The cricket ball was smaller than a baseball but larger than a golf ball, and it was white. Palm fronds were used for what appeared to be bases. The Mullets & Mohawks took to the field first. The pitcher stood back farther from the batter than in baseball, and he had a peculiar way of throwing, with a double wind-up, and he actually tried to bounce the ball before it reached the batter. Strange.

On the first pitch, a Green player hit a pop fly to Nipples, who proclaimed to everyone, "I'VE GOT IT!" then proceeded to drop the ball as it came to rest in, and then fall out of, her cupped hands.

"SHIT!" she screamed, to which the Greens chanted, "MULLETS & MO-HAWKS ARE WANKERS!"

Nipples seemed as upset with her performance as she was with the Green team's exhortation. Shaking her head, she slunk off the field, only to resurrect moments later as her team's beer maid. Armed with a clipboard, pen, bottle opener, and bucket filled with cold VBs, she made deliveries onto the field, popping open bottle after bottle while marking down on the clipboard who consumed how many. It was a great bar-tab system that, if employed in the United States, would, I'm sure, greatly increase interest in all amateur field sports.

The game went on with plenty of boos and some cheering. About halfway through, a rhubarb erupted that involved a prolonged interpretation of one of the game's more arcane rules. A series of consultations was conducted among many players on and off the field, including the captains of both teams, resulting in no resolution, which prompted once again a chorus of "MULLETS & MOHAWKS ARE WANKERS!"

Not satisfied with the tinny music sputtering out of the makeshift sound system, sweaty The Serb walked off the field and began fiddling with the car-battery generator wires attached to the tape deck, when, all of a sudden, the music stopped.

"WHAT THE FUCK?" Stabber shouted, joined by Captain Black, Wog Boy, and Diddy, whom I recognized as the guy who'd been sleep-drumming the imaginary guitar in the Darwin hangar two days earlier.

The Serb got the sound going again, and inserted a tape of heavy metal music, to which Nipples said. "TURN THAT SHIT OFF!" When the bar maid in any establishment speaks her mind, patrons listen.

The limit of beer consumption was six bottles. I'm pretty sure that wasn't Nipples's rule but either the company's or First Mate Phil's. Many players had reached their limit, and as Nipples continued to make her rounds, with clipboard and beer bucket, I heard her sweetly say to one player, "I'm sorry, Nicole. You've already 'ad your six. I'm cuttin' you off."

Indeed, as the game continued, play got sloppier. A medley of loud belches came from an assortment of players. A pop fly got dropped when FNG called it his own but refused to put down his beer. The descending ball promptly pinged off the bottle he was holding, allowing the Greens to score two more points.

In the end, the Greens won, although to some the match would forever be under protest. Crowded on a large motor boat to transport us back to the *Paspaley IV*, Piranha, Schmidty, and Arse sat on the boat's railing and bid adieu to the Greens by pulling down their pants and chucking moons.

The revelry lasted way into the night, getting louder and more raucous with each hour. The *Paspaley IV*'s fiftyish captain, Michael Kyriacou, a bearish guy who goes by the nickname Ernie (because of a striking resemblance to the *Sesame Street* character) came down from the bridge not to calm things down but to see the action in full swing. "Looks like day're 'avin' a goood time," Ernie said, like a father chaperoning a high school prom. In progress was an assortment of chugging contests, outrageous flirting, multiple rounds of robust high-fives, and a quintet of baritones dueling with a trio of sopranos. "It's goood fer dese kids ta blow off steam," Ernie said, sounding very old. "Day work 'ard. Good, clean fun. Worse thing onboard is a bunch of whisperers, da ones dat don't join. Day can turn a 'hole crew. Ya gotta weed 'em out early."

"Ever have moments when the fun isn't good and clean?" I asked.

Ernie, Phil, and Second Mate Billy pondered that one. For a moment, it seemed the question had stumped them, until the lightbulb went off in Billy's head.

"Well, aye don't know if dis qualafies. But what aye'm thinkin' 'bout wasn't bad and it sure was fun. It was *different*, aye guess, is what 'oo'd say." Billy couldn't help but break into laughter.

Ernie and Phil looked at him like he was nuts.

"'member da *German* girls?" Billy asked.

"Oh, da *German* girls," Phil said, nodding.

"Who could eveh forget da *German* girls?"

There was a moment of silence, a collective sigh, it seemed, of reverence and appreciation.

"Sor'y, mate," Billy said, shaking his head, as though someone had suddenly splashed sea water on his face. "Da *German* girls were deckies two or three 'ears ago."

"More like four or five 'ears, was'n it?" Ernie corrected.

"Actu'lly, it was four years ago dis month," Phil announced.

"*Whenever* it was," I stepped in. "What happened?"

"Who wants ta tell da Yank da story?" Phil asked patiently.

Billy nodded. "Da two of 'em shared a room, and ev'ry time day left ev'ry mornin', day'd 've full makeup on, lipstick, cream, da stuff day put around deir eyes, you know."

"Mascara," Ernie interjected.

"'nd eye shadow," Phil added.

"Aye think day even curled deir eyelashes," Billy said.

"Dese girls, day were stacked, way out ta 'ere." With that, both Ernie and Phil cupped their hands and held them in front of their chests. "Like dis," Ernie pointed out.

"We all looked at dem and were wond'ring, 'How long is dis gonna last?' I mean dis is hard, dirty work, and dese girls are dressed to the nines . . ."

"Ya say tat in America?" Phil asked. "Nines?"

"Course day say dat!" Ernie said.

Billy wanted no part of the linguistic one-upmanship. "Anyway," he continued, "over da course of da next two weeks, dese girls one by one did everyone on the ship, any bloke, and I dare to say, any girl—at least dose who wanted ta."

"Wonder if day evah paired up?" Ernie asked.

"Wouldn't 'ave put it past 'em," Phil said.

"No," said Billy firmly. "You gettin' dem mixed up with da two girls who used to go to dah top deck for nude sunbathin'. Rememba dem?"

Another sigh, until Billy got back to the story of the German girls.

They seemed to have an attack plan, going cabin to cabin, knocking off one by one, and when they were through, they got tired and left the ship. "Just like dat," Billy said, snapping his fingers.

"Neva seen anythin' like it," Ernie said. "Neva in me life."

"Ya 'ave either of 'em, Phil?" Billy asked.

"Whadyamean, *either*? Aye 'ad 'em both!"

"Whadabout you, Ernie?"

"Aye'm a married man!"

"Well, aye am, too, and dat didn't stop *me*!" Billy said.

To be sure, it was juvenile, sexist, and probably not in the least bit true. Boys-will-be-boys stuff. But these boys were sailors, and wasn't this the way sailors were *supposed* to talk?

The moon bathed the ship like a giant klieg light that night, casting all that lay below in a warm, protective glow. Groups of deckhands told jokes, girls gossiped about boys. Boys eyed girls across the deck. A lingering smile, a glance held with purpose, a laugh that enchanted, a stray hand draped on another forearm for just a moment. I spotted Nipples flirting with one of the cricket players, FNG or Random, I wasn't sure which. While these were workers whose labor allowed women thousands of miles away to drape precious pearls from their necks or to hang them from their earlobes, pearls for these deckies were nothing more than fruit cocktail had been for me so long ago. Pearls were the same as coal to the coal miner, perhaps how words are to the writer. Pearls were a means, a way to allow their pursuers to live.

By now, it was 1:00 a.m. I needed to get back to my room to take care of the prosaic task of writing up my notes. By then, the festivities had erupted into an uproarious free-for-all, with round after round of sloppy lyrics I couldn't understand, accompanied by a *batteria* of syncopated beats from plastic food tubs turned upside down and made into drums.

Despite the racket, I slept like a baby. Before the sun rose the next day, I was to go with five deckies on one of the *Paspaley IV*'s trawlers to haul up thousands of panels of wild oysters that had been caught and inventoried, to be inserted with beads by the ship's technicians. But how were the deckies ever going to be able to wake up on time?

25

At Sea

I

Despite the partying that lasted till 4:00 a.m., the deckhands assigned to go out to sea along with me assembled at the ship's rear deck promptly at 5:30 a.m. G'day mates, all around, clutching mugs of steaming coffee. There was something about the day's weather, chilly but humid and muggy. The expected swells could get pretty big.

"No 'ne gits seasick, 'ight?" asked Gary, the skipper of the *Vansittart*, the trawler that we were about to step onto.

No one bit. That'd be like a zookeeper saying he's scared of lions and tigers.

"Aye reckin it may git a lit'le rough out 'here t'day, mohr than 'sual," Gary said.

We all put on XXL hooded yellow slickers, matching pants, and workman's gloves, then climbed aboard the *Vansittart*, a twelve-meter boat with a flat area up front to allow room for stacking the oyster panels we were to haul from sea.

In addition to Gary, there were six of us:

• Bri, the aforementioned brawny woman with long, thick, tawny hair, from Vancouver. Bri was an Amazon of a woman, and knew it. Bri was an over-sized and hard-drinking woman in her early twenties. On the backside of her neck, she had a tattoo of three Japanese characters that, she said, translated to serenity, courage, and wisdom. "But my real motto is, 'Don't *screw* the crew!' It's askin' for trouble!" Bri announced, although no one had asked.

• Selena was a petite but muscular woman from Alberta with fine blond hair and green eyes, who'd been traveling with her boyfriend, Jordan, for the last eighteen months. They'd spent a night at an Australian youth hostel, where someone had recommended they sign up to be deckhands.

• Benny spoke with such an extreme accent, the equivalent of rapid-fire, jumbled Aussie-Cockney, popular among working-class blokes from South Queensland, that I never found out much about him. With the roar of waves slapping against the side of the trawler, about all I could follow were a couple of *mates*, lots of *bloody* this, *bloody* that, and a lot of *fuck!* He was a brute of a guy, a stocky and stout 220-pound fire hydrant with red hair, who could probably bench-press 300 pounds. When he and another deckie were on shore leave the week before, they got totally wasted, and at bar close, they were walking with a brick of twenty-four "tinnies" (Australian for cans) of beer when, they said, they were attacked by a group of fourteen Aboriginals, who "beat dah shit 'ut a us an' rahn a'way wit hour berh. Fuck 'ose fuckahs!" As a result, Benny had deep cuts and scratches on his face, a split lip, and a coal-black swollen left eye.

• Hannah, a tall, willowy woman with chestnut-colored hair from the Australian capital of Canberra. Her immediate goal in life, she said, was to open a bar and restaurant back home. "Aye wanna make it into a 'omey place, where people 'ill feel com-for-ta-ble," she told me. Hannah raised some eyebrows on the *Paspaley IV* because she was traveling with her partner, a smallish brunette whom some deckies said wasn't pulling her load.

• Joe, a handsome and bashful guy from Perth with an engaging smile and huge, oversized biceps, who didn't say much, and when he did, it was mostly directed to Benny.

Bri and Benny bragged that they'd pulled all-nighters, and I'm sure Selena, Hannah, and Joe couldn't have had more than a couple of hours' sleep, but no one seemed too worse for the wear. We had a two-hour trip in front of us to get to the nautical triangle where our pickups were—some two thousand tagged oysters submerged in flat panels, soaking up the nutrients of the wild sea. These were among the crop that had originally been scooped up by diver Sam Morton, inserted with beads, then returned.

We'd been traversing increasingly large swells, surging, lurching, then flop-ping against foamy whitecaps as the sun began its quick ascent. A fine rain started falling. Hannah, Selena (both catnapping), and I huddled inside the trawler's bridge while Bri, Benny, and Joe were the tough guys up front, chatting away, braving the rain, holding onto ropes to keep their footing. They seemed to be in a full-tilt animated discussion about last night's blowout. I could see Bri and Benny clinking imaginary glasses of beer, then clapping each other on the back of their slickers. They were yukking it up.

Suddenly, I saw Joe point toward the distant port side.

"'OOK!" he shouted excitedly, the electricity in his body short-circuiting. "WHALES!!!"

Joe's charged exclamation wasn't as dramatic as "Thar she blows!" but for all of us that day on the *Vansittart*, it served the same purpose. Gary and I immediately pivoted to our left and in the distance, we saw a cow and her calf, perfectly arching their backs, mother and child, breaching high above the water's gray-blue surface. These whales were huge, and no more than two hundred meters away.

I nudged snoozing Selena. "Whales!" I said, unable to conceal my excitement.

Selena's eyes went from slits to full rounds. Awakened, Hannah clutched my elbow and with a sense of urgency asked, "Where, where? Tell me!"

"Over there! Look!"

In one motion, the three of us panned west to the *Vansittart*'s port side, and this time, there was even more to take in. Not just the mother and her calf, but four more large whales followed, traveling in a school, stealthily and wearily traversing the sea like big gray submarines that every ninety seconds or so would surface. They surely sensed our presence, knowing we were trespassing their dominion. They gave us a wide berth, steering clear of us, wary of our intrusion.

"Wow!" Hannah, Selena, and I said, completely taken.

Every once in a while, a sudden gush of water shot vertically, as high as fifteen feet, from the whales' blowholes. Up front, from the trawler's bow, Bri raised her right hand high, cocked us a jubilant thumbs-up, and yelled "IN-FUCKIN'-CREDIBLE!"

For Skipper Gary, though, the cetaceans were hardly a welcome sight. He hated them. "Let 'em stay w'ere day 're," Gary said with surprising anger, shaking his head, his tongue for a second darting out to moisten his salty lips. He took his eyes off port side and grimaced straight ahead into the horizon as though to say, "Mayh-be, 'f aye don't 'ook at 'em, mayh-be day aren't really 'tere. . . . Dere fahr enuf away, 'nd dat's w'ere aye whan 'em ta stayh. Day come 'ny closa, 'nd we be askin' fer tro'ble."

Gary might have been a killjoy, but he also was a good skipper. The problem he foresaw was not trifling. Whales get tangled and caught in the nylon lines used to tether submerged oyster panels, flapping and fighting to free themselves. But that was the least of it. Some whales had a pesky habit of actually going after a boat, sidling up parallel, then rubbing their backs against the hull to scrape away barnacles that attach themselves to their tough skin. The action is akin to a whale's going in for a full body scrub with the boat as a giant loofah. It might be great for the whale, but it plays havoc with the vessel. It'll cause any sailor's heartbeat to max out, his brow to drizzle sweat, as a boat gets rocked side to side, taking on thousands of gallons of water. Whales have also been known to put on other impromptu shows. They'll swim within fifteen meters of a trawler, flapping their fin tails, slapping the water's surface, which makes for a colossal deluge, unlike anything Shamu is capable of. Within ten meters, the vessel and even its crew can get smacked by the leviathan's tail. A whale's close proximity to a ship as large as the *Paspaley IV* is cause for shuddering, and the *Paspaley IV* is four times as long and fifty times as heavy as the *Vansittart*.

Fortunately, these portside whales were bashful, content to be admired from afar; they veered westward, one final spout of water shooting out of a blowhole, in an elegant farewell. Gary was relieved, and stopped licking his lips.

"Was that *fuckin'* cool or what?" Bri asked, as we converged on the *Vansittart*'s deck, the weather suddenly clearing, the rain stopping. A hazy but goldish medallion was visible climbing the horizon. In the distance on our starboard side, we could even see the faint outline of a rainbow. I noted that in the Southern Hemisphere, ROY G BIV (a mnemonic for the order of the seven colors of a rainbow: red, orange, yellow, green, blue, indigo, violet) still held sway.

II

The *Vansittart* continued chugging west, and in about an hour, a large bobbing buoy signified that we had reached the first pickup point. Gary sank the *Vansittart*'s anchor and we started to work. At each of these underwater farms, we were to pull up some 250 panels, each filled with eight oysters. Joe was first to operate the ship's mechanical winch, attaching a cable to a thick guide rope threaded to hold each panel together, one by one, ten feet apart. Then he grabbed each seaweed-covered panel, unhooked it, and handed it off to Bri, who swung it to Benny, all the while spraying the deck with an assortment of ocean muck. Benny was in charge of operating a conveyer-belt washing machine on board. He sent each panel through this oyster-o-matic clean machine, which squirted jets of salt water at the precious charges in each panel's pockets, powering off debris like gnarled clumps of sticky seaweed, sucked-on barnacles and snails, gooey leachlike centipedes, and wayward starfish (oysters' natural predator: they wrap their tentacles around the hard shell, tenaciously crack it, and suck out the meat). Down the line, Selena pulled the panels off the end of the oyster-o-matic's rinse cycle, and then swung them to Hannah and me to stack on alternative sides of the boat. Each stop that day had us hauling, swinging, cleaning, rinsing, and stacking panels containing thousands of fan-shaped *Pinctada maxima* oysters. These loaded panels weren't light, about twenty-five pounds a piece—Joe, to Bri, to Benny, to Selena, to Hannah, and me. It was non-stop assembly-line work. If you let up for as little as a minute, you'd be facing a backup coming at you fast and furious. And no one wanted to mess with Bri. She was this trawler's de facto macha forewoman, shouting streams of profanities. She ran a tight ship. The last thing anyone wanted was for Bri to call us wankers.

There was a nice rhythm to the assembly-line process and speed, as there had been so many years ago when I worked at the cannery. I quickly synced the routine, and even while trading stories with Selena and Hannah over the din of Benny's oyster-o-matic and Bri's stream of scatological monologues, the six of us were one mean oyster panel-stacking machine. It took a certain amount of brainless concentration; still, if you let your mind wander, you'd end up like Lucy at the chocolate factory assembly line, only in our case, you'd be buried under heavy panels of slimy oysters.

"Eh Steve!" Selena yelled my way. And *whoosh*, a wiggling fish was headed directly for at my head. I threw the live fish to Hannah, who tossed it up front to Bri, then to Benny and Joe, a nautical version of Hot Potato.

We went to two more pickup sites, then broke for lunch (sandwiches Leigh had made for us), sitting with our backs to the sun, watching another whale and her calf, these way off, perhaps five hundred meters, make their journey westward, occasionally breaching, shooting seawater from their blowholes. These colossal grays off in the distance were breathtaking to behold, two heaving and plopping baleens, peregrinating at the bottom of the world.

We were in awe, still in a trance, when Bri suddenly jolted us with a great and sonorous burp, which sounded as if it could have come from deep within the bowels of one of the whales we were admiring.

"Back to work, ya deadbeats!" she said. "*Fuckin'* right!" Two more retrieval sites to pull up more dumped oysters, and we'd be done for the day.

By the time we got back to the *Paspaley IV*, it was 5:00 p.m. We'd been gone almost twelve hours. Phil took over the *Paspaley IV*'s huge boom, with Bri and Benny affixing to a cable line each of the panels we'd pulled from the sea, rinsed and stacked. They worked into the early evening, hauling 1,306 panels, for a total of 10,448 oysters we'd pulled from the sea that day. It would be into these oysters that technicians would insert shell beads the next morning. And when the technicians finished, other deckhands would stack the oysters into more panels, yet to be submerged to grow nacre that would (if everything went according to plan) turn the beads into pearls. In the meantime, Joe, Selena, Hannah, and I stacked the oysters just loaded onto the ship into heated vats of salt water to ease any shock they might be experiencing.

While working over the vats, quickly shifting oyster after oyster from panel to calming water, my fingers feeling puckered even inside wet gloves, it dawned on me again: Bri, Selena, and Hannah would probably never wear the pearls they were helping to create. Too expensive, but also not their style. I asked them about it, and Selena said pearls as fashion didn't interest her in the least. Hannah said her parents had given her pearl earrings for her sixteenth birthday, and she still cherished them, but seldom wore them. When Bri was finished unloading the last of the oyster panels, I asked her, too. "Yeah, right!" she boomed. "Me and pearls, a natural combo. *Not!*" Maybe that's how it always is—the guys on the Del Monte assembly line hated fruit cocktail, pastry chefs hate Napoleons.

By 7:00 p.m., Phil called for the workday's end. We had thirty minutes to dinner, late tonight, and there was a rush to the showers. The technicians had cut out early; they'd have a full day tomorrow, and now they were relaxing on the ship's top deck. Two were riding stationary bikes, another was doing a slow, deliberate jog around the ship, three practiced Tai Chi, two were doing stretching exercises, and one was kneading another technician's neck muscles. "Releases stress. Feels good. You try?" he offered genially.

At dinner, I noticed that Nabu, the new Japanese deckie, was sitting with the technicians on the port side of the dining hall, sharing a bottle of red Bunnamagoo wine, most of the men edging close to her, as though they were inmates crowding around a visitor.

When I got to the front of the food line, Leigh surprised me with kangaroo stew with mushrooms, prepared with what he described as a reduction marinade sauce. I felt a little uncomfortable eating a meal different from the rest of the crew (who were dining on beef bourguignon), but Leigh said he had only a pound of kangaroo meat in the freezer, and someone had to eat it, so why shouldn't it be me?

Despite Leigh's culinary pyrotechnics, he'd been right about the kangaroo. It was tough and chewy. With a sense of relief, I pushed the cubes to the edge of my plate.

Her hair matted wet and a meal under her belt, Bri was again flying high. To Joe, Benny, Selena, Hannah, and me, she made an impromptu toast. "You guys were great today! We live by the slogan: 'Work hard, party hard!' Deckies forever!" Bri slapped each of us with a high-five.

After dinner, deckhand Elodie Colas and I talked about her favorite movies. She was a huge De Niro fan, but also adored Daniel Day-Lewis. *In the Name of the Father* was about to play in the ship's entertainment center, and *Raging Bull* was queued to follow.

An English guy sitting on the rear deck, under a fluorescent light, pulled on a hand-rolled cigarette, thoroughly engrossed in the just-released Harry Potter book. By 10:00 p.m., Nabu had paired off with one of Japanese technicians, the youngest and most handsome, and they were just starting their second bottle of wine. I walked up to the top deck, where I spotted Hannah snuggling with her partner. They were sitting looking at the moon and stars, holding hands and giggling.

I was to leave the vessel next day, hopping onto the *Paspaley III* (the ship Nick Paspaley had assembled at George Levin's shipbuilding facility in Ise, Japan), which would be harvesting oysters, so I'd be able to see technicians extracting real pearls. There I was to rendezvous with the society ladies I'd first met at Roslynne Bracher's house, to take a first look at the cream of this year's pearl crop.

26

The Show

A most extraordinary thing happened the morning I was to leave the *Paspaley IV*. Fifteen minutes before Smoko was to begin, I heard a great commotion off the ship's starboard side. Hannah heard it and she came running. So did Tommy Kelly, although a macho guy like Tommy would never let on that anything alarmed him, so he ambled over, legs bowed like a cowboy. I can't readily describe the shipside clamor, except to say that it sounded like intense and massive flapping sounds. A school of whales? Sharks?

I rushed to the railing, and below me weren't whales or sharks, but thousands upon thousands of silvery fish flying through air. For the entire length of the ship, fish no more than four inches long were jumping out of the water en masse. They were everywhere and they were jumping halfway up the ship's hull. At the water's surface, some of the fish looked as though they were walking on the sea's glassine surface, their tails serving as feet. There were so many fish, and they were so densely packed, that the scene for a moment resembled a sparkling curtain pulled alongside the ship. As the morning sun bounced off the flying fish, the scene turned into thousands of prisms shooting through air—crisscrossing vectors of rainbow colors.

There was more. Within minutes, I heard a high-pitched, pulsating, giant-insect kind of sound. Hundreds of gulls had gotten wind of the flying-fish show. More and more gulls showed up for the free-for-all, executing daredevil acrobatics, snatching as many fish as they could. So many fish were flying helter-skelter that some gulls plucked out of the air a half-dozen at a time, swallowing a couple, keeping more for friends and family back home, all the while dropping one or two from their loaded beaks.

"Leigh, come 'ere" I yelled over to the kitchen.

Leigh had just finished setting out Smoko, looking very pleased.

"Look at 'em all. What's going on?" I asked.

Leigh seemed disappointed. "Dat happens ev'ry 'nce in a 'hile. Not a big deal. It's a chain re-ac-shun. Dhose fishes are doin' a sorta high-flyin' trapeze act, tryin' to save deir lives."

From what Leigh explained, a school of large predator fish must have just swarmed into the area, gobbling up as many fish as they could. That triggered smaller fish to eat even smaller fish, which triggered smaller fish to eat smaller fish, so on down the food chain, prompting the Masada scene playing out before our eyes.

Leigh shrugged his shoulders, disheartened that the seafaring action wasn't anything more newsworthy, then got back to the rear deck to make sure the gulls, after their feeding frenzy, didn't move in on his Smoko, which today happened to feature three herring dishes.

Within ten minutes, the fish-gull frenzy was over as though it never had happened.

"Dat was somethin'!" Tommy Kelly, who'd seen it all, announced.

"Dat was *amazin',*" Hannah added, not quite certain that the silvery tableau had been real.

With an hour left before I was to be ferried to a seaplane that'd take me to the *Paspaley III*, Leigh's Smoko was in full force. I sat with First Mate Phil and Second Officer Skippy, a slice of lamington, a dish of fried squid, and a cup of sweet lemonade before me. Johnny Kaye, the ship's domestic, came by and sat with us. Skippy estimated that up to 30 percent of this season's deckies would return next year for another season, and that 10 percent would eventually make a living out of pearling, advancing from deckhand to full-time crew, some to second and first officer, engineer, skipper, or captain.

"And God 'elp 'em if day do," Johnny cracked.

The schedule for full-timers at sea depends on their duties, but usually it's one month on, two weeks off.

"It 'itn't bad, rally," Johnny said. "Yoo git so used to it, dat 'nce yoo're on land, yoo can't wait till yoo git yoorself back on sea. It takes me a coup'e of daze to a' just to walkin' on land again."

Phil Mark and Skippy nodded. "Bein' out at sea ain't really any different from how it used ta be a 'undred years ago," Skippy said, chewing a triangular slice of watermelon, then machine-gun-fire spitting a half-dozen seeds overboard. "Oh, da tech-no-o-gy is betta, dat's fer sure, and the con-dis-shuns is betta, so's da pay. And somethin' else: Da women make it more plea-sant," Skippy said, raising his eyebrows à la Groucho Marx, sans cigar. I imagined if Bri had been anywhere near us, she'd have chimed in, "*Fuckin'* right!" but she was on the other side of the deck, facing off with Benny in what appeared to be a round of arm wrestling.

Skippy paused for a couple of seconds, looking out at the blue-gray sea. He pursed his lips. I could see he was lining up on his tongue another set of watermelon seeds to fire out. "Aye like it cuz it's constant. Datz it fer me. Aye got me a job ta do and aye do it. Aye like bein' out 'ere away from da shitty. It suits me." Philosophical riff complete, Skippy let fly a final volley of black seeds.

Ernie, the ship's skipper, just then strode onto the rear deck, late for Smoko. "Don't ev'ryone stand at once," he said, smiling.

The five of us sat for a farewell of sorts. These men, full-time sailors with good salaries, might have the wherewithal to purchase the coveted fruits of their labor, and I asked if they ever bought pearls for their wives or, in Phil's case, his girlfriend, an attorney in Broome.

"Yoo're away for a month, and it's nice ta bring 'em back somethin'," Phil allowed in a chivalrous sort of way. But even though Paspaley offers crew members a discount on personal purchases of up to 50 percent, Phil said it's off of a steep retail price schedule, so even for these guys, feet firmly on a top of the first third of the pearl ladder, pearls weren't something they could afford, at least from the Paspaley Company. Some crew members who do buy pearls for their sweethearts end up at a shop in Broome called Linneys, which discounts for crew members and substantially undercuts the Paspaley markup (even with the employee discount), these guys told me.

At some point in our discussion, we all heard a distant roar that sounded like a roll of thunder, and in a few seconds, the rumble grew louder and it got closer. The rolling roar wasn't a return of the flying fish free for all, but the arrival of the Paspaley Mallard, which came into view a quarter of a mile away, coming in quickly for a landing not far from our starboard side.

I made my way to a waiting motorboat, engine revving, threw my bags in, and waved good-bye. After a fire line to exchange bag after bag of the *Paspaley IV*'s garbage for boxes of apples, oranges, pears, lettuce, tomatoes, and condiments (Worcestershire sauce, Tabasco sauce, soy sauce, mustard, ketchup, mayonnaise: Leigh would be happy), I climbed aboard, took a seat, and, as the pilot sped down on aquatic runway, I instinctively put in my Day-Glo earplugs. I looked out my window. By now, Smoko was over, and the crew was in full-tilt work mode, prepping yesterday's haul for the technicians.

We flew low past a natural wonder the locals call a horizontal waterfall. Located in the middle of an aquamarine fjord in the Kimberleys between twin underwater rock formations, the submerged topography entices water to flow into a wide opening, and then fans out above a submerged chasm.

I had thus far seen how the pearl-culturing process worked in Japan, China, the Philippines, French Polynesia, and now Australia. The five countries supply—or processed—almost all of the world's pearls, and the flamboyant pearl lords I'd met in each were the product's most important players. The laborers continued to interest me, though, as much as the kingpins. That's why I'd worked as a deckie—to become a part of the humanity that produced these expensive orbs that'll eventually end up sitting on bosoms, or hanging from earlobes, of wealthy women halfway around the world. That was one of the reasons I'd embarked on this journey in the first place: to get at the equivalent of the workers who had farmed the fibers that would be transformed into fabric to make the rental tuxedo I'd tracked so many years earlier.

But as of yet, I hadn't yet seen a pearl harvest in Australia, and that's why I was flying on this deafeningly noisy, seaplane. On the *Paspaley III*, technicians were to commence the final harvesting stage—extracting pearls from oysters. I could hardly wait to see these babies. It'd be payoff time.

There was another element to my visit. I was to rendezvous with the VIPs I'd met earlier at Roslynne Bracher's house in Darwin—the coffee magnate, and the ex-politician's wife from Melbourne and her pretty teenage daughter. The three were on tour to see the wonders of pearl cultivation, but in reality, the trip was a junket, plain and simple. Each was expected to buy several pearl baubles, maybe more. That's the way these things worked. Paspaley wasn't going to wine, dine, sail, and fly these wealthy style- and opinion-makers to some of the most remote places on earth without an implicit understanding that they'd make it worth the company's while.

At first, I thought this to be a simple quid pro quo: We treat you like royalty; you buy our pearls. But there was more to the equation. It was a kind of product placement. These wealthy women go to a full circuit of gala society functions, at which they, of course, will wear the jaw-dropping Paspaley pearls. Other wealthy women notice the pearls, swoon over them, and covet them for their own. The VIP gushes about the luscious pearls. Also part of the junket was to extol the Paspaley family as being as Australian as shrimp on the barbie. For a fellow Australian, buying Paspaley is buying Australian. None of those inferior Philippine, Tahitian, or, God forbid, cheap Chinese freshwater pearls. That's at least how the scenario is supposed to play out.

Along with the VIPs would be Paspaley niece Christine Bracher, whose job was to coordinate such high-roller events, as well as Christine's aunt, Marilynne Paspaley, to assist in closing the deal. I was looking forward to contrasting the trio of VIP women to Bri, Hannah, and Selena, who'd worked (and partied) so hard to get those pearls to these and other deep-pocketed buyers.

A waiting motorboat picked us up from the seaplane and ferried us to the nearby *Paspaley III*, where Marilynne and Christine (who both were wearing outrageous pearl strands that retailed for more than $100,000 each) greeted me. After kissing on both cheeks the Sydney and Melbourne junketeers, we climbed to the top deck, to the captain's private dining room. An assortment of the ship's brass was awaiting including the skipper, first mate, two or three obsequious functionaries, and the ship's chief technician, Yagura Toshiyuki Shima.

"Let's get started," Yagura said, not wasting any time.

This was to be Yagura's show. He was to display the latest pearls he and his crew of technicians had extracted from the watery confines of tens of thousands of *Pinctada maxima* oysters. Some of these oysters had just been harvested that morning.

Yagura picked up a folded white tablecloth and, with a flourish, as though he were a magician (in many ways, he was), unfurled the thick cloth. The fabric seemed to hover, defying gravity, almost levitating, before slowly floating down onto a large Formica-topped table. The show had begun.

I flashed onto the scene that Jean Taburiaux had written about, of the Arab sheik lovingly displaying pearl after pearl to an incredulous, mesmerized guest, sitting cross-legged from the sheik. The sheik's pearls had been stored inside clear little jars that the sheik would place one by one in front of his wide-eyed guest. Each succeeding jar, and the pearl within, would be larger than the last, until the sheik would display his pride and joy, a huge, magnificent pearl that was more precious than all the rest combined.

In front of me in the captain's floating private dining room, Yagura was playing the Arab sheik, and we were his guests. Yagura opened a large metal box at the corner closest to him, lowered his head, and peeked inside. He smiled, then nodded, as much to himself as to all of us. He closed the lid and looked at each of us. "Are you sure you want to see what's inside?" he teased.

"No fair!" I said, playing to Yagura's hand. "Come on!"

Yagura removed the lid, lifted the box, then slowly spilled out onto the table hundreds of brand new, luminescent freshly harvested pearls. The force of pouring so many pearls onto the table made some plink against each other and skitter across the white cloth. It was a sight to behold: pearls just barely free of the confines of the oysters that had created them and stored them. They were as virgin as could be. They'd been touched by just one or two humans since coming out of their gelatinous source.

The politician's ex-wife gasped.

The coffee mogul sputtered.

The teenaged girl eked.

Yagura's trick had worked.

I wanted to watch Christine and Marilynne's reactions to the unveiling of the pearls, even more than I wanted to see the VIPs'. I was certain how the coffee baroness and politician's wife and daughter would react. But Christine and Marilynne were a different story. Surely, they'd been through such pearl acts hundreds of times. I wanted to see whether pearls by now would be mere props, whether the act would be just another part of the job, or whether they, too, would be mesmerized by such a multitude of sparkling fresh pearls.

What ensued was a split-second moment that seemed taken from *Mad* magazine's Spy vs. Spy. With one of my eyes focused on the pearls and the trio of VIPs, and the other eye on Christine and Marilynne, I could clearly see that Christine and Marilynne weren't looking at the pearls at all. They couldn't have cared less about the pearls. Their eyes were firmly fixed on the VIPs to see *their* reactions. And when Christine's, Marilynne's, and my eyes locked, there was a nanosecond of "gotcha!" I had made the two of them.

Perhaps Christine and Marilynne were gauging their clients' degree of interest before setting a price for these expensive babies. Maybe they were just wondering whether the junketeers had been worth all the feeding and care they'd be given. They surely hoped the pearls world make the VIPs' eyeballs pop.

I came to believe Christine's and Marilynne's couched actions were based on something else, though. Like the sheik who had hoped his collection would slay *his* guest, for anyone who loves pearls as much as Christine and Marilynne surely do, part of the enjoyment is simply seeing the giddy delight other people derive from them.

For a second or two, no one said a word. A recurring thought came to me as we sat momentarily speechless on this sun-drenched afternoon, on this elegant ship bobbing off the coast of northern Australia. In a different location, with a different set of people, we might not be looking at pearls, but a host of other expensive, scarce commodities: diamonds, opals, rubies, emeralds, cocaine, caviar, truffles—pick your *objet de fantaisie*—which, for a host of culturally constructed reasons, people simply adore and will pay just about anything to own.

And then, almost in unison, everyone started babbling.

"I love this one," the Melbourne VIP said, going immediately for the largest teardrop pearl on the table. "Sweetheart, it would look absolutely *gorgeous* on you as a pendant," she said, holding the pearl inches above her daughter's budding breasts.

"Yes, it *is* rathah nihce," said the girl, embarrassed by her mother's boldness.

"Hold it up and let us all see," the VIP instructed her daughter, who replied in an embarrassed way, "Mummy, *please*," but nonetheless did as she was told.

"I fancy this one," the coffee tycoon, said picking out an outrageous 18-millimeter perfectly round pearl.

"I suspect Nick will, too," Marilynne said, a touch disapprovingly. "This is really one of the finest pearls I've seen for a very long time."

"Oh, my," the coffee magnate said, red-faced, handing the pearl over to Marilynne like a girl who'd been caught with a pack of French cigarettes by her teacher.

"I do tend to have expensive taste, don't I?" the coffee baroness said, recovering awkwardly.

Marilynne's proprietary seizing of the coffee baroness's choice may have been a ruse to justify setting a stratospheric price for it; but, as I eyeballed the pearl, it was as perfect as Australian South Seas come, and probably could retail for at least $15,000.

The idea behind the show was that the junketeers could select the pearls they particularly liked and then have them set into a necklace, set of earrings, brooch, or bracelet by Paspaley designers back in Darwin. Marilynne's comment, though, seemed to signal that certain pearls were off limits until analyzed and appraised.

Of course, no one talked price. A bit crude, wouldn't you say? If you had to ask how much, you didn't belong in this tight little circle. The idea was to assist a few privileged souls to find the pearls of their dreams as close to the source as humanly possible (as long as the pearls weren't *too* perfect). How much the pearls might cost ought to be irrelevant, right? In this idyllic setting, to bring up money—indeed, even to *think* about money—how utterly garish! Choose your favorites; Christine would hold them for you, then, back on shore, the two of you could figure out how your choices could be turned into strands, brace-lets, brooches, or necklaces. Money and dreams should never be mixed.

To the casual observer, I suppose, these round little objects rolling around in front of us could have been strangely shaped marbles. If I hadn't spent three years on the pearl trail and, before that, enjoyed a lifetime adoration of them, I might not have understood the show. With the exception of the pearl the cof-fee baroness spotted, few of the five hundred to six hundred pearls on the table were perfectly round. Almost all were semiround and button-shaped, with the rest teardrop or baroque. There were several very large pearls—the larg-est we measured was a humungous 19.6 millimeters—but most were in the 13–15-millimeter range, larger than all but the rarest of Chinese freshwaters. Even to mention Chinese and Australian pearls in the same breath, though, was fundamentally wrong. It'd be like comparing Gallo to Dom Perignon.

All of us we were having marvelous fun. Picking out favorite pearls, holding them to the light, lining up similarly shaped pearls about the same size, color, lustre, radiance, and orient, making imaginary necklaces out of them. That task wasn't easy. When you have an opportunity to study a multitude of pearls, you realize that each is, in fact, unique, with slight variations, which makes perfectly pairing them for earrings challenging, for strands, extraordinarily difficult.

After an hour, each of the VIPs had collected a small assortment of favor-ites. Christine gathered those pearls and put them in silk pouches for safekeep-ing. I was uncertain whether anyone would eventually buy these pearl-filled pouches. In the meantime, they were like party favors from an afternoon tea party.

Yagura glanced over at Marilynne, who looked at Christine, who nodded. "We rally must git going," Christine announced. "The Mallard will be waitin'."

Yagura began gathering all the pearls, rolling them back into that big box of his. We headed down two flights to catch our motorboat back to the Mallard. As I had done earlier that morning, we formed a fire line, this time much shorter, handing off supplies to be couriered back to shore. Only this time there was a difference.

Yagura carried four heavy gray plastic boxes. Each was sealed with a black plastic band, threaded and strapped around a heavy metal closure. If someone were to open one of the boxes, the band would have to be broken. From the motorboat to the seaplane, Yagura passed me each of the boxes, which measured no more than nine by fifteen by six inches. The boxes were heavy; each had to weigh forty pounds. I passed them, one by one, to the Paspaley worker next to me, who carefully stored them deep in the airplane's hull.

Among all the chatter, I realized what was inside. The four boxes contained thousands of pearls, the bounty of the harvest. Their content was worth millions of dollars. All the technology, all the expertise of the ops room, Chef Leigh, First Mate Phil, Second Officer Tommy, Skipper Ernie, deckies Bri, Hannah, Benny, Selena, Tommy, the FNG, Nipples, Mon, and Random—all of it was inside these four boxes.

27

The Comer

Paspaley isn't the only name in Australian pearls. There are a dozen smaller farms and operations, and the fastest growing of these Davids to Paspaley's Goliath is a pearling firm called Autore, started by a determined Italian entrepreneur in 1991. To tell Autore's story is to tell the story of a consortium of spirited Australian pearlers bound by a single goal: to break the Paspaley pearl cartel. These smart and persistent pearlers are going after Paspaley and all he represents like a starfish trying to lock onto an oyster and crush it to pieces.

The anti-Paspaley story might very well start with Larry House, a forty-nine-year-old former wild man. When I met House on a muggy, overcast Sunday morning at his home in Broome's Mangrove Bay Apartments, we sat in front of his collection of twelve antique hardhat pearl diver's helmets. House was wearing an unbuttoned safari shirt with a Hard Rock Café singlet underneath. He has blue-gray eyes, a crooked nose that looks to be the result of one or more barroom brawls, and a receding hairline made all the more noticeable by stringy reddish-blond locks he pulled behind his ears. These days, House has a gut on him. He radiates the image of a once-fit tough guy who now doesn't give much of a shit. House looked like a washed-out Robin Williams who'd been on a bender for a couple of years.

Born in the port city of Perth, House was a competitive swimmer who once played on the Junior Australian Water Polo Team. In 1980, he got himself to Broome and started working as a deckhand and diver for PPL, the old Gerdau-controlled company. At the time, many of PPL's divers were huge Thursday Island natives who'd march down to the pearling luggers at Broome harbor, chanting war songs. Broome catered to a rowdy crowd then, but for its entire history, Broome has always been (and still is) a rough-and-tumble, drown-your-sorrows kind of town. On shore leave, divers, prostitutes, and deckhands partied hard at hotel bars such as the Broome Arms, Star, Central, Conti (short for Continental), and Roebuck Bay. Drunken sailors used to swing from bar chandeliers. Cue sticks and beer bottles got broken over patrons' heads; sometimes the heads were what broke.

In 1986, during a break in the bar action, Larry House and a partner wangled a pearling license from the Australian government, one of only twelve licenses at the time, for a relatively small number of oysters—ten thousand. The industry reaction to the upstart intruders—they called their company Clipper Pearls—was swift and direct. "They did everything they could to stop us," House told me over breakfast of bacon and eggs. "They first said there wasn't enough shell to support another license. Then they said we'd deplete the stock. Then they said we'd open the floodgates, that more and more would want to get into the industry and we'd be the cause of the Australian pearl industry's ruination. The short of it all was they were scared. They had had the pearling industry all to themselves, and then suddenly we were on board. They did not take kindly to us." House teamed up with Kim Male, who at the time had a partial interest in Kuri Bay (the majority interest was still owned by the Gerdau Co.). The deal between Male and Clipper Pearls was that Male would give House the use of his lugger to dive for oysters, which would be taken to Kuri Bay, where technicians would seed them. In return, Kim Male and Clipper would split the pearl crop fifty-fifty. All that changed when Paspaley bought out PPL and, several years later, bought out Male's portion of PPL, thereby wholly owning PPL and Kuri Bay.[1]

At which point House was pretty much screwed. Paspaley had begun to spread his tentacles, making life for House and other independent pearl farmers difficult. A cyclone in 1990 had destroyed much of House's crop; the only silver lining was that House had been able to salvage some beautiful pearls from the previous year's harvest. That's when a local pearler by the name of

Bruce Farley introduced House to Andy Müller. Müller liked the promise of House's crop of pearls (and didn't mind getting free of the Paspaley stranglehold), and over a cup of tea and a handshake at the Conti Hotel, gave House and his partner three million dollars to purchase their entire next year's harvest. Such auctions are common among pearlers and are known by the Japanese word *hama-age*.

"Dat first crop was nine 'undred pearls; dey were large and da quality was very good. When we made dat deal, we were over da moon. And, as we went along, the pearls got bigger and better, with all of 'em goin' ta Andy. We nevah woulda survived without 'is initial investment," House recalled.

With cash in his pocket, House bought an old shrimper, the *Trident Aurora*, and converted it into a pearling vessel and cranked up his business. At about this time, House met American Alex Ogg, a chef who'd been trained at the Culinary Institute of America and moved to Sydney to work at a restaurant a stone's throw from the Opera House on Sydney Harbor. Alex joined Clipper (by then, House had bought out his partner), where today he still works as manager, with a small percentage of ownership. Clipper continued farming pearls, selling his small quality crop to Müller. At this point, House was so small a player, if he was a mosquito buzzing around Paspaley's ear, Paspaley probably wouldn't even have heard him.

The story to break the Paspaley juggernaut shifts at this point. This is where Rosario Autore entered the Australian pearling industry and, within ten years, turned it upside down. Autore, in his mid-forties, is a fast-talking, gap-toothed salesman who could convince the Hasidim to invest in pigs. By his own admission, he can't sit still.

Autore's father was a jack-of-all-trades who imported coal from the U.K. and then sold it in Italy. The family moved to Australia when Autore was a toddler, staying for three years, then returned to Italy, where Autore lived till he was fourteen. In 1967, the family moved back to Australia, to Melbourne, this time for good. "I didn't speak a word of English," Autore told me in his downtown Sydney office across from the Queen Victoria Building on George Street, still speaking with a trace of an Italian accent. In Melbourne, his mother worked at a knitting factory, then as a seamstress, while his father got a job at the Australian department store Waltons and moonlighted cleaning pubs.

"Kids called me a wog," a derogatory term for a foreigner, Autore said still smarting at the word. A small child, Autore used to get picked on, and his worried parents transferred him to a series of schools. As much to get away from bullies as to make money, Autore worked with his father at nights mopping up pubs. In the mornings, he had a paper route, delivering the *Southern Cross* newspaper in Melbourne.[2]

Relying on connections back home in Naples, Autore's father began importing leather goods from Italy, and the Autore house doubled as a warehouse. Autore dropped out of high school, driving from town to town, selling Italian shoes and scarves out of the back of his car. When that failed, he worked as a concrete layer, then as a janitor. The family didn't quite know what to make of hyperkinetic Rosario, who couldn't stay interested in anything long enough to keep a job.

At nineteen, Autore's oldest brother talked Autore into joining him in the diamond trade, and Autore began selling Monnickendam diamonds in Australia. After a year, Autore and his middle brother got back into the import/export business; his family also started a sixty-seat Italian restaurant called Tiberio in Middle Brighton, a Melbourne neighborhood, where Autore served as chef. "I found out dhat I loved ta cook," Autore said. "We were usin' da best ingredients, and we were servin' dinners to a full house ever' night, but we weren't chargin' enough. By the end of da day, we weren't making any money." It was last in another in a series of disappointments, with a saving grace: Autore learned to make pasta and a variety of sauces from scratch, a skill that would serve him well.

At about this time, Autore got into the pearl business. Pearls hadn't meant anything to him, but one of his brothers had met English expat David Norman, whose father had been a major London pearl dealer, buying from among others, Allan Gerdau. Pearls seemed like an adventure. Norman convinced Autore to go to Japan with him to study pearls under the tutelage of John M. Jerwood, a mercurial, seminal British character who had no children and used to take in young men who'd apprentice under him through his Japanese firm, Cultured Pearl Export Co. Years earlier, Jerwood had met his future wife, who was Japanese, at a party at the Japanese Embassy in London just prior to World War II. After marrying, the two moved to Tokyo and lived in a house next to the Okura Hotel. Jerwood became one of handful of the first Westerners to export Japanese pearls.

For Autore, life in Japan was a little bit of déjà vu. He was once again in a foreign country and didn't know a word of the language. In the day, he worked for Jerwood sorting and stringing pearls. Jerwood had set up his apprentices in a Tokyo apartment in the Aoyama neighborhood. "We worked in the office during the day, but every night, we partied hard," David Norman told me over sushi at a restaurant perched atop the cliffs of Sydney's Bondi Beach. "We never missed a night." There was occasional intrigue along the way for the young men. On Norman's twenty-first birthday, Jerwood sent him to Bombay on a secret mission to spirit a cache of natural pearls back to Tokyo.

The cadre of young men Jerwood picked—Rosario Autore, David Norman, Robert Fawsett, Fran Mastoloni, Tony David, Paul Braunstein, Ariel Russo— would become among the world's the next generation of major pearl dealers. Jerwood paid for their airfare to and from Tokyo, lodging in an apartment, and he gave them living expenses.

After two years, David Norman came back to Australia to work with Braunstein for Jerwood's Australian operations, leaving in 1986 to work in Perth for Australia's other Greek pearling family besides Paspaley—Kailis; American Fran Mastoloni returned to New York to work with his family's pearl business; when Norman left to work for Kailis, American Paul Braunstein took over the Jerwood office. Braunstein eventually returned to the States to set up his own pearl dealership near San Francisco, ultimately becoming the largest U.S. importer of South Sea pearls behind Salvador Assael. Autore took over Queensland, Western Australia, and New Zealand as Jerwood's representative back home.

Like Allan Gerdau, John Jerwood was an eccentric, erudite global businessman who could talk endlessly about anything and at the same time nothing. In his letters, Jerwood took to quoting passages from *Macbeth* and *Othello*. He shared many of Gerdau's reservations about government, and wrote long missives about the erosion of individual freedoms, as well as the world's great religions. In a 1986 letter to David Norman, Jerwood wrote:

"Take comfort that with all the frightening changes we face, yet release comes in the end to some a shade earlier. Meantime there's much of worth in the daily round which I have enjoyed for 68 years now and for which I am, to humanity, most profoundly grateful."[3]

Jerwood prided himself on being an intellectual, whereas almost everyone else in the pearl-trading business was what he might term an instinctual trader. Jerwood used to tell salty jokes, and he loved to drink $150 bottles of wine and bet heavily on the horses. He was a bon vivant. "He once told me that if your wife ever catches you in bed with another woman, deny it until she thinks she's hallucinating," David Norman recalled. Jerwood amassed a huge Japanese tax bill, and left Japan in the dark of night, moving to Geneva, Switzerland, where he continued to run his company, which he called Devino.

Meanwhile back in Australia, Autore was selling up a storm for Jerwood.

Jerwood had advised Autore to develop a direct connection with pearling sources, and, outside of Paspaley's stranglehold in Darwin, just about all the pearling action in Australia took place in Broome, or the waters around Broome. If Autore was ever going to make his mark on the Australian pearling world, he'd have to leave the populated southeast of the country and wade his way into the production end of the business 2,500 miles to the northwest. That's what Autore did.

One day, Autore picked up the phone and called the dean of Broome pearl retailers, Bill Reed, who was a partner in the Broome jewelry store Linneys. Reed, a character who looks and talks as though he sprang to life from a Graham Greene novel, is punctilious and precise, it seems, in everything he does—from his jaunty gait to how he dresses, eats, and drinks. Trained as a biologist, he sold his French Polynesia pearling atoll Mangareva in 1974 to Robert Wan, who went on to make it world famous, and in the process make Wan a millionaire many times over. But Reed holds no grudges. His store, Linneys, probably sells a greater volume of pearls than any other independent jewelry store in Australia, maybe even in the world.

"'My name is Rosario Autore and I want to come up to Broome to talk to you 'bout pearls,'" Reed told me, recalling his first conversation with Autore more than a decade ago, while we were eating dinner at a Thai restaurant one sultry evening in Broome.

"I'm not interested," Reed replied tartly.

Then Reed asked, "How old are you, anyway?"

"Twenty-four," came the reply.

"Sorry, but if you are still in the business in ten years' time, call me again."

Autore persisted, calling Reed every few days, saying he was planning a trip to Broome and wouldn't Reed just sit down with him for a cup of coffee?

"Ten minutes, that's all I ask. I promise I won't bring up da subject of pearls."

As much to get rid of young Autore, Reed agreed. The two had coffee and did not discuss pearls. Every six months for the next several years, whenever Autore traveled from Melbourne to Broome, Reed and Autore would meet for coffee or lunch. Autore always picked up the check.

Autore persisted, pestering Reed until finally Reed caved in. Well, sort of. It happened one weekend Reed had planned a dinner party for some local pearlers. "I suppose if you're this insistent, you can come up and I'll introduce you. But don't think anyone's going to give you the time of the day."

Autore's ears perked up. "What are ya cookin'?" he asked.

"That was a rude question," Reed recalled telling Autore. "I cook reasonably well and you will eat what I cook."

"I'll cook for you," Autore said.

"You'll do *what?*"

"It would give me great pleasure to cook," Autore replied, in his sometimes fractured English. "I'll take care of everythin'. I'll even bring the food. What kind of wine da ya prefer? Tell me where ya live, and I'll let meself in. Dinner'll be waitin' for you and yer guests."

What the bloody hell? Reed figured. I'll give the Neapolitan upstart a test. Meanwhile, Reed made reservations at a local restaurant just in case.

Autore packed his bags with pasta, tomatoes, spices, olive oil, and after the eight-hour milk-run flight from Sydney-Perth-Geraldton-Karratha-Broome, Autore arrived at 3:00 a.m., slept for the rest of the morning, and by mid-afternoon, had found Reed's house and starting cooking.[4]

Reed said that when he and his guests arrived that night, the dining room table was set with flowers and serviettes in the colors of the Italian flag. Autore had antipasto, three homemade pasta dishes, and a whole roasted fish. It was one of the most memorable dinners Reed and his guests had ever eaten. One of the guests was Bruce Brown, a second-generation pearler who operates a family farm, Cygnet Bay Pearls, just north of Broome. Brown's brother Lyndon was one of the first Australian pearl farmers who had competed against the Japanese at Kuri Bay in the early 1960s.

"I liked Rosario," Brown told me when I interviewed him at his farm. "Immediately, ya got da impression that he was honest. He asked us what we weren't gettin' and how he could help us. We weren't used to dhat. We'd harvest large beautiful pearls and up till then, we'd have dealers who came in and told us what dhey'd pay us. It was a case of 'take it or leave it.' Autore asked what he could do to 'elp us sell our pearls at a betta price." What Autore did, was eventually offer Broome pearlers a system where every farmer would get a percentage of their pearls' selling price.

Autore flew back to Melbourne, thinking maybe he'd broken through. "I knew I had to get to da source, and 'ere were farmers with pearl licenses and they hadn't been treated right. Dhe farmers had no bargainin' power."

Autore's approach was different from Paspaley's, and not just in the size and scope of his operations. Paspaley was a producer of pearls at the source. He had a growing fleet of vessels, a wholesale business, and eventually a burgeoning retail operation. Paspaley also had two generations of pearling experience behind him. Paspaley had a name and a legacy from the time his grandfather arrived in Western Australia in 1919 from Kastellorizo, Greece. All Autore had was a small office he was operating for his immediate superior, Rudy Zingg and for this company's owner, Jerwood. That, and no small amount of colossal chutzpah.

Brown decided to give Autore a chance, offering his entire harvest to Autore (another *hama-age* deal). Autore flew to Broome, looked at Brown's pearls, and made an offer of $2.2 million AUD for Cygnet Bay's entire harvest. Autore said Brown wanted $2.5 million AUD, and was firm, so Autore came up with the extra cash, meeting Brown's price. "I was elated," said Autore, who added that he personally borrowed the extra money to make payment to Brown, even though he was wholly representing his employer, Jerwood. Autore had followed Jerwood's advice. Instead of being the second, third, or fourth buyer of pearls, with dealers at each rung jacking up the price, Autore now was the first. He had gotten as close to the source as possible without the cost of going out to sea.

But just before Autore was about to make the pickup, word reached Paspaley that upstart Autore had been making direct offers to farmers for their pearls. Brown told me that Paspaley offered him 10 percent more than any offer Autore put on the table. It was no contest. Brown stiffed Autore and sold his entire crop to Paspaley.

Paspaley had the resources to outbid anyone in a preemptive strike to maintain what amounted to an Australian pearl cartel of one. This upping of the ante signaled good news for the small, independent pearl farmers in and around Broome. Competition meant higher prices for the producers.

Autore got burned in the Brown deal, but kept going back to Broome, six, seven, eight times, still courting Brown and other farmers, including Steve Arrow, a young pearler who owns the eponymous Arrow Pearls Co. one bay over from Brown's farm.

At about this time, on a buying trip to New York, John Jerwood suddenly died. Jerwood's firm was taken over by Rudy Zingg.

The next year, Autore bid $6.8 million for Brown's bumper crop, close to seventeen thousand pearls of all grades. Autore wanted the deal to stay quiet, no use alerting and antagonizing Paspaley to the transaction, so he didn't fly into Broome, but instead flew to nearby Derby. Autore said before buying the crop he had already presold all of it to an assortment of Japanese dealers, but when he told his new boss, Zingg, Zingg hit the roof.

Autore promptly quit and started his own firm in Sydney, setting up a factory in a warehouse in Sydney's Surry Hills. By 2000, Autore says he was selling ninety million dollars' worth of pearls a year. Starting in 1995, he began holding auctions in Sydney, but stopped in 2003. Like the other pearl giants, Autore today sells directly to large retailers, such as Neiman Marcus, Fortunoff, and Mozafarian, as well as to dealers like Vock and Müller, who, in turn, sell to other dealers, wholesalers, and retailers around the world.

About his relationship with Paspaley, Autore said, "At first, he didn't say much, and then he started getting edgy. We'd run into each other and be civil with each other, but you could tell there was a lot of tension between us. There still is."

And how.

In the coming years, Autore would enter into a joint venture with an Indonesian pearl farm, and he now owns five farms in Indonesia. In 2006, Autore bought out Larry House's assets of Clipper Pearls, but then sold back 25 percent to House and 25 percent to Bruce Brown, with the American Alex Ogg owning a small portion.

Today, Autore says he's cornered 20 percent of the South Sea pearl market, or about six hundred thousand loose pearls a year, of which about a third go into strands. With Clipper, Autore joined in marketing and distributing pearls from Brown's Cygnet Bay, along with Arrow Pearls, Blue Seas Pearling, Coral Sea Mari-Culture, Toomebridge Pearls, and Arafura Pearls, as well as Atlas Pacific and PT Autore Pearl Culture in Indonesia. Today, Autore employs some four hundred workers worldwide.

When I visited Autore's headquarters, he was eager to show me blueprints for the firm's first retail store, scheduled to open in the heart of Sydney, less than ten blocks from Paspaley's showcase store.

Autore also took me on a tour of his processing plant. Indeed, it was different from any anything I'd seen. Autore's operations were more international, less formal than any pearling firm I'd visited. At 5:30 every evening, Autore often joins employees for a yoga class on the rooftop. Many employees aren't Australians, but from Switzerland, France, and Italy. "Rosario runs the company like a big Italian family. We're all very loud and very passionate about, it seems, everything," said Alessio Boschi, Autore's chief jewelry designer.

Like any astronomically priced good, whether it's a Ferrari, Rolex, or Learjet, the idea behind Autore's (and Paspaley's, Branellec's, and Wan's) large pearls is to create an aura of sublime elegance. Autore and Paspaley both publish sophisticated, high-end magazines similar in editorial content, but also in design and even the soft, thick quality of the paper. "Ever'thing we do has to have a strong and noticeable tactile impact—just like pearls," said marketing manager Sarah Young. This is true—from the smooth, fine-grain wooden boxes in which

Autore's pearls are packaged to the thick, embossed bags in which they go home with the client.

"It's all 'bout selling a dream, and in doing so, creating a demand for dhat dream," Young said, echoing Jacques Branellec's mantra. The marketer's goal is to transform what is merely a commercial product into a cultural and aesthetic icon. Autore and the other pearl lords I met spend millions of dollars on product placement. "You have to pay for what is essentially real estate on stars' wrists, necks, ears," Young told me. "Essentially, what we are doin' is rentin' a piece of dheir body fer several hours." It can be worth it. One well-timed photo at the Academy Awards, along with the name of the brand, can be worth an entire year's harvest.

Meanwhile, back at Autore headquarters, even though it was nine on a Wednesday evening, the place was in a frenzy. Clear plastic bags full of pearls had been laid out on tables, ready to be shipped the next day to Japan, the United States, France, and Switzerland. Autore told me he's an insomniac. It's a rare day when he is not up and dressed by 5:00 a.m. "Many of my employees consider me a lit'le crazy," he confessed. "I have a lot of energy."

As we talked, I noticed something unusual about Autore: he wasn't wearing any jewelry—not a watch, not a wedding band, even though he's been married since 1994. Strange, I thought, for a man whose business is jewelry. "I can't wear it. I'm too fidgety," Autore told me. "I'd take it off, play with it, break it, or lose it."

28

The Payoff

Women buy, wear, or collect pearls for all kinds of reasons. For most, it's because they believe pearls radiate a multitude of messages, and the wearer can choose which specific image or images she seeks to transmit. One of the triumphs of pearls is that they reflect an array of conflicting, culturally mediated meanings: success, respectability, wealth, and power. But paradoxically, pearls can also signal sexuality (as well as chastity), artiness (irregularly sized baroques do this), simplicity, and spirituality. For some, pearls are a politically correct adornment. There's no equivalent in the pearl world to "blood diamonds" or "conflict diamonds." There are no dark, calamitous, unsafe mine shafts when it comes to extracting pearls, as there are with gold, diamonds, and other ores and minerals. Today, the conditions under which pearl workers around the globe labor are reasonably good. Because of underwater breathing apparatus, marine protocol, and medical advances, the bends are largely a condition of the past for divers, and rare bites from marine creatures are treatable. Certainly, some pearl workers are poorly paid (in China and Indonesia, and to a lesser degree in the Philippines), but wages in most pearling venues are relatively high when compared to wages of other first-rung extractive workers.

Wherever pearls come from, the environmental conditions necessary to grow them must be pristine (again, with the exception of China); indeed, in order for seawater oysters to grow pearls, the water and air quality must be exceptionally clean. When compared to other forms of industries, pearl farms treat the environment reasonably well.

Of course, the reason most women wear pearls, though, has nothing to do with environmental or labor politics. It's because pearls simply make the wearer feel good.

When I started my journey, I set out to track a single pearl—from the moment a diver scoops an oyster off the ocean floor to the instant a woman fastens a strand with that oyster's pearl in it—and all the steps in between. Over the course of three hectic, globetrotting years, I found divers, deckhands, farmers, biologists, technicians, scrubbers, sorters, graders, polishers, drillers, stringers, designers, auctioneers, brokers, traders, dealers, wholesalers, and retailers (not to mention all the support personnel: skippers, captains, pilots, drivers, maids, managers, cooks, as well as the pearl lords overseeing the operations) who handled a multitude of pearls that followed the same trail. Now it was time to find the woman, the end user who makes the long, multi-continent journey that starts at a diver's hand economically worthwhile.

During one of my sojourns home, one November afternoon, I spoke before a quaint organization known as the Pearl Society of America, in the Chicago suburb of Evanston. A hundred or so women (and a handful of men) had given up an unseasonably warm Sunday afternoon to talk endlessly about their favorite gem. After my talk, I found myself face to face with Ricki Angelus, a lively, curly-haired woman in her mid-sixties who was wearing one of the most elaborate pearl necklaces I'd ever seen. It wasn't a simple strand, but a complicated combination of twists and turns, with pearls I immediately recognized as French Polynesian, Chinese, and one large centerpiece that looked Australian. Adorned with such an intricate necklace, Ricki was dressed casually, in a T-shirt, black stretch pants, running shoes.

"You *get* pearls," she said excitedly to me, beaming like I was George Clooney. "You're one of the few men who *gets* pearls." At that moment, Ricki's eyes glowed like two pearls plucked from a *Pinctada maxima* oyster.

Men—*if* they're attracted to gems at all, Ricki said rather dismissively—usually go for diamonds or gold. Diamonds are quantifiable in carats (one carat is the equivalent of 200 milligrams) and by the age-old three other Cs (clarity, cut, and color). Gold is measured by its purity, usually from 14 to 24 karats, but its aesthetic value rests squarely on how a designer crafts the precious metal while molten. But classifying pearls is totally intuitive. There is no universal classification system.[1] The standard variables for a pearl—size, shape, lustre, orient, surface quality—certainly have something to do with setting price, but a gorgeous pearl that makes one person's heart flutter might put another to sleep. For some reason, perhaps cultural, maybe inbred and genetic, most men seem to want *and need* a tried-and-true system that quantifiably rates luxury items. Maybe this is a way of justifying spending so much. Years of aging, horsepower, and gigabytes are allied quantifiers that men seem to latch onto for booze, cars, and computers. Ricki was absolutely enthralled that she'd discovered a man in love with pearls as much as she was, someone who could trust his own instincts instead of relying on some silly numeric grid. Ricki volunteered that she has dozens of pearl necklaces, rings, pendants, and drops, and when she started reeling off their names—*Mermaid's Tale, Homage to Matisse, Valley of the Lost Youth, Apple That I Ate in Solitude*, among others—I knew I had found my pearl woman.

The middle child of Hungarian-born Jews, Ricki's father owned a kosher poultry market in northwest Chicago. As a little girl, Ricki prayed with her family at the Humboldt Park synagogue across the street from her father's market, and she remembers seeing lots of pearls among the worshipers—multiple strands wrapped around, as Ricki recalls, the gizzardy necks of old women with double chins. "I had a love-hate relationship with pearls then. I connected pearls with controlling married women," she told me, the two of us squeezed into the backroom of the jewelry store where I'd given my talk. "I loved the beauty of pearls, but for the women wearing them, pearls were nothing more than status symbols. These women wore pearls for what the pearls meant to others, not to themselves." To these women, Ricki thought pearls signified one thing: wealth. Pearls' innate, luminescent beauty never entered into the wearer's mind. Or so Ricki thought.

Ricki led a pretty conventional life without pearls. She met her husband, Paul Angelus, at Chicago's Roosevelt High, and after graduating she became a stenographer. The couple had three children. Ricki's first pearls showed up in the early 1970s, when she went to Shelle Jewelers in Glencoe, to make sure the diamond in her engagement ring was securely set. While waiting for the ring to be repaired, Ricki glanced over to a display case, where she saw a 16-inch strand of 6-millimeter pearls. That's when she had an attack of sorts.

"This sounds rather strange now, but I remember the sensation as if it happened yesterday: I couldn't breathe. Literally. I started gasping for air. I realized I'd never seen anything so beautiful in my life," Ricki told me, still sounding as mesmerized by the strand today as she was thirty-five years ago. "But I was frightened to try the pearls on. They were something forbidden. I was afraid I'd covet them. I didn't want to be obsessed with something I couldn't afford."

Ricki distinctly recalls an out-of-body encounter of sorts she had that day in the jewelry store. She heard herself tell the clerk that she loved the pearl strand, but that what she really wanted was a longer necklace. She asked the clerk whether the strand in the display case could be lengthened. The price for such a strand would be two thousand dollars, he told her.

With three children and a blue-collar husband, that sum might very well have been twenty thousand dollars. Buying the strand was completely out of the question. But against her own judgment, she figured, "It won't cost anything to *try* the strand, so why not?" She did, and from that moment, she was a goner.

Ricki found herself perspiring and hyperventilating. Never before had she felt so viscerally and spiritually connected to anything. She couldn't get the pearls out of her mind. Once the pearls had touched her skin, she never wanted them to leave. She absolutely had to have them.

It was a complete turnaround. "For my whole life, I'd had such negative feelings about pearls. They represented prosperity. They represented acquisition. There was one reason women wore pearls, and that was to show off, usually their husbands' wealth. I wanted to run away from all that." But at the same time, her brain kept telling her, "If you can find a way to buy these pearls, you *must* have them."

Ricki responded by running out of the store.

After a sleepless night, she returned the next day and summoned the courage to ask the clerk if she could just hold the strand. She wasn't even going to try the pearls on.

Holding the strand, she remembers her whole being transformed. "I got this unmistakable sensuous feeling. The strand felt like it wanted to leap out of my hand and dance." She was fearful of the sensation, and it made her uneasy. But Ricki left the store that day determined that she'd save enough to buy the strand. As she walked through the door to the street, she had her second out-of-body experience in two days: The pearls were beckoning her to return. "Come back," the strand called to her.

In the early years of her marriage, Ricki kept a stash of savings—maybe she had $1,600 in it, certainly no more than $2,000. But she kept on adding to it, and in two months, she returned and purchased the strand, which the jeweler had lengthened to 33 inches. "I felt like I had just purchased a handful of magic stardust," Ricki remembers, smiling in a dreamy kind of way.

"I didn't tell my husband anything," she said, lowering her voice, talking as though she'd been carrying on an affair and in a fit of bravado had brought her lover home. Ricki was terrified to wear her purchase. She kept the strand hidden behind a stack of towels in the bathroom linen closet, and only when Paul and her children were gone would she put them on. Wearing the strand alone at home became a daily ritual. She'd vacuum, wash dishes, fix dinner wearing the pearls. But a half hour before her husband or children were to return home, she'd make sure she removed the strand, safely returning it to the back of the linen closet. On weekends, Ricki would lock the bathroom door and spend hours modeling the pearls for herself.

One evening, Ricki finally summoned the courage to wear the strand at dinner. And her husband didn't even notice! "I think he must have assumed they were fake," Ricki said, "just some costume jewelry I had." But Paul's reaction emboldened Ricki. If he hadn't noticed the pearls, maybe no one else would. So she started wearing the strand more and more, and again, no one seemed to notice. No one had made her or what was nestling atop her cleavage. "If someone asked, I'd tell them the pearls were fakes, beads. It was as though the strand and I were sharing a secret." That further empowered Ricki. "I had an incredible opportunity to surround myself with beauty every day, so I said, 'Why not?'" Soon, she began wearing the pearls as often as possible.

That was Strand One.

Strand Two came into Ricki's life when Eve Alfillé, the owner of an Evanston jewelry store, asked Ricki whether she'd consider looking at another pearl strand: a necklace of Chinese freshwater rounds. When Eve lifted the lid to the box containing the strand, Ricki says the experience was a "silent explosion." Again she couldn't breathe. "I'd never seen anything so beautiful. My heart started pounding. It was as if this strand was speaking to me." When Ricki tentatively held the pearls, her hand started trembling. She recalls an unmistakable powerful vibration that the pearls were sending her. "I don't care what anyone says. There was an energy that came out of those pearls that almost knocked me backwards. Each pearl was saying, 'Look at me! Look at me!' It was an emotional experience. The pearls evoked in me a sense that was deep and primal. I couldn't understand it at the time. I've come to believe that it had to do with realizing that such amazing beauty exists in the world, and that I was chosen to have the privilege of seeing that beauty, and eventually, that I'd have the opportunity to be a part of that beauty. It was difficult not to cry."

I need to interject something here for the skeptical reader. Ricki Angelus is not a woman who believes in multi-hue chakras, deep colonic irrigations, or Reichian orgone boxes. She looks conservative. She is a grandmother of three, and by all accounts, responsible, sensible, and mature. She carries with her a healthy skepticism. Looking at her, you wouldn't think there's a single New Age corpuscle in her body.

Now, back to her story.

It was at about this time that Ricki began thinking of pearls as signposts that will outlast our own mortality. She began to believe one doesn't *own* pearls but is a temporary steward of them and of their well-being. Jewelers, thus, wouldn't "sell" Ricki pearls; instead they'd "release" them to her when both she and her jeweler felt the time was right. Of course, Ricki would have to pay for her pearls, and Strand Three's price tag was $22,000. But there would be a time for everything, and that time hadn't quite arrived yet.

Ricki's husband, who now owns a business installing and repairing appliances, and who resembles a disheveled Jack Nicholson, went along with his wife's primal urges, saying, "I love everything about you, and everything you wear. Please, though, don't tell me how much any of these things cost."

Which was fine by Ricki, since she had already forged a relationship with each strand of pearls she fancied, and the last thing she needed was a jealous suitor trying to get between her and her pearls.

The time eventually became right, and Ricky bought Strand Three, which led her to another awakening. She became more spiritual, moving closer and closer to religion. She'd be at the movies, wearing her pearls, when up on the screen there'd be a scene with, say, a faucet in the background. Out from the faucet, instead of water, Ricki would see a stream of Hebrew letters pouring fourth. The pearls and combination of the celluloid hallucination were messages. In 1995, Ricki celebrated her bat mitzvah, a rite of passage reserved for thirteen-year-old Jewish girls, but one that hadn't been afforded her. During the ceremony, Ricki wore Strand One, the opera-length pearls, twisted and doubled over; during her *parsha* reading of the Torah, she gently touched the strand girding her neck, which relaxed her, bringing her a redolent sense of peace, serenity, and purpose.

There were more strands, and soon Ricki branched out into pearl pendants, drops, bracelets, and rings. Anything pearl she adored. A collection of five gold and black Tahitian pearls and a diamond pavé star cost $6,300. A pendant of thirteen diamonds and an assortment of small natural Mississippi River pearls cost $16,000. With each piece, Ricki had to feel just right. Timing was important, and only when Ricki felt a convergence of spirituality and beauty would she ask the jeweler to "release" the pearls to her. "At first, I'd be so taken aback, I felt my body couldn't withstand the spiritual vibrations." Sometimes it would take months, other times years. Ricki would take to visiting the jewelry store to check in on the pearls she fancied, and whenever she'd see them, she'd break out in tears.

Ricki maintains that she never shops for pearls, but that pearls magically appear—in a store window, display cases, at estate sales, when she's rushing to pick up her grandchildren. And always, the pearls stop her in her tracks. Each piece, she says, is sacred and somehow finds her. "Coincidence is God's way of remaining anonymous," she says.

Pearls, Ricki says, have helped steer her to a gentler, more spiritual side of her life. She started working in a hospice, and eventually developed a sense that she could heal people, whether in her presence or thousands of miles away. She performed a long-distance healing for a girl in Jerusalem who had a grave pulmonary disease. All the while, of course, Ricki wore her pearls, which she said helped focus her healing. Pearls, she says, are amulets from the Almighty, not unlike rosary beads. "God, I'm willing to do Your work, but I need to feel Your presence. Pearls help me in knowing You."

One of the best things about Ricki's collection is that no one (except her jeweler and me) probably knows that real pearls are hanging from Ricki's neck, encircling her fingers, dangling from her ears, or pinned to her blouse. "That's the way I like it. It's the total opposite of how I was introduced to pearls as a little girl, where the point was to shout, 'Look at me.' Now, I'm the only one who knows their value."

For a moment during our interview, Ricki allowed that perhaps those controlling, pearl-wearing women at her synagogue when she was a little girl weren't just showing off their husbands' prosperity. "Maybe they felt that by wearing pearls they were expressing their own spirituality," she mused. Perhaps, Ricki said, they were connecting in a similar way to the generations of Jewish women who light Shabbat candles every Friday night—women Ricki understands in her heart.

Today, pearls continue to find Ricky, including a ring made of breathtaking abalone. Another ring consists of two 13-millimeter pearls, one mauve, the other gold. All told, Ricki has forty-three pearl pieces and estimates their total value at over $100,000—certainly nothing compared to the Baroda Pearls or single strand that either Christine Bracher or Marilynne Paspaley would wear. Her collection comes from Burma, China, Tahiti, the Cook Islands, and Japan, and she has several single pearls from Australia. But provenance doesn't mean a thing to Ricki. "It's the beauty of the piece, that's the thing. Whenever I put pearls on, I'm overwhelmed with a sense of joy. When my body wants pearls, I'm drawn to wear them. I don't have to look at myself in the mirror. I just feel them," she said smiling beatifically.

The way Ricki was describing pearls wasn't any different from how New World Indians more than five hundred years ago would have described them—as a source of light, strength, energy, and power. Or how early Christians viewed pearls—as conduits to God's voice. Or how I felt as I first held those South Sea pearls at the Tucson jewelry show when I started my pearl trek. I, too, had been certain they were pulsating in my palm.

29

Where It All Began

I wanted the last stop on my pearl odyssey to be the first place where pearls had been found in the New World: an empty, pancake-flat island eleven miles north of the coast of Venezuela. The barren, sandy island, Cubagua, is where Nueva Cádiz, the first Spanish settlement in South America, was founded in 1509, only to be plundered, destroyed, and eventually abandoned. At its peak, 1,500 brave souls lived in Nueva Cádiz, and for a hectic nonstop twenty-seven years, the city served as the sole New World processing center for hundreds of thousands of exceptional pearls, spirited back to the Spanish crown and then to the rest of pearl-hungry Europe. In its heyday, Nueva Cádiz was a conglomeration of today's pearl powerhouses—Kobe, Hong Kong, Xuwen, Palawan, the islands of French Polynesia, and Broome. Pearls exceeded by ten times the value of all other goods combined that the Spanish brought back from the New World. For a short quarter of a century, the greatest number of pearls the world had ever known passed through this now forgotten island.

By 1543, not much was left in either Nueva Cádiz or on Cubagua, and pretty much that's the way it's stayed for the last 466 years. Today's population on this dot within the Leeward Islands chain, part of the Lesser Antilles, might total thirty fisherman and their families, but almost all live on the desert isle only part of the year in temporary shelters. Nueva Cádiz is a classic boomtown gone bust.

Cubagua is sandwiched between the Venezuelan tourist destination of Margarita Island, five miles to the north, and the Peninsula of Araya, on the Venezuelan mainland, twelve miles to the south. It lies not far from such popular Caribbean resorts as Grenada, Curaçao, and Aruba. Within Venezuela, more than a dozen commercial jets fly the forty-minute route from Caracas to Margarita's capital, Porlamar, every day, often packed with tourists looking for a close-by getaway.

But Cubagua is a wholly different world. To get there from Porlamar, you have to travel through a narrow isthmus to Punta de Piedras, a sleepy port town on the southwest side of Margarita. Then you need to find a fisherman and convince him it'll be worth his while to motor to Cubagua. Depending on the weather, how choppy the water is, when the boat captain wants to leave, and whether he's sober, getting to Cubagua can take as little as fifteen minutes or as long as two hours.

I had read that on Cubagua today, there were still traces of the original Nueva Cádiz, tangible proof of the once-flourishing pearl trade that so long ago defined the city. The half-millennium-old ruins certainly aren't of the magnitude of those at Machu Picchu or Tikal, but, unmistakably, remnants of the original pearl colony on Cubagua remain.

By the time Columbus left Spain on his third voyage to the New World, the once charismatic, irrepressible explorer had largely fallen out of favor with his benefactors, Ferdinand and Isabella. The settlement he'd established five years earlier on Hispaniola was overrun by bloody insurrections. News of the brutal treatment of the indigenous population, which Columbus had overseen, had reached the Spanish sovereigns. The king and queen, by all accounts, were appalled. Factions of Columbus's subordinates were grumbling about the wages the admiral had promised but never paid. The ship's crew was at each other's throats. Mutiny was no longer discussed in whispers.

Pressure was mounting for the explorer to come up with tangible commercial goods that would justify the extraordinary expenses his voyages had racked up for the Spanish crown and his commercial benefactors. Midway on his voyage, at the Canary Islands, Columbus split up his fleet of six ships, sending three to Hispaniola and three on an unscheduled exploratory voyage, which he was to lead. Columbus's flotilla sailed past the Portuguese Cape Verde Islands, then Trinidad, and finally to the Venezuelan coast. On August 8, 1498, while tracking the coastline, near the port of Cumaná, where the Orinoco River empties into the Caribbean, Columbus became the first European to find himself within miles of what was the world's largest virgin reserve of pearls.[1]

Or so the story goes.

The saga of Columbus's discovery of pearls, triggering a global Pearl Rush that has never really stopped, is filled with international intrigue, almost-certain deception, and profuse guile. There is compelling evidence that Columbus may have tricked Ferdinand and Isabella by not revealing the extent of the extraordinarily rich pearl beds in the area, as well as by delaying and obscuring news of their discovery. This blockbuster of a revelation became more than just speculation when an obscure diary found its way to the Library of Congress some seventy years ago. The manuscript, ostensibly written by a sailor under Columbus's charge, unequivocally states that the Genoese explorer was not the first European explorer to discover the vast numbers of pearls in the region. Known as the Trevisan Diary, after Angelo Trevisan, who sent it to Venice in 1502, the manuscript contends that Columbus nine years earlier had sent five caravels on a secret expedition from Hispaniola to survey the warm-water seas just north of the South American coast. The revelation of such a secret reconnaissance mission is significant because it places in context why Columbus may have understated the prodigious oyster beds and the bountiful pearls they produced when he wrote his own diaries. In part, it was to swindle Ferdinand and Isabella, as well as to delay announcing to the world the exact location of such a plentiful supply of priceless pearls. Why share the riches?

The diary, first written in Spanish and later translated into Italian, stokes one of the world's greatest unsolved mysteries. The manuscript reveals that Columbus's quintet of ships left Hispaniola in late September of 1493, traveling through the Windward Passage, skirting the coast of Cuba, and setting sail southeast. Accompanying the crew were native Indians seized from Hispaniola to serve as guides and interpreters. Almost immediately, there was a period of "intense and awful heat" with torrential rain, the Trevisan account reads, so the ships veered further south, where the weather moderated. As the caravels reached the high, steep banks of the Venezuelan coast near Cumaná, the Indians directed the crew to sail leeward, where soon the ships entered a tranquil harbor. Under a subheading in the Trevisan manuscript entitled "The Harbor of Pearls," the diary states that Columbus's crew was greeted by two dugout canoes filled with six men in each vessel, who welcomed the sailors with gifts of fresh fish. The sailors noticed legions of natives on shore waving for the mariners to join them. The men promptly lowered dinghies, and as they reached the sandy shore, groups of Indians waded and swam out to the ships to greet the foreigners, including "one young man with a string of pearls on his neck and arms," reads the account. Other Indians wore large clusters of pearls on their wrists, arms, and ankles, according to the diary.

One can only imagine the reaction the mariners had upon seeing so many pearls. Pearls such as these casually worn by Indians could fetch unbelievable sums in Europe. At the time, there was a surfeit of buyers for pearls, and European dealers could command unheard-of prices. The sailors traded little bells, pieces of mirror and earthenware, bits of copper, and assorted trinkets for as many pearls as the Indians could be convinced to part with.

The narrative details how several of the sailors followed the Indians ashore. The native man wearing the pearl strand around his neck led the mariners to his father, presumably a tribal chief, who lived in a home made of timbers, palms, and other broad leaves. There the sailors were offered a sumptuous banquet, along with wine made not from grapes but from sweet fruits the Europeans had never tasted before. The diary indicates that everyone conversed in an animated fashion, both groups seemingly realizing that a remarkable and apparently felicitous historical event was taking place in their midst and that they were its leading players, even though neither the Spanish nor the Indians understood a word of what the other said. Either the interpreters from Hispaniola were not invited to this monumental exchange of cultures or they were unable to understand the language the indigenous tribes spoke. When the feast was over, the sailors were led into a room where barely clothed women welcomed them with the tumult of ceremonial dances, incomprehensible singing, and thunderous clapping and shouting. Trevisan describes the women as bedecked with pearls on their ears, arms, wrists, and necks. More trading presumably took place, with the diary describing the jewels as resembling "very beautiful 'oriental pearls.'"

The five caravels eventually left the shore, returning to Hispaniola, where Columbus remained, "satisfied with what they had found, especially with the pearls," writes Trevisan. All told, the secret sortie lasted forty-five days.

Hardly anything else is known of this early journey or even whether the expedition ever happened.[2]

It wasn't until the summer of 1498 that Columbus contended in his own diaries that he made his first voyage to the same island. Perhaps Columbus had made earlier voyages to the pearl-rich area around Cubagua, but none has ever been officially recorded. According to Columbus's official diaries, the small-framed Arawak Indians paddled their canoes to greet the explorer and the other oddly dressed sailors aboard, who surely must have resembled giant men from the other side of the world (which they were). In a dispassionate manner, Columbus allows in the diary that he encountered Indians wearing strands of pearls. "Some women came who wore on their arms strings of small beads and among them pearls or misshapen pearls, very fine."

At this point, the veracity of Columbus's official record begins to crack and erode. The admiral notes in a rather self-serving explanation that he left the area almost immediately. "I would have remained there, but the provisions of corn, and wine, and meats, which I had brought out with so much care for the people whom I had left behind, were nearly wasted, so that all my anxiety was to get them to a place of safety, and not to stop for anything," Columbus writes. "I wished, however, to get some of the pearls that I had seen, and with that view sent boats ashore. And they likewise directed me to the westward and also to the north behind the country they occupied. I did not put this information to the test, on account of the provisions and the weakness of my eyes and because the ship was not calculated for such an undertaking."

Before pulling up anchor, almost as an afterthought, Columbus concedes that he and his men traded bells, beads, and sugar with the Indians for three pounds of pearls. On his way to Hispaniola, Columbus by August 15 sailed within sight of the eastern shores of Cubagua and Margarita, just ten miles from the richest pearl beds in the New World. But he never set foot on either island—at least that's what he wrote in his official diary.

Might Columbus have acquired more pearls than he admitted to procuring, and willfully omitted mentioning the rest?

Columbus most certainly knew that even this limited, declared quantity of pearls would bring a bounty in Europe. At the least he knew he had a taker of pearls when it came to Isabella. Elisabeth Strack writes that the most beautiful of the pearls Columbus acquired in this first exchange were fashioned into a magnificent strand worn by Isabella and became known as the Venezuelan necklace.[3] But, in his official diary, the navigator mentions nothing more about pearls.

With such certain riches before him, why did he leave? Could Columbus have acquired more pearls on this voyage and on earlier journeys for his own personal enrichment without ever declaring them to the crown? Did he, in fact, stop at the pearl havens of Cubagua, Margarita, and Coche and simply not mention it in his official diaries?

Over the years, speculation has grown that Columbus concealed from the crown his acquisition of massive quantities of pearls. However sickly the navigator possibly was at the time, whatever stench the spoiling food created below his flotilla of caravels, how could he turn his back on one of the greatest treasures the world had ever known?

Ultimately there was no way to keep the location and multitude of New World pearls a secret for long. As news of the fecund oyster beds filtered back to Spain, it aroused the same kind of frenzy repeated hundreds of years later in other historic events of discovery—after John Sutter and James W. Marshal spotted gold nuggets on the shores of the American River in Coloma, California, on January 24, 1848; or when oil was first unearthed in the Persian Gulf on October 16, 1931.[4]

Almost instantly, ships plied their way from Palos, Spain, to the New World, returning with massive quantities of white, yellow, pink, and occasionally black pearls to Seville (and later to Lisbon, Venice, Amsterdam and Genova), which became the European hub of international pearl trade. The Spanish crown skimmed off the most extraordinary pearls, leaving the rest for nobility and upper classes. A large percentage was exported, which flooded the capitals of Europe. Most of the New World pearls were fashioned into jewelry, but many found themselves on elegant, embroidered gowns, woven into silk and velvet, and accessorized on hats, cloaks, and gloves. Ten of thousands of pearls became part of elaborate tapestries, and a large number ended up as ornamentation in Europe's grandest cathedrals, particularly those in Seville and Toledo, which have whole walls and altars encrusted with New World pearls. In Seville, hundreds of pearl craftsmen and vendors set up shops close to the cathedral for the burgeoning industry at hand.[5]

The Cubagua pearls symbolically did something else. They carried tangible evidence of a faraway place that, save for a few adventurers, heretofore could only have been imagined. For years, the New World had been a fantastic place of wild tales. Now that place was real. "America's 'limitless' supply of pearls, its exotic geography, flora and fauna, 'bizarre' human inhabitants and the dangers of trans-Atlantic voyages, all enhanced the mythical 'otherness' as well as the commercial valuation of the gems," writes Nicholas J. Saunders.[6] New World pearls helped turn Spain into a global powerhouse. Pearls became a metaphor of imperial possession, these tiny shiny iconic jewels circulating thousands of miles from the exotic world where they had originated. Perhaps the best example of such blatant imperial display of pearls was that of the Spanish crown itself, embedded with a dazzling assortment of the best New World pearls. When worn atop the sovereign's head, it was a beacon of Spain's colonial authority. Outside Spain, pearls carried the same aura. As more and more dazzling pearls made their way into the sanctity of European churches, the more omnipresent Spain's ascendant wealth, glory, prestige, and power became.

As the demand for the world's newest and seemingly never-ending pearl supply mushroomed, the Spanish crown by 1512 set up its processing center on the nine-square-mile island of Cubagua. Once sorted and graded, the pearls would then be shipped to Havana, San Juan, or Santo Domingo for passage to Spain. The region formed by Cubagua, Margarita (the name is the Greek-Latin derivative of *pearl*), Coche, and the Araya Peninsula on the mainland of South America became known as the Costa de las Perlas, with Cubagua as its collection hub. From Cubagua, workers in canoes fanned throughout the pearl-saturated Venezuelan coast and were forced to dive by Spanish pearling masters. So voracious was the demand that soon the Spanish pushed their explorations west, and discovered pearl beds off Costa Rica (named the Rich Coast because of its pearls), along the Pacific coast of Panama, and farther west in the Gulf of California.[7] The economic incentives to find new pearl sources was so great that Spanish explorers traveled north to what was to become known as the United States, but found nothing worthy of commercial exploitation.[8]

In 1528, the crown recognized Nueva Cádiz as an incorporated city and an official administrative unit of the monarchy. It was the unchallenged axis of all pearl trade in the New World. The crown declared a monopoly on all pearls, and quickly instituted control over every aspect of their exploitation. The Royal Treasury kept 20 percent of all pearls, the so-called *quinta*. Because the plethora of pearls yielded such massive revenues (and because the New World was at such a distance from Spain), the crown required that elaborate and meticulous records be kept; oversight and tax officers were dispatched to Cubagua to safeguard the nation's profitable resources.[9]

Nueva Cádiz turned into a teeming center for slave trading, as well as a strategic outpost for the ensuing Spanish conquest of the South American mainland. For all its value, Nueva Cádiz was an expensive city for the Spanish crown to maintain. All drinking water had to be imported, as did almost all food (the exceptions were oysters, turtles, fish and birds) and construction material. Nueva Cádiz soon became a bustling frontier town. Pearlers on the island imported from home such delicacies as figs, wine, olive oil, almonds, and raisins. Venetian glassware, enameled and gilded façades, majolica earthenware, and fine furniture also came in the steerage holds of ships to Cubagua from Spain.

Nueva Cádiz soon was plagued by the same social conditions that beset almost every outpost whose existence is defined by a recent discovery of a scarce, sought-after commodity. Great sums of money were made by a very few people, which prompted greater numbers to flock to the settlement, with newcomers realizing little, if any, of the bounty. The rapid influx of profit-seekers, in turn, begat disease, filth, corruption, drinking, gambling, debauchery, rape, and murder. As journalist Peter Muilenburg, who explored Nueva Cádiz in 1991, wrote, "Cubagua was booming with anarchy, greed, and wealth."[10]

Nueva Cádiz's resident population swelled to 1,500, with Spanish sailors, clergy, Indians, slaves, traders, merchants, smugglers, and government assayers all taking up residence. The city had a plated central grid, with masonry buildings lining a main thoroughfare and a tentacle of side streets. The most elaborate of all buildings on the island was a Franciscan monastery, set off with elaborate carved gargoyles, as well as two churches, an expansive commercial plaza, and a City Hall.[11]

There were great sums of money to be made by few on the island. Aldermaro Romero, a biologist from Arkansas State University, using extant tax records, conservatively estimates the official record of oysters harvested at Cubagua to be *at least* 113 million, yielding more than 12 tons of pearls.[12] During the time the region's pearl beds were most abundant, Indians were forced to dive dawn to dusk, and in a year's time, each diver on average would harvest more than 33,000 oysters, according to Romero's estimates. In 1529, in just one month, more than 12,000 ounces of pearls were harvested from the beds near Cubagua, writes archeologist Raymond Willis.[13] Since Romero and Willis's figures are based on official records, the estimate of real pearl extraction is thought to be much greater. To reach such staggering levels, Romero computed that divers were forced to make on average nine dives per hour per day, at depths ranging from fifteen to a hundred feet. The divers dove nude without goggles, even though the salt water burned their eyes and constant exposure to it caused body sores.

In 1508, Lucayan Indians from the Bahamas were brought to Cubagua, based on their reputation for deep diving. The men were weighted down with ballast stones so they could descend quickly and stay submerged as long as possible. All the while, they held their nostrils and mouths shut, crunching their faces, blowing their cheeks into grotesque shapes, in an attempt to equalize the crushing pressure from the descent. They stayed submerged for anywhere from two to three minutes, gathering as many oysters as they could, placing them in net bags around their neck, before being pulled up by ropes operated by a men in vessels on the water's surface.[14] Like all pearl diving around the world, the work was deadly. Many divers died of what would three hundred years later become known as caisson disease, or the bends. Some divers spewed blood out of their ears and mouths from the rapid descent, which attracted sharks in the warm waters; others, after hyperventilating prior to diving, blacked out on the seafloor and drowned. By royal order, the monarchy eventually banned all Indian divers because of allegations of abuse, and African slaves took their place. The crown seemed not in the least concerned about the Africans' safety.

With such intense, nonstop harvesting, shallower oyster beds were soon depleted, forcing divers to go deeper and deeper, exacerbating divers' health hazards. To accelerate the harvesting of pearls, and thus to bring in more money to Spanish coffers, in 1528 the crown began authorizing dredging the *Pinctada imbricata* oyster beds surrounding Cubagua, Margarita, and Coche, reversing the age-old—and less efficient—practice of diving for pearls. The fragile oyster beds could not withstand the wholesale assault; two years after such practices were begun, fearing that dredging would completely deplete the supply of oysters, the crown reversed itself, and began instituting a series of reforms, but few were enforced. Fewer and fewer oysters were recovered from the waters surrounding Cubagua, and in 1536 the crown resorted to imposing a January-to-September moratorium on pearl fishing in hopes that the beds might replenish themselves.

But the damage had already been done. The plundering of the greatest source of virgin pearl oysters the world had ever known was inexorable and irreversible.

As word spread of pearls still stashed on the island, pirates made frequent raids on Cubagua, looting everything they could get their hands on. Violence escalated between the Indians and the Spanish, and to quell unrest, the crown sent a series of enforcers to the island. Scholar Enrique Otte describes a horrific event when a police agent of the Spanish crown arrested two Indian chiefs, hanging one in the plaza of Nueva Cádiz, and strapping the other to the muzzle of a cannon, blowing his head off and feeding his body to dogs. In retaliation, natives killed a notorious slave master and set Spaniards' homes ablaze; the settlers retaliated again with a massacre of hundreds, piling bodies on the beach, impaling heads on stakes.

Within twenty-five years of Nueva Cádiz's founding, the pearl beds had been so heavily fished that they virtually disappeared. With less and less to show for its investment, the Spanish crown became disenchanted with the cost of maintaining the outpost. Soon large deposits of gold were to be discovered in Mexico and Peru, which shifted attention and revenues from Cubagua. The crown, investors, and adventurers were through with Cubagua. By 1539 fewer than fifty hardly souls remained. Nueva Cádiz, once known as the pearl capital of the world, became a ghost town. As a final coda, in 1541 a hurricane leveled much of the island, and two years later, French pirates finished the job. By 1545 Spain's first capital of South America had been abandoned.

Today, Cubagua is nothing more than a curious footnote in history books. But to me, it represented my own voyage come full circle. The promise of setting foot on the island, walking through the ruins of a city's sudden rise and ignominious fall, finding pearl fishermen of today, long-lost descendants of Kino perhaps, buoyed me. My journey had led me all over the world—to imperial Japanese dealers, millionaire-dollar auctions, rural Chinese karaoke bars, cricket matches on remote Australian islands, stern Filipino health officers, pearl playboys who commandeered helicopters, Tahitian millionaires with lovers a third their age, impoverished but nonetheless optimistic pearl farmers, New York pearls dealers on the prowl for Cuban cigars in Hong Kong. In comparison to what I'd learned about Nueva Cádiz and Cubagua, those escapades seemed ordinary and commonplace. I was soon to set foot on the place where New World pearls got their start.

30

The Dogs of Cubagua

I

Traveling to Cubagua represented a coming home of sorts. Whereas my trips to Asia, the South Pacific, and Australia had been novel, I was an old hand when it came to South America. After graduating from college years ago, I bought a one-way place ticket from San Francisco to Lima and for nine months hitchhiked my way to the Strait of Magellan. Much later, I worked in Brazil as a foreign correspondent. I've been to every South American country, with the exception of Ecuador, for some reason. Life in Latin America was something that invigorated me, like a shot of espresso.

To get to Cubagua, I first had to go to Caracas. As my plane took off from Miami, wheels lifting from the tarmac, scores of passengers around me making the sign of the cross, a multitude of fingers touching forehead, mouth, chest, never once getting entangled with each other, I flashed back on living in Rio de Janeiro twenty-five years earlier. Whenever I'd take the bus, whenever we'd pass a church or cemetery, the same thing would happen. On a twenty-minute trip, passengers sitting and standing in packed buses would cross themselves at almost every block, a ballet of hands and arms in a whirl of motion.

Upon my arrival at the Caracas airport, I was met with winding lines of converging passengers. Still smarting from my near-calamitous episode with the Philippines health officer, I tried to blend in with the crowd. I inched forward with everyone else, as customs officers slammed down a mechanical device that stamped each passport. Click. Whomp. Click. Whomp.

Two hours later, when I exited the mess at Maiquetia airport, I noticed huge white banners with red lettering: *Por Ahora*—For Now. The banners lined the highway to Caracas, swaying and shimmying in the warm evening Caribbean breezes that floated up the forested mountainside. *Por Ahora* was a reminder of President Hugo Cháves's prophetic speech in 1992 when he was allowed to address the nation after his arrest for leading an aborted coup to topple the American-backed government of President Carlos Andrés Pérez.[1] "Unfortunately, *for now*, the objectives we had set for ourselves were not achieved," Chávez told millions of Venezuelans glued to their television sets. Seven years later, after Chávez became the nation's elected president, two words from that speech—*por ahora*—had catapulted into the national lexicon, turning into a battle cry all Venezuelans today recognize. *Por ahora* was a pledge of Chávez's social-change agenda, an oft-repeated epigram of hope, patience, equality, and revolution just around the corner.

The revolution aside, as soon as I got to my hotel, I needed to exchange dollars for local currency. I had contacted U.S. newspaper correspondents in Caracas, and they all had advised the same: Bring bucketsful of dollars. With my travel budget almost depleted, any leftover dollars I had barely covered the bottom of a kid's beach pail. Still, my journalist friends told me, the Venezuelan black market to convert dollars to bolívares was soaring, to two-and-one-half times the official exchange rate. A hotel that normally would run eighty dollars would cost thirty dollars.

For a moment, I thought myself a modern-day Columbus, infecting and exploiting the masses not with disease or trinkets but with imperialist greenbacks. As in Columbus's time, the locals enthusiastically embraced what I had brought and desperately wanted to trade for it.

The moment the front-desk clerk at my hotel saw my passport, she lowered her voice and asked, "Would you like to sell dollars, sir?"

Five minutes later, the hotel porter, who quite unnecessarily carried my beat-up suitcase to my room, asked the same question. Once in my room, the front-desk clerk called and again asked if I was interested in selling dollars. Five minutes later, she called again and upped her exchange bid.

I said no to all these offers. All my journalist friends had advised me to contact a local money changer named "Jim" when I got into town.

Like illegal immigration, smuggling, prostitution, and corruption, changing money on the "parallel market" is an activity virtually impossible to eradicate. However poorly they're doing worldwide, greenbacks are still king in all of Latin America, but in no nation more so than Venezuela. Soaring inflation has made Venezuelan currency denominations unmanageable. A ham-and-cheese sandwich and a beer could cost as much as 12,000 bolívares. The numbers were getting so ridiculous that on January 1, 2008, the day after I arrived, the government issued a new currency, the bolívar fuerte, that lopped off three zeros from each bloated bill.

As soon as I got through to Moneychanger Jim, I realized I had reentered the surrealistic world of Latin America money changing. Once, in Brazil, I had exchanged dollars for local currency with a money changer protected by a half-dozen bodyguards armed with pistols. When I left the dealer's office that day, my dollars converted into thousands of different-sized, multicolored bills, the pile of local loot was so tall that the money changer threw in a tote bag to carry it all in.

"You came recommended to me," I started on the phone with Moneychanger Jim.

Pause.

"You do change money, right?"

Pause.

Had I said something wrong?

"When discussing issues such as these, it's best to talk about *cases of beer*," Jim opened rather stiffly. "How many *cases of beer* would you like to buy?"

I needed local currency to pay for food, hotels, a plane ticket to Porlamar, and to hire a boat to Cubagua. "Eight hundred or so?" I replied. "I guess you could say I'm thirsty," a lame attempt at a joke.

"I've had guys much thirstier," Jim came back deadpan. "Let me see what I can do. Gimme ten minutes."

Twenty minutes later, Jim called back, saying he'd been able to find the beer and that we'd be able to meet and transact business at a neighborhood bakery in an hour. Jim's price beat the front-desk clerk and porter's offers by 20 percent.

This black market dollars-as-beer code wasn't too different from start-up negotiations between a prostitute and a john. Both parties, after all, need an out. "You want a blue jacket? It'll cost you fifty dollars. A full coat, now that'll run you a hundred. Which'll it be?"

I had no idea how Moneychanger Jim would recognize me. I thought to say something like I'd be the curly-haired man reading the *El Universal* newspaper, opened to page 20, but that seemed too cloak-and-dagger. Moneychanger Jim didn't describe himself. There was no mention of wearing a white gardenia in his lapel.

I got to the bakery and waited till a ruddy-faced, white-haired guy in his sixties, wearing a white guayabera and jeans, approached me. We shook hands and ordered *cafecitos* as Moneychanger Jim griped about garbage dumping ("It's happening all over the city"), government corruption ("It's much worse under Chávez"), Caracas pollution ("It's so bad, it makes my eyes water"), and El Commandante ("He must have a strong bladder to talk for six straight hours without getting up to pee"). Neither of us dropped a word about beer.

After a half hour, we got into Jim's cherry-red Dodge Ram, drove around the block a couple of times, then parked in a nearby grocery-store parking lot. Jim opened the glove compartment and handed me a bulging envelope stuffed with bills. The wad was four inches thick. It was bound together by an intricate series of connecting rubber bands.

I thumbed the stack, although I refrained from thumbing the roll next to my ear. Everything seemed to be in order, at least to my unpracticed thumb and ears. Moneychanger Jim and I shook hands and bid each other farewell.

Was the greenback transaction really any different from trading for sex, cocaine, or guns or pearls? Greenbacks have ready portability, are easily transferable, and fetch reasonable rates of return anywhere in the world—as do sex, cocaine, guns, and pearls. There's a veritable ticker price for each that fluctuates hourly. All four commodities are easily converted into any nation's currency. At their core, the trading of these services or goods is essentially the same: saleable units that effortlessly transcend their countries of origin, and which carry value anywhere in the world. They are global capitalist widgets.

With a bulging cache of bolívares as my traveling papers, I was ready to get myself to Cubagua, the New World's first capital of pearls.

II

The forty-minute flight to Porlamar was packed with Caraqueños happy to get away from nonstop Caracas. I didn't know where they'd be staying, but the only vacancy I could scrounge up had been a hole that euphemistically called itself Posada Hidalgo. I knew Hidalgo to be the honorific that preceded Don Quixote's name (*The Ingenious Hidalgo Don Quixote of La Mancha*); meant to denote Spanish nobility, Hidalgo derived from *hijo de algo*, literally "son of some" important family. But this particular Hidalgo was a long way from any pedigree. Perhaps after the Venezuelan revolution takes place, the Pousada Hidalgo would rise and turn into a people's stunner. For now, though, outside my room two dusty donkeys were swatting flies with their tails while making eyes at each other. The Posada Hidalgo reminded me of a down-and-out love shack, vying with the dump where I'd stayed in Papeete as the most likely lodging in which to come down with lice. I hoped the Posada Hidalgo wasn't worse than a pension I once stayed in Manaus where the desk clerk suggested I sleep with my shoes on since the local rats were known to have affection for leather, but only if it didn't move.

On the way to the dock early the next morning, I counted five dead dogs on the highway. A man at a bus stop executed the old Latin America standby—the one-handed nose clean, a loogie shooting downward with meteoric speed. Behind him, another guy peed against a truck tire. When I got to the harbor at Punta de Piedras, the skipper said he wanted more money before he'd pull anchor for Cubagua. After dickering for twenty minutes, El Capitán seemed satisfied with a newly negotiated rate, but just as we were about to put out, he said he needed gas, stepped onto a rubber dinghy, and putt-putted to an offshore filling station.

It seemed the harbormaster, a large woman with untamed hair, had to be paid off. That task accomplished, El Capitán turned the key to the boat's twin motors, which started up slowly but soon built to a roar. We finally left the waters of Margarita, traversing choppy currents. The wind was fierce. I imagined caravels in Columbus's time, plying the same waters, canvas masts rippling and billowing in anticipation of landfall at Cubagua.

Twenty minutes into our trip, the island came into distant sight, and as we got closer, I could see the unmistakable outline of ruins.

El Capitán cut the engine fifty yards from the shores of Nueva Cádiz. To my eyes, the remains looked to be eight to ten streets crossing a thoroughfare.

As we drifted closer, I could plainly see brown stone footings of what once had been walls. There appeared to be an intersection of sorts that looked to have once been a plaza. I excitedly kicked off my sneakers, rolled up both legs of my jeans, and began wading onto shore.

The clear, bluish water was surprisingly warm. I was transported a half millennium back, when Spanish navigators had made the same journey ashore. I approached the island cautiously, as I'm certain they had. Would locals beckon me, holding strands of pearls the size of hazelnuts, drawing me closer and closer? After a sumptuous meal, followed by a dance of bewitching sirens, would a tribal guide lead me to magnificent pearl reserves?

As I made my way onto the beach, water dripping from the rolled-up cuffs of my pants, my receiving party wasn't a circle of tribal elders. No half-naked women, either. Instead, six skinny dogs and three cats greeted me.

A quizzical-looking brown dog with white splotches seemed to be the leader. He cocked his head: "Why would anyone come *here*?" he seemed to be asking.

The dog sniffed at me, was not offended, and merrily started me on a tour, expertly pointing out every nook he intimately knew, as the five other dogs and trio of cats (for a while) followed as closely as they dared.

I stopped for several minutes to take in all there was. I took from my backpack a notebook and sketched the outlines of an outpost the size of four football fields laid out side by side. Where once streets were today was filled in with tens of thousands of brittle oyster shells that crunched when I stepped on them. I could only surmise that the shells had been placed by a conservation crew on a visit to the island. I had read enough to know that when Nueva Cádiz was a processing center, there was a constant, never-ending stench of rotting oysters. The multitude of shells crackling under my step gave me an indication of what residents must have breathed day and night.

Four hundred yards away, at a vista point close to the water, there was a modern concrete obelisk about five feet tall. On either side were inlaid metal numbers—1492 and 1992. No doubt a government agency or cultural foundation had erected the monument to commemorate Columbus's voyage. But there was no commemorative plaque, and the obelisk's backside was cracked and in pieces, two rusty bare rebar poles sticking out at acute angles. The monument looked as though someone had taken a pickax to it, the target of vandalism or perhaps a political statement, considering a renewed era of political awareness against Columbus and imperialism under President Chávez.

An adjacent monument, this one older and taller, made from hundreds of carefully mortared rocks, had also been the target of plunder. Souvenir hunters, vandals, or political activists had pried off its plaque, too. It wasn't surprising and seemed fitting. Cubagua had historically been the site of treasure seekers and marauders. As I was to learn, residents and builders from Margarita and the mainland for years had come to Nueva Cádiz to raid the stones that had built the Spanish colony on the island. The harbor I'd left from, Punta de Piedras (Point of Stones), got its name from years and years of geological expropriation.

Not everything in Nueva Cádiz had been ransacked. I could touch the footings of many original buildings, the work of a reconstruction team that had set out to restore the city to some of its onetime splendor. The tallest of the buildings came up to my chest, and I could walk inside the outlines of dozens of what once had been homes, trade offices, and government assay posts. The floors had been reclaimed by sand and scrubby weeds, but the stones of the buildings were still stuck together, some more wobbly than the others, the product of crumbling mortar that no longer held in the baking sun.

With the canine pack still serving as my guides, several hundred yards past the downtown grid of old Nueva Cádiz, I came to a fisherman's lean-to of rusted corrugated metal and a blue tarp strapped into place by fraying twine. A makeshift plywood door banged back and forth, and as I peeked inside, I saw torn, weather-beaten cushions on metal benches, probably scavenged from a wrecked motorboat. I walked inside, the dogs busily sniffing. Straight ahead in a place of honor I saw a ceramic shrine I knew to be La Virgen del Valle, the Virgin of the Valley, the patron saint of pearls.[2] Draped from the virgin's head was a robe, lined with a border of plastic pearls.

Nueva Cádiz seemed to be empty of people. I wanted to go farther, but as I pushed my boundaries, the dogs seemed to have reached their limit. They stood at the outskirts of Nueva Cádiz, a whooshing concert of wagging tails, uncertain why I had to leave.

31

El Señor Sixto of Cubagua

I said good-bye to the dogs and walked toward an abandoned, sunbleached lighthouse on the northernmost point of the island. As I got close, I saw a teenage boy off in the distance on a ridge. Up till now, it had just been the dogs, cats, and me. I felt a little like Robinson Crusoe upon finding Friday's footprint. My heart skipped a beat.

As I approached, I shouted hello. I asked the young man if he lived on Cubagua, to which he diffidently shook his head. *"Vivo en Margarita,"* he said. *"Estoy aquí hoy con mi familia."* (I live in Margarita. I'm here today with my family.)

"Do you know any fishermen who live on the island?" I asked a little breathlessly.

"Mi tio es pescador" (My uncle's a fisherman), the boy volunteered, pointing east to what looked like a covey of corrugated metal shelters on the far side of a sandy ridge.

"¿Pesca por perlas?" (Does he fish for pearls?)

"Pienso que sí. Pero no sé por certeza." (I think so. But I don't know for sure.)

I thanked the boy and hurried toward the hut, perhaps six hundred yards away, on my way passing a small dog skeleton. The dog likely had died of starvation, and birds had picked it clean. No wonder my canine buddies had been so eager to make friends.

As I turned the corner to the fisherman's shelter, I saw a stationary red baseball cap bobbing atop a sagging hammock. The hammock scene reminded me of the two guys at the seawater pearl farm in southern China, almost a year earlier. These men of the same profession, separated by thousands of miles, were members of the same global assembly line, and each had been taking a nap in a hammock when I approached.

"Excuse me, sir," I started tentatively, unsure of the protocol of waking a sleeping fisherman.

The red cap stopped bobbing. Then the hammock rustled and swayed. A slight, skinny guy with a leathery chest and blue-jean shorts presently looked out from under the brim of the cap. He rubbed his eyes, startled by my presence. Maybe he thought he was still dreaming. "Come forward . . . please," he said tentatively.

I introduced myself, as did the fisherman, and we shook hands. The man was Señor Hernandez Sixto, but, he quickly added, everyone just called him Sixto, which means the sixth. He was from a long line of Hernandezes, he said. Sixto removed his cap and held it in both hands as we talked.

Like the guys in China, Sixto seemed delighted to welcome a stranger who'd come so far to ask questions about pearls, even though he, like Xie Hong Wu and Xie Hong Chong, had no idea why I'd made such a journey. In Sixto's case, I was hoping he'd turn out to be the incarnation of the men centuries ago who dove, under penalty of death, for pearls that would be shipped to Seville, Paris, or Rome, to sit atop a queen's bosom, be encrusted in a king's crown, perhaps worn by the pope himself.

Swinging his feet to the sand below, Sixto said he fishes for oysters, but not for pearls. The only commercial use of oysters today, he said, is oyster meat. And to get at those oysters, Sixto said, he doesn't dive, but uses a dredge (*rastra* was the word he used) that attaches to the back of his boat. On good days, he picks up as much as eighty pounds of oysters. "Come," Sixto said, motioning me with his right hand, fingers flapping in toward his palm. "I have the dredge in the back. I'll show it to you."

I followed Sixto outside the hut. Leaning against the ribbed metal wall was a beat-up rusty dredge, the rope net a tangle of knots and dried seaweed. The contraption looked antique, and I imagined not all that different from what the Spanish had used to decimate the once-abundant pearl beds surrounding

Cubagua. In part, it was this kind of device that had killed the *Pinctata imbricata* oysters and all their glistening pearls. When I asked Sixto about diving for oysters, he pointed to a pair of fins and a mask hanging from single a nail, and then laughed. "Those I use for fun, when I play in the water with my children. But for business, it's the dredge." This way, he said, he stays in his boat and doesn't even get wet, at least not too wet.

"Diving is what they *used* to do. Today, no one dives. Why would anyone dive?" Sixto asked, shrugging his shoulders, turning his callused hands palms up.

Diving, Sixto said, brings dangers, particularly from sharks and stingrays. "You don't want to play with those guys," he said, looking at me straight on this time, then shuddering and pointing to a jagged scar on his leg. What caused the scar I wasn't sure. I sensed Sixto didn't want to relive that marine encounter. Diving was a dangerous occupation. Why *would* anyone trade collecting oysters from the safety of a boat for the possible dangers lurking beneath the water's surface? And how could any diver compete with the efficiency of scraping oysters from the seafloor with a dredge?

Sixto said the market for oyster meat these days is strong, in part because of oysters' reputation as aphrodisiacs. Much of the meat ultimately is dried, pulverized, and sold locally as brand-name concoctions such as "Broken Mattress," "Gimme More," or "Seven Times a Night." Sixto laughed heartily.

"Do you ever find pearls, though, while going after the oyster meat?" I asked.

"In a large haul, we might get ten or so pearls, but they're very small, almost specks."

"Do you have any here?"

"Not a one," Sixto said, shaking his head a little wistfully. "They're too tiny to have any value. If we do find something big, usually the fishermen keep 'em. No else wants 'em. Once in a great while, if we find a large pearl, we'll trade it for chocolate."

Not much had changed from the days of the uneven exchange of Columbus's era.

"What's the largest pearl you've found?"

"Oh, maybe three or four millimeters," Sixto said, "like this," putting his thumb and forefinger together, the flesh from each digit almost touching.

That was the biggest? It was miniscale, compared to what I had seen in my travels. I asked Sixto to draw the size in my notebook, and he took my pen and outlined a tiny circle, the size of a large kernel of rice.

I was determined to discover whether there were *any* pearls left from what once were the world's richest pearl beds. My determination wasn't because I wanted to buy such a pearl. That wasn't why I'd embarked on my pearl odyssey. My budget, even with the lopsided exchange rate Moneychanger Jim had given me, was now nearly tapped out. I had bought in China, Tahiti, and Australia all the pearls Iris could ever possibly want or wear. What propelled me was to get at their stories and, if I was lucky, to hold the pearls in my hand, to marvel at what they represent. It was just as Daphne Lingon at Christie's in New York had suggested as I was starting. "Come on, touch them," I remembered her taunting. "You gotta hold them, feel them."

But fishermen must find *some* pearls of size in the waters surrounding Cubagua every once in a while. "Aren't there *any* fishermen who keep pearls they find?" I asked Sixto, pushing.

Sixto thought for a while, then nodded. He fingered the brim of his baseball cap. "You need to find a guy who goes by the name Señor Johnny back on Margarita, near the port. He's got a ton of pearls from around here."

Sixto said Sr. Johnny lives in Nueva Punta de Piedras, adjacent to the old city on Margarita, near where El Capitán had moored his boat. "Ask around for him. People know him. Señor Johnny's the only one I know. He has a collection of natural pearls. Tell him I sent you."

I said good-bye to Sixto, who doffed his cap and bowed elegantly as we shook hands.

As I walked back to Nueva Cádiz, my canine guides greeted me once again. They sniffed my ankles, in unison backed up a couple of paces, and then yapped approvingly, as though stamping a visa and waving me through. I pulled off a half of the peanut-butter-and-jelly sandwich I'd brought with me and bent down to feed these customs officers, who gobbled up my bribe.

I walked some more and found one of perhaps thirty original stone structures in the abandoned city. I crawled inside a particularly pleasing one, with a view of the blue sea. I sat there, my back against a stone wall corner. It was quiet by midafternoon, the wind had died down, just breezes curling around the main street, gently lifting a flock of seagulls circling above. The brown and white dog joined me, curling up at my side, whimpering for more food. I still had a ribbon of crust from the sandwich, stuffed in my pocket. I wanted to keep the offering as a going-away present.

During an excavation of Cubagua undertaken in 1954–55, archaeologists found a number of artifacts within yards of where I sat. One was an olive jar half full of pearls that archaeologist Jose M. Cruxent had found inside the doorway of a residence. Overjoyed, Cruxent took the jar of pearls to Caracas to hand-deliver it to the president. The pearls, of course, had deteriorated and held no commercial value, but the political exercise proved to be priceless. News of the find spread throughout the nation, and the Venezuelan government increased Cruxent's funding for six more years of excavations. By 1966, all artifacts in Nueva Cádiz had ostensibly been recovered (many of them today are on permanent exhibition not in Venezuela, but at the University of Florida), and the team had stabilized the site. Cruxent's dig had been the last large-scale, comprehensive assay of Nueva Cádiz.

In their findings, Cruxent and colleague Irving Rouse reported that they had found remnants of oyster shells, housing structures, and evidence of burials. They found walls made from uncut stone, chinked with clay and plastered with lime made by grinding up coral. Among the glassware uncovered were green, clear, and crystal glass; brick-red glass; and lavender and dark blue glass, as well as goblets, perfume bottles, and medicine vials. They found portions of barrels thought to have been used to store fresh water. Perhaps most telling, though, was this: The archaeologists found a plethora of glass beads the Spanish had brought with them. The beads uncovered were clear, blue, yellow, white, and emerald-green—all presumed to have served as cheap barter for pearls.[1]

A remarkable architectural scale model of Nueva Cádiz has been created by Graciano Gasparini, and I'd seen it on Margarita at the Marine Museum. The city once had a bustling commercial district, along with warehouses with long rooms to accommodate ship masts. The church and monastery had a tall belfry. City Hall was split into two sections—a meeting room and an exchange room, where pearl auctions took place. A customhouse had also been built. The Gasparini model showed separate quarters for Indians and for black slaves who dove for pearls.[2]

I sat on the sandy floor of what once had been a house or office and peered through a doorway to the sea. El Capitán wasn't due back for another hour, and I welcomed the solitude. As I stared at the expanse of the sea, I imagined what the early inhabitants of this five-hundred-year-old city must have thought—those who had the fortune, or more likely the misfortune, to live here. What misery, greed, and sorrow this very building must once have housed. For the Spanish invaders, the vista toward the blue emptiness must have carried a terrible longing. I envisioned a lone Spaniard scanning the horizon from the exact same place where I sat. Perhaps he, too, had a wife and child far away. Besides the temptation of treasure, what had prompted him to travel such unfathomable distances to leave all that was safe and comfortable behind? While the invading Moors had been triumphantly turned back, Spain was about to descend into an inferno of religious persecution, with the beginnings of the atrocities of the Inquisition. Was this imaginary adventurer fleeing his nation? Was he an adventurer seeking fortunes that few of his fellow countryman could conceive? Perhaps he was a criminal, a family pariah, sent far away? Lighting out for the territories was what was to become a cornerstone of the American experience. To explore a new world was a temptation few could deny.

Day after day, week after week, month after month of waiting, and finally, in the distance, perhaps this man seated in the exact spot where I sat on this hot January day five centuries later spotted a flotilla of caravels cutting through the lilting Caribbean waves, bringing news, supplies, perhaps a family member, from across the Great Abyss. Imagine his glee upon seeing such a wondrous sight appearing on the horizon. Particularly after 1535, when Nueva Cádiz's star began plummeting, to be platooned on the island must have been hardship service of the worst order.

For the Indians or African slaves, likely chained in a dank and crowded thatched hut, the prospect must have been one of absolute despair, the total and complete absence of hope. I was hardly the first to speculate on such horrors, but it was impossible not to imagine vacant faces of utter desolation and never-ending exhaustion. Spurred by wanton expansionism, religious fervor, and a global spike in the demand for pearls, the Indians' and Africans' whole existence, the core of their being, had been debased and infected with disease, greed, cruelty, and death, all within a matter of two decades. And Nueva Cadíz had been the epicenter of such wretched despair.

While they provided no consolation, the soft rocking tides of the blue waters seemed to be the only constant for these vanquished souls. The view for the Indians and Africans, as it was for the Spanish, must have been one of terrible longing, a tragedy of epic proportions that few could then—or now—truly comprehend.

32

Nicholas El Gato's Legacy

I

El Capitán surprised me by showing up when he promised he'd arrive, flying across the water as though he was piloting a plane instead of a boat. He was traveling so fast that from a distance his boat seemed to be airborne, skimming the tips of the Caribbean sea caps. His arrival made such a ruckus that the dogs ran up and down the beach, barking in a most disagreeable manner. As I bid the pack adiós, I pulled from my pocket the crumbly sandwich crust, and gave it to my guide as a final offering.

We made the passage back to Margarita in record time. As we approached the dock, the tangled-haired harbormaster greeted us, probably with another attempt at extortion in mind. With El Capitán paid for his services, I tethered the boat's line to the dock, jumped onto the pier, nodded to both the harbormaster and El Capitán, and made my way to find Sr. Johnny and his amazing collection of pearls.

Sixto hadn't given me much to go on. I got myself to Nueva Punta de Piedras, adjacent to the port, and walked down the main residential street, which shot off diagonally from the plaza. The first people I spotted were a middle-aged woman and a girl I took to be her granddaughter.

"Excuse me, ma'am," I started. "Would you happen to know a Señor Johnny?"

The woman shook her head, almost defiantly. She said she had lived her entire life in Nueva Punta de Piedras and never once had she heard of anyone with the name Sr. Johnny. "I know every single person in town, and I will tell you there's no Señor Johnny here," she said with certainty.

I had to admit the name did sound pretty preposterous, as was my mission to find him. I was searching an entire Venezuelan city for a guy whose address I didn't know and who went by the moniker Mr. Johnny. This according to a guy named Sixto.

The woman scurried past me, pulling the girl by the hand, several times looking back at me over her shoulder.

I walked farther down the block, where I found four men. Actually, it was the grease-streaked, sweaty, bare backs of four men that I encountered. The men were peering under a hood at what looked to be the eviscerated engine of an old Ford. They were about to pull the transmission or weld something inside. One guy swiveled his head my way, and when I asked about Señor Johnny, he, too, came up blank. "But waita minute," he said, tapping the guy next to him, whose head was deepest in the engine.

That guy came up for air, positioned a set of goggles from his forehead to cover his eyes, and ignited a welding torch. The first man asked him, "Ja-eva cheer of sinnor Jon-nee?" or so it sounded in slurred, rapid-fire Spanish.

The blowtorch dude nodded. Dialing down the flame, then pushing the goggles back up on his grim-streaked forehead, he instructed me to go to the end of the block, past a baseball diamond. There, to my right, I'd see a dock. Go to the ninth or tenth boat. There'll be guys working there, shucking oysters. "Ask for Ishmael. He'll know where to find Señor Johnny."

The guy's cadence had been so fast and so full of slang, not to mention the hiss from the blow torch and its menacing blue flame shooting a couple of feet from my face, I wasn't sure I got everything.

I was sure about Ishmael, though. Could there be any more appropriate a name for a guy who knows pearls?

As I walked down the street, I found a plaza, where a pickup game of baseball was in progress, and just as the blow torch guy had advised, the dock was behind the baseball diamond. I counted nine boats. At the tenth, under a blue tarp, were three men opening oysters nonstop with short, stubby knives. As I got closer, a gut-retching stench hit me.

"Ishmael?" I asked. "Anyone know Ishmael?

All three men looked up. "Ishmael's gone," one of the men volunteered. "Who wants him?"

I recapped—about Señor Sixto on Cubagua, the trip to Nueva Cádiz, the mechanic down the block, my quest to find Señor Johnny.

To which one of the three men announced: *"Yo soy Señor Johnny."*

For a moment, I was speechless.

Alas, my eureka moment was short-lived. It turned out Señor Johnny no longer collected pearls. "I used to have some, but I gave 'em all to an old man," Señor Johnny told me, simultaneously splitting open oysters at an amazingly rapid pace, as many as twenty to twenty-five a minute, throwing the gooey meat into a large plastic bag and tossing the shells off to the side.

"You need to find Nicholas El Gato," Señor Johnny advised me. "That's the guy who has pearls. He's the only one left with any pearls."

"Where does he live?" I asked.

"Go to El Barrio Negro and ask someone there for directions," Señor Johnny advised, pointing back downtown, past the baseball diamond, past the blowtorch mechanic, past the lady who swore she knew everyone in town, past the harbor.

To recap: An unnamed teenager on a nearly deserted island had sent me to Sixto, who in turn had sent me to Señor Johnny on another island, whom I was to locate via Ishmael, who now was sending me to a guy named Nicholas the Cat.

I made my way back past the port, where by now the virago harbormaster and El Capitán had undoubtedly divvied up the exorbitant charter fee I'd paid. Five blocks further west, I found a bustling supermarket, with shoppers entering and exiting, hurrying to get home. In front of the market, I spotted a teenage girl, chatting with friends.

"Would you know a man by the name of Nicholas El Gato?"

Without a moment's hesitation, she said, "He lives on the same block as I do. He's an old man. I'll take you to his house, if you like."

The girl got on her bike and rode slowly so I could keep up as I followed her. Nicholas El Gato lived across the street from the girl, and, yes, he had worked as a pearl fisherman his entire life, she said.

As the day turned into dusk, I followed the girl down a maze of streets lined with one-story cement houses. "There," the girl said, pointing. "Nicholas El Gato lives there."

I knocked on the door, and within seconds, a large, red-faced woman in her midthirties appeared. She cranked her head back, squinted, and took a second look.

As soon as I said Nicholas El Gato, the woman nodded. "Nicholas El Gato is my uncle. He's here, in the back. Please, by all means, come in."

I followed the woman through three barely lit rooms, all painted various shades of pink, past two large framed portraits of Jesus, to an enclosed dirt patio. And there's where Nicholas El Gato sat.

II

Like Sixto, Nicholas El Gato was bare-chested, wearing blue-jean cutoffs and a baseball cap. He looked to be about seventy-five and weighed no more than 120 pounds. Folds of loose tanned skin gathered at his chest when he got up to shake my hand. I could see the outline to his shoulder bones almost protruding through his skin.

Since Nicholas El Gato was six, he told me, his singular passion in the world had been pearls. He'd been a diver, a crew member on hundreds of pearling vessels, and, later, when he could afford them, a collector of pearls. He was too old to work any longer, but in his youth, occasionally, he'd find pearls while opening oysters when he was in the employ of a pearl master. Whenever a crew member found a pearl, it was to be dropped in the hole atop a wooden lockbox, to be opened only by the pearl master.

That's what was supposed to happen. But when Nicholas El Gato was certain no one was looking, he'd slip a pearl into the lining of his shorts. Sometimes he'd feign a cough and place the pearl under his tongue. But stealing pearls was a perilous activity. Not only could Nicholas El Gato get fired, he could be arrested and thrown in jail.

"The owner of the boat always took the pearls," Nicholas El Gato told me. "The arrangement the owners made with the crew was that any pearls found would go to the boat owner, who'd sell them to a dealer in town, and then the crew members would get a percentage of the profits from the pearls. Or so it was supposed to go.

"But that seldom happened. The owner would come back to the crew and say he wasn't able to sell the pearls, or that they'd been stolen, or that the market was down and when it bounced back up, there'd be plenty of profits to be shared." Nicholas El Gato shook his head and allowed a smile, shrugging his narrow shoulders. "Sometimes an owner would hand out extra money after a particularly good haul, and if we found pearls, we'd get a little more. But we all knew the owners never gave us what they should have. It wasn't right, but what could we do?"

Nicholas El Gato's story reminded me of what Daniel Tavere and Jean Tapu had told me that afternoon a year earlier in Apataki, in French Polynesia.

I asked Nicholas El Gato why for more than a half a century it had to be that way. Hadn't there ever been an opportunity for the fishermen to share the fruits of their labor? It seemed only natural for several fishermen to have joined together to buy a boat and form a cooperative or partnership.

Nicholas El Gato laughed gently. "It wasn't possible," he said, shaking his head. "It was hard enough just to find a job as a crew member. Once you had a job, you worked hard. You felt lucky. You didn't dare ask for anything, or do anything, that would jeopardize that job. We lived in fear that if we didn't do what we were told, we'd lose the jobs we had."

For a moment, there was silence between us. I was reminded of an old Luchino Visconti film, *La Terra Trema*, about a fishing village in Sicily. A young fisherman has the audacity to challenge the town's greedy wholesalers, and as a result a tragedy strikes the fisherman and his family. "Everything falls on the backs of the poor," a line from the film goes. "You learn to live with injustice."

Nicholas El Gato's story was an updated version—minus the slavery, torture, and squalor—of what had happened to the Indians and Africans on Cubagua more than five hundred years ago.

By now, Nicholas El Gato's niece, a woman as large as Nicholas El Gato was slight, had joined us. She was making *arepas*, fried corn fritters, pounding them by hand, under a bare lightbulb hanging from a bamboo pole.

"Señor Johnny suggested you might show me some of your favorite pearls," I said, adding, "I don't want to buy any. I just want to see what natural pearls from Cubagua look like."

Nicholas El Gato nodded his head.

But then there came over his face a look of remorse.

"They don't exist any longer," he said, as though explaining the death of a child.

"I'm the only one around here who ever kept them, and I haven't seen a pearl for thirty or forty years. There aren't any left. They've all disappeared. I haven't a single pearl left."

I felt as though I ought to recite words from the Mourner's Kaddish.

Nicholas El Gato was the final link to the brilliant pearls of Cubagua, and they were no more. The lure that had brought Columbus to the New World, which prompted hundreds of flotillas to secure for kings, queens, popes, noblemen, and noblewomen these glorious tears of mermaids—today such pearls no longer exist. At least according to Nicholas El Gato.

"You don't have a one?" I pressed. "What about the pearls Señor Johnny sold you? You must still have some of them, don't you?"

Nicholas El Gato shook his head. "All gone," he said, almost in a whisper.

"But where?"

"There never were many to begin with, and the few I've had over the years, I sold to jewelers in Porlamar. You'd never get very much for them."

There was a moment of silence between us. Then, almost as an afterthought, Nicholas El Gato said, "I do have pearls that never separated from their shells, not many, but some. Would you like to see those?" He asked, I sensed, hoping I'd say yes.

Nicholas El Gato's niece dropped the *arepa* she'd been pounding and went into the house to retrieve the pearl shells.

She came back with a stack, placing them on my lap. These were the beginnings of what the Japanese call mabe pearls—pearl blisters that are tiny protrusions from the inside lining of oyster shells. The shells were native *Pinctada imbricata*, tiny compared to what I had seen in Australia, the Philippines, and French Polynesia. At their widest diameter, perhaps these shells were three or four inches. The pearl blisters inside were no more than 2 millimeters, specks really. These tiny blister pearls inside the shells were curios. They reminded me that even in Columbus's era, the pearls from the *Pinctada imbricata* had been small when compared to pearls that would years later be cultivated in the South Pacific.

When I gathered up the pile and handed them back to Nicholas El Gato, he protested. "No, they're yours. Please. A present. Keep them."

I couldn't possibly keep the shells, but Nicholas El Gato refused to take them back. When I asked how much I could pay him, he brushed my offer aside. I persisted, but he would not take money. "*Please,*" he said. "My present to you."

I asked him to recall when he'd last seen the kind of pearl that might have propelled Columbus to sail across the Great Abyss. He paused, then nodded, and, after a moment, began.

"Long ago, when I was a young man, I found one pearl like none other," he said in a reverie. "It was black, with a shade of brown that you could see if you held the pearl against the light." He smiled at the memory. "The pearl was round, not near-round or semi-round, but perfectly round. It was the largest pearl I'd ever seen.

"Oh, it wasn't *big.* Maybe five millimeters, but for pearls from here, that was big." Nicholas El Gato curled his forefinger, touching with the tip the fleshy skin in the crook of his thumb, and made a circle. "It was this big," he said, holding up his hand.

"How many years ago was that?"

"Fifty years ago, when I was eighteen."

"What did you do with the pearl?"

"I gave it to a businessman who promised to sell it, and that was the last I ever saw of either the businessman or the pearl. Someone told me that pearl would have sold for a million bolívares."

Nicholas El Gato's story was the same as Daniel Tavere's or Jean Tapu's. I couldn't begin to compute how much a million bolívares was a half century ago, but it surely would have changed Nicholas El Gato's life, perhaps in as positive a way as the great pearl that Kino found changed his in a negative way.

I hardly could imagine a pearl so small, however perfect, fetching close to a million of anything. Perhaps over the half century, Nicholas El Gato had added several zeros to what he said the pearl had been worth.

But I didn't challenge the story or the pearl's value. Nicholas El Gato's story was the saga of the pearl that got away, the same tale every fisherman needs to believe and needs to tell on evenings like this one. Whether it was true hardly mattered.

I took several photographs of Nicholas El Gato, backlit by the bulb hanging from the bamboo pole. Nicholas El Gato's niece put the blister pearl shells in a plastic bag for me. As I got up to leave, Nicholas El Gato and I exchanged an *abrazo,* then shook hands. I needed to get back to the Pousada Hidalgo before heading home early the next morning. My journey was over.

ACKNOWLEDGMENTS

In the United States:

Bo Torrey, the editor and publisher of the industry standard *Pearl World*, who helped set up many of the connections that made this worldwide odyssey possible. Bo, who packed a mighty snore when we split a room in Tucson to attend the Gem & Jewelry Show, earned my lasting admiration by asking women on elevators and in hallways about the provenance of the pearls hanging from their necks. Thanks also to Kumiko, Gigi, Toby and Tyler, Mr. Pickles, and Bella for putting up with so many questions.

Eve and Maurice Alfillé, who operate Eve Alfillé Gallery in Evanston, Illinois. Eve, a jewelry designer and pearl collector, is founder of the Pearl Society of America. Eve and Maurice (and their children and grandchildren) opened their home and hearts to me.

Daphne Lingon, Christie's consummate jewelry buyer (and rabid Wolverines fan), who ignored dozens of pesty e-mails about tracking a natural pearl necklace until I wore her down. Thanks also to Christie's public relations maven, Kate Swan Malin.

Alexandra Rhodes, Europe senior jewelry director; Carol Elkins, senior jewelry vice president; and David Bennett, Europe and Middle East jewelry chairman, all of Sotheby's.

Sonny, Depak, Anil, and Rene Sethi from Tara Pearls for trusting me to tell their story. Were they ever wary (and weary) of me! They probably still are.

Salvador Assael, the Pearl King, for spending time talking to me about his life. His assistants, Jale Turcihin and Albert Friedel, welcomed me with a wealth of introductions to pearl aficionados around the world.

Andres Babio, my first pearl doctor, who has worked for Assael for thirty years and has transformed thousands of ugly ducklings into swans. The pleasure he gets from pearls is reflected in his own shiny eyes.

Pearl veteran Henri Masliah, who immediately understood why I sought him out in his New York showroom, and shared with me his philosophy not only of pearls but of life.

Deborah Blum, Dale Maharidge, and Sam Freedman, first-class authors and world-class teachers of narrative journalism at the University of Wisconsin, Madison (Deborah), and at Columbia University (Dale and Sam), who supported this project from the beginning. Dale pushed me to apply for a residency at the MacDowell Colony, and for that I'll be forever grateful.

David Skorton and Michael Hogan, the former president and provost at the University of Iowa, friends who believed in me to pull off this multi-continent project, and weren't timid about allowing me to pursue it. David is now president of Cornell University and Mike is president of the University of Connecticut. To Catherine Ringen, a persistent professor of linguistics, for pushing me not to accept no for an answer, and to Linda Maxson, who beat me to Broome, Australia, by two decades.

John Loring, the design director at Tiffany's, for his precise vision of what constitutes elegant design.

Gina Latendressse, the president of American Pearl Company, for sharing stories of her pioneering father, John, as well as tales of Tennessee pearls.

Jeremy Shepherd, the president of pearlparadise.com, for allowing me to traipse along with him in the wilds of remote southern China.

Marc Freeman, of Freeman Gem Co. in Los Angeles, for trusting me to tell the story of Chinese freshwater pearls.

Alex Vock, the indefatigable president of ProVockative Gems, for his candor about the pearl business, and his jewelry designer wife, Donna, and his buying partner and sister-in-law, Jenine Kelly, whose modesty belies her eye for pearl color, orient, lustre, and shape.

Elisabeth Strack, the doyenne of pearl writers, for her encyclopedic book, *Pearls*, and for not turning up her nose at my impish temerity to embark on this journey.

K. C. Bell, who shared the thrill of finding natural pearls wherever it takes him.

Doug Fiske, a former surfer and writer with the Gemological Institute of America, who graciously shared with me numerous contacts and stories about his own pearl trail adventures.

Caitlin Williams, whose love for pearls and their pedigrees is nothing short of inspiring.

Zeide Erskine, who opened her home and her amazing pearl collection to me. Ricki Angelus for sharing both her pearls and her spirit with me.

Dave and Mia Thompson, who live in paradise with a Cook Island pearling boat hanging in their living room in Waimanalo, Hawaii, for navigating me through the pearl maze, as well as connecting me with pearlers in Tahiti and China.

Gilles Tisseraud, a Tahitian pearler in Hawaii, who opened up his thick book of friends and helped me connect to the world of pearls in Papeete, and Jennifer Howell for her expert French translation.

Richard Fassler, a prolific pearl writer, organizer of the famed Pearl '94 convention, expert on aquaculture, and inveterate economic development specialist for the State of Hawaii (and Martin Landau look-alike), for gilding the lily of my upcoming travels one delightful afternoon in downtown Honolulu.

Moshe Rapaport, a geographer whose dissertation on the Tuamotus was spellbinding, for waxing about everything from kayaking to whale-watching to child-rearing, as well as Leilani and Kainui.

Ken Schneider, travel agent extraordinaire of Worldview Travel, Beverly Hills, who never balked at any of my requests, except to say, "You want to go *where?*"

Kirsten Scharnberg, Bill and Savannah Hampton, Vanilla (a k a Waffey), for allowing me to crash at their Kunia, Oahu, home while I prepared to launch my trip to Asia. Kirsten, a former student, who used to work as a national reporter for the *Chicago Tribune*, again and again shows me why teaching is a noble endeavor.

Joan Rogers and her husband, Dick Rogers, of Portland, Maine, Cecilia Blewer and Carlson Gerdau, both of New York, who helped me piece together the remarkable lives of Otto and Allan Gerdau by sharing with me family trees and a treasure trove of letters and memories. Christine S. Windheuser, a volunteer reference assistant at the National Museum of American History's Archives Center, also assisted me in pursing the Gerdau story, as did Alice Gingold of the New York Historical Society.

Michael Judge, a terrific reporter and writer, whose network of friends and experts in Asia and Australia, helped me considerably.

To the administrators, writers, composers, and visual artists at the Virginia Center for the Creative Arts and at the MacDowell Colony, who nurtured me during the final stages. Special thanks to Anne Mills McCauley, Patricia Patterson, Mel Rosenthal, Marilyn Webb, Diáne Moser, and Bill Zavatsky.

Michael Flamini, my editor at St. Martin's Press, whose love for pearls shines through on each page of *Tears of Mermaids*; to Sally Richardson, St. Martin's editor, who took to the manuscript the way all elegant women take to pearls; and Vicki Lame, who shepherded the manuscript with care.

In Japan:

Mikio Ibuki, the executive director of the Japan Pearl Exporters' Association, for giving his time and expertise to introduce me to scores of pearl dealers in Kobe, as well as for accompanying me to Toba and Kashikojima one bright yet windy day in February.

Tomokazu Nakamura, a pearler for the ages and founder of Mikage Boeki, as well as secretary general for the South Sea Pearl Consortium and professor of English at Doshisha University, for his erudition on the trade.

Andy Müller, a legendary pearl dealer in Kobe for thirty-five years, for showing me the correct way to bow in Pearl City. Andy also shared with me lunches and dinners at neighborhood holes-in-the-wall and at the Kobe Club while expounding on his favorite subject.

Aki Ishida-Smith for helping me with navigational snafus.

Tasaki Shinju, the revered father of Kobe pearl dealers (known as the Emperor), of Tasaki Pearls, for submitting to a robust interview at his company headquarters.

Yasuaki Mori and Takashi Abe for squiring me through their company, Otsuki Pearl Co., and allowing me to ask intrusive questions about how Japanese pearling companies operate.

Yoshihiro Shimizu, president of the Japan Pearl Exporters' Association and chairman of Hosei Pearls, for our frank discussion, as well as a mutual affection for Macallan scotch.

Takuya Fujimura, a marine biologist with Wakasa Otsuki Pearl Co., for (literally) showing me the ropes while cruising through pearl farms on Ago Bay, and being forthright about the precarious future of Japanese akoyas. Thanks also to Deguchi Takafumi, a technician of great skill when it comes to the delicate task of nucleating akoyas.

Kiyoo Matsuzuki, the director of the Mikimoto Pearl Museum in Toba, for a personal tour of the museum, and Tatsuo Inoue, for negotiating the narrow roads of Mie Prefecture without getting us killed.

Misako Vemura and Hunae Vemura, two inveterate *amas* in Toba City, who continue the pearl-diving tradition (and who cooked me conch, abalone, oysters, and clams on an open-pit fire) and Toshiyuki Murayama, a municipal officer with Toba City, who shared his enthusiasm for the city's newly opened Amas Museum.

Takashi Mori, a towering historic figure whose pluck helped create demand in the 1950s among U.S. servicemen for akoya necklaces they brought back to the States, thus creating the pearl-strand standard in America.

Yuji Suto, the gutsy pioneering engineer growing akoya pearls in Port Stephens Bay, Australia.

In Hong Kong:

The Paspaley personnel who put on the Hong Kong auction, particularly Nick Paspaley, who spent hours with me, patiently explaining the nuances of his business. Thanks to Michael Bracher and Peter Paspaley poised to bring even greater presence to the Paspaley Pearl Group; Charles Cormack, head of retail sales; Mario Malfliet, the computer guru of the auction; and Dennis Hart, one of the auction coordinators.

Leung Sik Wah (life honorary president of the Diamond Federation of Hong Kong) and his brother Yuen Wang Leung, for guiding me through the intricacies of how the Paspaley and Wan auctions work.

Fran Mastoloni, for sharing with me his family's three-generation history in the pearl trade, on a plane ride from Osaka to Hong Kong. Also, to Fran's father, Frank, and uncle, Ray, for meeting me in New York on their busiest week of the year.

Alain Boite, a Paris jeweler, and one of the finest purveyors of pearls in the world.

Hugo Restall, editor of the *Far East Economic Review*, for conversation at the China Club with Shirley Syaru Lin, a Ph.D. student at Hong Kong University, Xiaohui Restall, a former *New York Daily News* reporter, and George Ho, a painter from Taipei.

Gene Mustain, a former *New York Daily News* reporter, who now teaches journalism at Hong Kong University, for welcoming me as a colleague (as well as recommending a terrific Hong Kong tailor).

In China:

The personnel at China Pearls & Jewellery, especially chairman Ricky Cheng, international general manager Dave B.K., Chow, deputy manager Maud Errerra, Jonathan Liu, and director Ruan Tie Jun.

Sonny Hung, a director at Man Sang Holdings; Limiao Wang and Quankang Zhan, president and general manager, respectively, at Zhejiang Sanshui Jewellery; and Tiebiaco Qi, CEO of Seven Continents Pearl Co. and Tears of Angel Pearl Co.

Faye Tian, who showed me the modern life of a Chinese pearl queen, in Joo-jee.

Other pearl enthusiasts who joined me in Joo-jee, including Melissa Wong, managing editor of *Jewellery News Asia*; and Jamil M. Ali Farsi, a jeweler from Jeddah, Saudi Arabia.

My inestimable colleague and all-around buddy China scholar Judy Polumbaum, who took me under her wing to explore Beijing's hidden pearls, including a wonderful foot message parlor.

Evan Osnos, former Beijing bureau chief for the *Chicago Tribune*, now a staff writer for *The New Yorker.*

Nathaniel Gao, for his stellar saxophone playing at Beijing's best jazz venue, Club D-22; Liu Jun, for showing me (and serving as my able translator at) the Hongqiao Pearl Market and the Guwancheng Antique Market; Tammy Cai of Stall 105 at the Hongqiao Market, who, at age twenty, shows a promising career in the pearl business, and Bai Rufang, president of Fanghua Pearls.

Shi Hongyue, the deputy secretary general in charge of pearls for the Gems & Jewelry Trade Association; and Shen Meidong and Han Xiao, managers at the National Gemstone Testing Center in Beijing.

You Hongqing, who owns a pearl-processing plant in Xuwen and two nearby pearl farms, for allowing me to visit his pearling operations (and his favorite karaoke nightclub and foot masseur), and Zhu Ping, who served as our capable translator.

Dave Bing, Sofinny Kovak, Ju-Ha and Jian Hao, who shepherded me around rural China and made me appreciate the universally understandable word, "wow."

To the many pearl shuckers and technicians who allowed me to interview them, in Xuwen and Xillan, including Huang Jin, Li Hung, Hu Xiao Mei, Fan Mi, Xie Hong Wu, Xie Hong Chong, Xiao Ling, Li Zhu Li, Xie Xian Hua, and Li Yu Ying.

In the Philippines:

Jacques Branellec, who leads a charmed life centered on pearls; Manuel Cojuangco, Branellec's partner and office mate, who plays Felix to Branellec's Oscar; Daniela Fenix, Jewelmer's marketing manager, who turned out to be honest, forthright, and a terrific shopper; Mel Zinampan-de Luna, for sharing the science of pearl farming; Pierre Fallourd, for a spirited discussion on the future of jewelry; Rowena Yu and Ana Marie Echevarria, for logisitical planning; and Cyril Brossard and his two children, Gwenaelle and Theophile, for welcoming me into their home on Bugsuk Island. Thanks also to the following pearl workers who trusted me with their stories: Glenn Lovitos, Nobuhiro Kano, April Niones, Joni Damiles, Rommel Aguirre, and Rogelio Bas.

Wall Street Journal correspondent James Hookway, for explaining how cavalier life in the Philippines can be, and Bruno Marcantonio Savron, for his exhilaration of that life; and Ariel Chio, for meeting me in a Puerto Princesa restaurant in spite of what his Muslim friends might have thought.

In French Polynesia:

Jean and Estelle Tapu, who live among 400 people and 1,200 dogs in Apataki and who treated me like family. Thanks also to their grandson, Tyrone, who represents the next generation of Apataki pearl farmers, and to Tyrone's gracious wife, Marlene.

Former general manager Martin Coeroli and logistics manager Lailani Allouche of Perles de Tahiti for arranging a raft of interviews in Papeete, Tahiti.

M. Alfred Martin, CEO of the pearl growers' cooperative, Poe Rava Nui; and Vaihere Mooria, chief of quality control for the Ministére de la Perleculture de Polynésie Français, who showed me thousands of inferior-quality Tahitian pearls about to be destroyed (what a shame!), as she checked for nacre thickness at the government's clearinghouse.

Robert Wan, for his willingness to allow me behind the curtain; Cuixia Mi, the export manager of Robert Wan Pearls, for access to the company's Hong Kong auction; and Papeete associates Merehau Anastas, Nadia Roustan, Vanina Pichevin, Jeanne LeCourt, and Mary Anne Leou. To Wan's son, Bruno, with whom I reminisced about San Francisco; Touria Spector, an international citizen who, although she always carries a sweater, is as warm as a Tahitian sunset; Chilean Francisco Miranda Reinares (and his wife, Shirley Hidalgo Chau, and their soon-to-be-born son, Javier), a man not afraid to swim with the sharks off Marutea Island; to Chloé and Eva Connolly, mother and daughter artists who see the world through a painter's palette, and Benjamin Hinniger, a Frenchman who, via Peoria, Illinois, made a life as a master carpenter in French Polynesia.

Dave Tavere and his son, Jacques Yves, who continue to struggle against impossible odds to produce Tahitian pearls on their family farm.

Pearl farm supervisors Rino Moearo and Nicholas Mace, who talked to me frankly and freely in the shadow of their employer, Robert Wan.

Franck, Halidjka Vainana, and Glenn Tehaamatai, the family that owns and operates pearl farms in French Polynesia, as well as the Tahiti Pearl Market. Jean-François Dilhan, a pearler who works for the Tehaamatai family, shared with me his deep historical knowledge.

Représentante Eléanor Parker, of the Assemblée de la Polynésie Française, who met me on two occasions to share her vision of what creation of a government-run Tahitian Pearl House could do for struggling small and medium-sized farmers. Michel Pedron served as our able interpreter.

In Australia:

The family of Nick Paspaley, Roslynne Bracher, George Kapetas, Christine Bracher,

Marilynne Paspaley, Clare Paspaley, Garry Grbavac, and Milan Grbavac, who showed me hospitality without limitations, as well as the Paspaley organization, including Richard McLean (who introduced me to three Australian favorite pastimes—cricket, rugby, and VB), Dave Parker, Sonni Butler, Annette Crossley, Sarah Carroll, and Virginia Brueckner.

Tony Searle who made me rethink my options about first aid when it comes to snakebites and encounters with crocodiles.

Farm manager Darren Burke, skipper Ringo Thomanson, technician Yagura Toshiyuki, fishing master Pete Dixon, deckies Michelle Shalders, Angie Goddard, Kate O'Maley, Jess Henggeler, and domestic Johnny Kaye, and many others aboard the *MV Roslynne*.

To the entire crew of the *Paspaley IV*, who allowed me to take part in harvesting thousands of South Sea pearls. Special mention goes to deckies Elodie, Hannah, Elliot, Bri, Benny, Selena, Bec, Jordan, and Tommy; cook Leigh Harding; skipper Michael Kyriacou; first mate Phil Mark; diver Sam Morton; Joe; "Skipper Gary" of the *Vansittart*; Australian bloke of blokes Skippy; and master pearl technician Minoru Tominaga.

Amanda Elliott, Alexandra Elliott, and Clelia Winton, intrepid travelers who accompanied me to Vansittart Bay, Talbot Bay, and Kuri Bay.

Bill Reed, a vintage Broome pearler, who shared with me his life story, from the Persian Gulf to Broome.

Penny Arrow, with whom I spent a wonderful day sorting pearls and watching whales aboard the *Trident Aurora*. Penny has an enthusiasm and knowledge of South Sea pearls unmatched anywhere. Everyone at Clipper Pearls in Broome, including: Alex Ogg, an ex-pat from Columbus, Ohio, who I traded e-mails with for more than a year—when we finally met in Broome, we got along like long-lost friends (thanks also to Sandy, Liam, and Addison Ogg); owner Larry House, a diver who became his own boss; Sarah-Jane Laing, who helped arrange my stay in Broome; *Trident Aurora* skipper Phil Bainbridge; and deckies Naruma Osaka, Naomi Yoshizawa, Virginie Rouby, and Anais Salbany, who showed me once again the exhilaration of travel.

Bruce Brown, a savvy pearler who owns Cygnet Pearls, and who flew me to his farm north of Broome; Bruce's smart son, James, and wife, Sarah (and their son, Dean), and Bruce's wife, Allison, who made me feel at home with a lunch of corned beef and potatoes.

Kim Male, who shared with me his life story as the grandson of Broome pearl master Arthur Male, the son of pearl master Sam Male, and a pearl master in his own right. Kim's recollections of the eccentric and unpredictable Allan Gerdau helped shed light on a crucial but little-known facet of South Sea pearling history.

Dr. John Norman, scion of a pioneering Broome family, who has written a definitive book on the city and its intertwined history of pearls and mother-of-pearl shell, *A Pearling Master's Journey*, and Liz Janney, the administrator of the Broome Historical Museum, who spent a morning sharing with me her enthusiasm for a remarkable city.

Rosario Autore, who trusted me to tell his story, and Lisa Mayne, of Autore Pearls, who kept up with my ever-changing schedule. Others in the Autore organization who opened their creative minds to me included Sarah Young, Justin Schwarz, and Alessio Boschi.

Pearl trader David Norman for his sunny disposition, deep knowledge of pearls, and his willingness to share his voluminous cache of letters from his father, pearl trader Boris Norman, and from his mentor John Jerwood, not to mention for his impeccable taste in restaurants in Bondi Bay.

George Levin, who was forthright, candid, and frank about his role in the transaction that catapulted Nick Paspaley to the mega pearl player he is today.

In Venezuela:

Joselin Hernández, a thoroughly knowledgeable guide, who shepherded me throughout Margarita island and to Cubagua, where she and I walked the remarkable ruins of Nueva Cádiz.

Professor Ivan Gomez, for his deep knowledge of Cubagua and Margarita history, and his wife, Ana Maria, for introducing me to Margarita hospitality and *arepas*.

Simon Romero, the correspondent for the *New York Times* in Caracas; Jens Erik Gould, a former Venezuela stringer for the *Times* and *Time*, now a reporter for Bloomberg News in Mexico City; and Phil Gunson, a correspondent for the *Miami Herald* in Caracas. All graciously helped a fellow journalist who parachuted onto their turf.

Señor Hernandez Sixto and Nicholas El Gato, two real-life descendants of John Steinbeck's fictitious yet brave pearl diver, Kino.

ENDNOTES

Introduction

1. Kan and momme are arcane Japanese measures still used in the wholesale pearl trade. One momme equals 3.75 grams, or 75 grains; one kan is the equivalent of 1,000 momme.

2. *Pavé* is the French word for pavement; in jewelry it is a technique of covering the surface of the jewel with small stones, usually diamonds, set into multiple holes level with the setting, thus creating a kind of cobblestone or paved covering.

Chapter 1

1. Columbus's account of his initial expedition to the New World comes from *The Diario of Christopher Columbus's First Voyage to America, 1492–1493*, transcribed and translated by Oliver Dunn and James E. Kelly, Jr. (University of Oklahoma Press, 1989). I also read hundreds of intriguing accounts of various aspects of the momentous voyage. The most interesting include: Vincent H. deP. Cassidy, "Columbus and 'The Negro,'" *The Phylon Quarterly* 20, no. 3 (1959); W. F. Keegan *The People Who Discovered Columbus: The Prehistory of the Bahamas*, (University Press of Florida, 1992); Kirkpatrick Sale, *Christopher Columbus and the Conquest of Paradise* (Hodder and Stoughton, 1991); and Margarita Zamora, "Christopher Columbus's 'Letter to the Sovereigns': Announcing the

Discovery," in *New World Encounters*, edited By Stephen Greenblatt (University of California Press, 1993).

2. A fact obscured by much of the history of this period is that when Columbus returned from his first voyage, he wrote a letter to Ferdinand and Isabella from Portugal on March 4, 1493, before returning to Barcelona, in which he pledged in seven years' time to conquer Jerusalem and the Holy Land for the Spanish monarchy. Columbus wrote that his share of the bounty seized in the coming voyages back to the New World would enable him to fund an army of "five-thousand cavalry and fifty thousand foot soldiers." His gesture is seen as both appreciation of the king and queen's support of his first voyage and a gambit to extract additional backing from the royal court for a series of new conquests.

3. Sanford A. Mosk, "Spanish Pearl-Fishing Operations on the Pearl Coast in the Sixteenth Century," *Hispanic American Historical Review* 18 (1938): 392–400.

4. As cited in Fernando Cervigón, *Las Perlas en las Historia de Venezuela* (Fundación Museo del Mar, 1998), 24.

5. Carl O. Sauer, *The Early Spanish Main* (University of California Press, 1969).

6. Nicholas J. Saunders, *Ancient Americas: The Great Civilisations* (Sutton Publishing, 2004); Saunders's "Stealers of Light, Traders in Brilliance: Amerindian metaphysics in the Mirror of Conquest," *RES: Anthropology and Aesthetics* 33 (Spring, 1998); and Saunders's "Biographies of Brilliance: Pearls, Transformations of Matter and Being, c. AD 1492," *World Archeology* 31, no. 2: 243–57.

7. Stephen Greenblatt, *Marvelous Possessions: The Wonder of the New World* (Clarendon Press, 1992).

8. A fascinating account of gift exchange between Columbus and the New World Indians appears in Elvira Vilches, "Columbus's Gift: Representations of Grace and Wealth and the Enterprise of the Indies," *MLN* 119 (2004): 201–25.

9. See Mosk, "Spanish Pearl-Fishing," 395, and Lesley B. Simpson, *The Encomienda in New Spain* (Berkeley, 1929).

10. Bartolomé de las Casas, *Brevsima Relación de la Destruyción de las Indias*, 1552.

11. This conservative estimate is based on Aldemaro Romero, "Death and Taxes: The Case of the Depletion of Pearl Oyster Beds in Sixteenth-Century Venezuela," *Conservation Biology*, 17, no. 4 (August 2003): 1013–23.

12. Information on the early settlement of Cubagua was found in Fernando Cervigón, *Las Perlas en la Historia de Venezuela*; Neil H. Landman, Paula M. Mikkelsen, Rüdiger Bieler, and Bennet Bronson, *Pearls: A Natural History* (Harry N. Abrams in association with the American Museum of National History and the Field Museum, 2001); R. A. Donkin, *Beyond Price: Pearls and Pearl Fishing* (American Philosophical Society, 1998).

Chapter 2

1. Centuries of lore celebrate Cleopatra's alleged pearl-in-wine drama, but the fact is there's no way the queen could have carried off the feat. If such a large pearl dissolved in the wine, the wine would have to have been rancid and turned into vinegar. Even so, it would take weeks for the pearl to decompose. To hasten dissolving, Cleopatra could pos-

sibly have boiled the wine-turned-vinegar, and that would have hastened the pearl's partial decomposition, but it still would have taken hours and hours. The only way the queen could have swallowed such a solution would have been for her first to pulverize the pearl, and then vigorously agitate the ground-up pearl and wine-turned-vinegar solution. Even then, the elixir would not have gone down very smoothly.

2. Jean Taburiaux, *Pearls: Their Origin, Treatment and Identification* (Chilton Book Company, 1985), 16.

Chapter 6

1. From Andy Müller's presentation at the European Gemological Symposium, in Berne, Switzerland, June 5, 2009, "A Brief Analysis of the Global Seawater Cultured Pearl Industry (Past, Present, Future)."

Chapter 7

1. Keshis are small, irregularly shaped pearls, the result of an oyster rejecting an implanted nucleus. The word keshi means "poppy seed" in Japanese.

Chapter 8

1. All information on Salvador Assael's three homes was obtained from public, city, and county appraisal records.

2. All quotes from Salvador Assael come from a personal interview conducted in his Manhattan office over the phone on June 27, 2006, as well as from an assortment of published articles, including "Lifetime Achievement Award: Salvador Assael," by David Federman, in *Modern Jeweler*, December 1994; "Pearls of Wisdom: Salvador Assael," in *Avenue*, October 1998; Zina Moukheiber, "The Pearl King," *Forbes*, April 24, 1995; Bruce Porter, "The Black-Pearl Connection: How One Man Cornered the World Market," *Connoisseur*, April 1991; and Joan Jedell, "Behind the Hedges—Salvador Assael: The Oyster Is His World," *The Hampton Sheet*, August 1998. Observations about Assael were obtained through more than a score of interviews with brokers, dealers, producers, wholesalers, and retailers.

Chapter 9

1. For a description of freshwater Chinese pearls, see Elisabeth Strack's authoritative, encyclopedic *Pearls*, published in English from the original German (Stuttgart: Rühle-Diebener-Verlag, 2006). Another source is Landman et al., *Pearls: A Natural History*.

2. Information on chemical treatments of pearls was obtained from author interviews conducted in Joo-jee, China, with corroboration from Strack, *Pearls*, and from *Pearl World*, the quarterly industry newsletter published in Phoenix by Bo Torrey. *Jewellery News Asia*, a monthly trade magazine published in Hong Kong, consistently covers the Chinese freshwater pearl industry and is another important source of information. Other, less consistent sources on the subject are *Jewelers' Circular Keystone*, *Gems & Gemology*, *Gem and Jewellery News*, *Australian Jeweller*, and *Journal of Gemology*.

Chapter 13

1. *Pearl World* 15, no. 3 (2006), published on the cover of its July/August/September issue a Q & A with Jeremy Shepherd, excerpted from the April 2006 issue of *Jewellery News Asia*. The *Pearl World* issue carried the pull-out line, "This is the story of an unusual young man who parlayed luck, determination, grit, and just plain *cojones* into a niche pearl empire that grossed US$11.8 million in 2005. His name is Jeremy Shepherd."

2. For an insight on how Shepherd travels with so many pearls, see Jeremy Shepherd, as told to Joan Raymond, "Spanning the Blue Globe, for Little White Ones," *New York Times*, November 13, 2007.

Chapter 16

1. Whichever you call it, the Pearl of Allah or the Pearl of Lao-Tzu has a wild history. This much is not disputed (although it sounds an awful lot like legend to me): A Muslim diver discovered it near Brooke's Point on Palawan on May 7, 1934, when a 160-pound *Tridacna gigas* clam clamped its muscles around the diver's leg. Attempting to pull his leg free, he reached into the clam and found the amazing pearl. American mining surveyor Wilburn Dowell Cobb tried to buy the pearl from a local Islamic tribal chief, who refused. But two years later, Cobb returned, to find the chief's son dying of malaria. Cobb was able to cure the son with a new antimalarial drug, quinacrine, and as payment the chief gave Cobb the pearl. Cobb kept the pearl despite numerous offers. Perhaps the most unusual came in the mid-1970s—ten million dollars from a consortium that included businessmen Victor Barbish, Henry Kyle, Robert Pease, Johnny Weissmuller, and Rudy Vallee. Cobb steadfastly refused. Cobb died in 1980, which prompted his heirs to sell the pearl for two hundred thousand dollars to Beverly Hills jeweler Peter Hoffman through a probate court sale. Victor Barbish at that time bought half ownership of the pearl. Barbish and Hoffman then formed a company called World's Largest Pearl Co., Inc., through which they sold shares of ownership of the pearl.

   Now things get complicated. In 1985, Barbish borrowed money from two of his investors, Joe Bonicelli and S. Mort Zimmerman, with Bonicelli keeping the pearl as collateral. When Barbish reneged, a federal judge split ownership of the pearl among Hoffman, Bonicelli's estate, Barbish, and Zimmerman (but only if the pearl were ever sold). Meanwhile, Bonicelli died in 1998, but prosecutors showed that he had hired a hit man to kill his wife in 1975, and in a subsequent wrongful death suit, a jury found in favor of Bonicelli's children, awarding them $32.4 million, then the largest wrongful death judgment rendered.

   There have been assorted media reports of offers to buy the pearl, including one from a consortium of Las Vegas casino owners, another from the sultan of Brunei, and yet another from an Iranian royal crown princess. Perhaps the most interesting offer to buy the pearl allegedly came in 1999 from a representative of Osama bin Laden, who Barbish said wanted to present the pearl as a gift to Saddam Hussein as a gesture of unity between al Qaeda and Iraq, in an attempt to unite the Arab world.

   The story of the pearl's connection to the ancient Chinese philosopher Lao Tzu, the father of Taoism, is just as outrageous. In 1939, Cobb had lent the pearl to be exhibited at Robert Ripley's Believe it or Not Odditorium in New York. Ripley and Cobb met with an elderly Hong Kong merchant who expressed interest in the pearl. The man told a fabled story about his long-lost relative, Lao Tzu, who, family lore had it, had carved faces of Buddha, Confucius, and himself on an amulet, and instructed a nephew to securely place the amulet in a large clam, transferring it every four years. The family would experience great fortune if such a protocol were followed. The amulet went from generation to generation, growing larger and larger. The descendants of Lao Tzu, fearing the pearl would get stolen, shipped it to Palawan, where it was to be secured inside a giant clam. In 1745, a typhoon sunk the ship, and the pearl was lost until the Muslim diver stumbled upon it two centuries later.

Chapter 17

1. Peter S. Goodman and Peter Finn, "Corruption Stains Timber Trade; Forests Destroyed in China's Race to Feed Global Wood-Processing Industry," *Washington Post*, April 1, 2007.
2. Barbara Goldoffas, *The Green Tiger: The Costs of Ecological Decline in the Philippines* (Oxford University Press, 2005).

Chapter 18

1. Christie's catalogue, *New York, Magnificent Jewels, Wednesday 25 April 2007*, 211.
2. *The Travels of Marco Polo*, in a modern translation by Teresa Waight from the Italian by Maria Bellonci (London: Sidgwick & Jackson, 1984), 154, 162.
3. Katherine Prior and John Adamson, *Maharajas' Jewels* (Paris: Éditions Assouline, 2000), 81, 126, 128.
4. Christie's catalogue, *New York, Magnificent Jewels, Wednesday 25 April 2007*, 211.
5. Edward St. Clair Weeden, *A Year with the Gaekwar of Baroda* (London, 1911), 310.
6. In addition to the Baroda Pearls, the Maharaja of Baroda, Gaekwar Khande Rao, in about 1865 commissioned a magnificent carpet, five feet, eight inches by eight feet, eight inches, made with a foundations of silk and deer hide, threaded with at least 1.2 million natural Basra pearls. The carpet was auctioned off in March 2009 for $5.5 million at Sotheby's facilty in Doha, Qatar, to the Qatar Museum Authority.
7. Sara Fox, Christie's public relations department, in an interview, April 16, 2009.

Chapter 19

1. While I was preparing this book in the summer of 2008, Coeroli was discharged from his job and no longer is director of Perles de Tahiti.

Chapter 21

1. Nicholas Way, "How the Land Lies," *BRW*, May 19–25, 2005, 78–83.
2. These property transactions were recorded in their respective shires, and reported in *The Australian*, July 17, 1998 (Fiona Cameron, "Sydney Money Retreats to the West"), as

well as in *The Australian Financial Review*, October 2, 1998 in (Lisa Allen, "Paspaleys Add Coolah Holding") by and in *The Bulletin*, September 17, 2002 (Anthony Hoy, "From Pearls to Wine").

3. Paspaley Family Seeks Pastoral Holdings, *Australian Financial Review*, July 24, 2009.

4. Daniel Bourchier, "'We had a blast'—Elton," *Northern Territory News*, May 18, 2008.

5. Gary Hughes, "Air Rescue Group Gave to Coalition," *The Australian*, January 22, 2008.

6. Real estate records maintained by the city of New York and the city of Portsmouth, Virginia. The subsidiary is the Otto Gerdau Company.

7. *BRW*, May 31–July 4, 2007, 184; May 29–July 2, 2008, 188.

8. *BRW*, May 31–July 4, 184; Shares.com.au, an Internet information provider, tracking share ownership of Australian public companies; Jubilee Mines N.L. Report, at the Australian Nickel Conference, October 18–19, 2006; and Bell Potter Securities Research, issue dated June 22, 2006.

9. Strachan Corporate Report, March 16, 2006, www.lefroyresources.com.au/net/documents/1/Strachan_Research_Report.pdf.

10. "Sandfire Raises $4.4 Million," *WA Business News*, August 31, 2006.

11. Kimberley Diamond Company NL, Notice of General Meetings, September 25, 2006, as well as the Kimberley Diamond Company Web site, http://www.kimberleydiamondco.com.au/overview/history.html.

12. Much of Greek immigrants' early influence on Darwin history came from the Official Hansard of the House of Representatives, Commonwealth of Australia's Parliamentary Debates, No. 13, Monday, August 9, 2004, p. 32541.

13. Details of Nikolas Paspaley's early years in Port Hedland and Darwin came from the Darwin Research Center and from John Anictomatis's Fifteen Eric Johnson Lecture 2000, "A Home Away from Home—the Aegean to Australia," Occasional Paper No. 54.

14. Much of Vivienne Lavinia Paspaley's life story was gleaned from newspaper and magazine articles, notably "Darwin's Mother of Pearl Family" *Sydney Morning Herald*, October 13, 2003, and "Pearl of a Partner," *Northern Territory News*, October 14, 2003.

Chapter 22

1. Notes from the Otto Gerdau Collection, 1876–1900, Smithsonian Institution, National Museum of American History, Behring Center.

2. The original Tontine Building, built in 1794, was established for members of the New York Tontine Society, a group of insurance and investment executives. The site is where the first Sunday newspaper in America (the *Sunday Courier*) was published in 1825. The original structure burned down during what is known as The Great Conflagration of 1835, and the present-day Tontine building was erected in 1902, three years before Gerdau moved in.

3. "Was Bachelor Circle Night," *New York Times*, January 11, 1895.

4. Obituary in the *New York Times*, March 15, 1960.

5. Jura Koncius, "Pediments and Pilasters: The New Neoclassics," *Washington Post*, October 18, 1984.

6. "Mrs. Allan Gerdau," *New York Times*, May 15, 1937; and "12-Room Penthouse Rented in E. 72D St.," *New York Times*, March 11, 1937.

7. "First Group of U.S. Traders," *New York Times*, August 4, 1947.

8. Cited in Register of Heritage Places—Assessment Documentation, Heritage Council of Western Australia, March 30, 2007.

9. Val Burton, *General History of Broome* (Broome Historical Society, 2000), 54.

10. "Pearl Contract Signed," *New York Times*, July 10, 1949.

11. E-mail exchange between the author and veteran Australian pearler Stephen Arrow, June 6, 2008.

12. Andy Müller, *Cultured Pearls: The First Hundred Years* (Golay Buchel Group, 1997), 58–60.

13. Based on an interview I conducted with David Norman, Boris Norman's son, in Sydney, August 7, 2007.

14. Müller, *Cultured Pearls*, 58–60.

15. "The Pearling Game," Bob Connolly, reporter and director, and John Sparkes, executive producer, ABC National Television (Australian Broadcasting Corporation), 1961.

16. Virginia Lee Warren, "'An Oasis of Charm' Thrives on Wall St.," *New York Times*, March 7, 1966.

17. "Deal Laid to U.S. by Cohn's Lawyer," *New York Times*, March 25, 1964.

18. "Importer Replies to Ad on Johnson," *New York Times*, September, 28, 1967.

19. Obituaries in the *New York Times* and in the *Redding Pilot*, October 23, 1986.

20. Private notes provided by Joan Rogers.

21. Ibid.

22. I interviewed Joan Rogers from the Rogerses' home in Portland, Maine, May 30, July 3, 6, 2008.

23. Private correspondence from Allan Gerdau to Boris A. Norman, of Australian Pearl Co. Ltd, Halton House, London, June 3, 1982.

24. Dick Rogers interview May 30, 2008.

25. Last Will & Testament of Allan Gerdau, State of Connecticut, Court of Probate, District of Reading, April 1, 1981.

26. I interviewed George G. Levin from his home and office in Fort Lauderdale, Florida, July 2 and 4, 2008.

27. I conducted interviews with at least four sources present during various stages of the Gerdau Co. negotiations. These informants requested that their names not be used, a condition I have honored.

Chapter 27

1. I interviewed Larry House at his home in Broome on July 29, 2007.

2. I interviewed Rosario Autore at his office in Sydney on August 8, 2007.

3. From personal correspondence between J. M. Jerwood and David Norman, June 18, 1986, supplied to me by Norman.

4. I interviewed Bill Reed in Broome on August 3, 2007.

Chapter 28

1. This is a hotly contested issue among pearl producers and dealers. Rosario Autore is a staunch advocate of a rating system for pearls, while trader Alex Vock is not. The Gemological Society of America has commissioned a study to develop criteria to rate pearls, and hopes to implement a comprehensive system by the end of 2009. Now, like all gems, pearls can be sent to a GSA laboratory for an appraisal of their qualities, but pearls do not automatically come with any independent certification, as diamonds often do. Appraisals for replacement or actual value of pearls are notoriously unreliable.

Chapter 29

1. Details of Columbus's third voyage to the New World are primarily from Cecil Jane's translation of *The Voyages of Christopher Columbus* (Argonaut Press, Empire House, 1930); and Sauer, *The Early Spanish Main*.

2. The author is indebted to the fine scholarship of William Jerome Wilson, who first wrote about the Trevisan diaries in *Geographical Review* 31, no. 2 (April 1941): 283–99.

3. The claim that one or more pearls Columbus bartered for in 1498 eventually became part of Queen Isabella's legendary Venezuelan necklace comes from Elisabeth Strack, *Pearls*, 187.

4. There is an interesting connection between oil and pearls. When oil was first discovered in 1931 in the Persian Gulf, it couldn't have come at a more propitious economic time for Bahrain. The waters surrounding the island had for more than a thousand years been fished for natural pearls, which for a millennium had been Bahrain's No. 1 commodity, but with the onslaught of cultivated pearls from Japan, the market for natural pearls had by 1931 almost completely collapsed. Today, few natural pearls are found in the waters surrounding the Gulf nation, in part because of the heavy pollution oil has created.

5. Information on the commercialization of Cubagua's pearls is from E. Wagner, "Neuva Cádiz," in *Christopher Columbus and the Age of Exploration*, edited by S. A. Bedini (De Capo Press, 1992); Carvigón, *Las Perlas*; Kunz and Stevenson, *The Book of the Pearl: Its History, Art, Science and Industry*; R. A. Donkin, *Beyond Price*; and Saunders, "Biographies of Brilliance."

6. See Saunders, "Biographies of Brilliance."

7. In September 1622, a flotilla of twenty-eight Spanish crown ships, carrying silver from Mexico and Peru, emeralds and gold from Colombia, and natural pearls from the warm waters north of Venezeula, set sail for Spain from Havana. The ships sailed into a hurricane upon entering the Florida straits, and all galleons were lost. In 1985, a team working with Mel Fisher, a Key West, Florida, entrepreneur who calls himself the "world's greatest treasure hunter," located sections of one ship, the *Nuestra Señora de Atocha*, off the coast of Key West; in 2007, a joint venture partner with Fisher, Blue Water Ventures, recovered a sealed lead box with more than 16,300 natural pearls inside the hull of an-

other ship in the flotilla, the *Santa Margarita*. The find is one of the largest recorded caches of pearls ever recovered from a shipwreck.

8. One of the world's most famous and largest pearls, The Peregrina (which roughly translates to The Incomparable), comes from the Gulf of Panama, and was found during the crown's westward expansion during the early 1500s. The drop-shaped, 204-grain pearl the size of a pigeon's egg was first found by a slave and later bartered to the Spanish explorer Vasco Núñez de Balboa, in exchange for the slave's freedom. Balboa gave the massive pearl to Isabella's successor, King Ferdinand V. By 1513 the pearl began a long and peripatetic journey, during which it was owned by a succession of nobility, including Philip II's second wife, Mary Tudor; Louis XIV's wife, Maria Theresa; Napoleon's brother, Joseph, and the duke of Abercorn. In 1969, the pearl showed up at an auction in New York conducted by Parke-Bernet Galleries and was bought by Richard Burton. The actor gave the pearl to his wife at the time, Elizabeth Taylor, for her thirty-seventh birthday, paying $37,000. Taylor still owns the pearl, but it has been reported (by Strack and Landman et al.) that she momentarily lost it in a plush white carpet in a hotel room, though she eventually found it in her dog's mouth.

9. The single and most complete account of life on Cubagua during the Spanish conquest is Enrique Otte's 620-page masterpiece, *Las Perlas del Caribe: Nueva Cádiz de Cubagua* (Fundación John Boulton, 1977). Other source materials are contained in James Lockhart and Otte's *Letters and People of the Spanish Indies: Sixteenth Century* (Cambridge University Press, 1976); *Cedulario de las Monarquia Española relative a la isla de Cubagua*, compiled and with an introduction by Otte (Fundación John Boulton and the Fundación Eugenio Mendoza, 1961); and Fernando Cerigón, *Cubagua 500 Años* (Fundación Museo del Mar, 1997).

10. Peter Muilenburg, "Fate and Fortune on the Pearl Coast," *Américas* 43 (1991): 32–39.

11. Irving Rouse and Jose M. Cruxent, *Venezuelan Archeology* (Yale University Press, 1963); Willis, "The Archeology of 16th Century Nueva Cádiz."

12. Much of the historic and economic information on Cubagua I learned from the excellent scholarship of Aldemaro Romero and his groundbreaking essay "Death and Taxes."

13. Willis, "The Archeology of 16th Century Nueva Cádiz."

14. Details of how native divers procured pearls comes from a variety of sources: Clyde L. MacKenzie, Jr., Luis Troccoli, and Luis B. León S., "History of the Atlantic Pearl-Oyster, Pinctata imbricata, Industry in Venezuela and Colombia, with Biological and Ecological Observations," *Marine Fisheries Review* 65 (Winter 2003); Cervigón, *Las Perlas*; Otte, *Las Perlas del Caribe*; De las Casas, *Brevsima Relación*; and William D. and Mary L. Marsland, *Venezuela Through Its History* (Thomas Y. Crowell, 1954).

Chapter 30

1. For a terrific, albeit pro-Chávez, account of the coup and Hugo Chávez's rise to power, see Bart Jones, *Hugo: The Hugo Chávez Story from Mud Hut to Perpetual Revolution* (Steerforth Press, 2007).

2. There's an apocalyptic story about the Virgin of the Valley that everyone in Margarita

seems to know. In 1912, a diver by the name of Domino got bitten by a deadly stingray. Doctors told him that he must get his leg amputated or he would die. Domingo and his wife prayed to the virgin, telling her that if she saved his leg and life, they would reward her with a priceless pearl. The first day back diving, Domino found a huge oyster, and inside it a 17-millimeter pearl in the shape of a leg. Instead of selling the pearl, Domingo gave it to the church. Today it sits in the Virgen de la Valle church museum on Margarita, where tens of thousands of Venezuelans make pilgrimages every year. When I made my visit, the pearl didn't look to me like a leg, but more like a large, misshapen kernel of corn.

Chapter 31

1. Rouse and Cruxent, *Venezuelan Archeology*; Willis, "The Archeology of 16th Century Nueva Cádiz." See also Enrique Bernardo Núñuz, *Cubagua* (Monte Avila Editores, 1987).
2. Graciano Gasparini, as cited in museum display and DVD (Nueva Cádiz de Cubagua 1521–1543, Reconstrucción de una Ciudad Perdida) created by the Fundación Museo del Mar, Boca del Río, Isla de Margarita, Venezuela.

INDEX

abalone pearls, 38
Abe, Takashi, 69–70
Aboriginal Australians, 245, 266
Abu Dhabi, in global pearl trade, 3
Adam and Eve, 26
Add-a-Pearl concept, 19
advertising, word-of-mouth, 133
African slaves, 327
Ago Bay, 56, 66, 73–74
Ahe, 228
Ahhotep, Queen, 20
airport security, for disease control,
    166–69
akoya oyster. *See Pinctada imbricata* oyster
akoya pearls
    Chinese knockoffs of, 62
    competition with, from other pearl
        varieties, 91, 253
    decline of production, 56–57
    maximum size of, 63
    price of, 69
Alatika, 228
al-Dur, 19
Alfillé, Eve, 31, 199, 315

Alonthias tapui (fish named after Jean Tapu),
    212
al Qaeda, 175
Amami Island, 61
Amazon company, online shopping model
    of, and decline of brick-and-mortar
    stores, 142
American Gem Trade Association, Tucson
    convention, 30
Americans
    buyers of pearls, 103
    GIs in Japan, spending of money by, 66
Angelus, Paul, 313, 315, 316
Angelus, Ricki, 312–18
Aniston, Jennifer, 106
Antiques Roadshow, 197
Anuraro, 222
Apataki, 208, 212, 215, 227
aphrodisiacs, oysters as, 26, 338
appraising of pearls, 5, 29, 147, 364n28.1
Arabs, collectors of pearls, 23–24
Arafura Pearls, 309
aragonite (calcium carbonate), 25
Aratua, 208

Araya Peninsula, 325
Arenberg, Princess Silvie d', 94
Arrow, Steve, 308
Arrow Pearls Co., 308, 309
art (painting), pearls in, 21
Arutua, 184
Asay, Lilibeth, 182
Assael, Arlette, 88
Assael, James, 90–91
Assael, Salvador, 37, 67, 86, 87–97, 209, 224
    biography of, 90–92
    interview with, 88
    opinions about, 87
Assael, Sophia, 88
Astor, Brooke, 94
Atlas Pacific, 309
auctioneers, 199–204
auctions
    attendees of, dealers vs. private clients,
        197
    conventional vs. silent, 82
    held in auction houses, 188, 197–99,
        201–5
    See also Hong Kong: pearl auctions
Aukena, 222
Australia, 230–310
Australian pearl industry
    differences from other countries', 269
    introduction of akoya oysters, attempted,
        71–73
    natural pearls in, 24
    oyster-farming leases/licenses let by, 231,
        269, 302
    pearl divers in, 230, 272–74
    smaller operations in, 301–10
Australian South Sea pearls, 63, 78, 81, 114
Autore, Rosario, 58, 68, 231, 303–9,
        364n28.1
    promotion by, 86
Autore company, 301
Ayoub, Mona, 94

Babio, Andres, 95
Bahrain, 42–43, 48, 205
    cultured pearls outlawed in, 42–43
    natural pearls of, 42–43, 364n29.4
Bai Rufang, 132, 152
Balboa, Vasco Núñez de, 365n29.6
Barbish, Victor, 360n16.1
bargaining over pearls, 40–41, 129–35

Baroda Pearls, 188–91, 197–99, 201–5
    provenance of, 190–91
Baroda state, India, 189–91, 361n18.6
baroque pearls, 99, 101, 106, 125
Bas, Rogelio, 182
Basel, Switzerland, in global pearl trade, 3
Bass, Mercedes, 94
bead insertion (nucleation), 3, 73–74, 157–58
bead nuclei
    Mississippi River Delta clamshells bits
        as, 24
    size of, in Chinese pearls, 181
beads (fake pearls), 25
Beibu Gulf, 141
beige coloration, 99
Beijing, 49, 126–35
Bell, K. C., 38, 44
the bends (caisson disease), 22, 327
Bennett, David, 196
Berger, Lois, 31
Berry, Halle, 220
Bezos, Jeff, 142
Bible, 26
bib strand, 25
bids at live auction, 199–204
bids at silent auction
    making, 79
    minimum, 79–80
Binder, Jeff, 263
Bing, Dave, 109–12
bin Laden, Osama, 360n16.1
bin Sulayem, Ahmed, Sheik, 242
The Birth of Venus (Botticelli), 21
Black Monday, 94–95
black pearls, 53, 91–92, 184, 206
    fashion of, 209, 224
    surfeit of, 214
Black Pearls perfume, 93
Blahnik, Manolo, 18
bleaching, 64
bling, 37
Bloom, Stephen (author)
    pilgrimage in seeking out the story of
        pearls, 4, 54–55, 187–88
    wife and son of, during his prolonged
        trip, 54, 114, 140–41, 187–88, 206
blue-green coloration, 99
Blue Seas Pearling, 309
Bobadilla, Francisco de, 12
body cavity searches, 78

body crevices, hiding pearls in, 244
body oil and scent, pearls' absorption of, 26, 33
Bombay, 22
Bonicelli, Joe, 360n16.1
Borrelli family, 68
Borrelli, Victorio and Louis, 67
Boschi, Alessio, 309
Botticelli, Sandro, 21
Bowers, Andy, 182
Bowles, Camilla Parker, 21
bracelets, comfortable length of, 194–95
Bracher, Christine, 296–99
Bracher, Michael, 99–101
Bracher, Roslynne Paspaley, 239, 245, 246, 264, 295
  biography of, 243
Bradley, Ernestine, 94
Branellec, Jacques, 165–66, 169–74, 181–84, 209, 210, 310
  biography of, 183–84
  personal life an open book, 239
  promotion by, 86
Braunstein, Paul, 68, 305
Brazil, 71
Breakfast at Tiffany's, 5
brick-and-mortar stores, 142–44, 147
Brink's, 39
Broome, Australia, 24, 31, 72, 230, 244, 257, 302, 306–8
Brossard, Cyril, 178–82
Brouillet, Jean-Claude, 92, 184, 209, 224
Brown, Bruce, 307–9
Brown, Lyndon, 255, 307
Bugsuk Island, 165, 173–84, 185
Bulgari, 86, 97, 107, 142
Bunnamagoo wine, 240
buoys, 215
Burmese pearls, 91
Burton, Richard, 365n29.6
Bush, Barbara, 18, 132
Bush, George H. W., 132
Busuanga, Philippines, 166
buttons, mother-of-pearl used for, 155–56, 244, 246, 252–53
buying of pearls
  bargaining in, 40–41
  theatricality in, 32–33
  from traders, not directly from producers, 86

calipers, 78
Callas, Maria, 17, 51
Cambodia, 71
"came to possess" phrase, 190
capitalist system, 160
Caracas, 329–32
Cargill, 60
Caribbean
  pearl rush in the, after Columbus's discovery of pearls, 10, 319–21, 324–28
  volume of pearls harvested in, in 16th century, 15, 319
Caribbean Indians, 7
Carter, Rosalynn, 93
Cartier, 52, 97, 142
Catherine the Great, 17
celebrities, showing off jewelry (product placement), 86, 310
certificates of provenance, 51
Chanel, Coco, 17, 19
Charles, Prince, 21
Charles V, Emperor, 15
Charterhouse hotel, Hong Kong, 97
Cháves, Hugo, 330
Cheney, Lynn, 132
Cheng, Ricky, 117
Chiasso, Switzerland, 68
China
  economy of, 75–76
  global dominance of, 108–9
  low wages in, 70
Chinese, in Tahiti, 210–11
Chinese pearls
  competition with Japanese pearls, 56–57, 62
  and democratization of pearl wearing, 17–18
  exports, 137–38
  flooding of market with, 70
  internal consumption of, 138
  mislabeled as Japanese, 62, 106
  sold in Kobe, 25
  total production of, 136–39
Chinese pearls, freshwater
  called "Baby South Sea Pearls," 53
  called "junk," 69
  dyed, 46
  production method of, 105–25
  surpassing Japanese pearls in size, 106–7

Chinese pearls, river, 50

Chinese pearls, seawater, 149–50

Chinese pearl workers, 112–13, 149–50, 155–59

Chinese producers, 64, 105–25

choker strand, 25

Christ, pearls representing, 20

Christianity, Indians converted to, 13

Christie's, 3, 86, 188–93
  auction of Baroda Pearls, 188, 197–99, 201–5
  jewelry auctions of, 191–93

Cisneros, Gustavo, 94

clams, purple-lipped giant (*Tridacna crocea*), 178

clamshells, beads from, 24

classification systems for luxury items (gems, liquor, etc.)
  men's need for, 312–13
  See also grading systems for pearls

Cleopatra, 17, 26, 45, 358n2.1

clicking sound of pearls, 33

clients
  loyalty of, declining with the Internet, 142–44
  pearl producers' direct contact with, 86
  poaching of, by dealers, 85–86
  preselling of jewels to, 85
  reasons for desiring pearls, 311–18
  society and celebrity, names of, 88, 93

Clinton, Bill, 18

Clinton, Hillary Rodham, 18

Clipper Pearls, 302–3, 309

Cobb, Wilburn Dowell, 360n16.1

cocaine trade, comparison of pearl trade with, 38–40, 79, 156, 214

Coche, 10, 325

Cocia family, 68

Cody's Beef n' Beans, Tucson, 35

Coeroli, Martin, 220–21

Cohiba Cigar Divan, Hong Kong, 101–2

Cohn, Roy, 256

Cojuangco, Manuel, 165–66, 172, 174, 183, 184–85

Colas, Elodie, 271, 277–78, 291

collectors of pearls, 23–24, 43–54

Colombia, 11

color of pearls, 32, 206

color-treated pearls, 32, 113

Columbus, Christopher, 7–15
  diaries of, 322–23
  discovery of pearls, 320–23
  500th anniversary of landing, political attitudes toward, 334
  letter to monarchs promising to conquer the Holy Land, 358n1.2
  political blunders of and loss of favor with king and queen, 11–15, 320
  reasons for voyages, to secure "pearls" etc., 7–9

commercial-grade pearls, 82

conchiolin (calcium carbonate), 6, 25

consumerism, of Western world, 1–2

consumption (sumptuary) laws, 21

Cook Islands, 24

cooperative of pearl farmers, of Tahiti, 215–16, 220–21, 225, 226

coral, trade in, 68

coral reefs, 177–78

Coral Sea Mari-Culture, 309

Coral Triangle, 173

Cosa, Juan de la, 10–11

Costa de las Perlas, 325

Costa Rica, 325

CP&J (China Pearls and Jewellery City), 108

Crane, Neville, 260–62

cricket game of deckhands, 279–82

crocodiles, saltwater, 233–35

Cruxent, Jose M., 339–40

Cruz, Penélope, 220

Cuba, 90

Cubagua, 10–11, 15, 319–41
  destruction of oyster beds around, 327

Cultured Pearl Export Co., 304

cultured pearls
  and destruction of the natural pearl market, 107
  invention of, 24
  outlawed in Bahrain, 42–43
  process of bead insertion (nucleation), 3, 73–74, 157–58

Cumaná, 321

Curiel, François, 201–4

cyanide poisoning, fishing by, 176–77

Cygnet Bay Pearls, 307–8, 309

Dagohoy, Christine Marie, 182

Darwin, Australia, 230, 232, 244, 266

Darwin, Charles, 232
Darwin Ship Repair and Engineering, 240
Datang, 109
David, Tony, 68, 305
Davis, Barbara, 94
dealers in pearls, 36–41, 82–83
    examining jewelry, 57, 64, 194
    in natural pearls, 35–36, 38
    not holding onto pearls too long, 94
    occasional dealing in other gems, 96
deckhands on a pearling ship (deckies),
        232, 246, 266–95
    R & R for, 279–84
    rules for, 274–75
    women as, 268
de la Renta, Annette, 94
D'Elia, Bart, 67
D'Elia family, 68
Denniss, Rory, 273
Desdemona (monkey), 170–71, 182
Desperate Housewives, 220
Devino company, 305
DeWitt, Clint, 182
Dholpur, Maharaja of, 190
diamonds
    four Cs of, 5, 312
    grading of, 64
Diana, Princess, 5, 17
Diankow, 109
Dimitri, Prince of Yugoslavia, 95
Dingo Island, 279–82
disease control, airport security for, 166–69
diving for pearls
    in Australian waters, 230, 272–74
    forced on Indians in the Caribbean,
        13–15, 325–27
    modern equipment, 23
    without modern equipment, 22–23, 212
    See also pearl divers
DNA, 33
dog collar strand, 25
dollars, exchanging, 330–32
Domino (diver), 366n30.2
Dotillus, Nena, 182
dredging, of oyster beds, 327, 337–38
drill holes, 32
drills for stringing, 11, 114
Dubai, 242
Dubai Pearl Exchange, 242
Duke, Doris, 17

Duke, Robin Chandler, 88, 93
Dureau, Keith, 254
dyed pearls, 32, 46, 64, 113
dynamite, fishing by, 176–77

earrings, dealers' gifts of, 89
e-Bay, 104
Econo Lodge, Tucson, 35
Egypt, 9, 19–20
Ehime Prefecture, 57
Eliot, T. S., 26
Elizabeth I, Queen of England, 8, 17, 45
emeralds, 96
environmental conditions for pearl
        cultivation, 175–78, 312
environmentalists, 72, 174
Erskine, Zeide, 43–54, 116
    Natural Pearl Queen, 52
    "Rana of Fresno," 147
European clients, 103
European courts, pearls in, 15–16
Evans, Linda, 94
exchanging dollars, 330–32
excommunication for wearing pearls, 21

Fakarava, 228
Fallourd, Pierre, 185
Fanghua pearl boutique, Beijing, 129,
        131–35
Fan Mi, 151–52, 164
Farley, Bruce, 303
farmers' markets of pearls, 114–16
fashion
    changing taste in size and color of pearls,
        106, 209, 224
    pearls and, 16, 21
Fawsett, Robert, 68, 305
Federated States of Micronesia, 227
FedEx, 39
Felsenfeld, Jack, 67
Fengqiao, 109
Ferdinand, King of Spain, 7, 320–21
Ferdinand V, King of Spain, 365n29.6
Ferguson, Sarah, Duchess of York, 94
Ferrante, Victor, 67
Fiji, 24
Fishburne, Laurence, 220
Fisher, Mel, 364n29.7
fishermen, natural pearls discovered by,
        345–48

fishing
illegal, using dynamite and cyanide poisoning, 176–77
traditional, 156–57
floating laboratories, in Australia, 270
flotilla, lost in a hurricane in 1622, 364n29.7
Flower Island, Philippines, 171, 182, 183
flying fish, 292–93
foot massage, 164–65
fortune seekers
in Australian pearl trade, 244
in Caribbean after Columbus's discovery of pearls, 244
Fortunoff, 309
Foster, Jodie, 18
Foster, Temauri, 221
French
nuclear testing by, 223
resentment of, in Tahiti, 210
French Polynesia, 24, 91, 206–29
cultured pearl farming in, 209
Fresno, Calif., 43–54
Friedel, Albert, 87–88, 95
Fujian province, 108
Fujimura, Takuya, 73
Furstenberg, Alexandra von, 94
Fysh, Sir Hudson, 245

Gaekwar family of Baroda, 190–91
Gaekwar Khande Rao, 361n18.6
Gaijin Club (Kobe), 58–59, 65
Gambier Islands, 209
Garcilaso de la Vega, 15
Gasparini, Graciano, 340
Gates, Bill, 226
Gauguin, Paul, 207
Gauguin Perles, 221
Gemological Institute of America, 147, 192, 364n28.1
gems, and pearl dealers, 96
Gems & Jewelry Trade Association of China, 136
Geneva, in global pearl trade, 3
Gerdau, Alane, 259
Gerdau, Allan, 249–50, 251–60, 304, 305
political views and advertisements of, 256–57
Gerdau, Carl, 251
Gerdau, Carlson, 251, 260

Gerdau, Clara Ehlermann, 251
Gerdau, Florence Ruperti, 252, 258–59
Gerdau, Otto, 250–51
Getty, Pia, 94
Gifu Prefecture, 71
Girl with a Pearl Earring (Vermeer), 21, 51
glass, from Venice, as luxury good, 16
glass trade goods, 12, 340
global economy, 160
impersonality of, 1–2
pearl trade, as emblematic of, 3
global warming, 74
Gloria, Princess (Princess TNT), 94
Golay Buchel, 58, 94, 254
gold, value of, 312
gold-colored pearls, 165–66, 181, 185
Golfo de Perlas, 13
GPS systems for locating pearl lines, 215
Grace, Princess, 5, 17, 19
grading systems for pearls
advocates and opponents of, 364n28.1
nonexistence of, 5, 63–64, 313
in the Wan auction, 80
graduated, or chute strand, 25–26
grafting, 246
Graham, Katharine, 17
Greenblatt, Stephen, 13
Greenleaf, Robert K., 256
Grumman Malland seaplanes, 242, 267–69, 294–95
Guangzhou province, 108
Guerra, Cristóbal, 11
Gulf of California, 43, 325
Gulf of Mannar, 22, 190
Gulf of Paria, 9, 13
Gulf of Tonkin, 141
Gump's, 86
Gutfreund, Susan, 93

Haian, 148
Haikou, 158, 166
Hainan Province, 141, 158, 168
Halonen, Tarja, 132
Hammell, George R., 12
hanks, 86
Harding, Leigh, 276–77, 289, 290, 293
Hardy, Johanna, 200–201
Harry Winston, 86, 91, 92, 97, 107, 142
Hart, Dennis, 76–77, 83–84

harvesting (extracting pearls from oysters), 295

Hasidic dealers, 194

Hebrew Union College, Jewish Institute of Religion, 260

heirloom jewelry, auctions of, 188

hens, feeding pearls to, 26

Hernandez Sixto, Señor ("Sixto"), 337–39

Hervé, François Mais, 209, 218

Hill, James J., 202

Hilton, Paris, 18

Hinata firm, 58

Hispaniola, 8, 10, 12, 320–21

Hoffman, Peter, 360n16.1

Holidome, Tucson, 35, 40

Holly Golightly (character), 5

Holy Land, Columbus's promise to conquer, 358n1.2

Hong Kong, 75–84
    described, 75–76
    in the global pearl trade, 3
    hotels in, 97
    pearl auctions, 57, 59, 76–84, 98, 102–4

Hong Kong International Jewellery Show, 57, 76, 86

Hongqiao Market, Beijing, 127–35, 144
    tourist season in, 129

Hosei Co., 59

House, Larry, 301–3, 309

Howard, John, 241

HSN cable network, 36

H. Stern, 97

Huang Jin, 149–50

hurricane in 1622, pearls lost in, 364n29.7

Hussein, Saddam, 360n16.1

Hu Xiao Mei, 155

Hyriopsis cumingii mussels, 106, 120

Ibuki, Mikio, 60, 70, 73–74

Indians (American)
    attitude toward pearls, 12–13
    converted to Christianity, 13
    diving for pearls, 13–15, 325–27
    exploitation of, 12–15, 320, 326–27
    pearls worn by, 322–23
    reported to be cannibals and sodomites, 14
    seven naked ones, brought to Spain, 8–9
    trade with, 11

Indians (East)
    collectors of pearls, 23
    dealers, 194

Indonesia, 24, 166, 173, 309

Internet
    pearls sold on, 36, 46–47, 52–53, 107
    shopping on the, 143–47

Iris (wife) and Mikey (son), 54, 114, 187–88, 206
    impatience of, 140–41

Irwin, Steve, 274

Isabella, Queen of Spain, 7–9, 17, 320–21, 323

Ise Prefecture, 66

Ise-Shima National Park, 73

ivory, 252

Jacobs, Lady Evelyn, 94

Japan
    foreign dealers in, 67–68, 304
    travel to, 67

Japanese
    hostility to, in Australia after World War II, 254–55
    technicians in Australian floating laboratories, 272, 277–79

Japanese Pearl Exporters' Association, 59, 60

Japanese pearls, arcane measurements used for, 357nIntro.1

Japanese pearls, cultured akoya, 19
    declining production of, 25, 57
    modest size of, 91
    production methods, 68–71

Japanese pearls, freshwater, 70–71

Japanese pearl workers, 70

JCK magazine, 31

JC Penney, 107

jellyfish, poisonous, 273–74

Jerwood, John M., 68, 304–8

Jewelmer, 165–66, 171–86

jewelry auctions
    at auction houses, 191–93, 199–200
    examination of jewels at, 194
    high prices at, 198

jewelry retailers
    buying jewelry from traders, not direct from producers, 86
    competition from the Internet, 143–44, 147

jewelry retailers (*continued*)
    family-owned, 142
    traditional way of doing business, 142–44
jewelry shows
    Hong Kong, 57, 76, 86
    Tucson, Ariz., 30–41
Jewelry Television, 36
jewelry thieves, 31
Jewish jewelry dealers, 67
Jewish refugees, 90
Jian Hao, 121
John, Elton, 240
Johnny, Señor, 339, 342–44
Jolie, Angelina, 18, 220
Joo-jee, 105–9, 117
Josephine Bonaparte, 17
Juan, Prince of Spain, 9
Juergens & Andersen, 19
Ju Hua, 119
June Cleaver, 18

Kadakia, Rahul, 201
Kailis, M. G., 260–61
Kailis Pearls, 240, 305
Kalleito, 228
kan (measure), 3
kangaroo, 276–77, 290
Kano, Nobuhiro, 179
karaoke, 161–63
Kashikojima, 73
Kashikojima Cultivation Farm, 73
Kastellorizo, Greece, 244
Kasumiga pearls, 71
Kaye, Johnnie, 271, 293–94
Kelly, Grace, 19, 67
Kelly, Jenine, 37, 97–101
Kelly, Tommy, 271–72, 274, 292–93
Kennedy, Jacqueline, 5, 17, 19, 67
keshi pearls, 279, 359n7.1
keystone price, 80
Khashoggi, Shalpari, 94
Kidman, Nicole, 18
Kimberley Diamond Company, 241–42
Kino (in *The Pearl*), 53, 212, 348
Kissinger, Nancy, 94, 132
Knocker Bay, 255
knotting of strands, 26
Kobe, Japan (Pearl City), 56–75
    auctions in, 81
    Chuo-ku pearl district, 57

foreign dealers in, 67–68
in global pearl trade, 3, 25
heyday of, in 1960s, 66–68
Port Island pearl district, 57
Kobe Club (Gaijin Club), 58–59, 65
Koran, 26
Kuri Bay, 250, 255, 261, 263, 265, 302
Kuribayashi, Tokuichi, 254–55
Kwok, Sofinny, 112
Kyriacou, Michael ("Ernie"), 282, 294

Lake Biwa, 70, 106
Lake Kasumigaura, 71, 106
lakes in China, producing pearls, 110
Lam, Simon, 102
Lang, Christina, 88–89
Lao Tzu, 360n16.1
Las Casas, Bartolomé de, 14–15
"last on, first off" maxim, 6, 26
Lauder, Evelyn, 88, 94
LeFrak, Karen, 94
Leizhou Peninsula, 145
Levin, George G., 260–65
Levine, Harriette, 94
Lewinsky, Monica, 18
Li, Kent, 229
light, pearls and, in Caribbean Indian belief, 12–13
Liguori, Genaro, 67
Li Hung, 155
Lingon, Daphne, 188–93, 197–99, 201, 205
Linneys jewelry shop, Broome, 294, 306
literature, pearls in, 26–27
Liu Jun, 128–35
logging, illegal, 176
London, in global pearl trade, 3
Lopez, Jennifer, 18
lots
    determining the winning bid, 83–84
    at silent auction, 78–79, 102–4
loupe, 78
Lovitos, Glenn, 177
Lucayan Indians, 13, 326

mabe pearls, 347
Mace, Nicholas, 225
Mack, Sondra, 94
Madonna, 18
Magnificent Jewels Auctions, 193, 199–200
maharajahs, 189

Malabar, 20, 189
Malaysia, 24, 173
Malca-Amit, 39
Male, Kim, 257–58, 260–64, 302
Male, Sam, 254, 258
Mangareva, 222, 306
Manila, 170, 176
    airport, 166–69
    in global pearl trade, 3
Manila Jazz Festival, 171
Man Sang jewelry company, 117
Marco Polo, 4, 9, 20, 189
Marcos, Ferdinand and Imelda, 166
Margarita Island, 10, 320, 325, 333
Maricar, Salih, 204–5
Mark, Phil, 274–75, 278–79, 282, 289–90,
    293–94
marketing, of pearls, 309–10
markup, 52, 80
Marsh, Stuart, 143
Marsh's jewelry store, 143
Martial, 20
Martin, M. Alfred, 216, 220–21, 225, 226
Masendo, Lucia, 182
Masliah, Henri, 95–96, 224
Mason, Alice, 93
Mastoloni, Fran, 68, 77, 81, 86, 97, 194,
    305
Mastoloni, Frank, 67–68
Mastoloni family, 68
matching of pearls, 32
matinée strand, 25
Maugham, W. Somerset, 26–27
McConaughey, Matthew, 220
McGreevey, Dina Matos, 18
McGreevey, James, 18
measuring cards, 78
Mehta, Zubin, 132
Melaleuca Station, 233, 240
men, types of jewelry preferred by, and
    their felt need for classification
    systems, 312–13
Messing, Debra, 220
metal trade goods, 12
Michael of Kent, Princess, 94
Micronesia, 227
Mie Prefecture, 56
Mikimoto, Kokichi, 24, 56, 73
    grandson of, 224
    original necklace by, 43, 44, 49

Mikimoto Island, 73
Mikimoto jewelry stores, 107
Miller, Chantal, 94
Miller, Chrisopher L., 12
Miller, Henry, 172
Miller, Marie-Chantal Claire, 94
Mindanao, Philippines, 175
Mississippi River Delta clamshells, 24
Miss Pearl (of China), 138–39
money changing, 330–32
Monroe, Marilyn, 17
Moorea, 207
Morand, Pierre, 255
Mori, Takashi, 65–67, 68, 73
Mori, Yasuaki, 69, 77
Morton, Sam, 272, 274, 286
mother-of-pearl, 34, 155–56, 244, 246,
    252–53
Mozafarian, 309
Muilenburg, Peter, 326
Müller, Andy, 57–59, 67, 68, 77, 81, 86,
    94–95, 224, 303, 309
    book by, 254
mussels
    adapting to pollution, 120
    differences from oysters, 110–11, 119
    pearls from, 71, 106

nacre, 22, 231
Nakamura, Tomokazu, 60
natural pearls
    in Australian pearl industry, 24
    of Bahrain, 42–43
    collected by fishermen, 345–48
    collectors of, 23–24, 43–54
    dealers in, 35–36, 38
    death of the industry, 25, 364n29.4
    distinguishing from cultured pearls, 25
    formation of, 22
    large collection of, in Fresno, 43–54
    niche trade in, 35–36
    poor quality of those discovered today,
        279, 338–40
    price of, 36
    rarity of, 2–3, 24
    where they can still be found, 38
neap tides, 232
necklaces
    ideally suited to a woman's neck, 127,
        198–99

necklaces (*continued*)
  method of examining, 32–34
  seldom bought finished by dealers, 86
Neiman Marcus, 86, 99, 309
Nengo Nengo, 222, 225–26
New Caledonia, 24
New Guinea, 24
New South Wales, 72
New Testament, 26
New World
  discovery of, 7–8
  and Spanish power, 324–25
New York
  diamond district (47th Street), 38, 67
  in global pearl trade, 3
  pearl dealers' building at 608 Fifth
    Avenue, 37
  price of pearls in, 133
Nicholas El Gato, 344–48
Niishi Zosen Shipyard, 262
Niño, Pedro Alonso, 11
Niones, April, 179–80, 182
Nippo Pearl Co. Ltd, 254
Norman, Boris, 255, 259
Norman, David, 68, 77, 87, 304, 305
Norm Marshall & Associates, 220
northern light, pearl dealers' preference for,
    57, 64
Northern Territory, 263
nucleators, 150, 178–79, 272, 277–79, 290
Nueva Cádiz, 15, 319–20, 325–28
  decline and abandonment of, 328
  ruins of, 333–35, 339–41
Nueva Punta de Piedras, 342–48
Nukuoro, 227
Nuutina, 209, 218

Obama, Michelle, 18, 106
Ogg, Alex, 303
oil discoveries, in Persian Gulf, 364n29.4
Ojeda, Alonso de, 10–11
Onassis, Jacqueline. *See* Kennedy, Jacqueline
one-of-a-kind pearls, 82, 188
online shopping, 142
opera strand, 25
organic farmers, 174
Orient, search for route to, 7
orient (attribute of pearls), 5–6
Oriental (natural) pearls, 23–24
Osaka, 56

Otsuki Pearl, 68–70, 73, 81
Otte, Enrique, 327
Otto Gerdau Company, 248, 249–65, 302
  bequest of, after Allan Gerdau's death, to
    three religious institutions, 259–60
  put up for auction, 260–63
oyster beds, dredging of, 327, 337–38
oysters
  as aphrodisiacs, 26, 338
  life cycle of, 179–80
  meat of, 337–38
  myths about, 72
  natural defenses of, and genesis of pearls,
    22
  picking them up from the seabed, 288–90
  sensitive to water pollution, 120
  wild, on the seafloor, 269
oyster shuckers, 154–55
Oy Vey Café, Tucson, 38

Pacific Pearls, 221
Palawan Island, 165–66, 360n16.1
  in global pearl trade, 3
Palawan Island pearls, 32
palming a gem, 31
Panama, 24, 325
Papeete, 207, 220, 227
Paris
  as center of pearl trade, 21–22
  in global pearl trade, 3
Parker, Eléanor, 227–29
Paspaley, James, 244
Paspaley, Marilynne, 239, 245, 296–99
  biography of, 243
Paspaley, Mylissa (Nicholas's second wife),
    243
Paspaley, Nicholas (Nick)
  biography of, 242–44, 246–48
  competitors of, 71, 231, 307–9
  interview with, 81–84
  operations of, 232, 236, 237
  opinions about, 238
  pearl auctions sponsored by, 57, 76–80,
    81, 98, 102–4
  promotion by, 86
  secret acquisition of Otto Gerdau
    Company, 249–65
  use of name, forbidden to dealers, 79
Paspaley, Nikolas (father of Nicholas), 242,
    245, 248, 255

Paspaley, Peter, 98–99

Paspaley, Theodosis (grandfather of Nicholas), 245

Paspaley, Vivienne Lavinia Barry (mother of Nicholas), 245–46

Paspaley family, 237–48

Paspaley III (ship), 262, 291, 295

Paspaley IV (ship and floating laboratory), 270–95

Paspaley Pearling Company, 237–44, 269

Paspalis, Michael (brother of Nikolas Paspaley), 245

Paterson, David A., 18

Paterson, Michelle Paige, 18

patron saint of pearls (Virgin of the Valley), 335

pavé, 357nIntro.2

The Pearl (Steinbeck), 2, 5, 24, 26, 44

pearl (word)
  in Greek-Latin (*margarita*), 325
  in Sanskrit, 189
  as verb, 19

Pearl Age (1524–1658), 21

pearl companies
  concentration of, 210
  vertical integration in, 60, 64–65

pearl divers, 22–23
  in Australian pearl industry, 230, 272–74
  declining number of, 25
  difficulty and dangers of the job (poisonous jellyfish, etc.), 22, 273–74, 311, 338
  equipment of, traditional, 22–23
  payment of, 23
  reason for diving nude, 22, 326
  See also diving for pearls

pearl farms, large commercial
  inaccessibility of, 4
  at sea, in Australian industry, 210
  in Tahiti, concentration of, 210

pearl farms, small family
  economics of, 210, 212–21, 225, 226–27
  farmers turning to drink and drugs, 219
  protection for, proposed, 227–28

Pearl House, Tahiti (proposed), 228–29

The Pearling Game (TV documentary), 255

pearl ladder, first rungs of, 141, 267

Pearl of Allah (world's largest pearl), 165, 360n16.1

The Pearl of Great Price (Mormon), 26

pearlparadise.com, 144

pearl-processing plants, in China, 112

pearl producers, and clients, 86

Pearl Proprietary Ltd. (PPL), 254–64, 302

pearl rushes, in the Caribbean, after Columbus, 10, 319–21, 324–28

pearls
  addictive nature of, and collecting, 40, 313–18
  aging of, and changing appearance or deterioration, 49, 339–40
  aura of elegance of, 309–10
  authorities on, 44
  bargaining over, 40–41, 129–35
  body oil and scent absorbed by, 26, 33
  casual use of, 19
  color of, 32, 206
  color-treated, 32, 113
  as commodity, 267–68
  compared to diamonds and gold, in value, 18
  display of, pre-auction, 77
  display of, to private clients, 296–300
  distribution of, 39, 238
  energy vibrating from, 33, 315
  in European courts, 15–16
  examination of, 36, 40, 78
  as fashion necessity, 16, 21
  gift of, appropriate and classic, 19
  glowing luminescence of, 18–19, 33
  handling them, and perspiration of hands, 32–33, 130
  harvesting of (extracting from the oyster), 295
  history of, to modern times, 17, 20–25
  image of, compared to other gems, 311
  largest ones, 94, 165, 365n29.6
  marketing of, 309–10
  as metaphors and prisms, 5, 52
  missing, stolen, 216–18, 346–48
  never held too long by dealers, 94
  numbers harvested in the Caribbean, 15, 319
  obsession with, 34
  one-of-a-kind, 82, 188
  patron saint of, 335
  perfect, many steps necessary to obtaining, 180–83
  perfumes and cosmetics, effect on, 26
  personality of, 99

pearls (*continued*)
 playing with, 6
 political statements made by, 18
 popularity in Europe after discovery of
  America, 15–16, 20–21, 324
 prices of, 18, 77, 80, 95, 98, 107, 115, 122,
  137, 181, 210, 221, 231
 as protection against evil spirits, 20
 provenance of, 2, 49, 69, 79, 179, 185–86
 recovered from shipwrecks, 364n29.7
 size of, 63, 91, 181
 sound of clicking and bouncing, 33, 198
 spirituality of, 20, 317–18
 stamping on, to distinguish from
  imitation pearls, 25
 storage, and longevity of, 26
 stylishness of, 67
 symbolic meanings of, 12–13, 18, 20, 311,
  318
 testing of (telling real from fake), 25
 theorizing as to formation of, 20
 transformative power of, to make a
  woman beautiful, 199
 treatment of (dyeing, polishing, etc.), 29,
  113–14
 women and, 127, 198–99, 311–18
Pearls (book, Strack), 31, 44
Pearl Shell Fishing Co., 254
Pearl Society of America, 31, 312
Pearls of Arabia pearl museum, 242
"pearls of wisdom," 26
pearl sorters, 112–13, 151–52
pearl-stringing protocols, 25–26
pearl technicians (nucleators), 157–58,
 277–79, 290
pearl traders, 85–104
"The Pearl Walk" (at Tucson convention),
 30–31
pearl workers
 Chinese, 112–13
 Filipino, 174–75, 178–79, 180, 181–82
 Tahitian, 224–25
 worldwide, wages and conditions of, 311
Pearl World, 28–29
Pelosi, Nancy, 18, 106
Peninsula Hotel, Kowloon, 97
People's Pearl Cooperatives, 117–18
The Peregrina (pearl), 365n29.6
perfumes and cosmetics, effect on pearls, 26
Perles de Tahiti, 220

Persian Gulf, 22, 43, 190, 364n29.4
 oil discoveries in, 364n29.4
personality in pearls, 99
Philippine pearls, 63, 114
Philippines, 165–86
 Communist rebels in, 175
 in global pearl trade, 3
 motto "Pearl of the Orient," 175
 Muslim rebels in, 169–70
 natural pearl fishing in, 24
 pearl workers in, 174–75, 178–79, 180,
  181–82
Phoenix, Ariz., 29–30
Pinctada imbricata oyster (akoya oyster), 63,
 327, 347
 cultivated outside of Japan, 71–73
 discovery of cultivation technique, 24
Pinctada margaritifera oyster, 91, 184
Pinctada maxima oyster, 3, 91, 165–66, 179,
 181, 230–31, 253
Pinzón, Martín Alonzo, 11
Pinzón, Vicente Yáñez, 11
plastic buttons, 253
Poe Ravi Nui pearl cooperative, 220
pollution, 56
 and declining production, 24, 68, 71, 74,
  175–76
 mussels adapting to, 120
Porlamar, Margarita Island, 320, 333
Poroi, Alfred, 223
Port Island, 61
Port Stephens, Australia, 71
Posada Hidalgo, 333
possession of territory, claimed by setting
 foot on land, 11
pressurized suits, 23
price of pearls
 at a Chinese farmers market, 115
 of Chinese pearls on the global market,
  69, 107, 122, 137
 compared to diamonds and gold, 18
 to dealers vs. to retailers, 77, 80, 98
 to final customer, 80
 fluctuation of, with stock market, 95
 insider price, 294
 ladder of, 213–14
 of natural pearls, 36
 in New York, 133
 obtained by small farmers in Tahiti, 210,
  221

size and shape as main determinants, 181
of South Sea pearls, 231
pricing of pearls, and difficulty of getting
    appraisals, 5, 147
princess strand, 25
private deals, 85
product placement of pearls, 86, 220, 310
Protestant Episcopal Church, Domestic and
    Foreign Missionary Society, 260
provenance of pearls, 2, 49, 69, 79, 179,
    185–86
    certificates of, 51
    impossibility of tracing that of necklaces, 3
ProVockative Gems, 37, 96
PT Autore Pearl Culture, 309
Pteria sterna pearls, 43
Punta de Piedras, 333, 335
purple-lipped giant clams (*Tridacna crocea*),
    178
Putin, Vladimir and Ludmilla, 132

Qatar Museum Authority, 361n18.6
Qiongzhou Straits, 145
QVC cable network, 36, 107

rainbow-colored pearls, 106
rainbows, 288
Rainier, Prince, 19
Rampur, Nawabs of, 189–90
Rana of Bophar breastplate, 51
"Rana of Fresno," 147
Rankin, Tish and Wes, 38, 44
Reagan, Nancy, 88, 93
Reagan, Ronald, 93
red pearls, 43, 48, 53–54
Red Sea, 22
Red Tide plankton, 56, 74
Reed, Bill, 224, 306–7
Renaissance Harbor View, Hong Kong, 97
Rhodes, Alexandra, 196–97
Richie, Nicole, 18
Ripley, Robert, 361n16.1
Rivera, Anabel, 182
Roberts, Julia, 18
Robert Wan Museum (store), 222
Roebuck Bay Pearls, 263
Rogers, Dick, 259, 262
Rogers, Joan, 258–64
Romano, Emma, 182
Rome, ancient, 20

Romero, Aldermaro, 326
rope strand, 25
Rosenthal, Léonard, 43
Rosenthal family (France), 184
Roskin, Gary, 31
Rothchild, Lady de, 94
Rouse, Irving, 340
royalty, pearls worn by, 21
rubber, 8, 120
Rubens, Peter Paul, 21
Rubinstein, Helena, 195
Russian Revolution, 22
Russo, Ariel, 68, 305

Safra, Lily, 93
St. Louis World Fair of 1904, 24
Sakha Diamond, 60
Saks Fifth Avenue, 67
Salazar, Michelle, 182
Samoa, 24
Sandu, 109
Sang, Gaston Tong, 221
Santa María, 11
Sauer, Carl O., 11
Saunders, Nicholas J., 12, 324
Savron, Bruno, 182
Schecter, Stanley, 67
Schiff, René, 67
Schuler, Gary, 199–200
Schwarzenegger, Maria Shriver, 132
scorpions, a prized delicacy, 148
scriptures, pearls mentioned in, 26
Sea of Cortez, 24
seaplanes, 267–69, 294–95
Searle, Tony, 233–36
seawater, clean, needed by oysters, 72, 312
security
    airport, for disease control, 166–69
    against poachers and rebels, in the
        Philippines, 175
semi-rounds, 100
Seville, 15, 324
Shakespeare, William, 26
Shanxiahu, 109, 117
sharks, 338
Shelle Jewelers, Glencoe, Ill., 313–15
Shemtov, Rabbi, 38
Shepherd, Jeremy, 36, 43, 44, 46, 118,
    141–63
    biography of, 144–45

Shepherd, Jeremy (*continued*)
  franchise Web sites, 146
  Internet sites, 107
  interview with, 145–48
Shiga Prefecture, 70
Shi Hongyue, 136–38
Shikoku Island, 57
Shima, Japan, 24–25
Shimizu, Yoshihiro, 59, 77, 81, 86, 224
Shinmei inlet, 24
shipwrecks, pearls recovered from,
  364n29.7
shopping online, 143–47
shucking oysters, 154–55
Sita Devi, 190–91
"Sixto," Señor, 337–39
size of pearls, 63, 91, 181
  fraudulently stated, 53
sizing (measuring) of pearls, 78
skin color, human, pearls suited to different
  types of, 181
skinning, 95
Skippy, Second Mate, 293–94
slash-and-burn fires, 176
Slutzky, Isadore, 67
Smith, Bradley, 172
Smith, Joseph, 26
snails, pearls from, 49
snakebites, 233–34
society figures, as clients, 93
Soderini, Pedro, 11
Sofia, Queen, 132
The Sopranos, 220
Soros, Daisy, 94
Sorrento, Italy, 68
sorting and grading, 3
Sotheby's, 3, 86, 193–97
  jewelry auctions of, 191
sound of pearls bouncing, 198
South Marutea, 184, 222–23, 224
South Orange, N.J., 143
South Sea pearls, 57, 91, 165, 230–31
  cultured, 253–55
  market in, 309
Soviet Union, 22
Spain
  in the 1500s, 340–41
  New World conquests, 8
  wealth from pearls from New World,
    15–16, 324–25

spat, 179–80
spice trade, 9
spirituality of pearls, 20, 317–18
Spitzer, Eliot, 18
Spitzer, Silda Wall, 18
Star, Charles, 67
Star, Morris, 67
starfish, 289
Steinbeck, John, 24, 26, 43–44
stingrays, 274, 338
stock market crashes, 94–95
storage of pearls, 26
Strack, Elisabeth, 31, 44, 323
strands
  knotting of, 26
  standard lengths and styles of, 25–26
Streep, Meryl, 18, 106
stringing of pearls, 114
"A String of Beads" (Maugham), 26–27
Swiss watches, 90–91
Sydney, Australia, 242, 308–9

Taburiaux, Jean, 23, 296
Tahiti, 4, 207–29
  racism in, 210–11
Tahitian pearls, 32, 40, 53, 57, 59, 63, 80,
  92, 114, 184, 208
  product placement of, 220
Tahitian pearl workers, 224–25
Taíno Indians, 9
Taizhou, 128
Takafumi, Deguchi, 73–74
Takapoto, 184
Takaroa, 227, 228
Taku Island, 224
Talavera, Fernando de, 8
Tapu, Estelle, 208, 211, 217, 218–19
Tapu, Jean, 208–19
  biography of, 209–10
Tapu, Marlene, 219, 227
Tapu, Tyrone, 218, 219, 226–27
Tasaki, Shunsaku (Tasaki-San), 60–65
  biography of, 61
  interview with, 61–65
  purchases from Robert Wan, 224
Tasaki Shinju, 60
  retail stores, 60
Taubman, Judy, 93
Tavere, Daniel, 212–17
Tavere, Jean Yves, 212, 215

Taylor, Elizabeth, 88, 93, 365n29.6
technicians. *See* nucleators
Tehaamatai, Franck, 228–29
  children of, Glenn, Halidjka, and Vaiana,
  229
The Tempest (Shakespeare), 26
Thailand, 71
Thatcher, Margaret, 88, 132
theft (pilferage), 70
thirtieth anniversary, pearls as traditional
  gift, 19
Thurn und Taxis, Prince Johannes von, 94
Thursday Island, 91, 302
Tian, Faye, 108, 117–25, 145, 150–51, 152,
  153
Tiananmen Square, Beijing, 126
Tiffany & Co., 52, 86, 97, 142
Timor Sea, 4, 230
toads, cane, 235
Toba, 73
toilet paper, 227
Tokyo, 69
Tominaga, Minoru, 272
Tontine Emporium, 256
Tontine Society, New York, 362n22.2
Toomebridge Pearls, 309
Top End of Australia, 232, 244
Torre del Greco, 68
Torrey, Bo, 28–30, 35
Torrey, Kumiko, 28–29
torsade strand, 25
trading of pearls, 51–52
  holding onto for any length of time is bad
  business, 75
"transformatrons" (treatment rooms),
  113–14
treasure chests, filled with pearls, 13
treatment of pearls (dyeing, polishing, etc.),
  29, 113–14
Trevisan, Angelo, diary of, 321–22
Trinidad, 14
Triossi, Amanda, 192
Tucson, Ariz., 35
  jewelry show at, 30–41

Umm al-Qaiwain, 19
uniform strand, 25
United Arab Emirates (UAE), 19, 71
United States Catholic Conference, 260
Uwajima, 57

Vaiatiki Perles, 221, 228–29
Van Cleef & Arpels, 86, 91, 92, 96, 107,
  142
Vansittart (ship), 285–89
Venezuela, 9, 24, 71, 320–21, 329–32
Venice, 9, 20–21
  glass from, 16
Venman, James W., 259
Venus Before a Mirror (Rubens), 21
Vermeer, Johannes, 21, 51
vertical integration in pearl companies, 60,
  64–65, 238
Vespucci, Amerigo, 11
Vietnam, 71
vinegar, dissolving a pearl in, 26, 358n2.1
Virgin of the Valley (La Virgen del Valle),
  patron saint of pearls, 335, 365n30.2
Vock, Alex, 37, 77, 81, 82, 86, 95–96,
  97–104, 193–97, 199–201, 309,
  364n28.1
Vock, Dorette, 88
Voridis, Doda, 94
Vreeland, Diana, 17

wages of pearl workers
  Australian deckhands, 268
  Australian divers, 273
  Australian nucleators, 272
  China, 70, 112–13, 149–50, 156
  French Polynesia, 224–25
  globally, compared to other workers,
  311
  Japan, 70
  Philippines, 175
Wan, Bruno, 222
Wan, Robert
  biography of, 223–24
  competition with small pearl farmers,
  214
  first pearl farms acquired by, 184, 306
  interview with, 224–26
  opinions about, 209–11, 227, 229
  pearl auctions sponsored by, 57, 76,
  80–81
  tour of operations, 222–26
  volume of production, 221
Wan, Tomás, 222
Wang Fong, 223
Ward, Fred, 31
Warhol, Andy, 198

WASP dealers, 194
The Waste Land (Eliot), 26
wearing of pearls, "last on, first off" rule,
    6, 26
Webb, David, 196
Web sites, controlled by Jeremy Shepherd,
    146
Weeden, Edward St. Clair, 190
weight of pearls, 32
Western Australia, 263
Western world, consumerism of, 1–2
whales, 287–88
white pearls, 103
White Russians, 22
Wickham, John Clements, 232
Williams, Caitlin, 44–45
Willis, Raymond, 326
wine, dissolving a pearl in, 26, 358n2.1
Winfrey, Oprah, 18, 220
women
    as deckhands on a pearling ship, 268
    necklaces ideally suited to bring out their
        beauty, 127, 198–99
    and pearls, 311–18
Woodward, Skip, 31
World Pearl Organization, 60
World's Largest Pearl Co., 360n16.1

World War II, 90–91, 254
Wrightsman, Jane, 94

Xie Hong Chong, 156–57
Xie Hong Wu, 156–57
Xie Xian Hua, 159
Xilian, 154
Xioa Ling, 157–59
Xujiacun, 154
Xuwen, 124, 161–64
Xuwen Pearl Paradise, 150

Yagura Toshiyuki Shima, 296–300
yen, Japanese, 39, 79, 132
Yokosuka, 66
You, Mr. (You Hongqing), 124, 145, 148–50,
    154–64
Young, Sarah, 309–10
Yu Perles, 221
Yuji Suto, 71–73

Zamboanga Peninsula, 175
Zhejiang province, 105, 108
Zilkha, Cecile, 94
Zimmerman, S. Mort, 360n16.1
Zinampan-de Luna, Melinda, 175–77
Zingg, Rudy, 308